Writing the Talking Cure

Also by Jeffrey Berman

Joseph Conrad: Writing as Rescue

The Talking Cure: Literary Representations of Psychoanalysis

Narcissism and the Novel

Diaries to an English Professor: Pain and Growth in the Classroom

Surviving Literary Suicide

Risky Writing: Self-Disclosure and Self-Transformation in the Classroom

Empathic Teaching: Education for Life

Dying to Teach: A Memoir of Love, Loss, and Learning

Cutting and the Pedagogy of Self-Disclosure (with Patricia Hatch Wallace)

Death in the Classroom: Writing about Love and Loss

Companionship in Grief: Love and Loss in the Memoirs of C. S. Lewis, John Bayley, Donald Hall, Joan Didion, and Calvin Trillin

Death Education in the Writing Classroom

Dying in Character: Memoirs on the End of Life

Confidentiality and Its Discontents: Dilemmas of Privacy in Psychotherapy (with Paul W. Mosher)

Writing Widowhood: The Landscapes of Bereavement

Writing the Talking Cure

*Irvin D. Yalom and the
Literature of Psychotherapy*

Jeffrey Berman

Cover photograph: Michael Zagaris.

Published by State University of New York Press, Albany

© 2019 State University of New York

All rights reserved

No part of this book may be used or reproduced in any manner whatsoever without written permission. No part of this book may be stored in a retrieval system or transmitted in any form or by any means including electronic, electrostatic, magnetic tape, mechanical, photocopying, recording, or otherwise without the prior permission in writing of the publisher.

For information, contact State University of New York Press, Albany, NY
www.sunypress.edu

Library of Congress Cataloging-in-Publication Data

Names: Berman, Jeffrey, 1945– author.
Title: Writing the talking cure : Irvin D. Yalom and the literature of psychotherapy / Jeffrey Berman.
Description: Albany : State University of New York, 2019. | Includes bibliographical references and index.
Identifiers: LCCN 2018021839 | ISBN 9781438473871 (hardcover : alk. paper) | ISBN 9781438473888 (pbk. : alk. paper) | ISBN 9781438473895 (ebook)
Subjects: LCSH: Yalom, Irvin D., 1931– | Psychotherapy.
Classification: LCC RC480 .B377 2019 | DDC 616.89/14—dc23
LC record available at https://lccn.loc.gov/2018021839

10 9 8 7 6 5 4 3 2 1

*To the future—our beloved grandchildren:
Audrey, Max, Nate, Skyler, Sloane, and Talia.
And to Julie, the sparkling jules of my life.*

Contents

Acknowledgments — ix

Introduction: Existence Pain — xi

1. *The Theory and Practice of Group Psychotherapy*: The Art of Self-Disclosure — 1

2. *Every Day Gets a Little Closer*: A Dual Perspective of Therapy — 15

3. *Existential Psychotherapy*: Living with Death Anxiety — 27

4. *Inpatient Group Psychotherapy*: Educating Observers and the Observed — 43

5. *Love's Executioner*: Living with Existence Pain — 49

6. *When Nietzsche Wept*: Gratitude and Its Discontents — 79

7. *Lying on the Couch*: The Threat of Sexual Boundary Violations — 117

8. *Momma and the Meaning of Life*: The "Smoldering Inner Compost Heap" of Creativity — 143

9. *The Gift of Therapy*: The Hazards and Privileges of Being a Therapist — 163

10. *The Schopenhauer Cure*: Searching for an Antidote — 169

11. *Staring at the Sun*: Novel Healing — 207

12. *The Spinoza Problem*: "A Sedative for My Passions" — 225

13. *Creatures of a Day*: Anticipating Endings — 267

Conclusion: *Yalom's Cure* and *Becoming Myself* — 285

Works Cited — 297

Index — 307

Acknowledgments

I am deeply grateful to Irvin Yalom for taking the time to read and comment on the manuscript for *Writing the Talking Cure* before I submitted it for publication. He pointed out factual errors, helped me to make connections I hadn't seen, and allowed me to include his comments in my study. Irv and Marilyn Yalom invited my wife, Julie, and me to dinner in the spring of 2017 when I was doing research at the Yalom Archives at Stanford University. It was a great pleasure meeting the Yaloms, who could not have been more gracious. Reading Irv Yalom's responses to my manuscript, I had the same feeling that I do when I read his books: he is one of the people, as Henry James observed in "The Art of Fiction," "on whom nothing is lost." I have long known, like countless others, that reading and writing are therapeutic; authoring a book on Irvin Yalom has been the least expensive and most effective psychotherapy in my life.

I am grateful to the staff at Stanford University's Department of Special Collections, who went out of their way to help me during my research at the Yalom Archives, which contain hundreds of letters testifying to the power of his writings. A typical comment, written by a woman grieving the recent death of her father: "I want to thank you for all of your generous literature. You have helped me to embrace death and understand death anxiety and the importance of living life to its fullest—and most important, to share the expression of love with those [with] whom we share common paths. Had I not drowned myself in your writing, I do not think I would be coping as well as I am. Thank you, thank you with all of my heart." One could write an entire chapter on Yalom's correspondence, especially his influence on mental health professionals, as can be seen in a 2004 letter from an Australian therapist: "You have been the most influential therapist in my training and I would hate to think that you weren't around anymore to share your wisdom and humour."

Part of the discussion of psychobiography in *When Nietzsche Wept* appears in my chapter "Hemingway's Suicides: A Psychobiographical Approach to Literature" in *Critical Insights: Psychological Approaches to Criticism*, edited by Robert C. Evans, published by Grey House in 2017. Some of the information about Anne Sexton's sexual relationship with her psychiatrist Frederick J. Duhl appears in the book Paul W. Mosher and I coauthored, *Confidentiality and Its Discontents: Dilemmas of Privacy in Psychotherapy*, published by Fordham University Press in 2015.

I'm grateful to the two anonymous State University of New York Press readers for their helpful suggestions for improving this book. This is my fourth book published by SUNY Press, and, as always, I am grateful to James Peltz for his unwavering support. Special thanks to Rafael Chaiken, assistant acquisitions editor at the press, who helped expedite production of the manuscript. I always take the time to correct my students' grammatical and stylistic errors, and for that reason I'm grateful to my superb copyeditor, Dana Foote, who pointed out my own grammatical and stylistic errors. Finally, I wish to thank Julie, who helped me in countless ways, including spending hours patiently removing the mysterious artifacts that appeared when she formatted the manuscript.

Introduction

Existence Pain

I belong to those readers of Irvin Yalom who know perfectly well, after they have turned the first page, that they will read all the others, and listen to every word that he has spoken. My trust in him sprang to life at once and has been the same for nine years. I understood him as though he had written for me (this is the most intelligible, though a rather foolish and conceited, way of expressing it).

The preceding sentences describe precisely how I feel reading Irvin Yalom's writings, though, truth be told, these are not my words but Friedrich Nietzsche's, appearing in his essay "Schopenhauer as Educator," to express his boundless admiration for his intellectual mentor. I came across this passage while reading both philosophers' writings for my research on two of Yalom's novels, *When Nietzsche Wept* and *The Schopenhauer Cure*.

I don't mean to imply that I'm a Nietzsche or that Yalom is a Schopenhauer. But Yalom has long been one of my heroes—and for longer than the nine years Nietzsche mentioned. I admire Yalom for his profound contributions to both psychotherapy and fiction and for his vast humanity. He is not the first to write about "existence pain," but few authors have explored the subject more incisively, over a longer period of time, in both nonfictional and fictional writings, than Yalom. Indeed, he has transmuted existence pain into a distinctive approach to both psychotherapy and the art of psychotherapy tales.

My aim throughout this book is to show Yalom's growth and development as both an existential psychotherapist and a storyteller. Nietzsche eventually turned against his former mentor, rejecting Schopenhauer's gloomy pessimism and nay-saying; by contrast my appreciation of the life-affirming

Yalom has grown deeper over time. My trust in Yalom sprang to life when years ago I read first *Love's Executioner* and then *When Nietzsche Wept*. Both works dazzled me. I then began to read systematically all of his writings. I am an English professor, not a psychotherapist, but I believe I understand him as though he has written for me. If such an admission could make Nietzsche feel foolish and conceited, I have no problem feeling the same way.

"Autobiographical Note"

Therapist self-disclosure is the cornerstone of Yalom's writings, so it's appropriate that we begin with his "Autobiographical Note." He was born in Washington, DC, in 1931 to parents who had immigrated to the United States shortly after World War I from a Russian village. Living in a tiny apartment above his parents' grocery store in a poor, black neighborhood—Washington was still a segregated city—Yalom reveals in his "Autobiographical Note" that reading was his refuge. Twice a week he made the "hazardous bicycle trek" from his apartment to the public library:

> No counseling or direction was available: my parents had virtually no secular education, never read books and were entirely consumed in the struggle for economic survival. My book choices were capricious, directed in part by the library architecture; the large, centrally placed bookcase on biography caught my attention early, and I spent an entire year going through that bookcase from A (John Adams) to Z (Zoroaster). But it was mainly in fiction where I found a refuge, an alternate, more satisfying world, a source of inspiration and wisdom. Sometime early in life I developed the notion—one which I have never relinquished—that writing a novel is the very finest thing a person can do.

Yalom knew that earning a living through writing would be perilously difficult. Based on his peers' decisions, he seemed to have only two choices: going to medical school or into his father's business. He chose the former, mainly because medical school seemed closer to Tolstoy and Dostoevsky, two unsurpassed psychologists. He decided on psychiatry because it seemed to him, then and now, endlessly intriguing. Yalom singles out the narrative element of psychiatry, the same element that drives fiction. "I have approached all of my patients with a sense of wonderment at the story that will unfold. I believe that a different therapy must be constructed for each patient because each has a unique story."

In 1954 Yalom married the woman who would turn out to be his soul mate, Marilyn Koenick. A professor of French for many years and then a senior scholar at the Clayman Institute for Gender Studies at Stanford, she is the author of many acclaimed books. The Yaloms have four children. Irv and Marilyn Yalom often refer to each other in their books, and each is an influence on the other's thinking and writing.

After graduating from the Boston University School of Medicine in 1956, Yalom completed a residency at the Henry Phipps Psychiatric Clinic of Johns Hopkins Hospital in 1960. In *Staring at the Sun* he writes about the deaths of two of his Johns Hopkins mentors, John Whitehorn and Jerome Frank, as well as the death of a third mentor who was also his analyst and friend, Rollo May. After a psychiatry residency at Mount Sinai Hospital in New York City, Yalom served as a captain in the US Army, stationed in Honolulu, Hawaii, and then began teaching in 1960 at Stanford University as an instructor in psychiatry. By 1968 he had risen through the ranks to become a full professor. He was medical director of the Stanford University Hospital Psychiatric Inpatient Unit from 1981 to 1984 and was also a fellow at the Center for Advanced Study in the Behavioral Sciences in Palo Alto, California.

During the beginning of his academic career Yalom wrote the groundbreaking psychiatric textbooks that brought him early fame. His first book, *The Theory and Practice of Group Psychotherapy*, was published in 1970 and is currently in its fifth revised edition, rare for a psychiatric text; it has sold over one million copies and has been translated into eighteen languages. Three years later he coauthored *Encounter Groups: First Facts*. His next book, *Every Day Gets a Little Closer: A Twice-Told Therapy*, coauthored with a patient pseudonymously called Ginny Elkin, was published in 1974. Yalom's 1980 book *Existential Psychotherapy* was influential in pointing verbal therapy in a new direction, one inspired by the therapist's love of philosophy. *Inpatient Group Psychotherapy* appeared in 1983.

Love's Executioner, the first of three volumes of psychotherapy tales, became a critical and popular success when it was published in 1989, establishing Yalom's reputation as a master of creative nonfiction. The ten psychotherapy tales, all based on patients whose identities have been heavily disguised, reveal Yalom's delight in storytelling. Basic Books has published all of his books, unusual in a profession where authors and publishers seldom make a lifelong commitment to each other. Commitment is a key word for Yalom: he has demonstrated a lifelong commitment to his family, patients, profession, and readers.

When Nietzsche Wept, Yalom's first and perhaps best-known novel, was published in 1992 and continues to enjoy critical and popular success. Four million copies of the novel have been sold, and it has been translated into twenty-seven languages and made into a film. *When Nietzsche Wept* is an historical and philosophical novel that imagines how two great contemporaries who had never met, Josef Breuer and Friedrich Nietzsche, might treat each other using a new form of therapy, "the talking cure," which Breuer helped to create. *When Nietzsche Wept* also represents a new subgenre of fiction, the "teaching novel," designed to illuminate different aspects of psychotherapy for young therapists. Yalom's challenge as both psychiatrist and storyteller is to teach and entertain—a daunting task in light of Jane Austen's sardonic observation in *Pride and Prejudice*: "We all love to instruct, though we can teach only what is not worth knowing."

Following *Love's Executioner* and *When Nietzsche Wept* have come two more volumes of psychotherapy tales, *Momma and the Meaning of Life* (1999) and *Creatures of a Day* (2015), and three more novels, *Lying on the Couch* (1996), *The Schopenhauer Cure* (2005), and *The Spinoza Problem* (2012). *The Yalom Reader*, edited by his son Ben Yalom, appeared in 1998, a five-hundred-page volume containing selections from his textbooks, novels, and psychotherapy tales. *The Gift of Therapy* was published in 2002, abounding in insights for psychotherapists and the general public. *Staring at the Sun: Overcoming the Terror of Death* appeared in 2008, a meditation on our deepest fear. *Yalom's Cure* appeared in 2014, a documentary of the therapist's present life as an octogenarian. Yalom's final book, *Becoming Myself: A Psychiatrist's Memoir*, was published in 2017. Yalom retired from teaching at Stanford in 1994, after thirty-two years in the department of psychiatry, but he continues to have a small psychotherapy practice in Palo Alto and San Francisco.

Receiving and Bequeathing Awards

Yalom has received many awards from literary and psychiatric organizations. The French translation of *The Spinoza Problem* received the Prix des Lecteurs in 2014. *When Nietzsche Wept* won the Commonwealth Gold Medal for best fiction of 1993, and in 2009 it was honored by the Vienna International Book Fair; one hundred thousand free copies were distributed to the citizens of Vienna. Yalom has received the Oskar Pfister Award for contributions to religion and psychiatry from the American Psychiatric Association in 2000, the Foundation's Fund Award for research in psychiatry from the American Psychiatric Association in 1976, and the Edward Strecker Award for significant contributions to the field of psychiatry patient care presented by the Institute of the Pennsylvania Hospital in 1974. The Department of Psychiatry and Behavioral Sciences at Stanford School of Medicine sponsors the Irvin David Yalom, M.D. Literary Award, given annually to a deserving student, active in undergraduate or postgraduate education, for an exceptional essay or creative writing piece describing his or her experience with medicine as a doctor, trainee, or patient.

Yalom's psychiatric textbooks, psychotherapy tales, and therapy novels have been reviewed in many professional mental health journals, and interviews of Yalom have appeared in several magazines and newspapers. He is one of the most famous living American psychiatrists. In a 2006 survey of the most influential American psychotherapists, undertaken by *Psychotherapy Networker* magazine on the occasion of its twenty-fifth anniversary, respondents were asked the question, "Over the last 25 years, which figures have most influenced your practice?" Respondents could list up to ten people. Yalom was ranked fourth, after such luminaries as Carl Rogers, Aaron Beck (the founder of cognitive therapy), and Salvador Minuchin (one of the founders of family therapy). Sigmund Freud did not make the list, and Carl Jung was ranked eighth. In the same survey, Yalom was judged the "country's best-known theorist and practitioner of existential psychotherapy." Yalom has also found his way into popular culture. In the TV series *In Treatment*, the therapist Paul, in a state of confusion about his work as a clinician, laments to his supervisor, Gina: "Maybe Yalom was right; maybe it is all about the relationship."

Yet apart from Ruthellen Josselson's 2008 study *Irvin D. Yalom: On Psychotherapy and the Human Condition*, which contains valuable interviews with Yalom, there have been no full-length studies of his work. Throughout the present study, I take a chronological approach, which allows us to see his growth and development as both an existential psychotherapist and writer of fiction and creative nonfiction. There are many more continuities than discontinuities in his writings, but there are also several surprises, particularly his evolution as a self-disclosing therapist. Sometimes Yalom discusses an anonymous patient in an early book only to disclose in a later book that the patient was himself. As often as not, he will make a partial self-disclosure in an early book and then elaborate upon it in a later book.

All of his books reveal the continuing chapters of his life. A chronological approach enables us to see how, when, where, and why Yalom changes his mind about certain subjects. To cite only one example, he is ambivalent enough about the word *existential* to place it in quotation marks in his first book, acknowledging that he doesn't like the term. Ten years later he published *Existential Psychotherapy*.

My Own Autobiographical Note

It may seem odd that an English professor rather than a psychiatrist or psychologist is writing a book on Yalom, but I have long been interested in the relationship between literature and psychoanalysis, and I have written several books on the subject, beginning with *The Talking Cure: Literary Representations of Psychoanalysis* (1985), which explores well-known literary authors who experienced psychological breakdowns, entered therapy of one kind or another, and later wrote about their experiences in fictional or nonfictional stories. Years ago I interviewed Allen Wheelis, the distinguished psychoanalyst and novelist, and I wrote a long essay on him that was published in a volume devoted to an appreciation of his work. I intended to do the same with Yalom, but I discovered that his writings are too vast and complex to be reduced to a single article. Thus, the present book.

I'm not quite as hoary as Yalom—I was born in 1945, and I'm now a septuagenarian, as I routinely inform my students. I've taught at the University at Albany for forty-five years, in addition to the five years I taught at Cornell as a doctoral student and lecturer. There's a special significance for me near the dawn and twilight of my career to write books on the talking cure, a subject that has long fascinated me.

Yalom's books have deepened my understanding of why some of my pedagogical practices are effective. Two examples readily come to mind. First, Yalom has long insisted that the most important element in psychotherapy is the patient-therapist relationship, an observation that has been supported by scores of empirical studies. I believe that the student-teacher relationship is the most crucial factor in education, far more significant than whatever knowledge a teacher imparts to students. I encourage my students to call me by my first name, as Yalom encourages his patients to do. My students know that I take a special interest in them. Just as teachers can make a difference in their students' lives, students make a difference in their teachers' lives. I've been fortunate in staying in touch with students for decades, and

I've been lucky enough to teach my former students' *children*. Perhaps one day I will teach their grandchildren.

Second, Yalom has been psychotherapy's most influential proponent of therapist self-disclosure. Teacher self-disclosure has long been the cornerstone of my teaching. Teacher self-disclosure begets student self-disclosure, and I try to model self-disclosure for my students. I know from the published reviews of my books that I'm in a tiny minority when it comes to encouraging self-disclosing writing in literature classes. My students tell me that most of their high school and college teachers do not allow them to use the first-person pronoun in their writings, mainly for fear of encouraging excessive subjectivity. It's true that students shouldn't begin every sentence with "I think" or "I feel," but writing in the first person emboldens students to engage in self-reflection, a process that is more difficult if not impossible in "objective" writing. My book *Risky Writing: Self-Disclosure and Self-Transformation in the Classroom* (2001) focuses on the ways in which an empathic classroom allows students to write about the most important issues in their lives. Literature classes are not support groups, but I do everything possible to create a safe, empathic classroom where students will support each other. "At best there exists," remarks a character in *The Schopenhauer Cure*, "only a vague boundary between education and therapy" (261).

Like Yalom, I've written several teaching books, each filled with students' writings on a wide variety of personal topics. To minimize the possibility of subtle coercion, I ask students for permission to use their writings after they have completed their course with me and received their final grade. They disguise their identities and create their own pseudonyms. I then show the students exactly how I comment on and contextualize their writings. I also receive permission from the University Institute Review Board, which oversees all campus human research. I've discovered, as Yalom has, that students, like patients, want to tell their stories. They also greatly benefit from hearing their classmates' and teachers' stories.

My life has been profoundly fulfilling, abounding in happiness in family and work. Paradoxically, many of my books are about the two tragedies in my life: the suicide of my college professor and mentor, Len Port, on Labor Day, 1968, and the death of my first wife of thirty-five years, Barbara, from pancreatic cancer in 2004, at age fifty-seven. Several of my books have the words *suicide*, *dying*, *death*, *cutting*, or *widowhood* in their titles. Reading Yalom's books has been a therapeutic experience for me. He has helped me realize that many, perhaps most, of my books have been an ongoing effort to understand and cope with my own death anxiety. Writing about Yalom has been fascinating, life affirming, and deeply healing. Reading Yalom's many philosophical sources, such as Marcus Aurelius, Spinoza, Schopenhauer, and Nietzsche, has also been rewarding.

The Plan of This Book

Throughout the book I offer detailed readings of Yalom's novels and psychotherapy tales. I also discuss his extensive and always meticulous use of philosophical, psychological, and literary sources. In addition, I consider the many reviews of his work published in professional journals, magazines, and newspapers. Yalom's writings appeal to experts in the mental health profession and to the general public. He has crafted a magisterial prose style that places him in the tradition of the greatest storytellers.

Respecting Claudius's observation in *Hamlet*—"For goodness, owing to a pleurisy, / Dies in his own too-much"—I have not commented on three of Yalom's coauthored works. These include *Encounter Groups: First Facts* (1973), *Concise Guide to Group Psychotherapy* (1989), and *I'm Calling the Police*, a forty-one page short story published in the United States in 2009 as an ebook.

Chapter 1 begins with Yalom's first and still most popular textbook, *The Theory and Practice of Group Psychotherapy*. My primary interest in the textbook lies in its emphasis on the *art* of self-disclosure, an art that leads him ineluctably to literature, where Yalom explores Hermann Hesse's novel *The Glass Bead Game* and Eugene O'Neill's play *The Iceman Cometh*. Yalom often uses literary examples to support his clinical insights. *The Theory and Practice of Group Psychotherapy* contains one of his most revealing self-disclosures, one that he was not willing to own until nineteen years later.

Every Day Gets a Little Closer, the subject of chapter 2, is Yalom's "twice-told" therapy tale, written with "Ginny Elkin." Yalom and his patient offer in alternating chapters their shifting impressions of the weekly therapy sessions. The structure of the book is unique in the history of psychiatric case study literature in that we receive a dual perspective of the patient-therapist relationship. The patient's method of payment for therapy is also unique, writing summaries of each therapy session. We discover, in a metaphor that Yalom uses for the first but by no means last time, that everything is "grist for the therapist's mill." We also discover that what may be important for a therapist is less important, perhaps even ignored, by a patient. One of the most bizarre moments in *Every Day Gets a Little Closer* occurs when Marilyn Yalom enters the story, resulting in her husband experiencing a conflict of interest, being torn between his patient and wife.

Chapter 3 focuses on *Existential Psychotherapy*, the textbook that urges a new approach to mental healing. It is also the sourcebook for all of Yalom's later writings. The major problem besetting his patients and fictional characters is death anxiety, a subject that our death-denying culture seeks to avoid. It is easy for writers to point out death anxiety in others, but few writers confess to their *own* death anxiety. Like Freud in *The Interpretation of Dreams*, Yalom uses himself as an example of a person suffering from conflicts he seeks to heal, but Freud rarely admitted he was writing about himself. Yalom does. He is not afraid to reveal that he has entered therapy to come to terms with the death anxiety he seeks to help his patients overcome. Such admissions make Yalom more human. He offers insights into the role of death anxiety in others' lives, including his contemporaries. Elisabeth Kübler-Ross's influential but flawed stage theory of dying betrays her own unacknowledged death anxiety. Yalom also discusses the role of death anxiety in Hemingway's life. Abounding in insights, *Existential Psychotherapy* offers a new theory of why a patient's quest for self-discovery is important in psychotherapy. Insights are valuable, but the major importance of the search for knowledge is that it strengthens the patient-therapist relationship.

Inpatient Group Psychotherapy, to which I turn in chapter 4, is the textbook that serves as a bridge from Yalom's early clinical writings to his popular psychotherapy tales. His major purpose in writing the book was to offer a unique approach to group psychotherapy on rapid turnover wards. The idea of inpatient group psychotherapy may remind some readers of the therapeutic horrors of Ken Kesey's *One Flew Over the Cuckoo's Nest*, where patients, incited by the staff, use psychotherapy as a weapon to expose each other's vulnerabilities. Yalom gives us a much more affirmative view of inpatient group psychotherapy. The book contains many clinical vignettes, though most are too short to be memorable. *Inpatient Group Psychotherapy* does offer, however, many useful techniques for creating a pedagogy based on an evolving understanding of observers and the observed. These techniques can be used in the classroom as well as in the hospital.

Chapter 5 focuses on Yalom's first literary masterpiece, *Love's Executioner*, whose haunting title heralds characters rarely seen in American psychiatric case studies. The ten vignettes cover a remarkable range of colorful characters, all of whom struggle with existence pain. They challenge Yalom's imaginative powers as both an existential psychotherapist and storyteller. Readers will find themselves, like Yalom and his patients, both tearing up and smiling as they witness the dramas enacted in psychotherapy. There is a century-long tradition of the psychoanalyst in literature as a master sleuth, a psychological Sherlock Holmes, but Yalom gives us a new and jarring image of the therapist, love's executioner, a figure who challenges all of our death-denying strategies.

Chapter 6 opens with a discussion of psychobiography, an art that Yalom has mastered in his three philosophical novels. *When Nietzsche Wept* offers riveting portraits of Josef Breuer, Friedrich Nietzsche, and the young Sigmund Freud, who is still a medical intern. Breuer remains a shadowy figure in the early history of psychoanalysis. Though Breuer was the coauthor of *Studies on Hysteria*, the first book on psychoanalysis, Freud later spoke condescendingly about his older colleague. According to Freud, Breuer was in the throes of obsessional love for his patient, "Anna O.," who coined the expression the "talking cure." Yalom does much to humanize Breuer, making him into a compelling character, in some ways more prescient than Freud. Nietzsche, too, emerges as human, startlingly brilliant but tormented by his dark love for a woman who has recently spurned him.

Chapter 7 investigates the many ironies and ambiguities implicit in the evocative title of Yalom's next novel, *Lying on the Couch*. The story contains two existential psychiatrists, one of whom is a consummate storyteller and con artist (the two are not always identical), the other of whom is an ethical therapist who survives the seductive wiles of a female patient intent on destroying him. Yalom is not the first novelist to explore the sexual temptations that exist in the patient-therapist relationship, but he is the first to show how these threats are heightened by therapist self-disclosure. *Lying on the Couch* remains Yalom's most comic novel, filled with surprises that are artfully plotted. It also remains his most sustained analysis of sexual boundary violations, a subject about which he is deadly serious.

Momma and the Meaning of Life, Yalom's second volume of psychotherapy tales, constitutes chapter 8. The six stories lack the exuberance of *Love's Executioner*, but they retain all of the earlier volume's irony and ambiguity. Yalom reveals not only the autobiographical basis of his stories but also the ways in which life is the "smoldering inner compost heap" of his art. He resurrects Ernest Lash in the last two stories of the volume. It becomes apparent that Flaubert's celebrated statement—"Madame Bovary, c'est moi"—is no less true of Yalom's relationship to Ernest: there are many similarities between the real and fictional existential psychotherapists. Yalom doesn't hide behind his fictional psychotherapists; instead, he reveals how they represent his different sides, not all of which he exposes to his patients.

Chapter 9 focuses on *The Gift of Therapy*, in which Yalom comments on his forty-five-year career as a psychotherapist. The book marks a turning point in Yalom's career: from this point on, he and his patients have an acute awareness of his advanced age. *The Gift of Therapy* is a treasure trove of insights for young therapists, about whom Yalom worries because of his fear that his beloved psychotherapy is in a crisis, beset by external and internal problems. The tone of the slender volume is not apocalyptic but reassuring, however; one senses that the profession will weather the storm, partly as a result of books like *The Gift of Therapy*.

Yalom's third novel, *The Schopenhauer Cure*, the focus of chapter 10, casts much light on one of philosophy's most misanthropic thinkers, as well as on the emotionally disconnected therapist-in-training who tries to pattern his life on a flawed philosophy. The early twentieth-century Viennese satirist Karl Kraus caustically characterized psychoanalysis as the disease of which it purports to be the cure. The same could be said about the cheerless philosophy of Arthur Schopenhauer, whose radical cure for the problem of life demands an equally radical antidote. Yalom creates in *The Schopenhauer Cure* a terminally ill existential psychotherapist who seeks to provide through group psychotherapy a life-saving antidote to a former patient whom he could not help years earlier. The result is a fascinating philosophical novel that offers valuable life lessons in the form of an emotionally charged story.

Staring at the Sun: Overcoming the Terror of Death occupies the center of our attention in chapter 11. The book reveals Yalom's unflinching examination of the role of death anxiety in his patients' lives. Death anxiety, he maintains, is bedrock anxiety: there is no deeper terror. Our major interest in *Staring at the Sun* lies in his brief memoir, "Death Awareness," where he discusses his early experiences with death, a subject that is never far from his present life. One cannot escape death anxiety, but one can live with it without seeking supernatural remedies. *Staring at the Sun* demonstrates how death anxiety can serve as the inspiration behind art, a faithful muse to which Yalom remains devoted.

Chapter 12 explores Yalom's fourth and final novel, *The Spinoza Problem*. The story offers psychobiographical insights into two characters who could not be more different: the seventeenth-century Dutch thinker who is philosophy's supreme rationalist, and a man who was the chief Nazi anti-Semitic ideologue, Hitler's right-hand man. Why was Alfred Rosenberg so preoccupied with Spinoza's writings that he sent an officer to the Rijnsburg Spinoza museum in the Netherlands in 1942 to confiscate the philosopher's writings? What was the "Spinoza problem"? Yalom never found any historical evidence linking Rosenberg with Spinoza, but he imagined a story that explains why the Nazi might have found the Dutch philosopher so threatening. Yalom raises an additional question: How would a Spinoza-oriented psychotherapist treat a repugnant character like Alfred Rosenberg? The task may prove impossible, but Yalom's fictional therapist convinces us that he has a penetrating understanding of a man who was instrumental in creating the ideology that led to the final solution.

Chapter 13 focuses on *Creatures of a Day*, which offers an insight into an octogenarian's life and work. Most of the patients Yalom discusses entered therapy because they had read one or more of his books. How do patients feel about a therapist who writes about treatment? Why do patients, including those who are dying, want Yalom to use their real names? *Creatures of a Day* is essential reading for anyone interested in these and related questions.

In the conclusion I focus on the 2014 documentary *Yalom's Cure* and his 2017 memoir *Becoming Myself*. The documentary provides a rare glimpse into Yalom's relationship with his wife, children, and grandchildren. Interestingly, Marilyn Yalom is more self-disclosing than her husband, and we see their disagreements over romantic love, including the gendered nature of love. One cannot watch *Yalom's Cure* without being aware of the approach of mortality, and yet Yalom implies that he enjoys his golden years, fulfilled in his twin passions, love and work, eager to pass along his insights to others. *Becoming Myself* appeared after I completed a draft of this book, but I comment briefly on Yalom's farewell to his readers after a writing career that spanned half a century.

A Dual and Sometimes Conflicted Identity

Many people struggle with a single identity, but Yalom has had to negotiate two identities, that of a psychotherapist and a creative writer. He reveals in *The Yalom Reader* with characteristic self-mockery that whenever he picks up an issue of the *American Journal of Psychiatry* and reads articles he cannot understand about psychopharmacology or brain imaging research, articles having nothing to do with patients' human concerns, he thinks: "I don't belong in medicine or even psychiatry; I'm a writer—that's where I really live." Yet whenever he is bruised by a negative book review, he soothes himself by saying, "I'm not a writer; I'm a physician. Always have been" (436–437). Notwithstanding this split, no one has written better about the art of psychotherapy and psychotherapy as an art—and no one has more deftly melded the two careers.

Chapter 1

The Theory and Practice of Group Psychotherapy
The Art of Self-Disclosure

"Never has any therapist, I believe, made a more earnest attempt to demystify the therapeutic process" (201). The statement, two hundred pages into the fourth edition of Yalom's first textbook, *The Theory and Practice of Group Psychotherapy*, accurately describes one of Yalom's lifelong goals. The book, first published in 1970 and now in its updated fifth edition, published in 2005, remains the standard textbook in the field. The *American Journal of Psychiatry* cited the textbook as one of the ten most influential psychiatry publications of the decade. Jerome Frank, Yalom's mentor at Johns Hopkins, hailed the work as the "best book that exists on the subject, today and for the foreseeable future." *The Theory and Practice of Group Psychotherapy* is Yalom's only textbook that he has repeatedly revised.

Ruthellen Josselson observed that when she was a clinical psychology intern in 1970 at the Massachusetts Mental Health Center, an "[a]ugust bastion of psychoanalytic thought," Yalom's textbook was "greeted with contempt" by her professors and supervisors, who regarded its radical approach as subversive to the prevailing orthodoxy of the age. The book slowly "heralded a sea change" in her generation, and it is now, she wrote in 2008, "probably the most widely read in all of mental health practice" (x–xi). It continues to be Yalom's most widely read textbook.

Yalom admits ruefully that his primary audience when writing *The Theory and Practice of Group Psychotherapy* was the Stanford University Promotion Committee. Upon being notified he had received early tenure and promotion, he radically changed his audience and writing approach. "I put the promotion committee out of my mind; I eliminated all jargon, all detailed research analysis, and all unnecessarily complex theoretical structures; and I wrote with only one purpose in mind—to interest and to educate the group therapy student" (*Yalom Reader* 5–6).

The primary interest of *The Theory and Practice of Group Psychotherapy* to practitioners lies in its hands-on approach to all aspects of the subject: a how-to book that explores in clear, jargon-free language every question one can imagine about the theory and practice of group psychotherapy. The book's primary interest to us lies in the ways in which it adumbrates Yalom's vision of self-disclosure and anticipates his emergence as a novelist.

Early in the preface to *The Theory and Practice of Group Psychotherapy* Yalom notes that psychotherapy is "both an art and science" (xiv; all references, unless otherwise noted, are to the fourth edition, published in 1995). He returns to the statement on the last page of the book: "Psychotherapy is a science as well as an art" (532). There is an unexpected meaning to these statements. Throughout the textbook Yalom refers to *literary* art, fictional stories and plays that illustrate writers' insights into the human condition. Two of his literary references are especially noteworthy: Hermann Hesse's novel *The Glass Bead Game*, published in German in 1943 and in English (sometimes under the title *Magister Ludi*) in 1949, and Eugene O'Neill's 1946 play *The Iceman Cometh*. An examination of these two literary works reveals the extent to which both psychotherapy and fiction depend upon narrative art.

A Deathbed Confession: *The Glass Bead Game*

Yalom refers to both literary works in the chapter called "The Therapist: Transference and Transparency." Investigating the therapist's relationship with group members, the chapter opens in an unusual way, with a form of address seldom used by textbook authors: an apostrophe to the reader. "Do you, as therapist, play a role? To what degree are you free to be yourself? How 'honest' can you be? How much transparency can you permit yourself?" (189). Yalom discusses near the end of the chapter whether therapists should admit their flaws to patients. He then quotes a fellow practitioner, M. B. Parloff, who remarked that the "honest therapist is one who attempts to provide that which the patient can assimilate, verify, and utilize" (214). In a footnote Yalom offers a vivid example of the necessity for proper timing. He summarizes the theme of a thirty-one-page chapter in Hesse's novel,

"The Father Confessor," about two renowned Christian penitents, legendary for their gift of healing, who befriend each other and heal themselves:

> Joseph, one of the healers, severely afflicted with feelings of worthlessness and self-doubt, sets off on a long journey across the Indian subcontinent to seek help from his rival, Dion. At an oasis, Joseph describes his plight to a stranger, who miraculously turns out to be Dion, whereupon Joseph accepts Dion's invitation to go home with him in the role of patient and servant. In time, Joseph regains his former serenity and zest and ultimately becomes the friend and colleague of his master. Only after many years have passed, and Dion lies on his deathbed, does he reveal to Joseph that at their encounter at the oasis, he had reached a similar impasse in his life and was en route to request Joseph's assistance. (214)

The story is quintessential Yalom, affirming the need for an authentic therapeutic relationship, the value of self-disclosure for both patient and therapist, the idea of a wounded healer, the possibility of change and growth, and the importance of engagement as an antidote to existential loneliness.

A brief footnote cannot capture the subtleties of "The Father Confessor," particularly Joseph's gift for empathic listening. Whenever a troubled soul visits Joseph, Hesse suggests, the healer "knew how to listen to him, to open his ears and his heart, to gather the man's sufferings and anxieties into himself and hold them, so that the penitent was sent away emptied and calmed" (Hesse 490). Adept at the talking cure, Joseph never expresses impatience when penitents talk at length without revealing the reasons they have sought him out. Nor is he judgmental about the confessions and qualms of conscience that he hears. His refusal to pass judgment not only enables the penitents' self-disclosures but also allows them to understand the significance of their words. Whatever was confessed to Joseph, Hesse declares, "seemed not to be spoken into the void, but to be transformed, alleviated, and redeemed in the telling and being heard" (491).

Yalom's consideration of *The Glass Bead Game* appears in the first edition of *The Theory and Practice of Group Psychotherapy*, and he continued thinking about the novel, returning to it thirty-two years later in *The Gift of Therapy*. He doesn't change his interpretation of Hesse's novel, but now he recognizes something he had not seen earlier about the relationship between the two wounded healers. "Perhaps they missed the opportunity for something deeper, more authentic, more powerfully mutative. Perhaps the *real* therapy occurred at the deathbed scene, when they moved into honesty with the revelation that they were fellow travelers, both simply human, all too human. The twenty years of secrecy, helpful as they were, may have obstructed and prevented a more profound kind of help. What might have happened if Dion's deathbed confession had occurred twenty years earlier, if healer and seeker had joined together in facing the questions that have no answers?" (10).

Yalom identifies with both Joseph and Dion, the younger and older wounded healers, respectively, in Hesse's celebrated novel, which was singled out for praise by the Swedish Academy when it awarded him the Nobel Prize in Literature in 1946. Yalom also identifies with the novelist, the creator of both fictional characters. Hesse wrote the novel as a warning against the rising Nazi menace. Set five hundred years into the future, *The Glass Bead Game* cautions intellectuals not to remain isolated within academic ivory towers, a warning that Yalom reveals in his own writings, where he urges thinkers like himself to engage authentically with the everyday problems of contemporary life.

Yalom conveys in his two references to Hesse the theme of "The Father Confessor," but there is a third character in the chapter on whom he doesn't comment. A "scholar or literary man" visited Joseph and Dion and "talked long, learnedly, and eloquently about the stars and about the pilgrimage which man as well as all his gods must make through all the signs of the zodiac from the beginning to the end of every aeon" (Hesse 509). The unnamed storyteller, referred to simply as the mythologist, sees universal meanings that transcend narrow ideologies or religious creeds. Joseph cannot understand why Dion listens in rapt attention to this man whom the former characterizes as a heathen, uttering false doctrines. Dion's explanation of his interest reflects Hesse's commitment to the wisdom found in mythology, literature, and the arts. When Joseph claims that his and Dion's Christian faith is superior to the heathen's outmoded doctrines, the older healer points out that the storyteller "lives in his wisdom of images and symbols," a wisdom surpassed by no one.

On one level, the mythologist may represent Carl Jung, whom Hesse knew and admired: Hesse was in Jungian psychoanalysis, and he was especially interested in Jungian archetypes and the collective unconscious. On another level, the mythologist is the novelist, the storyteller who can provide insight, hope, and inspiration to those who may lack religious faith. Dion sees in the mythologist a younger version of himself, and he tells Joseph that those who derive ancient wisdom from their forbears demand respect. On still another level, the mythologist is Yalom himself, who, in his development as a storyteller, will come to live in the wisdom of images and symbols, seeking wisdom that transcends narrow ideologies or religious creeds.

Dion's self-disclosure, in the form of a deathbed confession, illustrates the value of therapists admitting to the same human failings as their patients. Yalom affirms throughout *The Theory and Practice of Group Psychotherapy* the advantage of self-disclosure for both patient and therapist. Self-disclosing therapists who can acknowledge without defensiveness their limitations encourage their patients to accept their own shortcomings. "Research has shown that successful patients even adopt the complex value system of the therapist" (86).

Yalom also suggests that self-disclosure benefits college students as well as psychotherapy patients. He cites two researchers, D. Medeiros and A. Richards, who demonstrated in a 1991 study that undergraduate students who anonymously shared secrets with their classmates experienced many educational and psychological benefits. The two researchers, Yalom reports, did everything possible to ensure students' anonymity: the secrets were written on uniform paper and read by the instructor in a darkened room so that no one could see facial expressions indicating discomfort. The secrets involved sexual preferences, illegal or immoral acts, psychological disorders, or family problems such as alcoholism. The atmosphere in the classroom was emotionally charged during the readings, but afterward, the students felt the kind of relief experienced by psychotherapy patients. "Students reported a sense of relief at hearing their secrets read—as though a weight had been lifted from them. But there was even greater relief in the subsequent class discussion in which students shared their responses to hearing various secrets, exchanged similar experiences, and not uncommonly chose to identify which secret they wrote. The peer support was invariably positive and powerfully reassuring" (355–356).

Yalom might have cited the groundbreaking research of University of Texas experimental psychologist James Pennebaker, who in his classic book *Opening Up* (1990/1997) has shown the health benefits of self-disclosure among college students. Pennebaker observes in his edited volume *Emotion, Disclosure & Health* (1995) that "[d]isclosure of one's deepest thoughts and feelings is a powerful social phenomenon, whether in a therapeutic setting or in daily life" (7). Pennebaker doesn't advise students to share their personal writings with others, fearful that they will regret revealing their self-disclosures. I agree that such writing is risky, but I believe that teachers can put into place protocols that will make the classroom a safe site for sharing personal writing. Moreover, students learn a great deal from listening to each other's stories, and they are themselves good teachers. "Educators have long been aware," Yalom writes, "that the most effective teacher is often a near peer, an individual who is close enough to the student to be accepted and who, by identifying with the student's mental processes, is hence able to present material in a timely, accessible fashion" (172).

A Foolosopher's Self-Disclosure: *The Iceman Cometh*

What happens when self-disclosure is used cynically and recklessly, particularly in a group setting? Yalom raises this question in *The Theory and Practice of Group Psychotherapy*. He has in mind the faddish encounter group movements of the 1960s and 1970s, when many therapists manipulated patients' self-disclosures for selfish ends, often resulting in sexual boundary violations. Yalom cites one of the worst examples of a charismatic therapist who exploited his followers, the car salesman–turned–guru Werner Erhard, the founder of est. But Yalom chooses to discuss in elaborate detail a *literary* example of self-disclosure gone awry, *The Iceman Cometh*. O'Neill's play is about a group of derelicts who have lived peacefully in the back of a barroom for twenty years. The group has remained stable over the years because each man's life illusions, or "pipe dreams," have been respected by the other men in the group.

The group's survival is threatened by the arrival of the iceman, Hickey, a "traveling salesman," in Yalom's words, a "totally enlightened therapist, a false prophet who believes he brings fulfillment and lasting peace to each man by forcing him to shed his self-deception and stare with unblinking honesty at the sun of life." Encouraging each person in the group to attack and destroy the others' illusions, the iceman has a profoundly destabilizing effect, causing one man to commit suicide and the others to turn against each other. Only when, by the instinct of self-preservation, the group labels Hickey insane and expels him from their presence can the men reaffirm their old illusions and regain their former cohesiveness, though not without being forever changed.

Hickey ingratiates himself with the residents by calling them by their first names, buying them drinks, and pretending to take interest in their lives, but his pledge to help them give up their "damned lying pipe dreams" is nothing more than an effort to free himself from excoriating guilt. Hickey is undone by his own admission, for he admits at the end of the play that he has murdered his wife, Evelyn, in her sleep, allegedly to release her from grief over his womanizing behavior. His confession, in the presence of the men and two police officers he has invited to the bar, and his stated wish to end his life in the electric chair, betray an impulse toward suicide that has motivated his actions. Only after a reading of *The Iceman Cometh* can one appreciate the irony of Yalom's characterization of Hickey as a "totally enlightened therapist," a healer who is both wounded and wounding. Hickey and Yalom have little in common, but it's ironic that the latter regards himself, in his first volume of psychotherapy tales, as "love's executioner," the destroyer of the false illusions of love. We may thus see Yalom as a positive version of Hickey, an enlightened philosopher, not a foolosopher.

Yalom reveals in his discussions of *The Glass Bead Game* and *The Iceman Cometh* that there is an art to self-disclosure. Too little self-disclosure, too late, as *The Glass Bead Game* shows, can result in missed opportunities for growth and friendship. Too much self-disclosure, too early, as *The Iceman Cometh* shows, can result in personal and social disaster. The art of self-disclosure depends upon many factors, including timing.

Vertical and Horizontal Self-Disclosures

Yalom encourages careful self-disclosures throughout *The Theory and Practice of Group Psychotherapy*, distinguishing between vertical and horizontal self-disclosures. A vertical disclosure refers to the content about a secret and involves digging, stripping away, uncovering, excavating. By contrast, a horizontal disclosure refers to disclosure about the disclosure itself, or *metadisclosure*, the "interactional aspects" of disclosure. What is most important in group psychotherapy, Yalom argues, is how a self-disclosure affects the members of the group, the ongoing relationships, rather than the past relationships involved with the secret's contents. He offers, as an example, his patient John, who disclosed his transvestism to the group. The members' "natural inclination" was to obtain more information about the content of the disclosure: the age when John began to cross-dress, the clothes he wore, his sexual fantasies at the time. Yalom's approach, by contrast, was to obtain from John more horizontal information about the disclosure: whether it was hard for him to wait twelve weeks before sharing the self-disclosure with the group, whether he felt uncomfortable about disclosing the information, whether he could predict that some members of the group would be more accepting of the information than others. Yalom's conclusion is that "even more important than the actual unburdening of oneself is the fact that disclosure results in a deeper, richer, and more complex relationship with others" (122).

I had an "aha" (or Eureka) moment when reading about Yalom's distinction between vertical and horizontal self-disclosures. I've been teaching personal writing courses for over four decades. I don't grade students on the content of their essays, or on the degree of self-disclosure, but "only" on the quality of their writing. (I place *only* in quotation marks to indicate the teacher's challenge to help students improve the quality of their writing.) Because students often write on dark topics, such as suicide, depression, cutting, eating disorders, or sexual abuse, we don't discuss the content of their writings, at least not directly. After a student reads an essay aloud, the three students sitting to his or her right raise questions they want the author to consider—but not answer in class. If, for example, an author has written an essay about depression, classmates might raise the following content questions: When did the depression begin? What was responsible for the depression? When did the depression lift? Or classmates might raise a different kind of question, one involving the process of self-disclosure. How do you feel about revealing this to the class? Was it hard or easy to share this self-disclosure with the class? How do you feel about your classmates' responses to your self-disclosure? Until reading Yalom, I never realized that the questions in the first category are "content" questions, and that those in the second category are "process" questions. Since a writing class has more affinity to group psychotherapy than individual therapy, horizontal questions are often more valuable than vertical ones.

Ptolemaic v. Copernican Conceptions of Change

One of the humbling implications of Yalom's research on encounter groups also applies to group psychotherapy. As he points out in his 1973 coauthored study *Encounter Groups: First Facts*, those who lead encounter groups, and, we might add, psychotherapy groups, must "abandon a Ptolemaic conception of the process of change. Change does not revolve around the solitary sun of the leader: the evidence is strong that psychosocial relations in the group play an exceedingly important role in the process of change" (428). The shift from a Ptolemaic to a Copernican paradigm underscores the need for members' honesty and openness with each other along with the willingness to give and receive feedback about their interpersonal behavior.

YALOM'S SELF-DISCLOSURES

Yalom's self-disclosures in the first four editions of *The Theory and Practice of Group Psychotherapy* are infrequent, cautious, and always in the here-and-now. He credits his recognition of the importance of here-and-now therapy to a "very savvy psychologist," Dorothy Semenow Garwood, who led a group therapy session he attended at the National Training Laboratory after his army service. "I was floored when she started the group by saying, 'I want us to stay entirely in the here and now,'" Yalom told Ruthellen Josselson. "That was new for me" (39).

In his clinical vignettes Yalom usually writes in the third person about an unnamed therapist or male cotherapist who may be Yalom himself. Occasionally he writes about himself in the first person, offering negative details about the therapist that seldom find their way into psychiatric case studies. One of his most revealing self-disclosures occurs when he describes three female members of a group who expressed strong sexual attraction to him but not to the other male cotherapist. Yalom then asked the women to help him identify his blind spots that were unwittingly responsible for the patients' sexual response to him:

> My request opened up a long and fruitful discussion of the group members' feelings about both therapists. There was much agreement that the two of us were very different: I was more vain, took much more care about my physical appearance and clothes, and had an exactitude and preciseness about my statements that created about me an attractive aura of suave perfection. The other therapist was sloppier in appearance and behavior: he spoke more often when he was unsure of what he was going to say; he took more risks, was willing to be wrong, and, in so doing, was more often helpful to the patients. The feedback sounded right to me. I had heard it before and told the group so. I thought about their comments during the week and, at the following meeting, thanked the group and told them that they had been helpful to me. (208)

I'm not aware of any other male psychotherapist who has admitted in a textbook, case study, or memoir that female patients were strongly attracted to him in part because of the therapist's vanity. Even if therapists were willing to make this self-disclosure, it is unlikely they would use the self-mocking words "suave perfection." Nor would therapists attribute patients' sexualized behavior to the therapists' blind spots. To heighten the irony, Yalom acknowledges that his cotherapist, sloppy, uncertain, and willing to be wrong, was more helpful to his patients.

On another occasion Yalom refers to himself in the third person to describe his dissatisfaction with his behavior during a group session. "He felt he dominated things too much, that he was too active, too directive. No doubt this is due in large part to his feeling of guilt at having missed the previous two meetings and wanting to make up for it today by giving as much as possible" (435).

Sometimes patients' criticisms expose Yalom's human side. When, years earlier, patients asked him why he was wearing a copper bracelet, and were told it was for tennis elbow, their judgment was swift and merciless. "They felt angry that I should be superstitious or ascribe to any quack cures. (They had berated me for months for being too scientific and not human enough!) Some suggested that if I would spend more time with my patients and less time on the tennis court, everyone would be better off" (194). One page later he describes a situation when, attacked by group members for his perceived inaccessibility, he was defended by a patient who mentioned, in passing, that he had telephoned Yalom, a conversation the therapist had forgotten to mention to the group. "'Where is your unconscious?' they jeered."

"That Seems to Be the Way We're Built": A Belated Self-Disclosure

The most intriguing self-disclosure in *The Theory and Practice of Group Psychotherapy* is one that remains anonymous. The opening chapter of the first four editions of the textbook contains a section called "Universality" in which Yalom notes that most patients who enter psychotherapy fear they are "unique in their wretchedness." These patients experience relief when they discover that other members of the group have similar fears. The relief arising from the knowledge that "everyone is in the same boat" also occurs in individual therapy. Yalom then gives the following example of the importance of consensual validation:

> Once I reviewed with a patient his 600-hour experience in individual analysis with another therapist. When I asked what he recalled as the most significant event in his therapy, he described an incident when he was profoundly distressed about his feel-

ings toward his mother. Despite strong concurrent positive sentiments, he was beset with death wishes for her—he stood to inherit a sizable estate. His analyst, at one point, commented simply, "That seems to be the way we're built." That artless statement offered considerable relief and furthermore enabled the patient to explore his ambivalence in great depth. (10)

What sets this clinical vignette apart from scores of others in Yalom's first psychiatric textbook is that he returns to it nineteen years later, in *Love's Executioner*, where he reveals for the first time that he was referring to *himself*. Describing a patient who was "so ashamed of being ashamed of her own father," Yalom recalls something his first analyst, Olive Smith, said to him thirty years earlier. "(I remember it well, I think, because it was the only remotely personal—and the most helpful—thing she said in my six hundred hours with her.) I had been badly shaken by having expressed some monstrous feelings about my mother, and Olive Smith leaned over the couch and said gently, 'That just seems to be the way we're built'" (120).

What shall we say about Yalom's belated self-disclosure? He was not ready for public confession in 1970, when *The Theory and Practice of Group Psychotherapy* first appeared, nor was he ready in the second, third, or fourth editions of the textbook. He *was* ready when he published *Love's Executioner*, confident enough to reveal highly embarrassing details about his conflicted relationship with his parents. He refers in his textbook to the "Taboo trio" that is rarely broached in therapy: sex, money, and death (152). Now he is ready to share two of these forbidden subjects with his readers. Just as Olive Smith used the word *we* to describe her resemblance to Yalom, an admission of her shadow side, he is ready to comfort readers of *Love's Executioner* by admitting his kinship with them.

Those who encourage the risky art of self-disclosure must be sensitive to the lurking presence of shame. Silvan Tomkins, Helen Block Lewis, and Léon Wurmser have deepened our understanding of the dynamics of shame. Wurmser, for example, has identified three distinct meanings of shame: the fear of disgrace, the affect of contempt, and the character trait that prevents disgraceful exposures. Unlike these theorists, Yalom has repeatedly disclosed his own shame, thus serving as a role model for his patients.

Yalom's delayed self-disclosure is a gift to his readers, assuring them that dark emotions are part of who we are. In revealing the identity of the therapist who was prosecuting himself for his base impulses, he was putting into practice his belief in careful self-disclosure. We can speculate that, while writing *Love's Executioner*, he experienced the exhilaration of disclosing in print, for the first time, material that had been burdensome to him for years.

What has also changed about Yalom's self-disclosure is the method of expression. His prose throughout *The Theory and Practice of Group Psychotherapy* is always lucid and mercifully free of psychobabble, but the language does not sparkle as it does in his later writings. (Academics know that sparkling prose impresses few tenure and promotion committees!) Yalom's gift for metaphorical language is evident when he wryly refers to himself as "laid low" by the "prosecution," a metaphor that reminds us of Kafka's *The Trial*. Yalom doesn't simply refer to his hope for an inheritance: he "greedily" anticipates it. And he captures in a few monosyllabic words his analyst's power to acknowledge and defuse the potentially deadly nature of the shadow self.

Demystifying Therapy

The Theory and Practice of Group Psychotherapy announces the beginning of Yalom's lifelong effort to demystify the therapeutic process. It remains a landmark book for many reasons, including its urgent insistence upon therapist transparency. Yalom's realness comes across on every page of the book. Anything that stands in the way of realness becomes an impediment to therapy. For example, in the fourth edition of the textbook he takes issue with an article published in a 1993 issue of the *American Journal of Psychiatry* advising therapists to veer away from the "very humanness" that is the core of therapy. Written with a "high Victorian tone," the article, in Yalom's words, "warned psychiatrists not to offer their patients coffee or tea, not to address them by their first names, not to use their own first names, never to run over the fifty-minute time period, never to see *any* patient during the last working hour of the day (since that is when transgressions most often occur), never to touch a patient—even an act such as squeezing the arm or patting the back of an AIDS patient who, feeling like an outcast leper, needs therapeutic touch should be scrutinized and documented." These admonitions, Yalom insists, are "deeply corrosive to the therapeutic relationship" (212). The coauthors of the offensive article appear in the bibliography, though a name is misspelled: T. Gutheil and G. Gabbard. The same criticism of the two coauthors appears in the fifth edition, but now Yalom updates his commentary. "To their credit, the authors of the 1993 article recognized the antitherapeutic impact of their first article and wrote a second paper five years later aimed at correcting the overreaction generated by the first article" (226).

Devastating Self-Disclosures

Yalom never sugarcoats the truth or rationalizes his failures. Nor does he make statements that may be too disturbing for his patients or readers to accept. But this doesn't prevent him from revealing that the "ultimate, terrible secret of the psychotherapist" is that the "intense drama in the group room plays a very small, compartmentalized role in his or her life." Yalom exposed the secret only once—to a therapy group of psychiatric residents who were experiencing anticipatory mourning over his departure for a semester-long sabbatical. He presented to the group a fact that they knew but refused to acknowledge: "I was vastly more important to them than they were to me. After all, I had many patients; they had only one therapist. They were clearly aware of this imbalance in their psychotherapeutic work with their own patients, and yet had never applied it to themselves. There was a gasp in the group as this truth, this denial of specialness, this inherent cruelty of psychotherapy, hit home" (211–212).

Yalom could have softened this brutal truth by saying that he would return in a few months, that he still wished them well despite his absence, and that he was confident they would succeed without him. He could have said that he was simply the bearer of an unpopular message. He could have also said, quoting his former analyst, "That seems to be the way we're built." But one suspects that by demonstrating he was a part of the inherent cruelty of psychotherapy, Yalom allowed, indeed, encouraged his patients to deidealize him, thus making it easier for them to do without him.

Ironically, although Yalom never qualifies the "ultimate, terrible secret of the psychotherapist," his novels and psychotherapy tales present another, no less noteworthy secret. The dying psychotherapist in *The Schopenhauer Cure*, Julius Hertzfeld, needs the other members of the group as much as they need him. His wish to die in harness depends upon practicing his beloved work to the end. The members of the group, both individually and collectively, are as necessary to Julius as he is to them.

Even when he offers a radical idea, such as therapist self-disclosure, Yalom counsels "moderation in all things," as he states in the fourth and fifth editions of his textbook. "There is a proper place for therapist concealment; and the most helpful therapist is by no means the one who is most fully and most consistently self-disclosing" (fourth edition, 213). The literary Yalom cannot help adding, in a footnote to this remark, that many of the "wilder innovations in therapy" have sprung from Southern California. Yalom then recalls Saul Bellow's "fanciful notion in *Seize the Day* of someone tilting a large, flat map of the United States and observing that 'everything that wasn't bolted or screwed down slid into Southern California.'"

"Craving for a More Human Relationship"

After the publication of *Love's Executioner* and *When Nietzsche Wept*, Yalom received a "deluge of letters, from both patients and therapists, attesting to the widespread interest and craving for a more human relationship in the therapy venture" (205). The constantly updated editions of *The Theory and Practice of Group Psychotherapy* testify to its continued relevance. Each edition, he observes in *The Yalom Reader*, demanded two years of intense work (5). The textbook remains a superb guide for patients, therapists, and the general public. Yalom realizes, despite his best efforts, that the last word can never be written about individual or group therapy, and he urges readers to cast a skeptical eye, particularly when he tells a patient, "You imbue me with too much wisdom" (209). It is one of the few statements in the book with which his readers will disagree.

Chapter 2

Every Day Gets a Little Closer
A Dual Perspective of Therapy

Psychotherapists who have written about their own clinical experiences have confronted a vexing problem that may well be insoluble: how to preserve patients' confidentiality while exposing their deepest secrets. Too much disguise alters the meaning of their story; too little disguise compromises their identity. The problem bedeviled Freud, as he admitted at the beginning of *Notes Upon a Case of Obsessional Neurosis*—the story of the "Rat Man" (1909). "I cannot give a complete history of the treatment, because that would involve my entering in detail into the circumstances of my patient's life. The importunate interest of a capital city [Vienna], focussed with particular attention upon my medical activities, forbids my giving a faithful picture of the case" (*SE*, vol. 10, 155). All of Freud's patients have been identified, many during their own lifetimes—and some, as in the case of the "Wolf Man," by the patient himself.

What about the therapist's confidentiality, however? How much can analysts disclose about themselves without worrying that such personal information can complicate and perhaps even sabotage therapy? To avoid these and other problems, Freud emphasized the analyst's neutrality. "I cannot advise my colleagues too urgently," he warned in "Recommendations to Physicians Practicing Psycho-Analysis" (1912), "to model themselves during psycho-analytic treatment on the surgeon, who puts aside all his feelings, even his human sympathy, and concentrates his mental forces on the single aim of performing the operation as skilfully as possible" (*SE*, vol. 12, 115). Freud conceded that his recommendation implied "emotional coldness," but he was willing to take this risk.

A surgical model of therapy, Freud asserted, "creates the most advantageous conditions for both parties: for the doctor a desirable protection for his own emotional life and for the patient the largest amount of help that we can give him to-day." In the next paragraph he uses an even more impersonal metaphor of the therapeutic relationship. "To put it in a formula: he must turn his own unconscious like a receptive organ towards the transmitting unconscious of the patient. He must adjust himself to the patient as a telephone receiver is adjusted to the transmitting microphone" (115–116). Near the end of the essay Freud rejects the temptation of "young" and "eager" psychoanalysts to "bring their own individuality" into the treatment of their patients. "I have no hesitation, therefore, in condemning this kind of technique as incorrect. The doctor should be opaque to his patients and, like a mirror, should show them nothing but what is shown him" (118).

Freud made these recommendations partly because he wished to establish psychoanalysis as a medical science—he later changed his mind that analysts should be medical doctors but not his belief that psychoanalysis was a science rather than an art—and partly because he feared that analysts who became emotionally overinvolved would reveal aspects of themselves that would harm therapy. Freud's discovery of transference (the patient's unconscious projective tendencies), countertransference (the analyst's unconscious projective tendencies), and clinical resistance are among his greatest insights. He was right to remind analysts of the dangers posed by transference and countertransference. "The psycho-analyst knows," he wrote near the end of "Observations on Transference-Love" (1915), "that he is working with highly explosive forces and that he needs to proceed with as much caution and conscientiousness as a chemist" (*SE*, vol. 12, 170).

And yet tellingly, Freud never practiced what he preached. We know, for example, from the Wolf Man's account of his analysis that Freud did not hesitate to give him advice, such as not following his desire to become a painter, and to avoid returning to postrevolutionary Russia in what would have been a dangerous and probably futile quest to regain his lost wealth. Additionally, Freud gave the Wolf Man gifts and confided personal information about his family, friends, and colleagues. Many analysands who went on to become analysts themselves, and who wrote about their experience with Freud, confirm that he was never a blank mirror to them. From the beginning of his career Yalom has rejected Freud's surgical model of psychotherapy, arguing that it precludes authentic therapy.

"A Twice-Told Therapy"

One solution to the problem of confidentiality is to invite a patient to be the coauthor of a book and allow her to make the necessary disguises to conceal her identity. Yalom used this strategy in *Every Day Gets a Little Closer* (1974), coauthored with his pseudonymous patient, Ginny Elkin. Subtitled *A Twice-Told Therapy*, perhaps an allusion to Hawthorne's short story collection *Twice-Told Tales*, the book consists of Yalom's impressions of his weekly sessions with Ginny, followed by her own impressions. We thus receive a dual perspective of the therapist-patient relationship. Additionally, each wrote a foreword and afterword eighteen months after their last therapy session.

The book's structure is unique in psychiatric history, as was the patient's method of payment. In lieu of therapy fees she could not afford, Yalom asked her to write a summary of each session, "containing not only her reactions to what transpired, but also a depiction of the subterranean life of the hour, a note from the underground—all the thoughts and fantasies that never emerged into the daylight of verbal intercourse" (xviii). Would this "bold procedural ploy," as Yalom called it, enable Ginny to overcome her writer's block—a perplexing problem for a twenty-three-year-old aspiring novelist who had enrolled recently in a creative writing program at a local college?

Yalom is quick to add that the arrangement did not involve a financial sacrifice on his part, since he was a full-time faculty member at Stanford and was obligated to turn over to the university any money he earned from clinical work. Both Yalom and Ginny agreed not to read each other's reports for several months to avoid becoming self-conscious. The idea of publication was never a consideration when they began their work together.

Yalom was aware of the risks of his therapeutic experiment. He was far more comfortable with self-disclosure than she was, and she had more to lose if her confidentiality was breached. She was, after all, the vulnerable patient, and there was much about her life that filled her with anguish, guilt, and shame. But Yalom's daring self-disclosures placed his own public image at stake. He never shrinks from raising difficult ethical questions. Was their "contract" a form of exploitation? He wasn't sure. "I suspect I have great expectations for Ginny; am I really exploiting her writing talent so that she will produce something for me? How much of my asking her to write instead of paying is sheer altruism? How much is selfish?" (13). The wording of these questions suggests that altruism and selfishness are not mutually exclusive. Viewing the patient from a dual perspective, Yalom hoped that he was mainly interested in Ginny the person and had "only a mild flirtation" with Ginny the writer (43).

A Reluctant Writer

Ginny was never as motivated to write up her impressions of the sessions as Yalom was. Sometimes she procrastinated; other times she didn't know what to write about, particularly when she was depressed, which was much of the time. Yalom couldn't decide whether to exhort her to write or scold her for not fulfilling her part of the contract. If he chose the latter, would her depression deepen? Not surprisingly, he remains more forthcoming and reflective than Ginny. His entries are longer, more detailed, and greater in number than hers. In an effort to be as egalitarian as possible, he refers to her as "Ginny," but she refers to him as "you," unable to call him by his first name.

Ginny's reluctance to write self-disclosingly is evident throughout the story. Her refusal to write on demand recalls Bartleby the Scrivener, whose expression "I would prefer not to" has a maddening effect on the narrator in Melville's short story. Notwithstanding her contract, Ginny has a good reason to be cautious about written self-disclosure. "This whole write-up for sessions is word magic which I hide. Which I wouldn't want anyone to see" (46). She rarely looks forward to writing the therapy reports, and she never overcomes the fear that her boyfriend, Karl, will discover them. (As it turns out, Karl attends some of the sessions and offers his own written impression of therapy, creating a thrice-told therapy tale.) Ginny worries that her writings are self-incriminating and that neither Yalom's nor her own account of therapy conveys accurately her life.

Reading some of Yalom's comments proves unsettling to Ginny. Psychologists have long known that emotions are as contagious as germs, and Ginny's knowledge that Yalom has been infected by her dark emotions only deepens her gloom. In general, however, nearly all of Yalom's comments about Ginny are supportive, and she realizes that he is an ally. He affirms her literary talent, believing that his language is "clumsy and unimaginative" compared to hers. He doesn't single out particular sentences for praise, but there are many. She suspects that talking about her writing is a "ruse to talk about my muse" (96). One page later she offers a unique description of how the write-ups have affected treatment. "It seems like I am living in an 'if' clause in therapy; my life dangling from a hanging if." Toward the end of therapy, she writes a satirical essay called "The Misfit" in which she dreams of dedicating all of her future books to "Dr. Y. who gave me the freedom to cry, the oomph to fly, and ten reasons not to die" (168).

Ginny reaches several conclusions about her writing reports during her two-year therapy. The tamer the session was, the harder it was to write about it. Can we infer that conflict was both the source and inspiration of her writing? Perhaps, but she never elaborates on this. Nor is it apparent whether writing reduced her inner conflicts. She notes in her nine-page afterword that regardless of whether her write-ups were "deliberately somber and serious or sloppy and fluffy," she could not force herself to "reach for the healing words" that she knew Yalom wanted. She implies that writing about her own impressions of therapy and then reading Yalom's words did not lead to any particular insights or breakthroughs. Nor was such writing clinically helpful. She mentions finding a job that involves research and writing, though it's uncertain whether her new work was a result of therapy.

Despite her complaints about the write-ups, Ginny remained devoted to Yalom both during and after therapy. He helped her feel better about herself and more confident about her life. Generosity and gratitude are supremely valuable character traits for Yalom, and he reminded Ginny that she should feel good about her efforts to befriend other people. He cautioned her not to dismiss her compassionate instincts as vices, as she tended to do. "I in effect told her to stop this Freudian reductionism and accept generosity or gentleness as positive and important truths about herself which stand by themselves and don't require further analysis" (20). Yalom's comment, as we shall see, becomes the cornerstone of *When Nietzsche Wept*, where the philosopher learns to appreciate gratitude as a gift that enriches both benefactor and recipient.

Literary Self-Consciousness

One of Yalom's singular strengths is the ability to acknowledge doubts and insecurities that other writers would attempt to conceal. He admits on the first page of the book that speaking with Ginny reminds him of his recent conversations with the existential psychologist Viktor Frankl. The knowledge that other therapists have affected his treatment of Ginny makes him feel "like a chameleon with no color of my own" (4). A few pages later he makes the same observation but in a more self-lacerating way. "It always makes me disgusted with myself to read someone and then find myself using his techniques in my next therapy session" (8). These confessions seldom find their way into the vast literature on psychological case studies. Yalom is equally suspicious of the performative element of writing, uneasy about the need to impress the readers of his book. And yet he realizes that the desire to win his readers' approval does not negate the need to help his patient. The solution to self-consciousness, he concludes, is to "keep an eye on it—the third eye, the third ear" (11), the latter an allusion, perhaps, to Theodor Reik's *Listening with the Third Ear*.

Yalom's writings abound in literary references, yet in his early books he sometimes resembles a doctoral student preparing for his exams, guiltily reminding his teachers of how much he doesn't know. Feeling anxious about a presentation he is giving the next day at the Modern Thought seminar, he confesses that his "interest in literature is vastly exceeded by glaring gaps in knowledge" (18). The gaps are never glaring to the reader, however. He quotes literary writers effortlessly, as when he observes that Ginny sometimes romanticizes her plight in a tragic way, reminding him of a "Virginia Woolf who will one day fill her pockets with rocks and walk into the ocean" (4; to be more precise, Woolf drowned herself in the River Ouse behind her house in Sussex, England). Another time he warns himself about "getting sucked into a Proustian recircling" of Ginny's past (42). He's not afraid to admit to writers he hasn't yet read, as when he notes Ginny's enthusiasm over a series of novels by Anthony Powell.

Grist for the Therapist's Mill

Nearly everything is grist for the therapy writer's mill, including a subject that no other person would write about—how a therapist's relationship with a patient affects his marriage. *Every Day Gets a Little Closer* begins with the editor's foreword, written by Marilyn Yalom, who, speaking as a French professor, describes how she felt when she first read both her husband's and Ginny's dual perspectives. "Privately I wondered if the post-session reports might not constitute a publishable piece of literature, with two distinct characters and two recognizable literary styles, not unlike an epistolary novel" (x). Her literary judgment proved correct, and she helped convince her husband to coauthor the book, and he in turn convinced Ginny. Yalom assured Ginny that whatever they wrote would be joint property. They would both need to agree to submit the final manuscript for publication, and they would share the royalties equally if the book was published. Marilyn Yalom edited *Every Day Gets a Little Closer*, but she also became inadvertently a character in the story. Fourteen months after the final session, Yalom met with Ginny and his wife for what he calls a "work-social meeting." The situation is confusing for everyone. "My wife calls me Irv, Ginny cannot mouth the word and I continue orbiting as Dr. Yalom." Even more "bizarre," he confesses, "is my recoil at my wife's familiarity with me in front of Ginny. I forget, what was it I was planning to do for Ginny? Oh yes, 'to aid reality testing so that she would work through her positive transference'" (212).

What happens next is weirder. As Yalom is speaking to Ginny in his office, his wife knocks on the door, wanting to talk to Ginny about a few sentences in her therapy report. Yalom and Ginny try to ignore the interruption, but then his wife, growing impatient, knocks again, at which point Ginny, to Yalom's amazement, states sharply, "just a few more minutes," and then, with the door still closed, bursts into tears, wailing, "I just realized I really have only a few more minutes. It's not that your wife has you all the time but this time is really precious to me." Yalom's response? "She cried for both of us" (213). A few pages later Yalom returns to the "eruption" of his confused feelings when his wife tried to enter into his relationship with Ginny. "When Ginny left I was morose, diffusely irritated and sullenly refused my wife's invitations to talk about our meeting. Though my phone conversations with Ginny were generally brief and impeccably professional, I was invariably uneasy at my wife's presence in the room. It is even possible that I invited, ambivalently, my wife into our relationship to help me with my counter-transference" (232).

Yalom is always scrupulous in observing professional boundaries, but he depicts a situation where boundary violations are inevitable: a former patient who is now a coauthor, and who is working professionally with the therapist's wife on a writing project involving all three characters. Yalom exploits the situation for all of its literary richness, and the fact that his wife is a French professor heightens the tone of French farce.

Dual Perspectives

Yalom's twenty-four-page afterword summarizes his goals in Ginny's therapy, focusing on interpersonal theory, the belief that psychological disturbances stem from conflicts in interpersonal relationships. Using a term that appears in his later books, he argues that psychotherapy is a "cyclotherapy" in which therapist and patient "together ascend a rickety, low gradient, spiral staircase" (219). (In a footnote to *Existential Psychotherapy* he credits the word *cyclotherapy* to an oral communication he received from D. Hamburg [503, n. 71], who was the chair of the Stanford Department of Psychiatry when Yalom was hired as an assistant professor.) The dual perspective approach leads Yalom to a noteworthy conclusion: patient and therapist often value different aspects of treatment. The most important part of therapy for Ginny was her relationship with Yalom. She valued being with a person whom she trusted and respected and who provided her with the support she needed. Yalom also valued the patient-therapist relationship, but he was mainly concerned with helping Ginny discover the insights that would lead to personality change and therapeutic growth. "She rarely ever acknowledges, much less values my labors, and instead seems to profit from my simple, human acts" (222). Sometimes she accepts an interpretation only to preserve the closeness of the patient-therapist bond.

The dual perspectives in *Every Day Gets a Little Closer* create a Rashomon effect, where patient and therapist have strikingly different points of view about what occurs in therapy. "The book is an exercise in post-modern realism," Ruthellen Josselson remarks. "What we think is happening is only one version of reality and woe to the therapist who loses awareness that the patient may be having a completely different experience of the interaction" (70).

Yalom likens therapy to Tom Stoppard's play *Rosencrantz and Guildenstern Are Dead*, where the drama onstage is different from the drama offstage. "That the therapist is the protagonist in many, varied, simultaneous dramas *is* his ultimate terrible secret" (222). This proves to be a major revelation for Yalom, one that forever alters his vision of therapy. No writer has described more starkly the many paradoxes of psychotherapy, where patient and therapist achieve, if they are fortunate, an intimacy that does not exist either before or after a therapy session. "Our relationship is a deep and authentic one, yet it is antiseptically packaged: we meet for the prescribed fifty minutes, she receives computerized notices from the clinic business office. The same room, same chairs, same positions. We mean much to one another, yet we are characters in a dress rehearsal. We care deeply for one another, yet we disappear when the hour is up, we will never meet again when our 'work' is done" (222–223).

A Therapist Who Needs Treatment

Yalom's major self-disclosure in *Every Day Gets a Little Closer* appears near the end of the afterword, where he offers a statement that is somewhere between an admission and a confession. He invests the self-disclosure with as much suspense as possible, tantalizing us with a secret he can no longer conceal. He then reveals the countertransference he brought into his therapy with Ginny. "It is not entirely true that she was the patient and I the therapist. I first discovered that a few years ago when I spent a sabbatical year in London. I had no claims on my time and had planned to do nothing but work on a book on group therapy. Apparently that was not enough; I grew depressed, restless and finally arranged to treat two patients—more for my sake than for theirs. Who was the patient and who the therapist? I was more troubled than they, and, I think benefited more than they from our work together" (230).

Yalom doesn't use the term "wounded healer" in *Every Day Gets a Little Closer*, but it forms a central concept in his later fictional and nonfictional books. First used by Carl Jung and then expanded upon by later therapists, wounded healers are compelled to heal patients because they are wounded themselves. One of the paradoxes of therapy, then, is that healing others allows wounded therapists to heal themselves. Part of the analyst's countertransference, Yalom suggests from personal experience, is counterphobic motivation. Therapist and patient may be wounded in different ways, but each gains from working with the other.

Yalom's use of a dual perspective in therapy anticipated by three decades a similar approach used in "narrative medicine," a movement started around the turn of the twenty-first century at Columbia University in which physicians attempt to learn everything they can about a patient's story. Narrative medicine integrates the values and methods of literary study into clinical practice and education. The ultimate goal of learning about a patient's history of health and illness is the improvement of health care. One technique involves a physician writing up case study notes, which the patient then reads and responds to. Reading each other's writings in a "spirit of co-discovery," Rita Charon and Eric R. Marcus explain in *The Principles and Practice of Narrative Medicine* (2017), results in a "feeling of resonance" (283). Yalom conveys this feeling in *Every Day Gets a Little Closer*.

Wounded Storytellers and Teachers

The counterpart to the wounded healer is the wounded storyteller, which is also the title of Arthur W. Frank's influential 1995 book.

> As wounded, people may be cared for, but as storytellers, they care for others. The ill, and all those who suffer, can also be healers. Their injuries become the source of the potency of their

stories. Through their stories, the ill create empathic bonds between themselves and their listeners. These bonds expand as the stories are retold. Those who listened then tell others, and the circle of shared experience widens. Because stories can heal, the wounded healer and wounded storyteller are not separate, but are different aspects of the same figure. (xii)

Yalom is both a wounded healer and a wounded storyteller, and these two roles meld deftly in his writings.

One seldom hears about a "wounded teacher," apart from an increasing number of classroom shootings, but like the wounded healer and wounded storyteller, the wounded teacher uses his or her woundedness to create empathic bonds with students. The teacher's woundedness becomes an academic fact of life, appropriate for any subject that involves suffering. Wounded healers, storytellers, and teachers bear witness to the inevitability of suffering and the possibility of recovery, an insight that applies to patients, readers, students, and teachers alike.

The End of the Story

After reading *Every Day Gets a Little Closer*, we know much more about Yalom than we do about Ginny. Nor is this surprising. She has been reluctant throughout the case study to reveal too much about her life, perhaps because she does not feel she deserves personal or public scrutiny. She remains shy and private, not given to attention or exhibitionism of any kind, a woman with modest expectations of life. It is easy to understand why she believes that her therapeutic notes are "horribly" self-incriminating, though they are also insightful and brave. We can also understand why she is paralyzed by the expression of strong emotion, be it anger or indignation. Nothing in her life has prepared her to look at her life through Yalom's magnifying glass. She is a good patient but feels guilty that she is not an extraordinary patient, as Yalom hoped she would be. Aware of his disappointment, she cannot prevent herself from holding something back in her writing.

After completing the story, we wish for an update on her life, or at least a statement about how she felt years later rereading the dual perspective of her life. Did her post-therapeutic life revolve around her identity of being Yalom's first major patient, as some of Freud's patients felt, such as Dora and the Wolf Man? Did she overcome her writer's block and become the author she wanted to be? Did she reread the case study to reaffirm or revise her identity? Because we care for her as a character, these are the questions that linger after we complete the story. We have different questions for Yalom. Was it hard or easy for him to call attention to his overarching vanity? He reminds us repeatedly of his literary ambitions, his desire to become a great writer. He confesses early in the beginning that he found himself hoping that Ginny would notice that some of the books in his bookcases were nonpsychiatric ones. "O'Neill plays, Dostoevsky. Christ, what a cross to bear! The ludicrousness of it. Here I am trying to help Ginny with survival problems and I'm still burdened down with my own petty vanities" (11).

In an interview published in the *North American Journal of Psychology* in 2007, Yalom noted that he had lost touch with Ginny Elkin for several years until she sent him a volume of interviews she published, for the Texas Sesquicentennial anniversary, on Texans in their eighties and nineties. The next time he saw her was when she unexpectedly showed up at a talk he gave in a Berkeley bookstore. They had several long chats after that. An English teacher in the Berkeley school system, she died, Yalom added, around 2005 from Marfan syndrome, a genetic disorder that weakens the body's connective tissue, sometimes resulting in aortic aneurysm.

In his desire to unlock Ginny and himself, what is Yalom suggesting about the meaning of his title, *Every Day Gets a Little Closer*? Closer to what? On one level, the title is an allusion to the song "Everyday," written by Buddy Holly and Norman Petty. Ginny quotes several lines of the upbeat song, which implies that true love is around the corner. On another level, the title hints at Ginny's gradual therapeutic improvement. The last line in her afterword suggests the closeness and durability of her therapeutic relationship with Yalom: "As often as I curled up, you uncurled me." On still another level, the title announces the end of Yalom's literary apprenticeship and his emergence as a major writer. *Every Day Gets a Little Closer* generated little interest among reviewers. I was able to find only one published comment, from *Kirkus Reviews*; the anonymous critic didn't know what to make of the book. "Whatever conjectural value the book has for others, it does show the osmotic-catalytic process in action." Notwithstanding Yalom's moments of literary self-consciousness and the reviewer's befuddlement, the psychiatrist will soon be writing stories that rank among the classics of case study literature.

Chapter 3

Existential Psychotherapy
Living with Death Anxiety

Published in 1980 and nearly 550 pages long, *Existential Psychotherapy* is not for the fainthearted. Yalom told Ruthellen Josselson that he spent ten years reading philosophical works and writing the textbook. It was a "sourcebook for all that I've written since then. All the books of stories and the novels were ways of expanding one or the other aspects of *Existential Psychotherapy*." The textbook was written, he remarks dryly in *The Yalom Reader*, "for a course that did not yet exist, delineating a professional discipline that was both amorphous and controversial" (167).

Yalom begins *Existential Psychotherapy* with a clear definition: "Existential psychotherapy is a dynamic approach to therapy which focuses on concerns that are rooted in the individual's existence." He concedes without defensiveness that "of all the therapy vocabularies, none rivals the existential in vagueness and confusion" (5). All of Yalom's books demonstrate his commitment to clear writing and clear thinking, a commitment that is often honored in the breach by the existential thinkers to whom he is indebted. "The single most important philosophical text in the field, Heidegger's *Being and Time*, stands alone as the undisputed champion of linguistic obfuscation" (16). No such obfuscation mars Yalom's own work.

A cornucopia of philosophical and therapeutic wisdom, *Existential Psychotherapy* abounds in insights, but our interest lies mainly in what it reveals about Yalom as a person, therapist, and writer. Along with death anxiety, existential guilt, existential isolation, and the therapeutic relationship figure importantly into Yalom's discussion. Beyond this, the book casts light on other authors, including Yalom's fellow psychiatrist, Elisabeth Kübler-Ross. Throughout *Existential Psychotherapy* he draws inspiration from iconic fiction writers like Ernest Hemingway and Franz Kafka, while simultaneously increasing our understanding of them. References to Spinoza, Schopenhauer, and Nietzsche prefigure his later novels on each of the three philosophers.

Like Yalom's other books, *Existential Psychotherapy* derives its greatest insights into human nature from the humanistic worlds of literature and philosophy rather than from the domain of empirical psychological research. "The truth of fictional characters moves us because it is our own truth." Or as Picasso observed, art is a lie that tells the truth. Yalom then quotes a statement by Thornton Wilder. "If Queen Elizabeth or Frederick the Great or Ernest Hemingway were to read their biographies, they would exclaim, 'Ah—my secret is still safe!' But if Natasha Rostov were to read *War and Peace* she would cry out, as she covered her face with her hands, 'How did he know? How did he know?'" (21).

Academics learn to critique other academics, but seldom do they critique themselves, particularly in print. Yalom's skepticism of psychological research extends to his own books. He reveals how a few years earlier he and two colleagues conducted a large research project on the outcome of encounter groups. They published their research in *Encounter Groups: First Facts* (1973). Some scholars praised the book for its precision in clinical work, but other scholars from a humanistic background vigorously attacked it. Yalom's two coauthors wrote "robust and effective" replies to the published criticism, but Yalom remained silent, partly because he agreed with the critics. Despite his reservations, he remains committed to empirical research, but he is mainly interested in a phenomenological approach that seeks to understand the patient's inner world.

Existential Forbears

Yalom uses the metaphor of "family" to suggest his relationship with mental health predecessors. Existential analysts like Ludwig Binswanger, Viktor Frankl, and Rollo May are "old country cousins." Humanistic psychologists like Gordon Allport, Henry Murray, Gardner Murphy, George Kelly, Abraham Maslow, and Carl Rogers are "flashy American cousins." Humanistic psychoanalysts like Otto Rank, Karen Horney, Erich Fromm, and Helmuth Kaiser, who all trained in Europe and then immigrated to the United States, are "friends of the family." Existential psychotherapy, he notes wryly, is "rather much a homeless waif," not belonging anywhere (14).

Yalom has a low tolerance for academic pomposity, yet he is willing to give credit where it is due. Serious readers, he tells us, are often troubled by the many distractions in Viktor Frankl's writings. "In virtually every work there are numerous self-aggrandizing comments: self-citations, reminders about the many universities at which he has lectured, his many titles, the many eminent people who endorse his approach, the number of professionals who assist him, the occasions when medical students have broken out into unrestrained applause during one of his interviews, the foolish questions posed to him, and his pithy rejoinders" (442–443). These distractions, we should note, never appear in *Yalom's* writing. He is put off by Frankl's affectations, but he also recognizes the insights in his writings. For example, Yalom points out that although Frankl's use of the technique of dereflection, telling patients to stop focusing excessively on themselves, is simplistic and authoritarian, the idea behind the technique is valid. "The therapist must find a way to help the patient develop curiosity and concern for others" (474).

Death Anxiety

Mental health professionals rarely acknowledge in print that they have the same problems as their patients. Yalom is the exception. Early in *Existential Psychotherapy* he discloses his own problems with death anxiety, including a problem that arose from a head-on collision with another automobile. Both cars were demolished, and the other driver, who was at fault, suffered severe lacerations. Yalom was fortunate that he wasn't physically injured, and later that day he flew to another city where he delivered a lecture in the evening. Following the auto accident, he began to develop a number of psychological symptoms, including anxiety during luncheon discussions of scholarly issues with colleagues. "Would I have anything of significance to say? How would my colleagues regard me? Would I make a fool of myself?" His anxiety became so intense that he began to avoid the luncheons to which he had once looked forward. The death anxiety that had arisen from a near-fatal auto accident became "secularized" into "such lesser concerns as self-esteem, fear of interpersonal rejection, or humiliation" (44–45). Related problems developed, such as fear of driving, bicycling, and skiing. The world became a far more dangerous place to him.

Anxiety over a different issue, insomnia, drove Yalom to visit a behavior therapist before an upcoming lecture visit to Cleveland, a "bad sleeping city." He was not helped by the four or five sessions that focused on a systematic desensitization approach, but as he was leaving the office, the therapist made a casual remark that proved to be unexpectedly effective. "He said, 'When you're packing your bag to go to Cleveland, don't forget to put in a revolver.' 'Why?' I asked him. 'Well,' he replied, 'if you can't sleep you can always shoot yourself'" (335). Many patients would have been offended by the quip, but it turned out to be an "inspired therapeutic maneuver." The comment "clicked" deep inside Yalom and still resonates years later. Why? The statement helped him reframe the situation, allowing him to put his anxiety into a meaningful existential perspective. Nietzsche's observation, "The thought of suicide is a great consolation: by means of it one gets through many a dark night," would have been equally helpful, but the aphorism was not in the behavior therapist's armamentarium.

Death anxiety does not figure prominently in *Every Day Gets a Little Closer*, but Yalom hints at it in his foreword. "It always wrenches me to find old appointment books filled with the half forgotten names of patients with whom I have had the most tender experiences." His many-tiered file cabinets filled with case studies and mounds of tape recordings remind him of a "vast cemetery." Living with these "monuments" imbues him with a "keen sense of transience." Writing about his experience with Ginny is a way to "stave off decay, to prolong the span of our brief life together" (xi). He notes at the end of *Every Day Gets a Little Closer* that "[t]his book has insured that Ginny never will become a half-forgotten name in my old appointment book or a lost voice on an electromagnetic band. In both a real and symbolic sense, we have defeated termination. Would it be going too far to say that our affair has been consummated in this shared work?" (232). Writing a case study thus is a way to achieve immortality with a patient, or at least the illusion of immortality, a powerful motive for writing.

Yalom offers in *Existential Psychotherapy* a convincing analysis of the role death anxiety plays not only in himself but also in other theorists, beginning with Freud, who preferred to talk about castration anxiety rather than fear of death, which struck too close to home. Few people in history were better endowed to achieve immortality than Freud, Yalom reminds us: "he had great imagination, limitless energy, and indomitable courage." Freud came close to greatness several times, but each time he narrowly missed lasting success. Unraveling the structure of the mind became Freud's "mistress." He put all of his money on libido theory, even if it meant casting off disciples who could not accept his views. The role of death either as a cause of anxiety or as a component of motivation had little appeal to Freud. Even in his late works like *Beyond the Pleasure Principle*, which focuses on the repetition compulsion principle, the desire to master traumatic experiences, Freud ignored the most basic fear of all: human mortality. Death was, in Yalom's words, "old hat, Old Testament" to Freud, not an idea that would lead to eternal fame. Yalom quotes one of Freud's favorite jokes, about a man who says to his wife, "If one of us two dies before the other, I think I'll move to Paris" (58).

How do patients feel when their therapists are world-famous authors? How does a therapist's published self-disclosures affect a patient? In *Existential Psychotherapy* Yalom gives an example of a patient who responded to one of his books in the opposite way he intended. "Karen" was a forty-year-old patient, in treatment for two years, who developed a powerful positive transference relationship to him. One might expect a patient who mythologized her therapist into a larger-than-life figure, endowed with omniscience and omnipotence, to welcome a more human portrait. Not so. "She read a book I had written with a patient in which I had been highly self-revelatory about my own anxieties and limitations" (135). Reading *Every Day Gets a Little Closer* only heightened Karen's admiration of him. This may be less surprising than Yalom realizes: writing publicly about one's anxieties and limitations requires uncommon courage and strength. Treatment was successful, Yalom notes, in alleviating some of her problems, but there came a time when continued therapy appeared to impede further growth. And so he decided to set a termination date six months into the future. As the date approached, she became panicky and threatened to commit suicide if he ended therapy, but he held firm. She was able to work past her fears and regain control over her life. He saw her for a single session two years later. She had learned that, in therapy as in life, "there is an inescapable substrate of lonely work and lonely existence" (137).

A Counterintuitive Theme

Yalom's fictional and nonfictional writings demonstrate that death anxiety is inversely proportional to life satisfaction. The theme may be counterintuitive, he concedes, because one might expect those disappointed and disillusioned with life to welcome death as an escape. But the opposite is true, Yalom suggests, and then he quotes Nietzsche who, with "characteristic hyperbole," stated, "What has become perfect, all that is ripe—wants to die. All that is unripe wants to live. All that suffers wants to live, that it may become ripe and joyous and longing—longing for what is further, higher, brighter" (208).

Elisabeth Kübler-Ross: Dedeathifying Death

The Swiss-born psychiatrist Elisabeth Kübler-Ross was at the zenith of her popularity in 1980, already a cult figure, when *Existential Psychotherapy* was published. Yalom argues that although early in her career she rejected the religious practice of indoctrinating children with fairy tale images of heaven, God, and angels, this is precisely what she does when she informs children that at the moment of death people are transformed or liberated "like a butterfly" to a comforting future, as she asserted in a 1978 address at Stanford Medical School. Characteristically, Yalom criticizes the idea, not the person. "The current position of this remarkable therapist who once confronted death unflinchingly indicates how difficult it is to face death without self deception" (108).

Born in 1926, only five years before Yalom, Kübler-Ross was the most famous thanatologist of the second half of the twentieth century. She had much in common with Yalom. Both challenged the entrenched psychiatric conventional wisdom of the age, including the belief that physicians should conceal the truth from terminally ill patients. Both urged an empathic, nonjudgmental approach to end-of-life issues. Both suggested the interdependence of life and death. Yalom would agree with Kübler-Ross's statement in her groundbreaking 1969 book *On Death and Dying*, that "[t]he more we are making advancements in science, the more we seem to fear and deny the reality of death. How is this possible?" (7). Kübler-Ross would agree with Yalom's statement in *Existential Psychotherapy* that "[i]t is not possible to leave death to the dying" (30). Both stated that they learned the most not from their medical school professors or colleagues but from their patients, who continued to be their instructors. Both admired many of the same theorists, including Ernest Becker, who argued in his Pulitzer–prize winning 1973 book *The Denial of Death* that annihilation and death are humankind's deepest fears. Both believed that frank and open discussions of mortality will result in a healthier attitude toward life and death. Both studied psychoanalysis and underwent long personal analyses, but neither became infatuated with classical psychoanalytic theory. Both were critical of psychiatry's growing reliance upon psychopharmacology.

Kübler-Ross and Yalom were both prolific authors whose books contain hundreds of lively clinical vignettes that transcend the dry discussions of most psychiatric case studies. Their books, published by commercial rather than university presses, appeal to a large general audience and always avoid psychobabble.

Death was Elisabeth Kübler-Ross's muse, as it has been for Yalom. "Dying" or "death" appears in the title or subtitle of twelve of her books. She spent her entire life writing about the destructive consequences of the denial of death, including the isolation experienced by the dying. She raises the following question in *On Death and Dying*: "Who was it who said, 'We cannot look at the sun all the time, we cannot face death all the time'?" (39). The answer, which she never gives us, is La Rochefoucauld: "Neither the sun nor death can be looked at steadily." Yalom uses the same maxim for the title of *Staring at the Sun*. "I would recommend staring into the sun to no one," he writes in the afterword, "but staring into death is quite another matter. A full unwavering look at death is the message of this book" (275).

Kübler-Ross is known primarily for the "stage theory" of dying, which proposes that the dying person progresses through five sequential stages of grief: denial, anger, bargaining, depression, and acceptance. The stage theory remains one of the most influential yet flawed theories of modern thanatology. Kübler-Ross's theory has been criticized for the lack of empirical evidence supporting it; its neglect of other stages of dying, such as fear, guilt, hope, and despair; its privileging of the "final" stage, acceptance; and its failure to discuss the role of culture in shaping death practices. Despite these criticisms, the stage theory of dying has an aura of scientific credibility. Not so with Kübler-Ross's subsequent theories of death. Her late publications read like science fiction. She was one of the foremost proponents of "out-of-body" events, and she wrote about her own encounters with angelic spirits, cosmic consciousness, rebirth experiences, and conversations with Jesus. Nothing was too fanciful for her to believe, and even after some of her associates who claimed to have the ability to channel spirits from the world beyond life were exposed as charlatans, she continued to assert that she had scientific proof of the existence of immortality.

In her 1997 memoir *The Wheel of Life*, Kübler-Ross discusses how in 1969 she flew to Switzerland to visit her seventy-seven-year-old mother who, worried about her health, told her, "If I ever become a vegetable, I want you to terminate my life" (154). Angered by her mother's request, Kübler-Ross responded, " 'If something happens, I will do the same for you that I do for all my patients,' I said. 'I will help you live until you die' " (155). Not long after, her mother suffered a massive stroke. She remained alive, unable to move or speak, for four years. Why did God keep her alive for so long in a vegetative state, Kübler-Ross asks? Cursing God for her mother's situation, Kübler-Ross has an epiphany. "Then, as unbelievable as it sounds, I changed my mind and was actually thanking Him for his generosity. It sounds insane, right? It did to me too—until it dawned on me that my mother's final lesson had been to learn how to receive affection and care, something she had never been good at. From then on, I praised God for teaching her in just four years. I mean, it could have been a lot longer" (195).

Years later, when Kübler-Ross found herself in her mother's situation, her point of view changed. In the middle and late 1990s, she suffered a series of strokes that left her paralyzed and confined to a wheelchair. Divorced from her husband, estranged from her two children, and largely isolated from society, she ends *The Wheel of Life* waiting impatiently for death. Caroline Myss reveals in the foreword to the 2008 edition of *On Life after Death* that Kübler-Ross sought her assistance on how to die. "During her last two years, as her health was failing, she phoned me three times: not to learn what she could do to help herself heal, but rather to find out what she could do to help herself die more quickly. She found living in a wheelchair, slowly waiting for death to come, an unbearable suffering. She fought with God until the very end, angry that she could not determine her time of death. Even Elisabeth, it seemed, had to walk through the famous stages of death and dying" (vii). The last sentence implies that Myss remains committed to the stage theory of dying, but we'll never know how Kübler-Ross felt at the end of her life. She died in 2004 at the age of seventy-eight.

Yalom has never applied the insights of *Existential Psychotherapy* to Kübler-Ross's life and death, but her theories can be viewed as efforts to deny her own death anxiety. Yalom cites Robert Jay Lifton's observation that Freud's libido theory "dedeathifies death" (64), an observation that applies equally well to Kübler-Ross's theories. Indeed, she insists in *The Wheel of Life* that "death does not exist" (210). Her belief in past and future lives calls into question the importance of freedom, choice, and responsibility in the present life. Unlike Yalom, who argues, with the existentialists, that dying is a lonely process, and that no one can die for another person, Kübler-Ross maintained that the dying have a guardian angel who accompanies them to the "other side." The reason children die young is simple: "They have learned in a very short time what one has to learn, which could be different things for different people" (*On Life after Death* 11). If you live well, she adds, you never have to worry about dying. Her later writings abound in messianic imagery, as I point out in *Dying in Character*: "Rescue fantasies are common among physicians and mental health professionals, but they are especially strong in her work. She 'rescues' her patients and readers, first, by reassuring them they have nothing to fear about dying and death; second, by promising them they will ecstatically merge with God's unconditional love; and finally, by telling them they must resolve their unfinished business lest they be forced to return to life and relive painful experiences" (59–60). Yalom never makes these promises to his readers.

Hemingway's Death Anxiety

Hemingway's death anxiety differed from Kübler-Ross's, and Yalom makes a noteworthy observation about the novelist's vaunted code of heroism, which contains "no place for aging and diminishment, for they have the odor of ordinariness." Yalom then notes the paradox that one of the reasons for Hemingway's suicide was the fear of death. "Many individuals have said in effect that 'I so fear death I am driven to suicide'" (122).

A graphic illustration of the fear of suicide is Hemingway's most autobiographical novel, *For Whom the Bell Tolls* (1940), where Robert Jordan's impending heroic death at the end of the novel is a disguised suicide. Jordan's greatest fear in life was emulating his father, who committed suicide, as did Hemingway's own father. Yalom doesn't discuss this novel, though he does mention the John Donne sermon from which Hemingway took his title. Yalom quotes two lines from the sermon, "And therefore never send to know for whom the bell tolls. It tolls for thee," to emphasize how for many people "the death of a close fellow creature offers the most intimate recognition one can have of one's own death" (168).

Irvin and Marilyn Yalom coauthored an article on Hemingway that was published in the *Archives of General Psychiatry* in June 1971 and reprinted in *The Yalom Reader*. The article appeared before the publication of Kenneth S. Lynn's pioneering 1987 psychobiography, which revealed that Grace Hemingway raised her first two children, Marcelline and Ernest, born a year and a half apart, to be *twins of the same sex*. Grace Hemingway dressed her son in girl's clothes until he was six. Several literary critics, including Carl Eby, have argued that this act had a lifelong effect on the construction and negotiation of identity and gender in Hemingway's life and art. The new research strengthens the Yaloms' central argument over the radical split between Hemingway's ideal self and his real self. "When the idealized image is severe and unattainable, as it was for Hemingway, tragic consequences may result: the individual cannot in real life approximate the superhuman scope of the idealized image, reality eventually intrudes, and he realizes the discrepancy between what he wants to be and what he is in actuality" (290). The split fatally widened as Hemingway approached old age. "When we read of the inappropriate antics of Hemingway at 60, we feel compelled to cry out like Lear's fool: 'Thou shouldst not have been old till thou hadst been wise'" (302).

Some of the Yaloms' statements can be questioned, however. They assert that the protagonist's wife in Hemingway's misogynistic short story "The Short Happy Life of Francis Macomber" shoots her husband by accident, but this remains a controversial question, and there's much evidence that it was deliberate murder. The Yaloms suggest that Catherine Barkley, Frederic's lover, dies "rather pointlessly" following childbirth, but that was the point the novelist was making in the following Nietzschean sentences: "The world breaks everyone and afterward many are strong at the broken places. But those that will not break it kills" (249). There are other psychological reasons for the novelist's decision to kill off Catherine, including Leslie Fiedler's sardonic observation in *Love and Death in the American Novel* that had she lived, she would have turned into the familiar Hemingway bitch.

Contrary to Thornton Wilder's statement, endorsed by Yalom earlier in *Existential Psychotherapy*, that Hemingway would have felt that his life "secret" was safe had he read his biography, the novelist was horrified when Philip Young sent him an early draft of his psychobiographical study. In his analysis of Hemingway's major fictional characters, Young found that each suffered a traumatic physical or psychological wound, which the literary critic then linked to the near-fatal injury Hemingway received during World War I, when he was struck by a mortar shell. Hemingway maintained that Young's study not only was a breach of privacy but also damaged his ability to write. Living authors, Hemingway asserted angrily, should not have their lives become an open book for others to read and analyze. Hemingway threatened to block the publication of the psychobiographical study, but he finally relented, and the book appeared in 1952. Young ruefully recalls in the foreword to the revised edition published in 1966 the telephone calls he received on July 2, 1961, "congratulating" him on the accuracy of his prediction. As he notes in the foreword, Young did not "predict" in his 1952 book the suicide but rather described a "situation, a pattern, a process in Hemingway's life and work in which the act of suicide would not be altogether inconsistent" (3).

The Yaloms are careful not to claim too much in their article. They do not seek to explain Hemingway's genius, but they are persuasive in showing the counterphobic motivation behind his writing. They agree with his famous statement, which he confided to A. E. Hotchner, that his real "analyst" was his Corona typewriter. Counterphobic motivation is the driving force behind many writers, but in Hemingway's case it could not keep him alive, particularly when he found himself unable to write near the end of his life.

Insight's Role in Strengthening the Therapeutic Relationship

Like Freud, Yalom believes that knowledge is power, essential to psychological change and growth. Insight in therapy without change is not enough, Yalom suggests, and he quotes an observation made by Allen Wheelis in 1950: "Therapy can bring about personality change only in so far as it leads a patient to adopt a new mode of behavior. A real change occurring in the absence of action is a practical and theoretical impossibility" (286–287). Later in *Existential Psychotherapy* Yalom quotes a passage from a different Wheelis article published in 1956, about people who "sit at the crossroads of life," unable to make a decision that requires renunciation (318).

Yalom offers a new explanation of why insight strengthens the therapeutic relationship. "The search for understanding," he remarks in one of his most important statements, "provides a context for the formation of the therapist-patient relationship; it is the glue that binds patient and therapist together; it keeps them occupied in a mutually satisfying task" (340). Patients are gratified by the attention they receive from a therapist, who helps them to understand a previously unrecognized aspect of their behavior, and the therapist is gratified by the challenge of intellectual and psychological discovery. But does this mean that nonpsychological interpretations may be effective in therapy? Yes, Yalom admits, and then explains why. "If an astrological or a shamanistic or a magical explanation enhances one's sense of mastery, and leads to inner, personal change, then it is valid (keeping in mind the proviso that it must be consonant with one's frame of reference). There is much evidence from cross-cultural psychiatric research to support my position; in most primitive cultures *only* the magical or the religious explanation is acceptable, and hence valid and effective" (344).

Empirical Support

Contemporary research supports Yalom's belief in the centrality of the therapist-patient relationship. Bruce E. Wampold and Zac E. Imel have long studied the extensive empirical research, and their conclusion is that empathy "is more highly correlated with outcome than any other variable studied in psychotherapy" (211). The two researchers confirm Saul Rosenzweig's 1936 hypothesis that all therapeutic approaches when competently used are equally successful. In an allusion to Lewis Carroll's 1865 novel *Alice in Wonderland*, Rosenzweig called his conjecture the Dodo bird effect. "At last the Dodo bird said, 'Everybody has won and all must have prizes.'" As Wampold and Imel remark, "The Dodo bird conjecture has survived many tests and must be considered 'true' until such time as sufficient evidence for its rejection is produced" (156).

Yalom doesn't deny the importance of transference relationships, which involve a patient's projection of feelings, usually associated with a figure in the past, onto the therapist, but he maintains that it's the present relationship, in the here-and-now, that heals. Yalom's fictional analysts are much less interested in conducting archeological digs into a patient's past, as Freud did, than in investigating the details of the patient's present existence. What counts most for an existential psychotherapist is a patient's present and future choices, not the past ones.

Existential Guilt

Yalom provides a taxonomy of guilt in *Existential Psychotherapy*. Whereas traditional guilt involves a real or imagined transgression against another person, existential guilt arises from regret, an "awareness of the unlived life, of the untapped possibilities within one" (320). Pointing out that no one has depicted existential guilt more profoundly than Franz Kafka, Yalom offers a perceptive analysis of Joseph K.'s guilt in *The Trial*. "As the reader gradually realizes, Joseph K. is confronted with an internal court, one residing in his private depths" (283). Joseph K. never understands that he is guilty of the crime of living an unfulfilled life, of never seizing the opportunity to fulfill his destiny—a Nietzschean as well as Kafkaesque theme. All of Yalom's novels are, in effect, illustrations of this internal court. Interestingly, Marilyn Yalom wrote her doctoral dissertation at Johns Hopkins University on "The Myth of the Trial in Kafka and Camus."

In a later chapter of *Existential Psychotherapy*, "Willing," Yalom argues that existential guilt arises from the refusal to take responsibility for one's life. Responsibility, however, is a double-edged sword: "if one accepts responsibility for one's life situation and makes the decision to change, the implication is that one alone is responsible for the past wreckage of one's life and *could* have changed long ago" (320).

Creativity

Yalom makes only passing reference to creativity in *Existential Psychotherapy*, but the subject will become increasingly important to him in later books. He remarks that a creative life is always meaningful. He refers to several novelists, poets, painters, philosophers, psychologists, and astronomers who overcame physical or psychological disabilities to make singular contributions to the arts and sciences. He singles out Beethoven as one of history's greatest examples of creativity overcoming hopelessness. "Beethoven said explicitly that his art kept him from suicide. At the age of thirty-two, in despair because of his deafness, he wrote, 'Little kept me back from putting an end to my life. Art alone held me back. Alas, it seems to be impossible for me to leave the world before I have done all that I feel inclined to do, and thus I drag on this miserable life'" (435). Several of the historical characters in Yalom's novels, including Spinoza, Schopenhauer, Nietzsche, and Freud, would agree with Beethoven that the pursuit of creativity was the greatest goal of their lives, a goal that made their lives meaningful.

Existential Isolation

Just as there are different kinds of guilt, there are different kinds of isolation: interpersonal isolation, or loneliness, which refers to isolation from other individuals; intrapersonal isolation, in which one part of the psyche is separated or split off from another part, as in obsessional neurosis; and existential loneliness, which occupies Yalom's major attention. Existential isolation may refer to the "unbridgeable gulf" between oneself and other people, or it may refer to a more fundamental separation between oneself and the world. Yalom acknowledges his indebtedness to philosophers such as Martin Heidegger, novelists such as Albert Camus, and theologians such as Martin Buber for providing the most powerful descriptions of existential isolation. Like them, Yalom believes that one's relationships with others cannot eliminate existential isolation.

Paradoxically, though each of us is alone, we can share our loneliness with others, thus helping ourselves and others endure painful isolation. "I believe that if we are able to acknowledge our isolated situations in existence and to confront them with resoluteness, we will be able to turn lovingly toward others. If, on the other hand, we are overcome with dread before the abyss of loneliness, we will not reach out toward others but instead will flail at them in order not to drown in the sea of existence" (363). No statement in any of Yalom's books conveys more eloquently or succinctly his vision of life than this one. Without reducing his complex characters to a single idea, we can say that all of his stories are variations on this underlying theme.

To illustrate existential loneliness, Yalom turns to Martin Buber, who argued that existence is primarily relational, consisting of two forms of dialogue, I-Thou and I-It. Yalom affirms the I-Thou relationship, quoting Buber's statement, "each of the participants has in mind the other or others in their particular being and turns to them with the intention of establishing a living mutual relationship between himself and them" (366). Recognizing the need for a balance between the I-Thou and I-It relationships, Yalom recalls Rabbi Hillel's words: "If I am not for myself, who will be? And if I am only for myself, what am I?" (367).

Yalom respects the mystical tradition, which urges a heightened oneness with the universe, but he is wary of the resulting ego loss, the annihilation of the self. Such "fusion," be it with another individual, group, or cause, is a "pact with Satan" and leads to existential guilt, "that guilt grief which laments the unlived life in each of us" (381). Yalom makes no attempt to conceal his secularism, but he is not a dogmatic atheist, as Freud was, and his rejection of religion does not imply a rejection of spirituality. In his last novel, *The Spinoza Problem*, Yalom describes the philosopher's ecstatic casting off of identity as a loss of separation, but this experience, which seems close to mysticism, cannot be attributed to Yalom's personal experience.

Working with Cancer Patients

Yalom learned a great deal about death anxiety in the mid-1970s when he created the first support group for patients suffering from metastatic breast cancer. Some of the patients he writes about in *Existential Psychotherapy* were members of the outpatient group whom he saw weekly at Stanford Medical School. He found that "those patients who experience a deep sense of meaning in their lives appear to live more fully and to face death with less despair than those whose lives are devoid of meaning" (431–432). In her 1997 book *A History of the Breast*, Marilyn Yalom refers to her husband's work with breast cancer patients, noting that "the most basic anxiety for most of them was not so much the fear of dying but the loneliness that surrounded the road toward death—breast cancer was still a taboo subject in those days." A ten-year follow-up study, conducted by one of Yalom's coleaders, Stanford psychiatrist David Spiegel, found that psychotherapy improved the women's quality of life and survival rates. "The women in the support group," Marilyn Yalom writes, "lived on average twice as long from the time they entered the study as the women in a control group" (235).

Yalom's work with terminally ill cancer patients demonstrated the possibility of creating personal meaning in the absence of religious or cosmic meaning. Regardless of their religious beliefs or disbeliefs, many of the patients demonstrated altruism to the end of their lives. Yalom's purpose is not to assert that his patients achieved what Kübler-Ross called a final acceptance of death but to show how people invent their own life meaning and then commit themselves to achieving it. Creativity overlaps with altruism in the search for fulfillment.

Yalom's optimistic view of psychotherapy never blinds him to the pitfalls inherent in his profession. He remains skeptical of the slickly packaged pop psychotherapies that proliferated in the 1970s, many in his home state of California. He singles out for criticism Werner Erhard (born John Paul Rosenberg), who became a new age guru and prophet. The creator of est (Erhard Seminars Training), taken by an estimated seven hundred thousand people between 1971 and 1991, Erhard promised miraculous transformations. "It is sophistry to claim," Yalom warns, "as est presumably does, that a product of personal responsibility may emerge from a procedure of authoritarianism" (261). By contrast, real psychotherapy, Yalom acknowledges, is "cyclotherapy," a "long, lumbering process in which the same issues are repeatedly worked through in the therapy environment and are tested and retested in the patient's life environment" (307–308).

Yalom often quotes novelists and philosophers who are deeply pessimistic, not to endorse their worldview but to indicate what we can learn from them. *Existential Psychotherapy* is the first but by no means last book in which Yalom evokes Thomas Hardy's comment, "If a way to the Better there be, it exacts a full look at the Worst" (14). It is perhaps Yalom's favorite literary passage. Unlike Hardy's tragic characters, who never learn from their mistakes—the statement "What's done cannot be undone" becomes a leitmotif in his late novels—Yalom's characters usually learn from past failures and, with the help of psychotherapy, go on to lead fulfilling lives.

Chapter 4

Inpatient Group Psychotherapy
Educating Observers and the Observed

The book jacket of *Inpatient Group Psychotherapy* states that Yalom's 1983 clinical textbook is "especially suitable for the contemporary psychiatric ward where acutely disturbed patients are hospitalized for brief periods of time." Yalom's intended audience is the "'front line' clinician—the harried mental health professional who leads groups amidst the tumult often found on the acute psychiatric ward" (x). *Inpatient Group Psychotherapy* is a transitional work, marking the end of his influential clinical textbooks and the beginning of his career as a storyteller. For many people, the idea of inpatient group psychotherapy evokes the specter of the "pecking party" in Ken Kesey's 1962 novel *One Flew Over the Cuckoo's Nest*, where, like crazed chickens attacking each other, the psychotherapy patients in Nurse Ratched's psychiatric ward eviscerate each other. Yalom never mentions Kesey's novel, but the psychiatrist's vision of a therapeutic community in *Inpatient Group Psychotherapy* could not be more different.

Inpatient Group Psychotherapy is untypical of Yalom's other clinical books in that it offers a spectrum of psychopathology far broader than is usually seen in the characters in his novels and psychotherapy tales: florid psychosis, substance abuse, schizophrenia, psychotic breakdown, geriatric psychiatric syndromes, and severe crisis and decompensation. *Inpatient Group Psychiatry* reminds us of Yalom's extensive experience with nearly every type of psychiatric disorder before becoming a novelist. He is aware of all facets of psychiatry, including the presence of a powerful third party, the "financial denizen who has a shocking degree of influence over admission and discharge decisions" (x). *Inpatient Group Psychotherapy* is also untypical in that it ignores death anxiety and existence pain, both of which dominate Yalom's later writings.

Now more than three decades old, *Inpatient Group Psychotherapy* shows Yalom's ongoing commitment to the therapist-patient relationship, even in settings where there is little time for such relationships to develop. The book demonstrates his fascination for storytelling, though the stories are necessarily brief and incomplete.

Inpatient and outpatient group therapy, in Yalom's view, rests upon interpersonal theory, which posits that "one's character structure is shaped by one's previous interpersonal relationships and that a patient's current symptoms are a manifestation of disordered interpersonal relationships. Individuals seek help with a wide array of complaints, but they have in common a major difficulty in establishing and maintaining gratifying and enduring relationships" (45). Interpersonal theory implies that a therapist need not focus on a patient's past history or behavior outside the group; the patient's interpersonal difficulty will manifest itself in the therapy group. A therapy that focuses on the here-and-now will thus contribute to therapeutic change. Here-and-now (as opposed to there-and-then) group psychotherapy consists of two stages: the experiencing stage, where each member is introduced to the group, describing his or her life briefly, and the self-reflective stage, where each member's statements are studied for their impact on the group. Yalom uses the word *content* to describe the experiencing stage and *process* to describe the self-reflective stage. The therapist's task in the self-reflective stage is to clarify or illuminate the relational aspects among the group members. The self-reflective stage is the more difficult one to maintain, if only because of the temptation to allow members to bring in material that cannot be usefully analyzed by the group. *Inpatient Group Psychotherapy* concentrates exclusively on here-and-now comments. Addressing his readers in the second person and using a simile he has not used elsewhere, he exhorts group therapists to think and act only in the here-and-now. "You must be like a shepherd who is continually heading off strays—into 'outside' material, into discussions of past events of their lives, into abstract intellectual discussions" (181).

One of the major differences between inpatient and outpatient group therapy is that the average hospital stay in most acute wards is only one to two weeks. Consequently, there is not enough time, as there is in outpatient group therapy, for the working through of conflict. The inpatient group therapist's aim "must be rapid conflict resolution, not conflict evocation" (148). A therapist who demonstrates rapid conflict resolution must be content with brief stories that illustrate a clinical point. There is no time to tease out the ambiguities of each case study.

"Gentling" Anger

Yalom offers several valuable therapeutic suggestions for "gentling" anger among members of an inpatient group. One technique is to express anger "once removed" by using the subjunctive tense: "*If* you were going to express your anger," he says to one patient, "what might you say?" Another technique is to ask the others in a group to role-play for a moment or two, "to pretend that they are the angry person and to express the anger that they think he or she might be feeling." Still another technique is to give a person a time limit in expressing angry feelings, perhaps for sixty seconds. Advocating therapist transparency, Yalom suggests that cotherapists can serve as models by expressing their differences of opinion with each other to the entire group. If the cotherapists disagree with each other but continue working together, "they provide excellent modeling for patients" (154). Inpatients are fragile, Yalom reminds us, and a destructive *Who's Afraid of Virginia Woolf?* approach is not appropriate (187).

Interactions Between Observers and the Observed

One of the most intriguing sections of *Inpatient Group Psychotherapy* is the discussion of the "wrap-up" format, the final phase of working with higher-level inpatient therapy groups. Yalom recommends several ingenious therapeutic techniques that both demystify therapy and provide a model for self-disclosure that may be used in many forms of education, a pedagogy based on the interactions between observers and the observed.

Yalom raises a simple question that has bedeviled therapists for decades. How can students, therapists-in-training, observe hospitalized patients engaging in psychotherapy without the latter feeling like guinea pigs? The traditional observational format in psychotherapy is the two-way mirror, also called, oddly enough, the one-way mirror, one that is partly reflective and partly transparent, allowing viewing from the darkened side but not from the brightly lit side. People on the brightly lit side, the inpatient psychotherapy patients, are kept in the dark, unaware of those who gaze at them. Two-way mirrors are used for interrogation rooms and execution rooms, but it is unethical to use such mirrors for psychotherapy patients without disclosing to them they are being observed.

The two-way mirror conjures up an Orwellian and Foucauldian specter of surveillance, where inpatient group psychotherapy patients lose whatever freedom of privacy they might have otherwise had. Psychotherapy patients detest the two-way mirror, demanding to know "which side of the mirror the therapists are on." Everyone agrees that an essential part of student training is to observe the therapeutic process, but observation creates a number of difficulties. One problem is that the two-way mirror violates patient confidentiality. Some patients, particularly those with paranoid ideation, are so fearful of the loss of confidentiality that they refuse to attend group psychotherapy. Another problem is that some patients believe that the presence of onlookers robs therapy of its intimacy and dignity. Still another problem is that the observer inevitably influences what is being observed. Viewing psychotherapy patients behind a two-way mirror evokes the Heisenberg principle of uncertainty, where the "observer effect" influences what is being observed. In short, how can therapists-in-training witness inpatient group therapy without inadvertently sabotaging the process?

Yalom's creative solution is not only to make the observers part of the therapy process but also to have them switch roles, allowing the patients to observe the therapists-in-training. Patients were "intensively interested in the observer-therapist discussion," Yalom reports. "Over and over they commented on the many feelings and thoughts it evoked, and regretted having to end the meeting without the opportunity to air them. Furthermore, many patients wished to interact with the observers, either to obtain clarification of a comment one had made or to respond to a question one had posed" (262).

Yalom describes several other related therapeutic techniques that encourage the observers and the observed to exchange roles to understand the others' point of view, resulting in both the demystification of therapy and heightened self-disclosure. One of these techniques, Yalom points out, was devised in the 1940s when early sensitivity-training groups were formed. "Fishbowling" was a technique in which "one group sat in a circle around another group; and periodically chairs were switched so that the outer group became the inner and discussed the process of the inner group they had just observed" (264). Yalom summarizes two clinical reports of fishbowling used in inpatient groups. Patients met in an inner circle, and the staff observed from an outer circle. In the final fifteen minutes the groups exchanged places: the patients heard the staff discuss their leaderless session. Yalom had used the same technique in his long-term outpatient group to see how his student-observers discuss his patients.

A related technique is a shared, written group summary. "At the end of outpatient group sessions I write a detailed group summary (an editorialized narrative summary, including detailed process analysis and considerable disclosure of my strategic therapeutic plan) and mail it to the members before the next week's session" (264). Yalom had used a similar technique with Ginny Elkin in *Every Day Gets a Little Closer*. Another technique, cleverly called "Multiple Therapy," consists of several therapists, most of whom are trainees, who meet with one patient at a time. "During these meetings the therapists interact individually or jointly with the patient but often may engage in a discussion among themselves analyzing some particular aspect of the interaction of the entire group" (265). Patients invariably find "Multiple Therapy" helpful. The format has "no economic future," Yalom ruefully concludes, but it demonstrates his tireless efforts to develop new therapeutic techniques that will help psychotherapy patients, practitioners, and students.

Promoting Psychological Health

Throughout *Inpatient Group Psychotherapy* Yalom affirms the principles of therapist transparency, careful self-disclosure, the role of empathy, the use of here-and-now therapy, and the crucial importance of the therapist-patient relationship. What he most remembers about his own therapy years ago, he confides to us, "are the warm, caring, affirming statements that my therapist made to me" (127). He demonstrates the same writerly qualities that we see throughout his works. He strives to make therapy understandable and down-to-earth, citing Harry Stack Sullivan's definition of psychotherapy: "A situation in which two people meet together, one of whom is less anxious than the other" (121). Yalom is not afraid to revise earlier statements; what he had called in *The Theory and Practice of Group Psychotherapy* "curative factors" is more realistically expressed as "therapeutic factors" (40). He delights in expressing clichés in unexpected ways. "Therapy almost invariably requires some degree of stretching on the part of the patient, and stretching always implies tension. (It has been said, 'If the shoe fits, you're probably not allowing for growth')" (257).

Inpatient Group Psychotherapy did not receive many reviews, but the ones that appeared were jaw-dropping. "Attention all clinicians, teachers, supervisors, and administrators who work in psychiatric hospitals or psychiatric inpatient units," announced E. Mansell Pattison in *Psychiatric Services*. "This is the book you have been waiting for—a straightforward, clinical, how-to-do-it description of group psychotherapy designed specifically for inpatient treatment programs. More good news: the price is so modest that you should buy several copies for your staff" (500–501).

Even more good news: Yalom always comes across as a bold experimenter and storyteller. Some therapists are reluctant to analyze a patient's improvement, citing the "old story of a centipede who, when asked about how he could walk so well with all those legs, took to inspecting his pace so carefully that his spontaneous rhythm broke down, and he was no longer able to walk" (235). In Yalom's version of the story, the therapist would praise the centipede's legs, examining his own in the process, and then proudly walk with the centipede, each admiring the other's stride.[1]

---

1. There's still more good news, Yalom reported to me. "There has been a recent resurgence of group work with good outcome data based on the model I used for *Inpatient Group Psychotherapy*. See the work [on focused brief group psychotherapy] by Martyn Whittingham."

Chapter 5

Love's Executioner

Living with Existence Pain

"[A]ll is not exactly what it seems," cautions Randall Weingarten in the foreword to the 2000 Perennial Classics edition of *Love's Executioner and Other Tales of Psychotherapy*. "Although it appears to be a teaching tool, this book also heralds the creation of a new artistic genre by a genuine literary talent" (xii). Weingarten, a clinical professor of psychiatry at Stanford University, where Yalom taught for many years before retiring in 1994 at the age of sixty-three, makes another astute observation. Throughout *Love's Executioner* Yalom succeeds in demystifying therapy, yet paradoxically, the mystery of therapy deepens.

Yalom is not the first psychotherapist to pen stories that lie at the crossroads of art and science. Freud was a master of creating riveting case studies, many of which are best known to us not by their formal titles but by their vivid nicknames, such as the "Rat Man," the "Wolf Man," and "Little Hans." Other therapists have followed in that tradition, including Theodor Reik's *Listening with the Third Ear* (1948) and Robert Lindner's *The Fifty-Minute Hour* (1955). But Yalom has created a distinctive type of psychiatric case study in *Love's Executioner* where the therapist learns as much if not more than the patient, where therapy never proceeds as expected, and where the therapist's apparent failure proves to be ultimately a success. *Love's Executioner* is unique in other ways. No therapist has been more self-disclosing than Yalom is here; and no therapist has portrayed himself to be more stumbling and bungling. Yalom plays many roles in the book, including that of a stand-up comic, always ready to laugh at his own failings and foibles. Yet he also comes across as a magician and wizard, unlocking the healing power of therapy.

The Journey from Case Histories into Short Stories

After completing his clinical textbooks, Yalom found himself at a crossroads, eager to continue writing about psychotherapy but frustrated by formal psychiatric prose. As he observes in *The Yalom Reader*, he began searching for a more evocative prose style. He had two purposes in writing *Love's Executioner*: to teach the fundamentals of clinical psychotherapy, and to give voice to his literary aspirations. He decided to reverse the strategy he had used in his textbooks. Instead of "smuggling" illustrative stories into his theoretical discussions, he would "give the story center stage and allow theoretical material to emanate from it" (340). To do this, Yalom relied on the extensive journal notes he had kept for each patient. He has always scheduled fifteen or twenty minutes between patients to record his impressions of each session. He likens these journal notes to Joycean epiphanies, "clarifying moments of luminous thought."

Yalom's original literary model for *Love's Executioner* was Lewis Thomas's *The Lives of a Cell*. Yalom planned to describe a therapy event in a couple of pages and then in a few more pages relate its significance to an aspect of therapy. The result, however, disappointed him: the creation of flat instead of round characters who never came to life off the page. The solution was to write longer vignettes with "one foot in fact, another in fiction." But then another problem developed. The stories seemed to take on a life of their own. He had the "remarkable writerly experience" of his unconscious taking over. As he approached the end of one story, another one appeared: "it was as though I didn't choose the story—the story chose me" (342).

The stories themselves were easier and faster to write than the theoretical afterwords. He eliminated eight of the afterwords and kept two, which he combined into a single lengthy foreword. Yalom reluctantly acceded to his editor's suggestion that he eliminate all of the afterwords and limit the prologue to eight pages. The decision represented a "watershed personal struggle that permitted me to abandon the didactic mode and let the story speak for itself" (343).

Published in 1989, six years after *Inpatient Group Psychotherapy*, *Love's Executioner* gave Yalom the opportunity to write in depth about a small number of patients, exploring their complexity in a way that was impossible in his earlier clinical textbooks. The ten clinical vignettes demonstrate a new vision of the talking cure based on a relational model of therapy and the idea of existence pain. The book is notable for another reason. We see Yalom developing here his gifts for character, point of view, dialogue, irony, wit, and paradox, gifts that achieve their greatest fruition in his three volumes of psychotherapy tales and four novels. *Love's Executioner* transmutes the talking cure into literary art and introduces psychotherapy to a wide audience.

Yalom was careful to preserve the confidentiality of the ten patients appearing in *Love's Executioner*. They read every sentence of the story in which they appeared to make sure their identities were adequately disguised. Except for the one patient who died before completion of the book, all gave their approval for publication. It would have been fascinating to learn how they reacted to seeing themselves in his book, particularly when the therapy did not succeed, at least from Yalom's point of view. Did they, for example, later form their identity around the idea of being one of Yalom's famous patients, as Freud's patients did?

The prologue to *Love's Executioner* expresses Yalom's belief that psychotherapy is always about existence pain, even if few therapists had pointed this out before him. Our deepest desires can never be fulfilled: "our wants for youth, for a halt to aging, for the return of vanished ones, for eternal love, protection, significance, for immortality itself" (4). Despite the inevitability of death, we act as if we can somehow escape the ending of life. The therapist's role is to point out the delusions patients may have about escaping death. Yalom sees himself as a *dis*illusioner, reminding his patients that this life is all we have, and that while there is no solution to existential loneliness, "therapists must discourage false solutions" (11).

A Momentologist

Beginning with Freud, authors of psychiatric case studies have placed the analyst in the position of the sleuth, the master detective of the inner life who uncovers the clues of the patient's problematic past that explain present-day illness. In this model, the analyst is a Sherlock Holmes figure, analyzing slips of the tongue, other symptomatic acts, dreams, fantasies, and free associations. The Holmesian analyst knows patients better than they know themselves, using that knowledge to unlock their secrets. Sometimes Sherlock Holmes is himself in need of a Sigmund Freud, as Nicholas Meyer imagines in his ingenious 1974 novel *The Seven-Per-Cent Solution*, where the master detective is addicted to cocaine, a problem that Freud knew about from painful personal experience. In this case study and others, a past revelation explains present behavior, leading to therapeutic cure.

But this is not Yalom's vision of psychotherapy. Interpersonal theory suggests that patients' difficulties manifest themselves in their present relationships. And existential theory postulates that time is the implacable antagonist in life. Emphasizing the here-and-now, Yalom gives us a new vision of the therapist, a figure who is not interested in archaeological excavation, as Freud was—ancient statuettes lined his desk in Vienna—but in the ticking clock of mortality. Death anxiety, not castration anxiety, sickens Yalom's characters, and therapists must come to terms with their own death anxiety before they can help patients deal with the same fear. Yalom's emphasis in therapy is on the moment—he is a therapist who might be considered a momentologist. To seize the moment, affirming carpe diem, the therapist must first analyze the moment, an act filled with momentous implications. Yalom does not use a stream of consciousness prose style to create the moment, as Virginia Woolf does in her novels; instead, he shows how the therapy moment is filled with surprises, reversals, and unexpected developments. The therapist can never be sure what the next moment will bring. Nor can the reader.

Existence Stories

Yalom's opening question to his patients in *Love's Executioner*—"What ails?"—affirms existence pain. In this dark universe, engagement, commitment, and authenticity are necessary to avoid succumbing to despair. Therapists must be attuned to a patient's anxiety without being paralyzed by it. "The more the therapist is able to tolerate the anxiety of not knowing, the less need there is for the therapist to embrace orthodoxy" (39). Yalom would agree with F. Scott Fitzgerald's observation in *The Crack-Up*: "The test of a first-rate intelligence is the ability to hold two opposed ideas in the mind at the same time and still retain the ability to function" (69). Yalom would also agree with Shakespeare's line from *King Lear*, "Ripeness is all." Yalom might add, "Ambiguity is all."

The ten vignettes in *Love's Executioner* are all existence stories, reminding us not only of existential pain and the inevitability of death, both of which produce a gaping wound in all the patients in these everyman and everywoman stories, but also that intimacy is possible, however short-lived it may be. Yalom's characters are *in extremis*, and the therapist's task is to help them lead a more authentic life. He knows that the past influences the present and often shapes the future, but therapy is not, he insists, an endless examination of ancient personal history. Just as Yalom rejects Freud's blank screen image of the analyst, he repudiates one of the central metaphors of Freudian psychoanalysis.

> I've learned that the therapist's venture is not to engage the patient in a joint archeological dig. If any patients have ever been helped in that fashion, it wasn't because of the search and the finding of that false trail (a life never goes wrong because of a false trail; it goes wrong because the main trail is false). No, a therapist helps a patient not by sifting through the past but by being lovingly present with that person; by being trustworthy, interested; and by believing that their joint activity will ultimately be redemptive and healing. (242)

Yalom's inclusion of an aphorism in a parenthesis is deceptive: there is nothing parenthetical about this insight.

Yalom is an ironist, aware of the contrast between appearance and reality. Like life, the outcome of therapy is unpredictable. Anything can happen in Yalom's world. The therapist is as surprised as the patient—sometimes more surprised, because the former cannot read the latter's mind. Character is mysterious, unpredictable, unknowable: the best we can do is capture a fleeting glimpse of another person's inner world. We can never take anything or anyone for granted. Occasionally we learn something important about a character's life only after his or her death. At the beginning of a story, Yalom the therapist doesn't know as much as Yalom the writer. The reader, too, remains in the dark until the story's end. The unpredictability of Yalom's case studies recalls the American short story writer O. Henry, who delighted in surprise endings, often with an improbable twist.

The ten vignettes in *Love's Executioner* all involve learning experiences for Yalom and his patients. The stories involve clinical conflicts that challenge Yalom's inventiveness as a therapist and writer. The tales demonstrate Yalom's role as disillusioner, revealing his identification with aspects of his patients' lives. We see Yalom's bold and often risky self-disclosures that have the effect of helping his patients realize they are not alone in struggling with a problem. Throughout *Love's Executioner* Yalom aims for maximum transparency, showing his patients' subjectivity as well as his own.

A Lovesick Patient: "Love's Executioner"

By far the longest and most complex story in the volume, the title story, with its haunting title, begins with perhaps the most startling opening of any published case study. "I do not like to work with patients who are in love. Perhaps it is because of envy—I, too, crave enchantment. Perhaps it is because love and psychotherapy are fundamentally incompatible. The good therapist fights darkness and seeks illumination, while romantic love is sustained by mystery and crumbles upon inspection. I hate to be love's executioner" (17).

What shall we say of this stunning opening paragraph? It is Yalom's finest paragraph and, as he remarks in *Yalom's Cure*, probably his favorite. He could have avoided the confession of envy, but that would have made him less human. To admit his envy, his craving of enchantment, places him in the same position as his patients, suggesting that he is a wounded healer. And to say that he doesn't like to work with patients who are in love implies that he is revealing not only a prejudice but also a countertransference issue, the first of many to which he confesses. As love's executioner, Yalom may feel the need to dispel his patients' enchantment with love, but their therapy stories never lose their sense of enchantment.

Yalom is different from other psychiatric case study authors because he always draws attention to himself, not because he is more narcissistic than others—he is not—but because his major interest lies in the relationship between therapist and patient. Modeling the kind of self-disclosure he asks of his patients, he takes pleasure in admitting, as concretely as possible, his human qualities, even if these qualities, often associated with shame, are seldom revealed by other therapists.

For many of his patients, Yalom is the therapist of last resort, the one to whom they turn when other therapists have failed them, and when some of them believe that the only option left may be suicide. This is especially true of Thelma, the seventy-year-old lovesick woman who is still infatuated with the handsome young psychology intern forty years her junior, Matthew, with whom she had a twenty-seven-day fling a year after her eight-month therapy with him ended. Thelma rhapsodizes about Matthew throughout her treatment with Yalom. "He introduced me to the spiritual, religious dimension of life," Thelma enthuses. "He taught me to care for all living things" (19).

Yalom is understandably horrified. Nothing is more harmful to treatment than a patient or ex-patient sleeping with a therapist, regardless of who initiated the seduction. It's always the therapist's fault, never the patient's. Sex in therapy can never be "consensual" because the patient may fear that if she—the victim is usually female—refuses, the therapist will terminate treatment. Lovesick patients are under the spell of transference-love, which blinds their judgment, and which an unscrupulous therapist can easily exploit. That's why all mental health organizations have banned sex in therapy, which is regarded as a symbolic form of incest. Sexual and nonsexual boundary violations dominate Yalom's most satirical novel, *Lying on the Couch*, but he implies in "Love's Executioner" and elsewhere that there's nothing funny about a patient who is harmed by sexualized therapy.

Matthew's behavior in "Love's Executioner" infuriates Yalom. "I've seen too many patients badly damaged by therapists using them sexually. It's always damaging to a patient" (25). Impervious to Yalom's statements that Matthew's behavior was irresponsible and destructive, not to mention self-destructive, Thelma maintains that lying in Matthew's arms was one of the greatest moments in her life. She believes this even after his coldness to her when they accidentally met six months after their affair ended. Still obsessed with him, the lovesick woman swallowed a bottle of sleeping pills and nearly died. "For eight years I haven't stopped thinking about him."

Early in "Love's Executioner" Yalom includes two details whose significance becomes apparent only at the end of the story. The first is that Thelma is married to a man, Harry, who, if he were to know about her affair with Matthew, would probably kill him. There's little love and no sex in the marriage, but they have remained together for many years, and Thelma is not prepared to leave him. Harry's "large, strangler's hands" display his potential for violence. The second detail is that Yalom and Thelma sign a treatment contract: she agrees to meet once a week with him for six months, with a possible six-month extension if they both think it necessary. She also agrees to participate in his psychotherapy research project, to study the impact of psychotherapy on the elderly. The project entailed a "research interview and a battery of psychological tests to measure outcome, to be completed twice, at the beginning of therapy and six months after termination" (32). The ending of the story will thus involve three different evaluative points of view, that of the patient, the research team, and the therapist—and a fourth point of view if we count Harry.

Yalom dutifully chronicles all of his mistakes in treating her. A moment after he expresses amazement to Thelma that she has never spoken to her previous therapists about her sexual relationship with Matthew, Yalom realizes he has blundered. "Bad technique! A beginner's error—but I could not suppress my astonishment" (24). Yalom's belief that he can succeed with her when other therapists have failed later strikes him as hubris, defined by the pre-Socratic philosophers as "insubordination to divine law," which the secular Yalom then qualifies: insubordination to the "laws that govern the flow of events in my professional field" (31). And yet the more Yalom tries to deprive Thelma's obsession with Matthew of the fuel that energizes it, the more she defends him. Even when Yalom tutors her on the basic feelings—bad, sad, mad, and glad—she falls back on her formidable distancing mechanisms.

Becoming more desperate, Yalom reveals, from wrenching personal experience, how a love obsession drains life of its reality, making real love impossible. He then makes the most startling confession found anywhere in his writings:

> At a conference approximately two years prior to meeting Thelma, I had encountered a woman who subsequently invaded my mind, my thoughts, my dreams. Her image took up housekeeping in my mind and defied all my efforts to dislodge it. But, for a time, that was all right: I liked the obsession and savored it afresh again and again. A few weeks later, I went on a week's vacation with my family to a beautiful Caribbean island. It was only after several days that I realized I was missing everything on the trip—the beauty of the beach, the lush and exotic vegetation, even the thrill of snorkeling and entering the underwater world. All this rich reality had been blotted out by my obsession. I had been absent. I had been encased in my mind, watching replays over and over again of the same and, by then, pointless fantasy. Anxious and thoroughly fed up with myself, I entered therapy (yet again), and after several hard months, my mind was my own again and I was able to return to the exciting business of experiencing my life *as it was happening*. (A curious thing: my therapist eventually became a close friend and years later told me that, at the time he was treating me, he himself was obsessed with a lovely Italian woman whose attention was riveted to someone else. And so, from patient to therapist to patient goes *La Ronde* of obsessional love.) (34–35)

Other writers have confessed to being attracted to or repelled by a patient, but I am not aware of another therapist, particularly one with a spouse and children, who has confessed in a case study to being overcome by a love obsession that has resulted in the necessity to return to treatment—and then discovering, to his astonishment—that the therapist was simultaneously suffering from lovesickness! Yalom's revelation raises several questions. How did his wife, children, friends, and colleagues feel about his self-disclosure? Did he have second thoughts after the book's publication? Or was this simply one more example of everything being grist for the therapist-writer's mill?

Self-disclosure is important for Yalom because it emphasizes the therapist's dual role of participant-observer. Unlike classically trained psychoanalysts, who are taught to disclose little if anything to a patient, Yalom believes that insufficient self-disclosure is more problematic to a patient than excessive self-disclosure. "I have erred consistently on the side of too little, rather than too much, self-disclosure; but whenever I have shared a great deal of myself, patients have invariably profited from knowing that I, like them, must struggle with the problems of being human" (176).

Thelma is not impressed with Yalom's efforts to free her from her obsession. In retrospect, he can understand why. "Generalizing from my experience to hers, I had mistakenly assumed her life to have richness that she was missing because of her obsession. Thelma felt, though she did not explicitly say so at the same time, that the obsession contained infinitely more vitality than her lived experience" (35). However successful Yalom's self-disclosure is from a literary point of view, it proves to be singularly unsuccessful from a therapeutic point of view. And yet all is not lost, in part because therapy (or re-therapy) has helped Yalom, and his therapist, overcome lovesickness. Thelma, too, becomes convinced, through the sheer force of Yalom's persistence, that she must be released from her obsession with Matthew. The question remains, however, how to free her from its baleful spell. Yalom has another task: to keep alive the story of being love's executioner.

Yalom succeeds in both efforts by describing the many mistakes he inadvertently makes in his treatment of her. The mistakes reveal that psychotherapy is as much of an art as a science, proceeding through improvisation and trial and error. Yalom asks Thelma to role-play, imagining that she is Matthew. A mistake: hearing "Matthew" talk about her suicide attempt only depresses her further. She also feels like a "foolish adolescent" while role-playing. Yalom asks her to consider Matthew's countertransference. Another mistake. She is not comforted by the possibility that she is merely an "innocent bystander" in a conflicted maternal countertransference. Knowing that her fear of aging and death is powering her obsession, Yalom hopes that by strengthening her real relationship to him she will be released from her idealized relationship with Matthew. Still another mistake. Thelma turns the tables on him by asking a theoretical question: "Wouldn't psychiatrists rather treat a thirty-year-old patient than a seventy-year-old patient?" (45). Yalom finds himself outmaneuvered once again.

But being outsmarted is part of the process of therapy, particularly when treating a patient whose resistance is so strong. The more challenging the case, the more interesting the story. Yalom sees ironies that other therapists miss, such as his growing identification with a therapist he otherwise detests. When Yalom tells Thelma that her impersonal questions have the effect of pushing him away, she responds, "This is exactly the sort of thing Matthew used to say," to which Yalom can only smile and silently gnash his teeth.

Finally, with time running out—they have only two months left—Yalom plays his final card: a single three-way session with Thelma and Matthew. She bolts upright in her chair, suddenly anxious about the opportunity to test her image of Matthew against reality. She lists all the reasons she thinks it's a bad idea. Yalom offers his single most important therapeutic credo: "the unimagined life is not worth living." Thelma ponders the question for a week and then, returning to the next therapy session looking ten years younger, agrees to a three-way session. Soon Yalom springs his biggest surprise on the reader. Matthew turns out to be nothing like the irresponsible therapist Yalom had imagined. Yalom was prepared for his directness and simplicity—"sociopaths often present themselves well"—and perhaps for his interest in Yalom's writings—"I've read your books for years. It's an honor to meet you"—but not for Matthew's explanation.

Matthew's story is a head-spinner. Upon finishing his clinical training eight years earlier, he considered becoming a Buddhist monk, traveled to India for an eight-day meditation retreat, and, as a result of total silence and isolation, began to lose ego boundaries. By the third week he was hallucinating, and, after an Indian physician placed him on antipsychotic medication, Matthew was flown back to San Francisco where, by pure accident, he encountered Thelma. Still in a fragmented state, and under the influence of the Buddhist spirit of universal oneness, he gave her everything she wanted, including the experience of "perfect oneness and love." Matthew soon realized he had made a grave mistake, and he followed his psychiatrist's recommendation to sever all contact with Thelma both for her sake and his own. What she perceived as heartlessness was his attempt at reparation.

After listening to Matthew's story, Yalom finds himself unnerved: none of his hypotheses to explain the transgressive therapist's behavior were even remotely true. As a result of his psychotic breakdown and his transgressive relationship with Thelma, Matthew decided to end his career as a psychologist; he now works as an administrator of a Christian health maintenance organization. Both Yalom and Thelma listen to Matthew's story with rapt attention—and the reader, too.

Yalom revels in interring the reader's expectations, and everything about Matthew proves stupefying, including his conversion to a fundamentalist Christian sect. Thelma doesn't believe a word of Matthew's story, further confounding Yalom. Now furious at both Matthew and Yalom, Thelma takes no comfort from the fact that what was a love experience for her was the aftermath of a psychotic experience for her former therapist. She sees the Matthew of eight years earlier not as a wounded healer, confused and vulnerable, genuinely sorry that he has caused her harm, but as manipulative and evil. "What a fool I was to have protected him for eight years!"

Thelma's anger enlivens the story. Trying to convince Thelma that what she and Matthew had together was not a shared experience of love, Yalom observes, "I don't think I've ever said a crueler thing, but to make myself heard, I had to speak in words so strong and so stark that they could be neither twisted nor forgotten" (63). Thelma rejects Yalom's statements about the value of no longer being in the throes of obsessional love and, to his dismay, now that she has completed six months of therapy, refuses to consider an extension. Yalom has succeeded in his efforts to be love's executioner, with disastrous results, from the patient's point of view.

The irony of Yalom's image of himself as love's executioner, a therapeutic disillusioner, is that few psychotherapists have been more optimistic about life and the possibility of achieving genuine love. His hopefulness shines through all of his writings: his clinical textbooks, his psychiatric case studies, and his novels. Yalom's hopefulness, which is never shallow or naive, remains one of his greatest strengths as a therapist and writer. Nobody's fool, Yalom may remind us, in his role of disillusioner, of another ironist, Freud, who, in the conclusion to *Studies on Hysteria*, responded to a patient who questioned how she can be helped when her illness is connected with the events of her life. Freud's answer is a masterpiece of wry wisdom. "No doubt fate would find it easier than I do to relieve you of your illness. But you will be able to convince yourself that much will be gained in transforming your hysterical misery into common unhappiness" (*SE*, vol. 2, 305).

Yalom has not exhausted all of the ironies of "Love's Executioner." At the end of Thelma's last session, Yalom briefly speaks with Harry, who has no use for therapy. "Give me back my wife, Doctor, the old Thelma—just the way she used to be" (69). Harry fails to realize that the old Thelma was madly infatuated with her former therapist and symbolically absent to her husband. Harry speaks in a pleading voice, but Yalom cannot help glancing at his large, strangler's hands. Musing over Harry's plea, Yalom thinks, "Harry, no less than Thelma, chose to embrace illusion. Cervantes asked, 'Which will you have: wise madness or foolish sanity?' It was clear which choice Harry and Thelma were making!" (70). A few days later Yalom telephones Thelma, casually informing him that she has seen Matthew the previous day; she remains convinced that he has helped her "immeasurably." They have agreed to meet every month or so "for a chat." The information drives Yalom into a frenzy of curiosity, but she declares she is no longer his patient and that he doesn't have a right to ask her personal questions.

Thelma honors her commitment to the research project, and six months after the termination of therapy she met with a research psychologist to complete a battery of questionnaires. The tests concluded that Thelma had "improved significantly" as a result of therapy. Of the twenty-eight geriatric patients in the research study, Thelma had the most positive outcome—but for reasons that could not be further from the truth, as Yalom notes in bemusement. "It appears that the therapist successfully employed a pragmatic symptom-oriented treatment plan designed to offer relief rather than deep insight or personality change" (72).

Has flawed reasoning ever led to a more accurate conclusion? No one reading "Love's Executioner" will believe, as the research team does, that Yalom employed a "pragmatic symptom-oriented treatment plan." Nor should we accept at face value Yalom's admission in the droll final sentence of the story that the results of the research report afforded him little comfort. It's true that Thelma's therapy did not go as expected and that Yalom may have felt that he had "botched this case beyond belief" (70), but it's doubtful that she felt this way. She tells him, in fact, that if she went back into therapy, Yalom would be her first choice as a therapist. Moreover, like all the patients in *Love's Executioner*, Thelma read the case study in manuscript form and approved its publication. However angry she may have been at Yalom for being love's executioner, she entrusted her life story to him, and, in doing so, she gave him a precious gift—and his readers, too.

A Parent's Last Gift: "If Rape Were Legal . . ."

The next story in *Love's Executioner*, "If Rape Were Legal . . . ," ends on an epiphany that readers will long remember. Only twenty pages long, the story is about a man who, though dying of cancer, cannot prevent himself from making crude sexual comments to the other members of his therapy group, predictably infuriating the women, one of whom had been raped. "Carlos is a cat with nine lives, but now it looks as if he's coming to the end of his ninth life," an oncologist tells Yalom. Carlos's aim in life, he admits shamelessly to Yalom, "was to screw as many different women as he could" (76). Yalom is not sure why he is so drawn to Carlos, who has been struggling with cancer for a decade, and now that death is close, Yalom wonders whether his patient can achieve anything ambitious in therapy. Complicating Yalom's challenge is that Carlos's offensive behavior intensifies when his cancer appears to be in remission.

To achieve his therapeutic goal of allowing Carlos to remain aware of the potentially liberating implications of the idea of death, Yalom finds himself acting more like a philosopher or religious teacher than a therapist. Yalom invades Carlos's "two innermost temples: his love for his children and his reincarnation beliefs" (87). He asks Carlos how he would feel if his beloved daughter lived in a society where rape is legal, as he desired. Carlos suddenly becomes serious and admits that he wouldn't want that to happen. Yalom then helps Carlos interpret a dream about a green Honda Civic, a color and car model he detests. The dream symbolizes a future life that will be a punishment for his action in this life.

What's remarkable about the ending of "If Rape Were Legal . . ." is not only Carlos's transformation in the last months of his life, becoming the most supportive member of the group and a devoted father to his children, but also Yalom's recognition of how the dying can help the living. "I have always felt that the way one faces death is greatly determined by the model one's parents set. The last gift a parent can give to children is to teach them, through example, how to face death with equanimity—and Carlos gave an extraordinary lesson in grace" (92). Caring for a dying person can be a gift, though it is often a mind-numbing one, particularly if dying is difficult and protracted, but even those thanatologists who acknowledge this gift may forget that this gift comes from the dying, who struggle with all their might not to burden their loved ones. Carlos gave this gift to his children, and Yalom conveys this gift to his readers through his moving story.

Confessing Prejudice: "Fat Lady"

Yalom's admission at the beginning of "Love's Executioner" that he doesn't like working with patients who are in love pales in comparison to a confession of a different prejudice at the opening of the next story, bluntly called

"Fat Lady," where he graphically dramatizes a quality that he had never considered a blind spot until his treatment of Betty. "I have always been repelled by fat women. I find them disgusting: their absurd sidewise waddle, their absence of body contour—breasts—laps, buttocks, shoulders, jawlines, cheekbones, *everything*, everything I like to see in a woman, obscured in an avalanche of flesh. And I hate their clothes—the shapeless, baggy dresses or, worse, the stiff elephantine blue jeans with the barrel thighs. How dare they impose that body on the rest of us?" (94).

How does a psychotherapist supposedly free from such hateful prejudice regain his reader's respect after such a damning confession? Yalom's task becomes more daunting because he depicts his repellent feelings in vivid, emotionally charged prose. He doesn't merely *tell* us about his contempt for the obese, but he also *shows* it in shocking detail. Holding nothing back, defying the prudence of both political and psychiatric correctness, Yalom analyzes the origins of his revulsion, confessing, "Obesity, endemic in my family, was a part of what I had to leave behind when I, a driven, ambitious, first-generation American-born, decided to shake forever from my feet the dust of the Russian shtetl" (94). His self-analysis in no way minimizes his responsibility for owning these shameful feelings.

Yalom's major challenge in "Fat Lady" is to regain his readers' sympathy, and if he succeeds, it's because of his determined efforts to help his patient. Betty offers him an opportunity to hone his skills as a therapist. "It was my hope that I would change as Betty and I progressed in her (our) therapy" (98). He reminds us that it's the relationship that heals—"my professional rosary" (98). A Jewish therapist must be desperate if he invokes a rosary!

"Fat Lady" elevates a therapist's countertransference to an art form. As with his other stories, everything is grist for the therapist-writer's mill. Yalom can't help thinking that Betty is the most boring patient he has treated, so boring that he must sit upright in his chair to prevent himself from falling asleep. Then he realizes that when he was in analysis with Rollo May, the therapist used to sit in a straight-backed wooden chair. "He said he had a bad back, but I knew him well for many years afterward and never heard him mention back trouble. Could it be that he found *me*—?" (99).

"Fat Lady" is filled with details like this. It is poetic justice, or therapeutic justice, that Yalom's countertransference feelings come back to haunt him. Patient and therapist take turns playing the role of psychological sleuth to the other. Yalom helps Betty realize that her behavior is a defense against her fears of dependency. When she admits that as soon as she meets new people, she imagines what it will be like to say good-bye to them, he immediately recalls one of Otto Rank's most arresting observations: "Refusing the loan of life in order to avoid the debt of death" (107). Yalom teaches Betty engagement, and she points out his blind spots.

Therapy proves to be almost as painful for Yalom as it does for Betty. While treating her, he began to feel guilty eating, as if he were acting in bad faith toward her. Finding himself passing the upper weight limit he had imposed on himself, he went on a three-week diet, which forced him to understand, more intensely than he wished, her anguish over losing weight. Betty succeeded in losing a hundred pounds, overcoming her long depression and low self-esteem, but at the end she pointed out something to him of which he had been unaware. He had been so repelled by her body that for the first six months he hardly looked at her, and for eighteen months he never shook her hand. Amused by his discomfort, she cut off his rationalizations lest, she told him wryly, his nose "grow longer and longer like Pinocchio." Betty confesses that from the beginning she knew how Yalom felt because, like him, she couldn't stand fat people. The story ends when Yalom hugged her good-bye. "I was surprised to find that I could get my arms all the way around her" (125).

"Fat Lady" is fascinating for its many therapeutic insights. As Betty loses weight, she "re-experienced the major traumatic or unresolved events of her life that had occurred when she was at a particular weight" (115). Yalom never endorses the now-discredited "recovered memory movement," where the therapist, consciously or not, implants ideas in patients, but he is sympathetic to the idea that the body can remember what the mind has long forgotten. Another insight is that conflicts are never entirely resolved in therapy—which explains Yalom's fondness for comparing psychotherapy to "cyclotherapy" (122). "Fat Lady" is also fascinating for its therapist self-disclosures. Yalom hides little about his own life. He is never loath to identify with a patient, as when he admits that he knows personally "how difficult it is for highly educated adults to relate to uneducated blue-collar parents" (120).

Unfreezing Grief: "The Wrong One Died"

"The Wrong One Died" focuses mainly on bereavement, examining perhaps the most painful loss of all, the death of a child, but the story also raises a question seldom discussed by psychiatric case study authors. Should a therapist's primary commitment be to research or to a patient? The answer, most readers would conjecture, is *both*, but what happens when a therapist begins interviewing a research subject who desperately needs treatment that the therapist is unable to provide? Yalom's response to this question makes "The Wrong One Died" especially interesting.

The story begins with a brief ad Yalom placed in a local newspaper seeking to interview people who have been "unable to overcome their grief." Penny was the first of thirty-five people to telephone for an appointment. A thirty-eight-year-old divorcée who drove a taxicab sixty hours a week, Penny was still grief-stricken over her daughter's death four years earlier. Penny looked both rough and vulnerable. Evidently in crisis—she experienced a blackout when she was driving, almost resulting in her death—Penny presented Yalom with a dilemma. On the one hand, the top priority in his life at the time was meeting an approaching deadline for a grant proposal for a new research project. Moreover, he was leaving for a year-long sabbatical in three months, not enough time for the long-term psychotherapy Penny probably needed. On the other hand, he found himself involved with her story, drawn toward her ruggedness and resilience. He could also imagine himself distraught over the loss of one of his own children.

Fearing that he might become inundated by the depth of Penny's emotions, Yalom resolves, like Odysseus, to lash himself to the mast of reason. True to his word, he asks challenging questions that allow her to narrate a story of multiple losses. He interviews her for two hours, sees her for two more hours, and then, when he realizes that the three "research" sessions have also been therapy sessions, agrees to meet with her six more times. When she tells him that she cannot pay for the sessions, he reassures her that there will be no fee: "since we had started to meet as part of a research venture, at this point I could not, in good conscience, suddenly change our contract and charge her" (138). During the ninth and final hour, Yalom sacrificed the rest of his credibility and offered to see her for three more sessions, until the time of his sabbatical departure. Asking himself why he found it difficult to terminate with Penny, he admits that he was "transfixed by the unfolding drama, as each week offered a new, exciting, and entirely unpredictable episode" (143).

Yalom conveys this unfolding drama by showing Penny's multiple losses, beginning with her daughter Chrissie's death from a rare form of leukemia one day before her thirteenth birthday. But there were other, less obvious losses. Her alcoholic husband walked out on their marriage, and her two sons, both in their teens when their sister died, appeared beyond help and dropped out of school, one getting into trouble with the law and landing in jail, the other becoming a drug addict. Each therapy session brought a new bombshell, such as the existence of illegitimate twins Penny had given away at birth when she was sixteen years old; she had never told anyone about the twins.

Penny's multilayered grief brought with it inexhaustible guilt and rage. She felt guilty that she was not with Chrissie when she died (Penny had blacked out during her daughter's final hours), guilty that she hadn't encouraged Chrissie to talk about her fears of death, guilty that she could not let her go, guilty that she was a bad mother, and guilty that she believed the wrong child, the idealized Chrissie, died rather than one of her worthless sons. Attempting to stop time, Penny makes Chrissie's bedroom into a shrine, keeping all of her clothes and possessions in their familiar places. One thinks of Miss Havisham's frozen grief and rage, a result of being jilted on her wedding day in Dickens's *Great Expectations*. The only difference is that Penny takes Chrissie's bed into her own room and sleeps in it every night, an act that Yalom at first believes, in his naivete, is unnatural and bizarre but later realizes is commonplace among parents who have lost a child.

Yalom learns much about chronic bereavement from Penny's story, as does the reader. When she admits that the wrong child had died, a confession that strikes her as inhuman, Yalom disagrees, reminding her that it is only human to feel that way. "I hear only human feelings. Maybe they don't sound good, but that happens to be the way we're built" (137). His words to Penny recall his analyst Olive Smith's similar words to him when he judged himself guilty for wishing to inherit his parents' money. Yalom praises Penny for being an excellent teacher of bereavement, and he learns from her a concept that proves to be a cornerstone of his future work with the bereaved: *"if one is to learn to live with the dead, one must first learn to live with the living"* (138). In return, Yalom teaches Penny about point of view, asking her to imagine how her sons must have felt when she devoted all of her time and energy to her dying daughter.

"Don't worry about me," Penny tells Yalom after the twelfth and final session, "I'll be all right," reminding him that she was a latchkey kid. Yalom reports in the epilogue that he saw Penny one more time a year later, when he returned from his sabbatical. "Never have I had a patient who was willing to uncover such painful material in such a short time" (147). Much had changed in her life. She was still a haunted woman, but now she was fighting demons in the present, not in the past.

Yalom concedes that although her limited time in therapy was too brief to address death anxiety, he was able to help Penny see that in many ways her sons were the real victims of the family tragedy—an insight he had to convey gently, lest she feel additional guilt. Penny accomplished much in her brief therapy, though much more work needed to be done. Yalom's final words emphasize the value of realistic goals in brief therapy. He ends the story by reminding readers of an insight he learned from one of his teachers: "Remember, you can't do all the work. Be content to help a patient realize what must be done and then trust his or her own desire for growth and change" (153).

"The Wrong One Died" is less self-disclosing than the other tales in *Love's Executioner*. Yalom is "tough" but never a disillusioner. Nor does he excoriate himself for his therapeutic failures. Other therapists in his situation might not have undertaken to interview a distraught research subject, but Yalom doesn't take an all-or-nothing approach. He remains committed to Penny both as a research subject and as a patient. He also succeeds in his role as storyteller. "The Wrong One Died" abounds in revelations. Each loss in Penny's life conceals a deeper one, and we begin to see how a mother's tragedy affects her entire family. Everything depends on point of view; only near the end of the story do we imagine the two sons' perspectives. The story offers lessons for clinical and nonclinical readers, including the importance of being as open-minded and alert to detail as possible. Grasping only part of the story of bereavement may be the best we can do.

Showing Me Everything: "I Never Thought It Would Happen to Me"

Yalom contrasts the dark emotions of "The Wrong One Died" with the lighthearted "I Never Thought It Would Happen to Me," the shortest and most comic of the therapy tales. The story resembles "Fat Lady" in that it contains a therapist's sheepish countertransference confession. Elva entered treatment with Yalom eight months after her husband died, and she had been doing well in therapy until a recent setback. "I never thought it would happen to me," she recounts to Yalom on the first page of the story. A thief ran up to her in a parking lot, snatched her purse, jumped into his car, and drove away. A few hours later the police found her purse, without the three hundred dollars that had been in it, dangling from a roadside bush. The robbery changed everything in her life, leaving her bereft in new ways.

Yalom unexpectedly found himself disliking the elderly woman, "part gnome, part sprite, part toad, and each of these parts ill tempered" (156).

Another reason he dislikes Elva is because her anger reminded him of his mother's vicious tongue. The only person his mother didn't hate was his father, who was "really part of her, her mouthpiece, her animus, her creation who . . . could not turn against his maker—despite my prayers that he would once—just once, please, Dad—pop her" (157). Yalom conjures up his childhood self to show how the past still influences the present. He mentions "Asimov's first law of robotics," a reference to the set of rules devised by the science fiction writer to prevent robots from turning against their human creators. Two other allusions come to mind: Mary Shelley's *Frankenstein* and Charles Dickens's *Great Expectations*, where Pip vainly seeks the good-hearted Joe's help in defending him against Mrs. Joe's assaultive violence. How can Yalom treat Elva if he still cannot come to terms with his childhood rage?

Yalom struggles to forge a positive therapeutic relationship with Elva. To his surprise, he began to enjoy her company. Traumatized when her purse had been stolen, an act that shattered her security, she regarded the loss as a reminder of her husband's death. The purse becomes both a symbol and a symptom of her bereft life. Over time the purse once again became full, posing a risk of being stolen again. In an inspired moment, Yalom suggested that Elva empty the contents of the bag, an act that evokes slapstick comedy. As she empties the purse, they quarrel over every item. Must she keep, he asks incredulously, a plastic sack of old orange peels, a bag of sourdough starter, three pairs of sunglasses? The humor of the situation arises from Yalom's voyeuristic pleasure in gazing at the contents of Elva's purse. Few novelists or creative writers would reach Yalom's conclusion that looking into an elderly woman's purse was a transformative act, yet the ending of the story is perfect. "Our time of intimacy—call it love, call it love making—was redemptive. In that one hour, Elva moved from a position of forsakenness to one of trust. She came alive and was persuaded, once more, of her capacity for intimacy. I think it was the best hour of therapy I ever gave" (162).

Secret Letters: "Do Not Go Gentle"

Yalom opens "Do Not Go Gentle" with a problem he has never confronted before: whether to be the keeper of a sixty-nine-year-old man's secret love letters. Dave's lover died thirty years earlier, and he has preserved hundreds of her letters about their clandestine affair. Now, however, he is worried that his wife may come across the letters after his death. And so he asks Yalom to hide the letters that are stashed in a bulging briefcase. Yalom thinks of many reasons for Dave to give up his foolishness and destroy the letters, but there are limits, the therapist confesses ruefully, to his hypocrisy. "I, too, had my sack of letters from a long-lost love. I, too, had them cutely hidden away (in my system, under B for *Bleak House*, my favorite Dickens novel, to be read when life was at its bleakest). I, too, had never reread the letters. Whenever I tried, they brought pain, not comfort. They had lain there untouched for fifteen years, and I, too, could not destroy them" (166).

Yalom never told his patient about these hidden love letters, but he tells his readers, a risky self-disclosure. This is not the first time Yalom has hinted at marital difficulties. Writing in *Every Day Gets a Little Closer* about Ginny's communication problems with her boyfriend, Yalom reflects on "comparable debacles with my wife" (185). And earlier in "Love's Executioner" Yalom confesses to a love obsession a few years earlier that required him to return to therapy. Publicly acknowledging hidden love letters in "Do Not Go Gentle" is another risky confession, one that Yalom is prepared to make because of his conviction that patients learn the most from therapists who confide that they have faced similar struggles.

"Do Not Go Gentle" raises several thorny therapy questions that Yalom explores in great detail, including whether he should agree to Dave's request to keep the secret love letters. "If I kept the letters, they could act as a guy line: he couldn't simply float away and disappear. At the very least, he would have to be up front about terminating: he'd have to face me and request the letters back" (168). On the other hand, accepting the letters might be a "pact with his shadow—an alliance with pathology" (168), a form of "colluding, in a countertherapeutic way, with his penchant for secrecy" (170). The question is further complicated when Dave accepts Yalom's suggestion to switch from personal to group therapy, which will give him an opportunity to investigate the interpersonal implications of his secretiveness, objectification of women, and mistrust of men. The switch to group therapy poses a problem for Yalom, however, because he doesn't know how much of his intimate knowledge of the patient he should share with the group.

All of these questions are related to the primary one, the psychological meaning behind Dave's need to preserve the clandestine love letters. Yalom agrees to store the letters in a safe place only if Dave agrees to tell the group about their bargain. Dave delays a decision, but he unexpectedly reveals to the group his morbid fear of illness and death. At the next meeting Dave shares the following dream. "*Death is all around me. I can smell death. I have a packet with an envelope stuffed inside of it, and the envelope contains something that is immune to death or decay or deterioration. I'm keeping it secret. I go to pick it up and feel it, and suddenly I see that the envelope is empty. I feel very distressed about that and notice that it's been slit open. Later I find what I assume was in the envelope on the street, and it is a dirty old shoe with the sole coming off* (173).

Group therapy is generally not the place to probe existential issues, yet the meaning of the dream is so fraught with death anxiety that Yalom struggles to find a way to help Dave and the others interpret the dream. Dave continued to act in a cloak-and-dagger way—and Yalom found himself becoming increasingly impatient. Yalom asks Dave for permission to reveal the meaning of the dream to the group, and the patient agrees. Yalom then states that the dream answers the question why the letters were "loaded" for Dave. Yalom doesn't tell the group that the dream also explains why Yalom's own letters were loaded for himself. "But of my letters I did not speak," he tells us: "there are limits to my courage."

Dave's dream is one about death, Yalom informs the group. "It began with 'Death is all around me. I can smell death.' And the central image was the envelope, an envelope that contained something immune to death and deterioration. What could be clearer? The love letters were an amulet, an instrument of death denial. They warded off aging and kept Dave's passion frozen in time" (176). One detail of the dream remains obscure, the meaning of the "sole" coming off the shoes, but another member of the group figures out the explanation. "The shoe is losing its *soul,* spelled S-O-U-L" (177). Yalom implies to us, though not to the group, that this interpretation explains the meaning of why he also has preserved for years a stash of love letters, but there is another meaning of the story on which he does not comment. As a man of letters, a writer, Yalom demonstrates the ways in which creativity is an amulet, an instrument of death denial, immune to death or decay or deterioration. Writing a book creates a form of immortality for the writer, or at least the illusion of immortality, a belief that not even a *dis*illusioner can entirely dispel.

Dave abruptly leaves therapy, never to return, and so the question of whether to store the letters becomes moot. Yalom typically blames himself for Dave's departure. The degree of his self-blame, here and elsewhere, may strike us as exaggerated, but his sadness over Dave's departure is heartfelt.

The title of Yalom's story alludes to "Do Not Go Gentle Into That Good Night," Dylan Thomas's iconic poem. Yalom's story, however, is not an injunction to defy death, to postpone the inevitable, but a meditation on the need to appreciate every minute of life. Contrary to his claim, Dave's life is not an open book, and he disappears from therapy, perhaps because of a recognition, to quote from the poem, that his words had "forked no lightning." By contrast, Yalom implies that the wise, those who have led fulfilling lives, will have less need to rage against the dying of the light.

Falling in Love with Our Own Creations: "Two Smiles"

"Two Smiles" is the most philosophical story in *Love's Executioner*, and the one that perhaps best illustrates the ways in which literary writers have enriched Yalom's imagination. "How disquieting to realize that reality is illusion," he muses, "at best a democratization of perception based on participant consensus" (185). The sentence defines not only reality but also the theme of "Two Smiles," a story as enigmatic in its own way as the *Mona Lisa*.

Marie has been in therapy with Yalom for three years, unable to move forward in her life since the accidental death of her surgeon-husband seven years earlier. Like Penny in "The Wrong One Died," Marie remains frozen in grief, but unlike Penny, she has reached an impasse in therapy. Four weeks earlier Marie had been thrown from a cable car in San Francisco and suffered serious injuries, including extensive facial and dental damage. A woman of intimidating beauty, she has entered treatment with an oral surgeon, Dr. Z., to repair her teeth. She had first met him when they were in college together in Mexico City, where he had tried unsuccessfully to woo her. Decades later he moved to the United States and worked in the same hospital as her husband. Shortly after her husband's death, Dr. Z., despite having a wife and five children, made unwelcome sexual overtures to her, which she angrily rebuffed. Now she needs his professional treatment, but he continues to harass her, and, in an attempt to punish and exert control over her, he refuses to prescribe adequate pain medication. To help control her pain and overcome the stalemate in therapy, Yalom recommends a trusted hypnotherapist, Mike.

Honesty compels Yalom to add a couple of details that other therapist-writers would discreetly omit. First, he is sexually attracted to the regal Marie, imagining himself embracing her and feeling her body unfreeze in his arms. She reminded him of a beautiful aunt who wore her hair in the same way and who "played a major role in my adolescent sexual fantasies" (180). Second, in recommending that Marie see a hypnotherapist, he confides in us that he has an ulterior motive. He wants Mike to bear witness that Marie is a difficult patient. "Yes, I admit it, a part of me was rooting for Marie to give Mike a hard time: 'Come on, Marie, do your stuff!'"

(182). To Yalom's amazement, Marie proves to be a model patient. Without knowing anything about her history, Mike makes two recommendations to her: to discuss pain management with her oral surgeon, and to cut down on her heavy smoking. To accomplish the second task, Mike urges her to imagine giving a much-loved dog a can of food labeled "poison." During both suggestions she and Mike "locked eyes," each time Marie smiling and apparently nodding in agreement.

Transfixed by these two smiles, Yalom wonders what they signify. Later, he asks Mike about Marie's two smiles. He remembers them well. "The smiles, appearing at points of power in his presentation, signified that Marie had understood and was affected by his message" (185). Mike's response surprises Yalom, for he had interpreted them not as moments of concurrence but as ironic smiles, indicating Mike's naivete in making simple suggestions that she knew would be impossible for her to fulfill: Marie hated the lecherous Dr. Z. and was, like Yalom, no dog lover. Marie also remembered her two smiles, but her meaning is different from Mike's and Yalom's. Both smiles indicated her intense discomfort: her fear that Mike might believe she was a "slut" for encouraging Dr. Z.'s lecherous behavior, and her embarrassment that Yalom might have overstepped his role as a psychiatrist by giving her direct advice to dispose of her dog.

The two smiles in this Rashomon-like story have broad psychiatric, linguistic, and philosophical implications, as Yalom discusses in the epilogue. He cites Flaubert's lament in *Madame Bovary* about the failure of language to convey reality: "none of us," writes Flaubert, "can ever express the exact measure of his needs or his thoughts or his sorrows" (194). To demonstrate that reality is distorted by both translation error and bias error, Yalom cites Proust's insight that we fall in love not with others but with our own creations. Yalom then cites Julian Barnes's doomed efforts in *Flaubert's Parrot* to find the "real" stuffed bird that the novelist claimed to use in a story.

Unlike his colleagues, Yalom has little confidence in personality tests or psychiatric diagnosis, though he believes that diagnosis may be useful for major organic psychiatric disorders such as schizophrenia and bipolar disorder. He marvels that anyone can believe that diagnosis is anything more than a reductive cluster of symptoms and behavioral traits. "Even the most liberal system of psychiatric nomenclature does violence to the being of another" (199).

"Two Smiles" affirms the need to look at others, patients and nonpatients alike, through fresh eyes, but we are always gazing at subjective reality, narcissistically seeing our own creations. Each of us has a strikingly different perspective of reality, even when we believe that we see what others see. Locked gazes imply that we are locked into and often imprisoned by our own vision of reality. Always mistrustful of "union" or spiritual "melding," Yalom suggests, in one of his most arresting metaphors, that people who "feel empty never heal by merging with another incomplete person. On the contrary, two broken-winged birds coupled into one make for clumsy flight" (197).

An Ambiguous Ending: "Three Unopened Letters"

Given the subjective nature of reality, the best conclusion to a story is an ambiguous one, as we see in "Three Unopened Letters." Saul, an accomplished sixty-three-year-old neurobiologist, returns to Yalom after an absence of three years. During that time Saul had received a generous award from the Stockholm Research Institute in Sweden: a six-month fellowship and a fifty-thousand-dollar stipend. Saul felt honored to work with a renowned Scandinavian cellular biologist, Dr. K., but collaboration only diminished Saul's fragile self-esteem. He had hoped that he and Dr. K. would publish an article together, but he encounters rejection after rejection from journal editors. Saul published a different article in a prestigious journal, but through no fault of his own he was unable to mention his collaborative research with Dr. K. Saul now dreaded the publication of the article, fearing that Dr. K. or the institute would regard him as both a fraud and thief.

Sure enough, Saul receives over the course of a few days three envelopes from the Stockholm Institute that send him into a panic—and back into therapy. Unable to summon the courage to open the letters, Saul succumbs to his catastrophic fears, concluding that he has only one option: to return the fifty-thousand dollars. Yalom realizes that Saul's overwrought reaction is irrational, but he also identifies with Saul's relentless obsession with work: similar demons chase both therapist and patient. Yalom has an intimate understanding of the menacing Dr. K., whose initial evokes Kafka's anguished protagonist in *The Trial*. Saul fears that both Dr. K. and the Stockholm Institute have put him on trial. The unopened letters, he senses, are his final judgment and death sentence. The Officer's statement in Kafka's "In the Penal Colony"—"My guiding principle is this: Guilt is never to be doubted"—is true in Yalom's world.

Worried that Saul might commit suicide, Yalom makes a rare house visit in an attempt to convince the bed-ridden patient that he suffers from massive guilt without having committed a crime. Yalom persuades Saul to agree to a no-suicide contract, even though such agreements are ludicrous ("If you kill yourself, I won't treat you ever again"). Yalom helps Saul realize that the intimidating unopened letters have a larger significance in his life, symbolizing his lifelong struggle for acceptance and approval.

It is not therapy, however, that rouses Saul from his deep depression but the discovery that Dr. K. had recently died—*before* he could have received the journal containing Saul's article. The three letters instantly lose their terror to Saul, and he opens them to find nothing reproachful in any of them. Therapy ends, and three years later Saul dies. In the last paragraph of the story, Yalom meets a young man at a party who recently returned from studying at the Stockholm Institute, a fellowship made possible indirectly by Saul's generosity. The final sentence contains the young man's startling question to Yalom. "Had I heard that, in his will, Saul had left the Stockholm Institute a bequest of fifty thousand dollars?" (226).

Like any good story, "Three Unopened Letters" leaves us with tantalizing questions. Did Saul bequeath the money out of gratitude or guilt? Did he die believing that he finally earned the recognition he craved? Or did he die believing that he had failed to fulfill his professional goals? Yalom raises two additional questions. Did Saul realize how deeply Yalom cared for him? And was Saul able to forget about work from time to time and enjoy the leisure of an afternoon stroll? The last question may be asked about Yalom himself, who earlier in the story tells us that he has "continued to work compulsively and to impose a professional schedule on myself that makes that stroll impossible" (210–211). The ending of the story remains ambiguous. "Three Unopened Letters" becomes a metaphor of *Love's Executioner*: the more carefully we read a psychological case study or short story, the more questions we have. The storyteller allows readers to reach their own interpretations. Or, as a character observes in Henry James's *The Turn of the Screw*, "the story *won't* tell . . . not in any literal, vulgar way."

Patient Devotion: "Therapeutic Monogamy"

Marge White, a thirty-five-year-old lab technician, is the kind of patient a therapist doesn't want. His first impulse after seeing her is to "get the hell away, far away." Yalom accepts Marge into treatment for a reason probably no therapist has acknowledged publicly. "Recently I had been asking myself how, in all good faith, I could go on teaching students to do psychotherapy and at the same time refuse to treat difficult patients" (228).

Yalom does his best to help Marge realize her many good qualities, such as compassion, but he inadvertently makes her feel worse about herself, exposing his ineptitude. Urging her on the telephone, during one of her frequent late-night desperation calls to his home, not to compare herself to highly successful women such as his wife, who had been featured in the *Stanford Daily*, he recommends that she liken herself to one of the homeless people whom she has helped. A "colossal blunder," he immediately realizes. Sure enough, during her next therapy session she points out that he conveyed his true feelings by associating her with the "most hapless souls on earth" (230).

Therapy reaches an impasse until a strange new voice emerges from Marge. "You don't know me," the "other" Marge says. She was right, Yalom declares. "I didn't know the voice who talked. The voice was so different, so forceful, so authoritative" (236). Yalom calls Marge's dark self a "Belle Dame sans Merci," an allusion to John Keats's 1819 poem. This new, assertive, seductive voice calls herself "Me," and suddenly we are in a story where a single personality has split into two.

Yalom regards the existence of "Me" in "Therapeutic Monogamy" as a Siren or Lorelei figure seeking to lure him into betraying Marge. Yalom's credo is that although therapists are not "monogamous" because they have several patients, a patient has the right to "expect fidelity *during* the hour" (239). He remains devoted to Marge, not to her seductive alter ego, an embodiment of Marge's rage and self-hatred. Whereas another therapist might have been beguiled by "Me," Yalom remains focused on the here-and-now. His therapeutic strategy is to integrate "Me" into Marge's personality. Yalom admits without guilt or regret that he has served as love's executioner to the Marge who no longer exists, a phantom who was born to demonstrate Marge's uniqueness as a person. But Yalom shows how Marge is unique in her own quiet, unassuming way. Yalom has not forgotten the specter, he tells us in the final sentence: "she avenged herself by burning her image into my memory" (244)—and into the reader's as well.

Wonderment: "In Search of the Dreamer"

Yalom ends *Love's Executioner* with a sixty-four-year-old accountant, the "two Marvins," but "In Search of the Dreamer" is not another story of multiple personality. Rather, Yalom distinguishes between Marvin the man and Marvin the idea. "It was the flesh-and-blood Marvin who was irritating and uninteresting. But Marvin the *project* was intriguing" (250).

About six months earlier Marvin began experiencing disabling migraine headaches that appear to be related to recent sexual problems. A neurologist could not explain or control Marvin's migraines and referred him to Yalom. The story opens with Marvin carefully unrolling a three-foot chart in which he has methodically recorded every recent migraine and sexual experience. "Every migraine of the last four months was preceded within twenty-four hours by a sexual failure" (247). Marvin is convinced that there's a causal relationship between the two. Yalom is not. Unable or unwilling to engage in the introspection that is necessary for psychotherapy, and deeply mistrustful of psychiatry, as is his wife of forty-one years, Phyllis, Marvin appears to be, in Yalom's judgment, a candidate not for psychotherapy but for brief cognitive-behavioral therapy or perhaps marital therapy, despite the fact that he claims to have an idyllic, harmonious marriage. But we know, like all the stories in *Love's Executioner*, that revelations await Yalom and his readers. Marvin's impending retirement and his decision to sell his accountancy firm, after a lifetime of working, are more problematic than he realizes, and perhaps responsible for his paralyzing migraines. Retirement, Yalom observes, "is a time of life review, a summing up, a time of proliferating awareness of finitude and approaching death" (250). Marvin doesn't realize this.

Freud said famously that dreams are the royal road to the unconscious. The key to Marvin's feelings about the future lies in his own dreams, which belie his account of a conflict-free marriage. Many of Marvin's dreams have an existential message. One dream reveals his fear that he is approaching the end of his life's work and that only sexuality will keep him alive—and even that is now failing him. Another dream signifies, more hopefully, that his therapist is giving him the opportunity, in Yalom's words, "to paint his life all over again on a blank canvas" (265). Another dream evokes the threat Yalom poses to Marvin, Phyllis, and their fraught marriage. And still another dream contains a striking literary (or filmic) reference that surely intrigued Yalom, a dream in which a woman reminds Marvin of a "Madame Defarge in the movie *A Tale of Two Cities* who knitted at the guillotine as heads were lopped off." The dream, in Yalom's view, signifies that Marvin has become aware of death too quickly, without the time to process it.

With his new openness, honesty, and curiosity, Marvin continues to surprise Yalom. The story proceeds in an unexpected direction when Phyllis, long housebound, enters therapy, and the three discuss how her agoraphobia has worsened as a result of Marvin's therapeutic progress. Yalom deploys a new and counterintuitive therapeutic strategy, one based on paradox. He instructs Marvin to call his wife punctually every two hours from work with the words: "Phyllis, please don't leave the house. I need to know you are there at all times to take care of me and prevent me from being frightened" (283–284). Both husband and wife stare at Yalom in disbelief, but Marvin faithfully carries out the instructions. "Marvin was irritated with me for making him promise to keep repeating the same stupid statement. Phyllis, even though she knew Marvin was following my instructions, grew irritated with him for ordering her to stay at home. After a few days she went to the library alone, then shopping, and in the next few weeks ventured farther than she had for years" (284).

A Bestseller

Love's Executioner spent many weeks on bestseller lists and was eventually translated into twenty-seven languages. The book received overwhelming critical praise, establishing Yalom's reputation as an inspired storyteller. The paperback edition quotes the *San Francisco Chronicle* reviewer: "Yalom writes with the narrative wit of O. Henry and the earthly humor of Isaac Bashevis Singer." The *Washington Post Book World* reviewer likened Yalom to Freud, a "graceful and canny writer." This was high praise, indeed, for the only major award Freud received in his own lifetime was the prestigious Goethe Prize in 1930.

The two reviews of *Love's Executioner* published in the *New York Times* reached different conclusions about the book. Writing in the Sunday *Times*, Eileen Simpson, was troubled by the blurring between fact and fiction. "An avid reader of both case histories and short stories, I go to the one and the other for different reasons. As psychologizing in fiction puts me off, so dramatic liberties in reports of psychotherapeutic treatment make me uneasy." The other *Times* reviewer, Eva Hoffman, observed that Yalom "demonstrates once again that in the right hands, the stuff of therapy has the interest of the richest and most inventive fiction." She added that Yalom never reduces his patients to a collection of symptoms.

Rereading *Love's Executioner*

How did Yalom feel rereading *Love's Executioner* when he was eighty? "I personally feel shocked," he wrote in the afterword to the 2012 paperback edition about confronting his younger self. "How dare he disclose so many of my private matters? My secret cache of love letters, my compulsive work habits, my inexcusably unkind, judgmental attitudes toward obese people, my love obsession that prevented me from being fully present at a family beach vacation. Despite such behavior, I am nonetheless proud of his putting nothing in the way of forging a true therapy encounter; I would do exactly the same today. I remain convinced that a therapist's judicious self-disclosure facilitates the course of therapy" (280). Yalom's only regret is that several obese women were offended by "Fat Lady." He acknowledges putting himself "on trial" several times and finding himself guilty. In his own defense, he adds, he is the major character in the story, which shows his honest efforts to understand his shameful feelings so that he could work more successfully with his patient. He ends the afterword by disclosing an unanticipated benefit of the inevitable memory loss that occurs when one is an octogenarian. "As I turned the pages of 'Three Unopened Letters,' 'Love's Executioner,' 'The Wrong One Died,' among other stories, I felt myself burning with delicious curiosity. I had forgotten how they ended!" (285).

Chapter 6

When Nietzsche Wept

Gratitude and Its Discontents

Published in 1991, *When Nietzsche Wept* is an historical novel based on real characters: the Viennese physician Josef Breuer (1842–1925), the German philosopher Friedrich Nietzsche (1844–1900), and the two women with whom they became dangerously infatuated, "Anna O." (1859–1936), the first patient in psychoanalysis, and Lou Salomé (later Lou Andreas-Salomé) (1861–1937), an alluring Russian who became a psychoanalyst and whom Nietzsche and the German poet Rainer Maria Rilke found bewitching. A young Sigmund Freud (1856–1939) also appears, still under the influence of his mentor Breuer. Yalom captures the intellectual, artistic, and cultural excitement of fin de siècle Vienna, the center of Europe during a turbulent historical moment.

When Nietzsche Wept is a philosophical novel, bringing to life perhaps the greatest philosopher of the nineteenth and twentieth centuries, a man whose stunning ideas continue to shape contemporary thought. Yalom distills the essence of Nietzsche's iconoclastic philosophy, highlighting the stark contrast between his radiant thoughts and grim life. Avoiding caricature, hagiography, and clinical case study, Yalom's Nietzsche is a complex, three-dimensional character who remains human, all too human.

When Nietzsche Wept is also a psychological novel, dramatizing the birth of psychoanalysis. Yalom raises an intriguing question. How would the despairing Nietzsche have reacted if he were treated by a physician, his exact contemporary, who was experimenting with a new form of verbal therapy, and who was experiencing his own emotional crisis? *When Nietzsche Wept* explores many contentious psychological issues, including the nature of gratitude and sympathy. Nietzsche and Freud both believed that the benefactor-beneficiary relationship was based on an unconscious struggle for power and therefore fraught with resentment and aggression. This dark view of gratitude strained both men's relationships with those to whom they were indebted. Yalom offers his own vision of gratitude, one that informs all of his writings.

The historical Nietzsche is an apt subject for a philosophical-psychological novel because the distinction between philosophy and psychology was blurred before the twentieth century. Nietzsche not only fused the two disciplines together but also became the greatest prose stylist in German after Goethe. The youngest professor of classical philology in the history of the venerable University of Basel, in Switzerland, Nietzsche was expert in Greek and Latin. He was also one of the world's first and most formidable cultural critics. Nietzsche was only fifty-five when he died; the last ten years of his life were lost in insanity, a result, most medical historians have concluded, of tertiary syphilis, a frequent and incurable illness at the time (late stage syphilis is still incurable). Some scholars have speculated that Nietzsche suffered from manic depressive illness for much of his adult life. It's likely that he experienced a series of strokes around the time of his collapse in early 1889, followed by permanent dementia. Confusing genius for madness, a few scholars have concluded from his final illness that his writings were also the product of insanity, a judgment that Yalom wisely rejects.

Above all, *When Nietzsche Wept* is a profoundly moving and ambitious novel, offering insight into the lives of two deeply troubled men who, struggling with existence pain, find themselves in a situation where each teaches and learns from the other. Their friendship is based on reciprocity, an idea central to Yalom's vision of psychotherapy.

Yalom and Psychobiography

When Nietzsche Wept is the first of three Yalom novels to offer psychobiographical portraits of major European philosophers and physicians. Only a century old, psychobiography is the effort to understand the life of a person through the use of psychological and biographical theory. Psychobiography is "multimethodological and essentially theoretically anarchistic," as William Todd Schultz admits in the introduction to his 2005 edited volume *Handbook of Psychobiography* (16). The psychobiographer seeks to learn the personal, historical, and cultural factors that contribute to a person's identity, and then to show the relationship between the subject's life and work.

Psychoanalytically oriented psychobiographers emphasize the importance of childhood experiences, the influence of one's parents in the shaping of personality, the role of the unconscious, and the ways in which the past shapes the present and future.

The subtitle of Alan C. Elms's 1994 book *Uncovering Lives* evokes the tense relationship between two discrete but interrelated disciplines: *The Uneasy Alliance of Biography and Psychology*. Elms begins by citing the columnist George Will's sneering definition: "In 'psychobiography' the large deeds of great individuals are 'explained' with reference to some hitherto unsuspected sexual inclination or incapacity, which in turn is 'explained' by some slight the individual suffered at a tender age—say, 7, when his mother took away a lollipop" (4). Elms reassures us that he has never encountered an example as ludicrous as Will's Lollipop Hypothesis, but he is mindful of the strengths and weaknesses of psychobiography.

Psychobiography can shed much light on the elusive relationship between the biographical subject and his or her work, but complete knowledge is an impossibility. Or as William James pointed out in the conclusion of his aptly titled "On a Certain Blindness in Human Beings," "neither the whole of truth, nor the whole of good, is revealed to any single observer, although each observer gains a partial superiority of insight from the peculiar position in which he stands" (149). We always need to ask ourselves what we know and do not know about a subject. Often we don't know what we don't know. There's much that remains mysterious and unknowable about Yalom's sketches of Nietzsche, Schopenhauer, and Spinoza.

Elms offers many helpful suggestions for writing and judging good psychobiography, suggestions that Yalom has intuitively followed. Psychobiography should avoid theoretical narrowness and reductiveness. "No one psychological theory can effectively elucidate every personality we want to understand. Therefore psychobiography needs to incorporate as much eclectic diversity as it can find" (Elms 10). Good psychobiography should be theoretically and methodologically cautious, avoiding what Freud calls "wild analysis," the tendency toward polemical, speculative, or crude interpretation. Psychobiography should emphasize psychological health, not pathology. The artistic impulse is a sign of health, not illness, an effort to understand and come to terms with inner conflict. Good psychobiography, as Freud reminds us, avoids the twin temptations of idealizing and devaluing the subject. Bad psychobiography, by contrast, spends too much time searching in vain for key biographical events, resulting in the fallacy of "originology," which Erik H. Erikson defines in *Young Man Luther* (1958) as a "habit of thinking which reduces every human situation to an analogy with an earlier one, and most of all to that earliest, simplest, and most infantile precursor which is assumed to be its 'origin' " (18). Yalom avoids the error of originology even as he suggests that certain psychobiographical events have had transformative impacts on his subjects' lives.

Finally, we should heed Dan P. McAdams's observation about the value of the psychobiographer's engagement with the biographical subject. "Psychobiographers' third-person accounts of their subjects' lives should aim to uncover, interpret, incorporate, and critique subjects' first-person narrative identities; the story the psychobiographer tells should creatively engage the story the psychobiographer thinks the subject told" (75). Yalom has taken this lesson to heart. His novels not only bring to life Nietzsche, Schopenhauer, and Spinoza, but the stories also show how the philosophers' writings influenced the lives of readers, including Yalom himself.

Two Flesh-and-Blood Characters

Much has been written about Breuer and Nietzsche, but Yalom is the first to transmute the two men into sympathetic flesh-and-blood characters interpreted by a novelist intimately familiar with both psychoanalysis and philosophy. Breuer and Nietzsche never met in real life, but each remains true to character throughout Yalom's story. More importantly, Breuer and Nietzsche remain fully believable in the novel, and each bears Yalom's authorial imprint. The two characters reveal as much about their creator as they do about their historical progenitors.

Nietzsche had few intellectual equals. As he noted in the preface to the second edition of *The Gay Science*, he was "still waiting for a philosophical *physician* in the exceptional sense of that word—one who has to pursue the problem of the total health of a people, time, race or of humanity— to muster the courage to push my suspicion to its limits and to risk the proposition: what was at stake in all philosophizing hitherto was not at all 'truth' but something else—let us say, health, future, growth, power, life" (35). Nietzsche encounters a philosophical physician in Breuer, who seeks nothing less than healing the philosopher's body and mind.

The novelist's original intention, as he observes in *The Yalom Reader*, was to invent a fictional lapsed priest-therapist to treat Nietzsche, but then he realized that the historical Breuer would be his model. "I knew Breuer's work particularly well because, for a decade, I had taught a Freud appreciation course in which I discussed the contributions of Breuer" (387). Once he selected Breuer as Nietzsche's therapist, "the rest of the plot quickly fell into place."

Breuer was a highly respected physician known as the finest diagnostician in Vienna. He was a researcher who made pioneering neurophysiological discoveries on the role of the vagus nerve: the "Hering–Breuer reflex" prevents the overinflation of the lungs. He was also known for his research on the role of the inner ear in the regulation of equilibrium. Breuer wanted to become a medical professor, for which he was superbly qualified, but Vienna's virulent anti-Semitism ended the possibility of an academic career, the same fate that would befall Sigmund Freud. Students of psychoanalysis know Breuer mainly as Freud's early collaborator. Breuer's case study of a young woman suffering from hysteria first appeared in a psychiatric journal in 1893 and then in 1895 in the coauthored *Studies on Hysteria*, generally regarded as the first psychoanalytic publication.

1882

The year 1882 was momentous for Freud, Breuer, and Nietzsche. Freud was a medical intern in his mid-twenties in 1882, when the novel opens, and he regarded Breuer, fourteen years his senior, as his mentor, friend, and admired father figure. In *An Autobiographical Study* (1925) Freud identified 1882 as a "turning-point" in his career, when Ernst Brücke, a professor of physiology for whom Freud had the greatest esteem, "corrected my father's generous improvidence by strongly advising me, in view of my bad financial position, to abandon my theoretical career" (*SE*, vol. 20, 10). Freud followed Brücke's recommendation, left the physiological laboratory, and entered Vienna General Hospital, where he worked in various departments. Freud had met Josef Breuer in the late 1870s, but their relationship was perhaps never stronger than in 1882, when Freud often had dinner at Breuer's home. Freud became secretly engaged to Martha Bernays on June 17, 1882.

In 1882 Breuer broke off treatment with the first patient in psychoanalysis, whom he called in his published case study "Fräulein Anna O." He had been treating her for a variety of symptoms, including paralysis and disturbances of speech and vision. Breuer was at this time married and the father of five children. His growing involvement with his patient strained his marriage and led ultimately to his abrupt termination of the case.

Beginning between the winter of 1882–1883 and the end of 1888, Walter Kaufmann points out, "Nietzsche came into his own," completing eight books (*Basic Writings of Nietzsche* xiii). The year 1882 saw publication of one of Nietzsche's greatest works, *The Gay Science*, which, along with *Human, All Too Human*, published in 1878, plays a key role in Yalom's novel. By 1882 Nietzsche had long resigned, for reasons of ill health, his professorship at the University of Basel, having been appointed in 1869 at the age of twenty-four. Living off a meager pension, he traveled from physician to physician seeking medical relief from problems that had plagued him his entire life.

This was the fateful year Nietzsche met Lou Salomé, with whom he had a brief, chaste affair. In Ernest Jones's view, Lou Salomé "attached herself to the greatest men of the nineteenth and twentieth century: Nietzsche and Freud respectively. Freud greatly admired her lofty and serene character as something far above his own, and she had a full appreciation of Freud's achievements" (vol. 2, 176–177). Salomé appreciated Nietzsche's achievements, but he hardly regarded her as lofty and serene. Nietzsche, Salomé, and the philosopher Paul Rée lived together briefly in a *ménage à trois*, but when Nietzsche, smitten with love, hastily proposed marriage to Salomé, she turned him down, precipitating Nietzsche's suicidal crisis—on which Yalom's novel opens.

Fact and Fiction

A reader can appreciate *When Nietzsche Wept* without an understanding of the historical Breuer, Freud, and Nietzsche, but the novel takes on added significance when we realize how closely Yalom has modeled his characters on factual reality. In the beginning of the story, Breuer and Freud enjoy a warm if not overly close relationship. It's odd to read a novel where Freud is overshadowed by Breuer, whom history has largely forgotten. Why did Yalom decide to center his novel around a man who now appears to be largely a footnote in the development of psychoanalysis? In 1882 the twenty-six-year-old Freud lacked the maturity and experience to understand the depth of Nietzsche's anguish and solitude.[1] The forty-year-old Breuer, by contrast, less intellectually driven than Freud but more warmhearted and worldly-wise, could begin to empathize with a man like Nietzsche, some of whose conflicts he experienced himself.

---

1. Yalom would have much preferred to have a therapeutic meeting between Freud and Nietzsche, he told me, but the dates did not work out. "By the time Freud became a psychiatrist Nietzsche was non-communicative and beyond help."

Yalom shows how Freud's idealization of Breuer prevented him from understanding the older man's disappointments with his career and marriage. Freud is too young to sense Breuer's growing midlife crisis, including the compromises he was forced to make in anti-Semitic Vienna. Breuer has a deeper insight into Freud's life than Freud has into Breuer's. He recognizes Freud's evolving genius, and he predicts the younger man's worldwide fame. As he watches Freud scan the bookshelves in his office, Breuer asks, "Shall I save a shelf for your future books, Sig?" to which the younger man replies, "How I wish! But not in this decade, Josef" (37).

The historical Freud's time would soon come, as would Nietzsche's. Freud admired Nietzsche's genius, as Jones points out. Freud said many times, Jones relates, that Nietzsche "had a more penetrating knowledge of himself than any other man who ever lived or was ever likely to live." To which Jones adds, "From the first explorer of the unconscious this is a handsome compliment" (vol. 2, 344). But Freud's indebtedness to Nietzsche was more complicated than Jones implies. Despite Freud's claims that he did not read Nietzsche to avoid being influenced by him, Yalom observes that Freud had a complete set of Nietzsche's books, a gift from Otto Rank. Referring to the "unfinished business between Nietzsche and the field of psychotherapy," Yalom suggests that the "entire field of psychotherapy has followed Freud's lead and ignored Nietzsche's contribution." One of Yalom's intentions in *When Nietzsche Wept* "is to address this oversight and to begin to harvest, more explicitly, Nietzsche's psychological insights" (*The Yalom Reader* 383).

Until the end of the twentieth century, most of our knowledge of Breuer came from Freud, hardly an unbiased source of information. Freud was a harsh and tendentious judge of others, especially those who never fully accepted his psychological theories. Freud's judgment of Breuer was based on their brief and conflicted collaboration in the 1880s. Breuer wrote "Fräulein Anna O." in 1882, but it took Freud more than a decade to convince his reluctant coauthor to include the case history in *Studies on Hysteria*, which contains five case studies, four of which were written by Freud.

According to Freud, Breuer was captivated by his young patient, who exhibited a number of bewildering hysterical symptoms. Anna O. famously described her treatment with Breuer as a "talking cure," cleverly referring to verbal therapy as "chimney-sweeping" (*SE*, vol. 2, 30). Breuer misleadingly implied at the end of the case study that she was cured completely, though he admitted enigmatically that he had "suppressed a large number of quite interesting details" (*SE*, vol. 2, 41). She was far from cured, however. James Strachey, the general editor of *The Standard Edition*, reveals in a much-quoted footnote to the case study that Freud confided to him that Breuer abruptly terminated treatment when the patient suddenly made manifest, in Strachey's words, the "presence of a strong unanalysed positive transference of an unmistakably sexual nature. It was this occurrence, Freud believed, that caused Breuer to hold back the publication of the case history for so many years and that led ultimately to his abandonment of all further collaboration in Freud's researches" (*SE*, vol. 2, 40–41, n. 1).

An Untoward Event

Using an English expression, Freud referred to this "untoward event" in *On the History of the Psycho-Analytic Movement*. He hinted that it was Breuer's intellectual timidity, his refusal to acknowledge Anna O.'s erotic desire for him, and Breuer's guilt and anguish, that signaled the end of treatment. In Freud's view, Breuer lacked the courage of his convictions. Expressed differently, Freud believed that Breuer lacked the courage of *Freud's* convictions.

Ernest Jones provides further details of the story, including the name of Anna O., Bertha Pappenheim, who later became Germany's first social worker. (Jones's disclosure appalled Bertha Pappenheim's family.) Jones also includes information, true or not, about Breuer's countertransference. According to Freud, when Breuer made an emergency visit to Anna O.'s home, he found her, in Jones's words, in the "throes of an hysterical childbirth (pseudocyesis), the logical termination of a phantom pregnancy that had been invisibly developing in response to Breuer's ministrations. Though profoundly shocked, he managed to calm her down by hypnotizing her, and then he fled the house in a cold sweat. The next day he and his wife left for Venice to spend a second honeymoon, which resulted in the conception of a daughter" (vol. 1, 224–225).

How accurate is the Freud-Jones account of Breuer's relationship with Anna O.? Did she experience a delusional pregnancy? Did Breuer terminate treatment because of his panic over her love for him? *The Story of Anna O.*, Lucy Freeman's 1972 biography of Bertha Pappenheim, agrees with the Freud-Jones account. Writing during the "golden age" of psychoanalysis, Freeman, the author of many popular books on the talking cure, including memoirs about her own prolonged experiences in psychoanalysis, never challenged orthodox Freudian theory. She believed that the story of Anna O. changed the destiny of human history. "Bertha Pappenheim has been described by some who knew her as 'almost saintlike,' as Breuer was called 'Christlike.'

It was the strange drama of healing played by these two over a period of eighteen months that led the way to psychic salvation for man" (230).

Albrecht Hirschmüller's 1978 biography of Breuer, translated into English in 1989, offers the most accurate portrait of the physician's relationship with Bertha Pappenheim. Hirschmüller observes that Freud's account is an "interpretative reconstruction," one that changed "under the influence of the advances of psychoanalytic doctrine over a period of several decades" (131). There's little evidence that Anna O. suffered from an hysterical pregnancy—if so, Hirschmüller asks, why did Freud not include this information in his published writings? Nor is it likely, the biographer suggests, that Breuer fled Anna O. and Vienna the summer of 1882. Nevertheless, Hirschmüller concludes that like most "myths," the Freud-Jones account contains a "germ of truth amongst all the errors and half-truths." It seems probable, Hirschmüller adds, that Breuer experienced a conflict between the "personal and medical interest in the case and a certain fear of the consequences of such a deep relationship" (130). The biographer believes it's possible Mathilde Breuer learned about her husband's attraction to Anna O., precipitating a marital crisis. Citing Hirschmüller's research in the author's note to *When Nietzsche Wept*, Yalom uses these two plausible conjectures—Breuer's attraction to Anna O. and his wife's horrified discovery—to explain his protagonist's personal and professional predicament in the novel. Yalom also includes the less plausible part of the myth, Bertha Pappenheim's hysterical pregnancy, and Mathilde Breuer's demand that her husband transfer the patient to another physician.

Freud's Ambivalence Toward His Former Mentor— and Mistrust of Gratitude

Freud made several disparaging statements about Breuer. The image of Breuer as an intellectual coward became inscribed in psychoanalytic lore. Part of Freud's wariness of his former benefactor had to do with Freud's ambivalence toward gratitude, one of the major issues in Yalom's novel. Freud recalls in *On the History of the Psycho-Analytic Movement* lecturing at Clark University in 1909 during his only visit to the United States. He was so moved by the momentous event that he declared, "It was not I who had brought psycho-analysis into existence: the credit for this was due to someone else, to Josef Breuer, whose work had been at a time when I was still a student engaged in passing my examinations (1880–1882)." Freud then mentions gratuitously that others thought his praise was hyperbolic, expressed "too extravagantly on that occasion" (*SE*, vol. 14, 7–8).

Freud has it both ways here: first he expresses unrestrained gratitude to Breuer for creating psychoanalysis, then he uses unnamed surrogates to point out that his praise is exaggerated. Freud concludes by saying that it doesn't matter whether the history of psychoanalysis began with Breuer or himself, a statement he contradicts in the first paragraph of the book when he asserts without qualification that "psycho-analysis is my creation; for ten years I was the only person who concerned himself with it" (*SE*, vol. 14, 7). Ernest Jones is only partly correct when he observes that the "bitter animosity" Freud developed toward Breuer, antagonism which is reflected in Freud's correspondence in the 1890s, is a sentiment "he never betrayed in any of his published writings, where he always spoke of Breuer in terms of praise and gratitude" (vol. 1, 168). On the contrary, Freud's deep ambivalence toward Breuer is clear in *On the History of the Psycho-Analytic Movement*, where his expression of gratitude toward Breuer is followed immediately by faint/feigned praise.

Freud's resentment over being financially indebted to Breuer, despite (or perhaps because of) the latter's willingness to forgive the debt, appears in a letter to his friend Wilhelm Fliess written on January 16, 1898. "Recently Breuer pulled another brilliant stunt," Freud begins, and then details the exchanges with Breuer over the loan. Freud bitterly concludes, "It is enough to make one extremely ungrateful for good deeds" (*Complete Letters of Sigmund Freud to Wilhelm Fliess* 294).

One can understand Freud's exasperation along with his hurt pride that he had to borrow a substantial amount of money from his older colleague to whom he was financially beholden. There may be some truth in Freud's cynical interpretation of Breuer's motives, but one may interpret Breuer's actions more generously, as Yalom does when he tells us near the end of the novel that Breuer forgave Freud's debts. The benefactor-beneficiary relationship was strained for Freud, perhaps even intolerable, but it's likely that Breuer was doing his best so that Freud would not feel in his debt. Their relationship ended badly, each feeling disappointed in and hurt by the other.

Breuer's Dilemmas

As *When Nietzsche Wept* opens, Yalom wastes no time in revealing Breuer's twin dilemmas. While vacationing with his wife in Venice, which allows him a temporary respite from seeing dozens of patients a day, as well as an opportunity to end his two-year treatment of Bertha Pappenheim, Breuer receives an impertinent letter from a young woman named Lou Salomé who insists on seeing him the next morning at the Café Sorrento on a matter of great urgency. "The future of German philosophy hangs in the balance." Breuer reluctantly agrees to the request, and while waiting for her, he continues to think about the former patient with whom he is obsessed. Spellbound, Breuer recalls her final words when he told her he could no longer be her physician. "You will always be the only man in my life" (2). Thoughts of her enticing beauty invade his waking and sleeping moments. "Am I destined to be merely a stage on which memories of Bertha eternally play out their drama?" (2). From where do such maddening thoughts spring, he wonders.

As Breuer broods over these questions, Lou Salomé imperiously strides into the café and implicates him in a vexing ethical dilemma. She uses her vast charm to convince him to take on a patient he has never heard of, Friedrich Nietzsche. Fearing that Nietzsche might commit suicide if he doesn't receive medical help, Salomé warns Breuer that the philosopher's death "would have momentous consequences—for you, for European culture, for all of us" (3).

Yalom devotes only a few pages in *When Nietzsche Wept* to Lou Salomé, but she comes across as supremely self-assured, aware of her own destiny as well as Nietzsche's. Breuer agrees to a second meeting with Salomé at his office in Vienna a month later, where she supplies him with additional information about Nietzsche. She insists that Breuer must not reveal to Nietzsche that she was the one who set up the examination because the philosopher cannot forgive her for spurning his marriage proposal. Nor must Breuer tell Nietzsche that she gave the physician two of his books to read, *Human, All Too Human* and *The Gay Science*, along with a letter written to Nietzsche by the German composer Richard Wagner. She shows Breuer a photo in which Nietzsche and Rée are standing before a cart while she is kneeling inside it, brandishing a small whip, symbolizing her power over the two men—three men, if we count Breuer, who is also under Salomé's hypnotic spell. Yalom's portrait of Salomé evokes the biblical Salome, the embodiment of fatal female seductiveness.

Breuer is intrigued by the challenge of treating Nietzsche, who has been examined by twenty-four of Europe's best physicians, none of whom can figure out the origin of his mystifying physical and psychological symptoms. Breuer is also intrigued by Nietzsche's startling description of himself as "born posthumously," a thinker for whom the world is not yet ready. Like Nietzsche, Breuer is passionate about philosophy. The historical Breuer had a thorough knowledge of classical and contemporary philosophy, including familiarity with Yalom's favorite philosophers, Schopenhauer and Spinoza. Additionally, Breuer hopes the case might free him from his obsession with Bertha Pappenheim. Healing Nietzsche may help him heal himself.

Explaining Nietzsche's need for a "doctor for despair," Salomé informs Breuer that she has heard about his treatment of Anna O.—"a woman who was in despair and whom you treated with a new technique, a 'talking cure'—a cure based on reason, on the unraveling of tangled mental health associations" (9). How could Salomé have known about this if Breuer and Freud did not publish *Studies on Hysteria* until more than a decade later? Yalom plausibly imagines that Salomé learned about Anna O. from her brother, a medical student who heard Breuer lecture on hysteria. Yalom's careful plotting, historical accuracy, and skillful characterization contribute to the novel's success. Breuer accepts Salomé's challenge, though he fears that, alluding to a line by Macbeth's physician, he cannot minister to a mind diseased. Breuer's relationship with Nietzsche thus begins with an element of duplicity. Priding himself on his integrity, Breuer is burdened with guilt until the end of the story, when he exposes the secret to the dismayed Nietzsche.

Breuer's willingness to accept Nietzsche as a new patient suggests his boldness as a physician. Treating such a patient may demand the need for a new therapy, a psychological therapeutics. One can never be sure of the consequences of a medical experiment. The historical Freud asserted, with self-fulfilling irony, that psychoanalysis brings out the worst in everyone. Will Breuer's experimental treatment of Nietzsche bring out the worst in the patient? In the therapist? More positively, can a physician heal himself while healing another? In a relationship based on reciprocal treatment, how can we know the healer from the healed?

Breuer: A Signature Character

Yalom's Breuer is less conventional than the historical Breuer, less constrained by traditional medical procedures, less cautious about insulating himself from risk. In the foreword to the 2000 edition of *Studies on Hysteria*, Yalom calls Breuer "history's first dynamic psychotherapist" (xiv)—and then vividly demonstrates Breuer's psychological insights. In light of our understanding of *Every Day Gets a Little Closer* and *Love's Executioner*, we can see that Yalom's Breuer resembles Yalom himself in several ways.

Breuer is, indeed, a signature character, a portrait of the psychiatrist as he imagines himself in Breuer's situation. Both are willing to experiment with new forms of psychological therapy that involve risks for therapist and patient alike. Both feel the need to heal others in part to heal themselves. Both affirm the value of self-disclosure and are willing to open up their lives to others, realizing that self-disclosure begets self-disclosure. Both dislike the inflated self-importance of physicians, the pompousness of high society, the narrow-mindedness of those who are convinced they worship the only true God. Both men are devoted to their wives, but they know what it's like to be in the throes of obsessional love for other women who have invaded their thoughts and dreams. Yalom understands Breuer's admiration of women, his desire to "merge with their bodies, to suckle at their nipples, to slip into their warmth and wetness"(15), a desire that both physicians resist with all their might. Yalom closely identifies with Breuer's fear of death—the impossibility of escape from the "prison of time" (48). Both value psychological therapies that avoid excessive medication; echoing Yalom, Breuer believes he has discovered a "psychological equivalent of pharmacologic replacement therapy" (7). A doctor of despair compels both Breuer and Yalom to become doctors of the soul, a search that leads both of them to Nietzsche and existential healing.

Haunted by his terrible desire for Bertha Pappenheim, Breuer cannot talk about his obsession with anyone, not even with his young protégé Sigmund Freud, who is too callow to understand the complaints of a middle-aged man. Moreover, the historical Freud greatly admired Breuer's wife, Mathilde—Freud named his oldest daughter after her—and he would be judgmental about the older man's all-consuming passion for a patient. Further complicating the situation, Freud's fiancée, Martha Bernays, is a good friend of Bertha Pappenheim. No wonder Breuer cannot confide in Freud.

Anticipating one of Freud's greatest discoveries, Breuer suspects that his obsession for Bertha Pappenheim must arise from a part of the mind that is inaccessible to consciousness. Breuer is not yet ready to accept, however, a revolutionary new theory of consciousness that is germinating in Freud, who has been studying the meaning of dreams. "When you start talking of another, separate mind," Breuer admits to Freud, "a sentient elf inside of us designing sophisticated dreams and disguising them from our conscious mind—that seems ridiculous" (39). Nevertheless, unable to free himself from thoughts of death and sex, Breuer becomes increasingly convinced that there must be a part of the mind that is inaccessible to consciousness. In 1882 the historical Freud was years away from postulating the existence of an unconscious self as a repository of repressed sexual and aggressive impulses, a discovery that arose from his self-analysis.

Lost in Back Alleys and Trapdoors

Breuer slowly embraces this idea when he finally meets Nietzsche, who forces him to call into question every aspect of his life and work. Like Freud, Nietzsche, too, is developing the idea that the psyche does not function as a single entity. "Parts of our mind may operate independently of others," Nietzsche suggests to Breuer. "Perhaps 'I' and my body formed a conspiracy behind the back of my own mind. The mind is, you know, fond of back alleys and trapdoors" (97).

Nietzsche's own mind abounds in back alleys and trapdoors that have resulted in a personality close to suicidal fragmentation. Throughout the novel Yalom conveys Nietzsche's anguish, isolation, and mistrust. A creature of dark, volatile moods capable of soaring to the heights of existence one moment and plunging to the depths of despair the next moment, Nietzsche is wracked by crippling migraines, nausea, partial blindness, gastrointestinal problems, dizziness, and insomnia—problems from which the historical Nietzsche suffered. In addition, he is dangerously addicted to morphine and chloral hydrate, two drugs he takes to excess. Complicating the situation is that he is an uncooperative patient, unsure whether he wants to give up his illness that drives him to despair while simultaneously serving as his muse.

How can Breuer treat a man who is so ill that he has recently resigned his professorship at the University of Basel, left his relatives and home, and traveled throughout Europe in search of relief from devastating pain? Nietzsche's nomadic existence left him rootless and friendless. Betrayed years earlier by his mentor, Richard Wagner, and now by Paul Rée and Lou Salomé, as well as by his sister, Elisabeth, who sought to destroy his relationship with Rée and Salomé, and who later, as his literary executor, twisted his writings to fit her anti-Semitic agenda, Nietzsche is contemptuous of sympathy, pity, and gratitude, all of which are a part of a relational world that he believes enfeebles the self. How can Breuer treat a patient who associates humankind with a herd mentality, women with duplicity, gratitude with revenge, and altruism with weakness?

Yalom's early descriptions of Nietzsche capture the striking contrast between his gentle, deferential demeanor and the startling, often strident voice in his writings. Yalom's portrait neither elevates the philosopher to saintliness nor reduces him to caricature. Yalom never whitewashes the historical Nietzsche, never sanitizes his writings to make them more appealing. We see the nobility of Nietzsche's spirit warring with his abject self-loathing. Avoiding small talk, Yalom's Nietzsche condenses his present existence into a few sentences. "My whole life has become a journey, and I begin to feel that my only home, the only familiar place to which I always return, is my illness" (51). No patient has spoken more eloquently about his illness—and part of Yalom's artistry is his power of compression. The historical Nietzsche was himself a master of brevity. "It is my ambition," he declares in *Twilight of the Idols*, "to say in ten sentences what everyone else says in a book—what everyone else does *not* say in a book" (556).

Breuer is no less impressive in his own authority and voice. Declining to read the voluminous medical reports Nietzsche offers him, Breuer gives an explanation Nietzsche can readily understand. There is "great *disadvantage* in my beginning with them," he explains to his patient. "Too much authority, too many prestigious opinions and conclusions oppress one's own imaginative synthetic powers. For much the same reason, I prefer to read a play before seeing it performed and certainly before reading reviews. Have you not found that to be the case in your own work?" (51) We realize from the opening dialogue that both men have a formidable intellect and that reading is a central activity in their lives. Each man reads the other's character—and Breuer reads the philosopher's books in an effort to understand the author's life.

Yalom succeeds in using only a few brushstrokes to sketch Nietzsche's pioneering ideas. The opening discussion of reading texts, be they medical or philosophical, leads to Nietzsche's statement that he mistrusts all interpreters because they cannot step outside their personal and historical point of view. When asked how he avoids this problem himself, Nietzsche admits that he acknowledges this limitation—and then learns to "see oneself from afar," adding, "sometimes, alas, the severity of my illness impairs my perspective" (52).

Illness seems to have explosively expanded Nietzsche's own perspective—at least when he is not too ill to read or write. Illness, particularly depression, often renders people mute, imprisoning them in a world of suffering, but Yalom's Nietzsche speaks about his melancholy with singular insight. "I have black periods. Who has not? But they do not have *me*. They are *not* of my illness, but of my being. One might say I have the courage to have them" (56).

Creativity and Madness

"Great wits are sure to madness near allied," quipped the seventeenth-century English poet John Dryden, "And thin partitions do their bounds divide." Nietzsche had a keen insight into the mysterious relationship between creativity and mood disorders. How did he feel about his own illness? His most extended statement about his health—and perhaps the most difficult to interpret—appears in *Ecce Homo*, written in 1888 and published posthumously in 1908. "There is no pathological trait in me; even in periods of severe sickness I never became pathological; in vain would one seek for a trait of fanaticism in my character. There is not a moment in my life to which one could point to convict me of a presumptuous and pathetic nature." Walter Kaufmann admits that it is impossible to know whether this comment is "starkly ironical or, on the contrary, totally lacking in self-awareness" (*Basic Writings of Nietzsche* 713).

Breuer's thorough medical examination of Nietzsche, followed by a careful medical history, allows Yalom to offer his own perspective of being a physician. Patients secretly enjoy a close examination of their lives because of the need for recognition. "The joy of being observed ran so deep that Breuer believed the real pain of old age, bereavement, outliving one's friends, was the absence of scrutiny—the horror of living an unobserved life" (55). Existential isolation and loneliness, Yalom implies, intensify near the end of our lives, making the need for human connection greater. A writer without readers, Nietzsche has been suffering from the horror of living an unobserved life. That's why he appreciates Breuer's questions about his health.

Harsh Truths

An internist, Breuer often thinks like a psychotherapist. Should he ask probing questions that evoke his patient's resistance? Or should he raise other questions that strengthen the doctor-patient relationship by being empathic? He usually chooses the latter strategy, knowing the impossibility of having too much empathy. The fictional Breuer foreshadows psychotherapists like Carl Rogers, Heinz Kohut, and Yalom himself, all of whom insist on the importance of empathy.

Nietzsche consents to the lengthy examination, but as Breuer rises to leave, the patient makes an unusual request: the opportunity to raise three blunt questions. Breuer agrees. Will Nietzsche go blind? Will his attacks increase? Does he have a progressive brain disease that will culminate in paralysis, madness, or dementia? Breuer welcomes the brutally direct questions, which, he believes, give him an opportunity to insist on the *patient's* obligation to be truthful to a physician. The reader recalls Yalom's tough questions to Penny in *Love's Executioner*. But Nietzsche presses the point when Breuer affirms a doctor-patient relationship based on reciprocal honesty. Nietzsche raises a question that goes against Breuer's medical training. What about a *physician's* obligation to be truthful to a dying patient?

Suddenly the roles are reversed: the philosopher has the physician on the defensive. Breuer, voicing the traditional medical point of view that continued until the last quarter of the twentieth century, declares that he does not have the right to impose a painful truth onto others. Nietzsche objects: "Who can determine what one wishes *not* to know?" (66). This brief conversation becomes a pivotal moment in the novel, allowing Nietzsche to instruct Breuer on the necessity for harsh truths. "'Sometimes,' Nietzsche responded, 'teachers must be hard. People must be given a hard message because life is hard, and dying is hard" (67). Nietzsche is a *dis*illusioner, as Yalom was throughout *Love's Executioner*.

As their conversation continues, Nietzsche expresses core insights that reflect both his and Yalom's vision of life. One of the philosopher's granite truths, "Become who you are" (68), reveals the need to fulfill oneself. Nietzsche derived the injunction from the ancient Greek poet Pindar, who affirmed, "Become such as you are, having learned what that is." Another Nietzschean granite truth is the need to come to terms with death. The question "how to live" presupposes the question "how to die." One must decide "*how* to face death," Nietzsche instructs Breuer, and then he offers examples of how people might talk back to death, reaching their own conclusions about life's central mystery. Nietzsche's voice here is unmistakably authorial. Like Yalom's other writings, *When Nietzsche Wept* is a contemporary *ars moriendi*, revealing the art of dying.

Nietzsche is perhaps the most quoted and misquoted philosopher in modern history. To distill in a few sentences the essence of a great writer's work is an art in itself. To avoid the obvious danger of using Nietzsche only as an authorial mouthpiece who ventriloquizes existential truths, Yalom presents the doctor-patient exchange not as a lecture but as a chess match, with each character trying to outsmart the other. Yalom invests the Breuer-Nietzsche relationship with keen personal and disciplinary competition, and the reader is never certain of the outcome.

Seeking to maneuver the philosopher into the role of the patient, Breuer suggests that a physician should always sustain a dying man's hope, but Nietzsche explodes in anger, asserting, "Hope is the final evil," a statement that appears in *Human, All Too Human*. When Breuer raises the question of suicide, Nietzsche responds aphoristically, "I've always felt the final reward of the dead is to die no more," a statement that also appears in *Love's Executioner*. Nodding appreciatively, Breuer jots down the words, compelling Nietzsche to observe that the statement comes from *The Gay Science*. When Breuer expresses interest in buying the two books, withholding the observation that Lou Salomé had given them to him without Nietzsche's knowledge, the obscure author observes that no one buys his writings. He then jots down for Breuer the name and address of his publisher. Later he gives Breuer personal copies of *Human, All Too Human* and *The Gay Science* filled with handwritten marginal notations. Breuer cannot believe his good luck, for now he can refer to the two books openly without subterfuge.

"What Are Your Motives?"

How should Breuer treat a patient as uncooperative as Nietzsche, who clings to his illness as tightly as he wishes to be released from it? Breuer consults with Freud, discloses the results of his medical examination of his patient, and asks for advice about how to proceed. Freud offers three suggestions: establish a strong doctor-patient relationship, hospitalize the patient for a few weeks, and have frequent in-depth discussions of his despair by using the chimney sweeping technique Breuer had used with Bertha Pappenheim. Breuer readily accepts Freud's recommendations and ends the conversation by saying, "The student has taught the teacher" (86). Breuer might have quoted one of Nietzsche's most astute statements: To remain a student is to repay a teacher badly.

Freud's recommendations, however, do not have the desired effect, for when Breuer praises Nietzsche's writings, the philosopher pointedly makes no reply. Nor does he seem satisfied by Breuer's forthright answers to the three medical questions. After giving his word that he has concealed no medical facts, Breuer reminds Nietzsche of their contract for reciprocal honesty, to which Nietzsche retorts a conversation with nothing concealed is "hell." He then begins to "bless" his illness, stating, "Whatever does not kill me, makes me stronger" (96–96), his most memorable affirmation. Asked whether one chooses an illness, Nietzsche responds, "I'm not sure; perhaps one *does* choose an illness. It depends on who the 'one' is. The psyche does not function as a single entity. Parts of our mind may operate independently of others. Perhaps 'I' and my body formed a conspiracy behind the back of my own mind. The mind is, you know, fond of back alleys and trapdoors" (97). Breuer is startled by the striking similarity of Nietzsche's statement to Freud's. Yalom conveys for his readers the drama of discovering from the history of ideas that two astonishingly similar theories may arise independent of each other.

Yet despite Nietzsche's recognition of the need to unlock the mind's mysteries, he has no interest in discussing his own subterranean unconsciousness. Nietzsche firmly rejects the Breuer-Freud recommendations. He leads a stress-free life, he claims, now that he has a nomadic existence, and whatever neurological hyperalertness he feels is necessary for his work. Nietzsche spurns the idea of hospitalization, not wishing to spend further time in cold Vienna. And he dismisses Breuer's offer to treat him without a fee, which would have left him further indebted to the physician.

Breuer tries everything at his disposal to convince Nietzsche to accept his help, including quoting the philosopher's words from *Human, All Too Human*. "*Psychological observation is among the expedients by means of which one can alleviate the burden of living*" (106). Nietzsche agrees that he has spent his life performing such a psychological dissection, but he is not willing to be the physician's subject. The philosopher then demands to know, "What is *your* motivation in this treatment project?" Breuer gives several evasive answers, none of which is satisfying. He cannot reveal three of his motives for wishing to treat Nietzsche: being bewitched by Lou Salomé's beauty in Venice; loving the music of Wagner, whose letter to Nietzsche Breuer had read without permission; and craving the intellectual challenge of being close to genius. Breuer can think of only one explanation with which Nietzsche might agree. Quoting Nietzsche's sentence "Become who you are," Breuer asserts that it may be his destiny to contribute to medical science and the relief of suffering. Breuer's destiny, he then adds, may be to help Nietzsche become who he is. Unexpectedly, Nietzsche contemptuously rejects the explanation, which he finds self-serving. "And if I am, as you say, to become great, then *you* as my animator, my saviour, become even greater!" (109). He then bolts out of the stunned Breuer's office, terminating treatment.

An innkeeper summons Breuer a few days later, informing him that Nietzsche has collapsed in his room, a victim of an overdose of chloral hydrate. Nietzsche recovers, with Breuer's help, but he insists on paying the physician for his services and leaving Vienna immediately. "My feelings about debts and payment are unchanged." Breuer makes one more attempt to keep Nietzsche in treatment, realizing that he cannot outwit the philosopher who is far cleverer than he is. Nietzsche refuses to change his mind, but, softening, concedes that he has never met a physician like Breuer. If Breuer wants to know why the idea of gratitude is so appalling, Nietzsche declares, the physician must read his books, which are rooted in his essence. To Breuer's regret, Nietzsche then departs.

Gratitude and Revenge

We may accept Nietzsche's invitation to read his books and turn briefly to his writings on gratitude. He never devoted an entire book to the vexed subject, but he often referred to gratitude elliptically in his writings. His earliest pronouncement appears in *Human, All Too Human*, published when he was thirty-four. "The powerful man feels gratitude for the following reason: through his good deed, his benefactor has, as it were, violated the powerful man's sphere and penetrated it. Now through his act of gratitude the powerful man requites himself by violating the sphere of the benefactor. It is a milder form of revenge" (46).

Nietzsche implies that gratitude is motivated by a secret desire to expose and exploit another person's weakness by asserting his position of inferiority. In Nietzsche's world, those who give and receive gratitude, the powerful man and the benefactor, respectively, are engaged in a power struggle that lies beneath the thin veneer of civilization. The adversaries never acknowledge their secret warfare. Deception and hypocrisy characterize this antagonistic relationship, which takes place, in Nietzsche's view, under the guise of morality. That which appears "good" is, in reality, evil, at least to the person who is victimized by gratitude. Nietzsche sees himself as the exposer of this underground warfare that is sanctioned and enabled by society. His attack on gratitude is a part of his larger assault on Christianity that he came to associate with "slave morality."

Many questions arise from Nietzsche's cynical view of benefactor gratitude, part of his hermeneutics of suspicion. Are there not more altruistic motives in gratitude? Is gratitude *always* and *only* a form of revenge? What happens when the giver and receiver of gratitude are both equally powerful? Few can doubt that gratitude can *sometimes* become burdensome, but why does Nietzsche assert that gratitude is motivated only by egoism?

Striking a Bargain

Refusing to give up the idea of treating Nietzsche, Breuer makes one final attempt when the philosopher returns briefly to the medical office to pay his bill and receive his medical report. Breuer proposes a unique professional exchange, one that has never been attempted in the history of medicine—or fiction. The professional exchange lies at the heart of Yalom's novel. Breuer proposes that he treat Nietzsche for one month for hemicrania, a primary headache disorder, at a clinic, without any fees on the patient's part. In return, Nietzsche will treat Breuer, acting as a physician to heal his diseased spirit. Puzzled, Nietzsche cannot imagine what Breuer means. For the first time in his life, Breuer discloses the nature of his anguish. His despair may not be apparent on the surface, where he appears to be leading a contented life, but beneath the surface reign despair and chaos:

> You ask what kind of despair? Let us say that my mind is not my own, that I am invaded and assaulted by alien and sordid thoughts. As a result, I feel self-contempt, and I doubt my integrity. Though I care for my wife and my children, I don't *love* them! In fact, I resent being imprisoned by them. I lack courage: the courage either to change my life or to continue living it. I have lost sight of *why* I live—the point of it all. I am preoccupied with aging. Though every day I grow closer to death, I am terrified of it. Even so, suicide sometimes enters my mind. (138)

Breuer's confession is, to begin with, an expression of his ambivalence toward his wife and children, a subject about which the solitary, childless Nietzsche had no personal knowledge. But Breuer knows that his reference to feeling besieged by "alien and sordid thoughts" is bound to intrigue Nietzsche, who is in the process of formulating his own theory of the unconscious. Breuer's admission of self-contempt is also likely to pique Nietzsche's interest, a subject that he knows all too well. Breuer is still too ashamed to disclose his obsession for Bertha Pappenheim, but he does reveal what is for Yalom perhaps the central fear in life, existential dread over approaching death.

To what extent is Breuer's obsession with Anna O. a reflection of the obsession Yalom speaks about in *Love's Executioner* when he encountered a woman at a conference who invaded his thoughts and dreams? In the beginning, Yalom admits, he "liked the obsession and savored it afresh again and again," but eventually it dominated his life, ruining the "rich reality" of existence. The dark obsession required Yalom, we recall, to reenter therapy, where he regained control over his life. Ironically, while he was being treated by a therapist, the therapist was himself obsessed with a woman whose attention was riveted to someone else. This is *precisely* the situation in *When Nietzsche Wept*.

The Motives Behind Confession

What is the motivation behind Breuer's proposition? Is he being sincere or disingenuous in proposing a professional exchange? The plan admittedly contains an element of duplicity because he makes no mention of being approached by Lou Salomé or having fallen, like Nietzsche, under her spell. Seeing the impact of his words on Nietzsche, Breuer congratulates himself on the elegant trap he has set. Appealing to Nietzsche's suspicion of human nature, he tells the philosopher what he wishes to hear. Breuer knows that if his proposal is to be accepted, he must not emphasize the altruistic nature of this professional exchange. "My motivation is entirely self-serving. I need help! Are you strong enough to help me?" (142).

Breuer's despair is real, as is his admiration for Nietzsche. The physician's search for relief from his terrible obsession with Bertha Pappenheim is palpable to the reader. Yalom knows, as did Nietzsche, that motivation is complex, a cauldron of altruistic and self-interested impulses. Breuer may desire to exert power over Nietzsche, but he also wants to take advantage of the philosopher's power. Nietzsche accepts Breuer's offer. Yalom thus masterfully sets the stage for an unusual therapy based on reciprocal self-disclosure—unusual for Breuer but not for Yalom, who used a version of it in *Every Day Gets a Little Closer*, where he and Ginny Elkin both wrote up their accounts of the therapy hour and shared them with each other.

The Art of Therapy

Danger lurks, however, for both Nietzsche and Yalom. How does Nietzsche attempt to apply his daring philosophy to a physician who is looking for pragmatic advice about how to live? How does Yalom attempt to convey Nietzsche to readers without domesticating complex ideas? The problem is daunting for several reasons. How does a storyteller convey aphoristic language and pithy pronouncements, filled with ambiguities, paradoxes, and aporias, without sacrificing other elements of fiction: characterization, plot, irony, and point of view? How does one craft a novel of ideas that is not cerebral? How does a storyteller avoid didacticism?

One way Yalom avoids the problem of abstraction is by immersing us in the details of late nineteenth-century Vienna, the birthplace of psychoanalysis. The novelist uses what the anthropologist Clifford Geertz calls "thick description" to recreate the cultural and intellectual ethos of Viennese life. Yalom shows us in detail the medical clinic where Nietzsche was treated for hemicrania, and he lists the medications the historical Nietzsche was prescribed. Yalom recreates the coffeehouse where Breuer shares details about his migrainous professor with Freud—and then the novelist transports his two characters to Demel's, the legendary Viennese pastry shop, established in 1786, where Breuer enjoys a chocolate torte and Freud a lemon torte *mit Schlag*.

Another way Yalom avoids abstraction is by grounding the novel in conflict. Freud is incredulous when Breuer tells him about the remarkable bargain struck with the philosopher. "You ensnared him by suggesting he begin to heal Western civilization by starting with a single specimen—you?" (149). The strategy may appear ludicrous, but this was what the historical Breuer attempted with his case study on Anna O. The fictional Breuer's evolving treatment plan, to persuade Nietzsche to help him while slowly manipulating the philosopher into the role of patient, abounds in ironies the physician cannot yet imagine.

Still another way Yalom avoids abstraction is through the complexity of characterization. Despite his profound insights into psychology, the historical Freud lacked *Menschlichkeit*, an understanding of the properties that make one, to use the German/Yiddish word, a *Mensch*, a man. Like the historical Freud, the fictional Freud comes across as psychologically naive and puritanical when he insists that he tells everything to his fiancée, Martha—and that he has never sexually fantasized over another woman. Breuer comes across as smug when he imagines that Nietzsche will fall easily into the role of compliant patient. Breuer does not yet realize that his situation is in some ways more desperate than Nietzsche's. Breuer's situation is complicated by his keen sense of integrity, which has already been compromised, perhaps fatally, by his complicity with Lou Salomé. How can he behave honorably given the circumstances of his relationship with the philosopher? And Nietzsche comes across as—Nietzsche, to Yalom's great credit as a novelist.

Few geniuses in history have had more blind spots than Nietzsche, and he remains noble in spirit yet tormented. The "great Immoralist," as he liked to call himself in his writings, was unfailingly polite and deferential in his behavior with others, perhaps never guilty of a single immoral action.

A Meeting of Minds

As a physician, Breuer is authoritative and self-confident, but as a patient, he is confused and resistant. He doesn't like Nietzsche's systematic clinical approach, even though it closely follows his own. Breuer is particularly troubled when Nietzsche wishes to begin with the most *fundamental* problem, fear of death. Breuer squirms over the therapy-in-progress, not even sure what to call it—"maybe despair therapy or philosophic therapeutics, or some name yet to be invented" (157).

In what follows, the fictional Breuer and Nietzsche invent a novel form of treatment, psychotherapy, to relieve psychological conflict. Responding to Nietzsche's question whether he has treated psychological illness, Breuer starts to relate the story of Anna O., but Nietzsche stops him, saying that he doesn't want to hear anything embarrassing or humiliating. Yalom highlights a glaring contradiction between Nietzsche's intensely private, secretive personality and his writings, all of which urge honesty and openness. Breuer convinces Nietzsche that he must hear all the details about Anna O., no matter how wrenching. He begins by summarizing his use of the chimney sweeping technique with her. This helped her temporarily to feel better, Breuer tells Nietzsche, but it had no effect on her hysterical symptoms. Breuer then relates how he stumbled on an effective treatment when he traced all of her symptoms to what he thought was the original source, her father's death. The discovery is nothing less than extraordinary to Nietzsche, and he recommends that Breuer use the technique on himself. Breuer refuses, partly because he claims that hysteria is a female disease; partly because he is not capable of being hypnotized, as she was; and partly because he believes that his own unhappiness is closer to normal human angst or misery.

A Turning Point

As Breuer relates his mad obsession with Bertha Pappenheim, Nietzsche responds with an aphorism: "Perhaps . . . only by being a man does a man release the woman in woman" (162). Does Nietzsche imply here a physician's right to exploit sexually a woman? For a man to take advantage of a woman? That all women are femmes fatales, as he believes Lou Salomé is? The cryptic statement gives Breuer an opportunity to affirm the Hippocratic Oath, to which he is firmly committed. He then discloses that he was sexually attracted to another woman, his former nurse, Eva Berger, who, worried about his attraction to Bertha Pappenheim, offered to give herself to him to "release" his pent-up desire. Nietzsche, whose mistrust of women bordered on misogyny, is skeptical and calls Eva Berger a "predator." The scene establishes the two men's strikingly different attitudes toward women, differences that remain unresolved by the novel's end.

As Breuer bares his soul, he enumerates his many symptoms of conflict, such as unwelcome thoughts that plague him and emotions like jealousy that bedevil him. He instructs Nietzsche, who is holding a notebook, to add these vices to his growing list. There's something comic about Nietzsche's laundry list of Breuer's character flaws. The physician holds little back, including enjoying the power given to him by virtue of his profession. Though Breuer's confession was motivated in part by the desire to coax Nietzsche into confession, the physician is surprised "by how easy—in fact, exhilarating—it was to reveal so much." The session marks a turning point in their relationship. Afterward, each writes up case study notes about the other, as Yalom and Ginny did in *Every Day Gets a Little Closer*. The Breuer-Nietzsche therapy notes reveal radically different perspectives, again similar to *Every Day Gets a Little Closer*. Breuer comments on Nietzsche's "prodigious blind spots" and "barbaric, hardly human" feelings about women; Nietzsche comments on Breuer's willingness to "wallow in that muck" when it comes to women. Each man believes he knows the other—and each is in for a surprise. During their next session, Breuer recounts his troubled dreams, and the two men agree that they are both fascinated with the subject. It will be years before the historical Freud issued his oft-quoted statement that dreams are the royal road to the unconscious, but Yalom's Breuer and Nietzsche anticipate his insight. Breuer discloses his many weaknesses and failings, all of which Nietzsche dutifully records in his notebook.

Like an empathic psychologist, Nietzsche reminds Breuer that he must not be so harsh on himself. Frustrated by Nietzsche's refusal to disclose his own fears, Breuer listens impatiently as the philosopher lectures him about the need to have the courage of one's own convictions: "One must have chaos and frenzy within oneself to give birth to a dancing star" (179–180). Nietzsche might have also reminded Breuer to have the courage to *overcome* his own convictions. Breuer finds the encomium too abstract but agrees to view his life from a different perspective, a cornerstone of Nietzsche's philosophy. "A cosmic perspective always attenuates tragedy," he later tells Breuer. "If we climb high enough, we will reach a height from which tragedy ceases to look tragic" (209).

Nietzsche's transformation from philosopher to clinical psychologist is one of Yalom's artistic triumphs. "You have grown physician's ears," Breuer exclaims in admiration. "Nothing escapes you" (189). Nothing escapes Yalom, either, including offering a plausible explanation for Breuer's ambivalence over advancing his career. Yalom's Breuer speculates that he delayed writing and publishing scientific articles because of a fear of competition. The thwarting of his academic career, he sadly concludes, was the "first wound of mortality, the first assault on my myth of infinite promise" (190).

Nietzsche's clinical strategy in treating Breuer is to trace his obsession with Bertha Pappenheim to fundamental existential concerns: the irreversibility of time, the illusions of infinite promise, and the approach of death. Breuer resists the process of chimney sweeping, preferring to be the overseer rather than the sweeper. His despair deepens, thus calling into question the value of the talking cure. Nietzsche's health, however, seems to be improving, perhaps as a result of his new role as therapist. Breuer begins to suspect that Nietzsche may have the power to heal him, if only Breuer will trust the philosopher's authority.

Yalom's therapy sessions in *When Nietzsche Wept* capture the philosopher's poetic speech, iconoclastic proclamations, and wry humor. We never feel that the novelist is simply placing into his character's mouth a list of famous or infamous statements culled from Nietzsche's writings. "If you kill God," he reminds the secular Breuer, "you must also leave the shelter of your temple" (179). "Grow hard," he exhorts Breuer. "You are no cow, and I am no apostle of cud chewing" (198). When Breuer admits that lovesickness for Bertha Pappenheim has made him suicidal, Nietzsche reminds him that all serious thinkers contemplate suicide. "It's a comfort that helps us get through the night" (208). When Breuer uses the word *bliss* to describe his obsessional love for Bertha Pappenheim, Nietzsche responds that "we are more in love with desire than with the desired" (227).

Nietzsche the Therapist

When Nietzsche Wept reflects Yalom's central ideas about existential psychiatry, ideas that are sometimes closer to Nietzschean philosophy than Freudian psychoanalysis. Unlike Freud, who believed that he was discovering immutable truths applicable to everyone, Nietzsche emphasized the importance of perspectivism. Changing the perspective changes the truth. Mistrustful of any system espousing universal truth, Yalom embraces Nietzschean subjectivity. One of Yalom's favorite Nietzschean statements was also Freud's favorite, a statement that foreshadows the psychoanalyst's discovery of repression: "'I have done that,' says my memory. 'I cannot have done that,' says my pride, and remains adamant. At last—memory yields" (*Beyond Good and Evil* 91). Yalom affirms Nietzschean risk-taking. No one was more fearless gazing into the abyss than Nietzsche—and he was prepared to accept the consequences. "He who fights with monsters," he observes dryly in *Beyond Good and Evil*, "should look to it that he himself does not become a monster. And when you gaze long into an abyss the abyss also gazes into you" (102).

Yalom endorses Nietzsche's command to live fearlessly—and die fearlessly. "Many die too late, and some die too early. Yet strange soundeth the precept: 'Die at the right time!'" (*Thus Spake Zarathustra* 74) Yalom admires Nietzschean blood-letting: "Of all that is written, I love only what a person hath written with his blood. Write with blood, and thou wilt find that blood is spirit" (*Thus Spake Zarathustra* 39). He admires Nietzsche's refusal to endorse supernatural religion. And he agrees with Nietzsche's perhaps most-quoted statement: "What does not kill me, makes me stronger." Unlike Freud, who was born at the right time, Nietzsche recognized that he was "born posthumously," a man whose ideas have remained controversial more than a century after his death. As Robert C. Solomon points out, Nietzsche had two short lists of virtues, one in *Daybreak*, where he affirms "[h]onesty, courage, generosity, politeness," the other in *Beyond Good and Evil*, where the list is slightly different: "Courage, insight, sympathy, solitude" (145). Yalom agrees with all of these virtues, though he would place less emphasis on solitude than Nietzsche did. Missing from Nietzsche's list is empathy, which is precisely what Solomon values most in *When Nietzsche Wept*. Solomon praises Yalom's "wonderfully empathetic fictionalizing," which allows us the "intimacy with Nietzsche and the knowledge of the details of his sad and lonely life that one cannot easily glean from his manic and polemical published works" (14).

Yalom's admiration for Nietzsche does not prevent him from seeing the philosopher's many blind spots. Yalom is closer to Breuer's temperament than to Nietzsche's. Breuer remains open and friendly by nature, like Yalom, unlike the secretive and aloof Nietzsche, who cannot endure being in the company of others. Breuer readily confesses to making mistakes, as does Yalom, a quality that is less apparent in Nietzsche. Yalom never minimizes

Nietzsche's mistrust of women, which is hardly softened by the end of the story. For all of his daring, Nietzsche remained puritanical about sexual pleasure, which Yalom and Breuer celebrate. And Nietzsche's impersonal, distant, and aloof way of relating to others could not be more different from Yalom's gift for relationships.

Perspectivism

One of Nietzsche's first therapeutic strategies in attacking Breuer's obsession is to change his perspective of Bertha Pappenheim. Nietzsche insists that Breuer compose a list of ten insults and then hurl them at her. Imagine living with the invalid, Nietzsche commands, sitting across the breakfast table with her, with her legs and arms in spasm, "cross-eyed, mute, wry-necked, hallucinating, and stuttering" (212). The therapeutic strategy, which recalls Yalom's use of paradox therapy in helping Phyllis to overcome agoraphobia in *Love's Executioner*, is based on one of Nietzsche's core beliefs: people are filled with resentment (he uses the French word *ressentiment*), hostility arising from unreleased anger and aggression. Yet none of Nietzsche's experiments in "bleaching the magic out of Bertha's image" succeed. Both men conclude that a frontal attack on Breuer's symptoms is an abysmal failure. They need to find another therapeutic strategy where patient and therapist feel elevated, not lowered.

Messengers of Meaning

The two doctors of despair devise a more successful strategy in the next chapter. Nietzsche suggests that the reason for their recent failure is that they were searching for the origins of a symptom rather than for its meaning. "Perhaps symptoms are messengers of a meaning and will vanish only when their message is comprehended" (220–221). Nietzsche then sits back in his chair and begins grooming his mustache—a moment of comic relief in a scene charged with intellectual energy. During the next few pages Breuer proceeds to chimney sweep, another word for the use of free association, a technique that, in Yalom's novel, Breuer and Nietzsche jointly discover.

The philosopher plays the role of analyst perfectly, encouraging Breuer's difficult struggle to understand the meaning of the spell that Bertha Pappenheim has cast over him. She conjures up desire and magic for Breuer,

Dionysian passion, as well as escape from the trap of time. How is Breuer trapped? He admits that he longs to escape from his present life, which he finds stultifying. Both men agree that living safely is dangerous—a central Nietzschean idea. In the presence of Bertha's beauty, Breuer confesses, he feels that he is in the "bowels of the earth—in the center of existence" (224). He imagines her lips clouded in an affectionate half smile that, in response to Nietzsche's prescient question, reminds him of both his wife's smile to their son and a smile that a girl gave him when he was infatuated with her thirty years earlier. Nietzsche asks two additional questions, supplying an answer to the second. "Who else? Have you forgotten your mother's smile?" Breuer reminds Nietzsche that his mother died at the age of twenty-three, after having given birth to his younger brother, when he himself was only three, information that will be explored in the novel's next chapter. Nietzsche intuits the overwhelming significance of maternal loss, an insight not generally recognized until the second half of the twentieth century.

Each man calls the other by his first name during this crucial scene, and, for the first time, Nietzsche reveals how his migraines freed him from the professorship that he had secretly regarded as a death sentence—a recognition of what Freud later called the "secondary gain from illness." Breuer then shows Nietzsche a photo of Bertha Pappenheim, dressed for riding, carrying a long riding whip. Suddenly the two men change roles. "A formidable woman, Josef," Nietzsche declares, adding, "she has great beauty—but I don't like women who carry whips" (224).

As important as chimney sweeping is, the patient-therapist relationship is more important—and here Breuer and Nietzsche express Yalom's familiar theme. Breuer notes the importance of the "relationship," though he realizes ruefully that observing a relationship is not easy when you are part of it. Suddenly he grows hopeful about his life. Instead of competing with and setting traps for Nietzsche, Breuer basks in the new warmth of their relationship. Breuer also intuits the phenomenon of idealization. "What Nietzsche is to me, I was to Bertha" (231). Such idealization, he realizes, must be explored, though he is not yet ready to do so. Curiously, Breuer forgets the contents of their discussion only an hour after his therapy session. "Could there be such a thing as an active forgetting—forgetting something not because it is unimportant, but because it is too important?" (231). Yalom intimates here the role of resistance, the unconscious forgetting of a painful truth.

Nietzsche, too, is cheered by the therapy session. The entire direction of their discussions has changed. The two men must look to the meaning of a symptom, not its distant origins. "The symptom is but a messenger carrying the news that Angst is erupting from the innermost realm!" (232). Nietzsche already grasps the meaning of Breuer's obsession with Bertha Pappenheim. "She is the great liberator bearing the reprieve from his death sentence" (233).

The Cemetery

In the next chapter Nietzsche accompanies Breuer on his monthly visit to the Jewish section of the Vienna Central Cemetery to pay his respects to his deceased parents and his only sibling, who had died eight years earlier. The cemetery visit is the perfect setting for the physician and philosopher to discuss death—and for the novelist to suggest the existential truth that anxiety arises from the recognition of our mortality. Respecting Breuer's need for solitude, Nietzsche wanders down a path lined with granite and marble tombstones. Minutes later Breuer catches up with his humming companion, who has been amusing himself by composing what he calls "doggerel": "Though no stones hear and none can see/ Each sobs softly, 'Remember me. Remember me'" (237). Nietzsche realizes that the past is never over, just as the dead remain alive to the living. The chapter is one of the most moving in the novel, evocative and lyrical. Breuer explains the Jewish custom of placing pebbles on tombstones as a ritual to memorialize the dead, and he then gives his definition of life, a "spark between two identical voids, the darkness before birth and one after death" (238), a Schopenhauerian (and Epicurean) idea to which Yalom returns in a later novel.

The pebbles on the Jewish tombstone, symbolizing remembrance, recall a footnote in *Existential Psychotherapy* in which Yalom reflects on Alan Sharp's 1965 novel *A Green Tree in Gedde*. The novel describes a small Mexican cemetery that is divided into two parts, the "dead," whose graves, in Yalom's words, are "still adorned with flowers placed there by the living," and the "truly dead," whose gravestones are no longer maintained—"they are remembered by no living soul" (46). Remembrance is often tricky, even for someone with a prodigious memory like Yalom: he misspells the novelist's first name and the last word of the title. He refers to the same novel in *Staring at the Son*, declaring, "Certainly there will come a time when the last living person who has ever known me dies" (179).

Yalom waits until his two protagonists are in the cemetery to reveal the name of Breuer's mother, "Bertha," the same name of one of his daughters, a fact the physician believes has nothing to do with his obsession over

Bertha Pappenheim. Nietzsche disagrees. "Yesterday we learned that your Bertha fantasy protects you from the *future*, from the terrors of aging, death, oblivion. Today I realize that your vision of Bertha is also contaminated by ghosts from the *past*" (240). Whereas Breuer believes that his relationship with Bertha Pappenheim involves only two people, Nietzsche suggests otherwise, asking, "*How many people are in this relationship?*" (240). Those who are obsessed with another person, Yalom suggests, may also be haunted by a revenant of the past. Breuer is not convinced, however, and the two men grow silent, each lost in his thoughts.

Throughout the cemetery scene, Yalom dramatizes the ebb and flow of his characters' thoughts and the shifting dynamics of their relationship. One moment each feels close to the other, believing he understands and is understood by the other. The next moment each emotionally retreats from the other, feeling isolated and misunderstood. Like a master pianist, Yalom knows how to play silences. Sometimes the silence between Breuer and Nietzsche indicates that they are lost in thought, reflecting on ideas they have never considered before, such as whether dreams may have meaning. Both agree on this issue, but whereas Breuer dreams about a woman *rescuing* him from death, Nietzsche dreams about a woman *leading* him to death. Sometimes their silence suggests unwillingness to raise a question that may be too painful or difficult for the other. They must learn the art of knowing when to raise a question: when to press forward and when to retreat. And sometimes their silence conceals their reluctance to express anger toward or suspicion of the other, fearful of endangering their evolving relationship.

The cemetery visit opens up both men's early childhood wounds, Breuer's loss of his mother when he was three and Nietzsche's loss of his father when he was five. How does early parental loss affect a child in later life? Yalom offers a compelling psychobiographical speculation. The fictional Nietzsche suggests that the early death of his father, a Lutheran minister, may have helped his own growth and development as a thinker. "Could I, the antichrist, have exorcized false beliefs and sought new truths with a parson-father wincing with pain at my every achievement, a father who would have regarded my campaigns against illusion as a personal attack against *him*?" (244).

Yalom next turns to Breuer's early loss of his mother, citing in the author's note George Pollack's suggestion that Breuer's powerful emotional response to Bertha Pappenheim may have been influenced by the death of his mother who bore the same name. Breuer's "deepest motivations as a psychological researcher and a human being," Pollack writes, were shaped by his "ties to a beautiful young mother who died in childbirth when he was between the ages of three and four, confronting him with a disastrous loss at the height of the oedipal period" (728). Pollack concludes that when Breuer's external involvements "threatened the eruption of repressed conflicts and existing defenses, flight mechanisms including avoidance and withdrawal occurred" (738). Yalom presents Pollack's theory as a possible explanation of Breuer's obsession with Bertha Pappenheim. The haunting cemetery visit allows Yalom to explore the extent to which early losses influenced his two protagonists' lives.

The chapter then moves to Nietzsche's ideas about death. "Die at the right time," the philosopher urges and then, because the injunction jolts Breuer, Nietzsche elaborates. "Live when you live! Death loses its terror if one dies when one has consummated one's life! If one does not live in the right time, then one can never die at the right time" (247). Nietzsche raises a question that frustrates both men, as the dialogue suggests: "Ask yourself, Josef: *Have you consummated your life?*" (248). Nietzsche's question anticipates one of Yalom's signature themes, the belief that death anxiety is inversely proportional to life satisfaction. "The fear of death," Yalom writes in *Love's Executioner*, "is always greatest in those who feel that they have not lived their life fully" (119).

There are moments in the cemetery chapter when Nietzsche is tender and warmhearted but other moments when he comes across as an angry preacher hurling thunderbolts. The historical Nietzsche cultivated in his writings the prophet's voice, a barbed prose and stiletto style that are not always appropriate for therapy. Yalom knows that authors of jeremiads may not realize they are overwhelming their audience. Nietzsche later senses that he has been too harsh with Breuer, though he is not sure what he could have done differently. Yalom uses an apt metaphor to describe Nietzsche's relationship to Breuer: "a guide must be a railing by the torrent, but he must not be a crutch" (253). Nietzsche's hammering questions have caused Breuer to be momentarily swept away by the torrent, and he feels vertiginous and faint, on the verge of collapse, symptoms with which Nietzsche has long been familiar. Yalom doesn't sugarcoat the talking cure: it is not for the fainthearted. Acknowledging painful truths may take one's breath away, as Breuer discovers. Nevertheless, Yalom implies throughout this chapter, effective therapists rarely use hammers.

Breuer is receptive to the importance of dying at the right time, living a fulfilled life as a way to overcome death anxiety, but he is skeptical about another Nietzschean idea, eternal recurrence. An ancient idea that is a cornerstone in Indian philosophy and that Spinoza appeared to believe in, eternal recurrence, or the eternal return, is the belief that because time and space are infinite, everything that will happen has *already* happened and will continue to happen again. Breuer reflects Yalom's skepticism over eternal recurrence. Nor is Yalom interested in two other Nietzschean ideas, the will to power, the title of a book based on Nietzsche's unpublished writings that he probably did not intend for publication, and the idea of the Übermensch (superman). Both of these Nietzschean ideas remain problematic.

Breuer's Trance Session

Convinced he is entombed in a lifeless existence, Breuer informs his wife in the next chapter that he is leaving her, his children, and his profession. Accepting Nietzsche's demand for a clean break, Breuer confronts a terrifying freedom. From a cosmic perspective, he rationalizes, his absence will make no difference to anyone. Trying to walk in Nietzsche's shoes, he thinks, "Better to break wedlock than be broken by it" (263). The aphorism sounds right but feels wrong. The historical Nietzsche insisted that one must not follow blindly in another's steps. "Be a man and do not follow me—but yourself! But yourself!" he exclaims in *The Gay Science* (155). Without knowing what he's doing, Breuer boards a train to visit Bertha Pappenheim in a Swiss sanitarium, but when he arrives, he sees that she has already transferred her affections to a new physician. Transfixed, Breuer watches as she attempts to seduce the agitated physician who can scarcely resist her advances. All seems lost—until Breuer hears a voice, that of Sigmund Freud, who has been attempting to awaken him from a hypnotic trance. Suddenly Breuer realizes, as does the reader, that the physician has been in a trance state induced by hypnosis, only imagining the events of the preceding seventeen pages. It is not too late for Breuer to change his life.

If this chapter in *When Nietzsche Wept* reminds readers of the Ghost of Christmas Yet to Come, the bleak vision of the future that Scrooge encounters in *A Christmas Carol*, it is because of Yalom's belief that literature and psychotherapy can in their own ways change a person's life. Breuer has the time and motivation to regain control over his life. Nietzsche's life of nomadic wandering, devoid of family and friends, is not right for Breuer, just as Breuer's domestic life of marriage and children is not right for Nietzsche. One must embrace in one's own unique way Nietzschean *amor fati*, love of fate, which the philosopher considered the formula for greatness in a human being. Each person will reach different conclusions about the command to "[b]ecome who you are."

Breuer can change only within the limits of his character, and Yalom must work within the constraints of the real Breuer's life. Nevertheless, Breuer has learned much from his conversations with Nietzsche. He has learned to will his destiny to happen, to love his fate. Feeling a surge of love and desire for his wife, whom he long ignored, Breuer has learned that she, too, is a "combatant in the war against time" (275). The real enemy, Yalom suggests, is destiny: time, aging, and death. Breuer has learned to separate Bertha Pappenheim's image from the transferential symbols and specters he has associated with it, freeing himself from the obsession that has dominated his thoughts. He has learned to affirm what he has failed to appreciate: his wife, children, and work. And he has learned that his way is not Nietzsche's way, the life of the lonely seer.

Breuer conveys both his discovery and recovery to a surprised Nietzsche in the last chapter. Yalom could have imagined the philosopher responding differently. Will Nietzsche be disappointed or angered that the physician chooses to remain with his present life? Will the philosopher lose respect for the man whose way is not his own way? Will he bitterly turn away from Breuer, as he has turned away from Lou Salomé and Paul Rée, convinced that he has been betrayed again? Another novelist might have imagined these scenarios, but Yalom's belief in the possibility of change leads to a more affirmative ending. Yalom presents us with a generous, magnanimous Nietzsche who praises the distance Breuer has traveled in his self-analysis. Each man admires, without envy or resentment, the strength of the other. Breuer acknowledges that, unlike Nietzsche, he cannot stare too long at the sun; Nietzsche acknowledges that, unlike Breuer, he has not found the shade. Each validates the other's aspirations, affirming their relationship. Breuer has internalized Nietzsche's wisdom, and when he cites the philosopher's words—"I know that the key to living well is *first to will that which is necessary and then to love that which is willed*" (282)—he reminds the philosopher of the importance of loving his fate, which will be the theme of his next book.

Yalom's own book is not yet over, however, and in the novel's emotional climax, each man confesses that he has betrayed the other. Nietzsche admits that though he had often unburdened himself in his letters, he turned away in shame when he met people face to face. Nor did he allow others to unburden themselves to him. "I was unwilling to incur the debt of reciprocation" (283).

Nietzsche also admits that whenever Breuer described his obsession with Bertha Pappenheim, he thought about his own obsession with Lou Salomé. "I concealed myself—like a woman—then crawled out after you had left, placed my feet in your footprints, and attempted to follow your path" (286). Nietzsche has not overcome his lifelong suspicion of women, a prejudice he took with him to the grave. Breuer then reveals his own betrayal: his secret meetings with Lou Salomé, her plea on Nietzsche's behalf, his reading of Wagner's letter to Nietzsche, and her request to invent a new treatment for a psychological ailment. Breuer conceals nothing, including Lou Salomé's recent visit, though he refused to tell her anything about his treatment of Nietzsche.

Opening Rusty Gates

Breuer's confession proves so devastating that it quickly precipitates in Nietzsche a severe migraine, a deft plot detail that allows the physician to resume his healing role and defuse his patient's anger. Breuer convinces Nietzsche that though his relationship with the philosopher began in duplicity, he has honored the spirit of their relationship. Breuer admits that he is being cruel by pointing out that Salomé never loved Nietzsche, never considered him as anyone other than a friend, but he justifies his harsh words by reciting the advice of a great teacher: " 'Offer a suffering friend a resting place, he said, 'but take care it be a hard bed or field cot' " (295). Yalom has taken the statement from *Thus Spake Zarathustra* (95), Nietzsche's renowned philosophical novel published between 1883 and 1891. Breuer's assault on the false illusions Nietzsche has associated with Salomé releases the philosopher from his terrible obsession. " 'Today I am the anvil,' Nietzsche interrupted, 'and it is *your* words that are hammer blows—crumbling the citadel of my love' " (294). In a spirit of reciprocity, the two men have each served as the other's hammer and anvil. Each has delivered and received from the other painful but transformative truths.

"Isolation Exists Only in Isolation"

Breuer's strategy at the end of *When Nietzsche Wept*, deidealizing and thus exorcizing a deadly obsessional phantom, would not be used by psychoanalysts until well into the twentieth century, but Yalom's readers have no trouble suspending their disbelief. Nor will readers have difficulty accepting Yalom's interpretation of the fictional philosopher's deepest fear, namely, that despite his bravado about being born posthumously, he is haunted by the fear of dying alone. Filled with despair over the loss of his last illusion, Lou Salomé's desire for him, Nietzsche is bereft, but Breuer knows how to rouse him from the depths of self-loathing. It wasn't Lou Salomé that Nietzsche wanted, Breuer suggests, but someone like her to rescue him from the claws of time. As Nietzsche bursts into sobs, Breuer asks him to imagine a thought experiment: giving voice to his tears. With his physician's help, the philosopher reaches a momentous truth, the paradox, in Breuer's words, that "[i]solation exists only in isolation. Once shared, it evaporates" (300).

Yalom is careful not to exaggerate what Nietzsche learns from Breuer. Nietzsche's mistrust of women hasn't changed, despite Breuer's efforts to convince him that Lou Salomé is a fellow sufferer. Breuer wonders whether Nietzsche's antipathy toward women was formed during the early years of his life, when he grew up in a household dominated by women. Whatever the reason, Nietzsche remains suspicious of all women. Nor has Nietzsche expressed a wish to change his solitary life in exile. He has spent too long living by himself to consider the possibility of living with another person. But what has changed is Nietzsche's feeling of freedom. If his tears could speak, he tells Breuer, they would say, "Free at last! Bottled up all these years. This man, this tight dry man, has never let me flow before" (299). Breuer's chimney sweeping has resulted in a genuine housecleaning, Nietzsche exclaims, and then, changing metaphors, declares that the Viennese doctor has "opened the rusty gate."

A Unique Friendship

One of Yalom's most singular accomplishments in *When Nietzsche Wept* is the new bond between two men of vastly different dispositions. Nietzsche wrote much about friendship, though he had few friends in his own life—and felt betrayed by some of them. There's nothing gushing or inauthentic about Breuer's friendship with Nietzsche, which has evolved from mistrust and misunderstanding to genuine intimacy. Implicit in their new friendship is Nietzsche's revaluation of sympathy, pity, and gratitude. The philosopher and physician are too astute to deny the existence of self-centered motivation when one person helps another, but they also affirm the ability to rise above self-interest. Breuer speaks for Yalom when he states that it's possible for two people to become dear friends. Both Breuer and Nietzsche have participated in the other's "self-overcoming," leading to recovery from despair. Yalom avoids sentimentality at the end when Nietzsche gently turns down Breuer's invitation to stay with him and his family. "No, my friend, my destiny is to search for truth on the far side of loneliness. My son, Zarathustra, will be ripe with wisdom, but his only companion will be an eagle. He will be the loneliest man in the world" (301). The two men embrace and depart from each other forever. Breuer, Yalom tells us, will practice medicine for another thirty years but abandon the talking cure, allowing Freud to make pioneering discoveries. And Nietzsche, Yalom reveals, tying up loose biographical ends, will travel to Italy for a fateful rendezvous with his greatest literary creation, the Persian prophet Zarathustra.

Yalom ends his novel with his hero pregnant with his greatest offspring, but the novelist knew as well as anyone that Nietzsche's life effectively ended in 1889, when, witnessing a horse being flogged in Turin, he threw his arms protectively around its neck and collapsed. He was never the same. Yalom briefly offers this information in the author's note, which serves as a poignant footnote to the story. If there were poetic justice in life, Nietzsche would have been able to enact his injunction in *Beyond Good and Evil*: "One ought to depart from life as Odysseus departed from Nausicaa—blessing rather than in love with it" (95).

Yalom titled his novel *When Nietzsche Wept* to emphasize the philosopher's celebration of the affective dimension of human life. The belief that philosophy is mainly about reason is at least as old as Socrates, but Nietzsche affirmed the role of the passions. Excessive reason, he believed, can blind us to our emotions. Yalom's Nietzsche prods Breuer into examining his emotional life, particularly his obsession with Bertha Pappenheim, and finally, under pressure from the physician, the philosopher reciprocates by examining his own obsession with Lou Salomé.

Praise for Yalom's Novel

When Nietzsche Wept has enjoyed international critical and popular success, and it remains Yalom's best-known novel. The *Boston Globe* praised *When Nietzsche Wept* as an "intelligent, carefully researched, richly imagined novel." The *Chicago Tribune* called *When Nietzsche Wept* the "best dramatization of a great thinker's thought since Sartre's *The Freud Scenario*." The *Washington Post Book World* described the novel as "magical, jolting." Acknowledging his lack of enthusiasm about novels that put historical characters into situations that never existed, James Joll conceded in the *New York Review of Books* that Yalom "shows considerable ingenuity in using his thorough knowledge of Nietzsche's writings to put plausible words into Nietzsche's mouth." Joll whimsically hoped that Yalom would write a sequel in which Breuer cures Nietzsche, enabling him to complete *The Will to Power* without the help of his anti-Semitic sister. Indeed, the historical Nietzsche and Breuer almost met. One of the great surprises in Yalom's life, he observes in *Becoming Myself*, occurred eleven years after the publication of *When Nietzsche Wept*, when a researcher in the Weimar archives sent him a newly discovered letter written in 1880 to Nietzsche from a friend urging him to consult with Dr. Breuer for the philosopher's medical problems. The letter convinced Yalom that he had remained true to André Gide's observation that "[f]iction is history that might have happened" (245).

When Nietzsche Wept appeals to readers interested in the intersections of philosophy, psychology, history, and biography. The novel is about reading: reading books, reading people, reading oneself. Though Nietzsche had few readers during his lifetime, he never lost faith that his books would appeal to future readers. "That a psychologist without equal speaks from my writings," he declaimed in *Ecce Homo*, "is perhaps the first insight reached by a good reader—a reader as I deserve him, who reads me the way good old philologists read their Homer" (722). Nietzsche was fortunate to have Yalom as both a reader and a novelist. Yalom succeeds in capturing the historical Nietzsche's nobility of spirit and, in doing so, conveys his own nobility as well.

Chapter 7

Lying on the Couch
The Threat of Sexual Boundary Violations

Yalom could not have chosen a more ironic title for his second psychotherapy novel, *Lying on the Couch*, where reclining analysands narrate their dreams, desires, fears, and fantasies. The title contains a rare *triple* entendre, a phrase capable of three distinct meanings, beginning with analysands reclining on the therapist's couch, the archetypal setting for talk therapy. (Few people know that Freud requested his patients to lie on his office couch because he disliked being stared at all day.) Lying on the couch also signifies the ambiguities of truth-telling in psychotherapy, the difficulty of determining the accuracy of patients' stories. And lying on the couch also conjures up sexualized psychotherapy, the most serious boundary violation in therapy. Yalom explores all three meanings of lying on the couch in his witty and sly novel.

Truth-Telling and Lying on the Couch

Patients' stories may be reliable or not, examples of truth-telling or lying. The binaries, however, are not always distinguishable. Narrative truth and historical truth, as Donald P. Spence observed in a 1984 book of that title, cannot always be separated. The meaning of a patient's life is cocreated by both the patient and therapist, culminating in a story that is a reconstruction shaped by the therapeutic process.

In "Lying on the Couch," the penultimate chapter of his 1976 book *Lying, Despair, Jealousy, Envy, Sex, Suicide, Drugs, and the Good Life*, the psychoanalyst Leslie H. Farber contrasts two different types of truth, one that is "problematical, partial, modest—and still breathing," and the other that is "revelatory," usually "attended by—indeed identified by—considerable emotion, which is often understood to have been repressed or denied and is only now breaking through to the surface." Farber is more interested in the first kind of truth than in the second. "I think that speaking truthfully is a more fitting ambition than speaking the truth" (211). Ordinary, fragmentary truth is not as dramatic or "aesthetic" as revelatory truth, but it is more genuine and enduring. The paradox of psychoanalysis, Farber notes, is that while it is predicated on a person's capacity for truth-telling, the "very devices and strategies traditionally employed for facilitating his search for truth . . . all seem to encourage the patient's capacity to embellish, to dramatize—in short, to lie" (214). Farber's conclusion is that the imagination, the "ally of both lying and truth-telling," is double-edged: "it has its uses and abuses, its privileges and penalties" (218). Yalom is well aware of Farber's writings. The protagonist of Yalom's *Lying on the Couch*, the young existential psychiatrist Ernest Lash, mentions reading Farber's writings when preparing for a grand rounds presentation on paralysis of the will, the subject of Farber's first book, *The Ways of the Will*.

Embellishment's close cousin, suggestibility, is also implied in lying on the couch, where therapists, consciously or not, create or implant memories in patients. The 1980s and 1990s were decades in which psychotherapy became embroiled in controversies over "recovered memories." Patients claimed, with the encouragement and sometimes manipulation of their therapists, that they could recall being victimized by sexual abuse, particularly incest, which sometimes occurred during early childhood, a time when the brain, according to most contemporary researchers, cannot accurately record and store information. Even more astonishing was the development of "past lives" therapy, where therapists helped patients understand their existences hundreds or thousands of years in the past—or future. The memory wars also involved "satanic ritual abuse," where thousands of patients recalled being involved in the ritualistic sacrifice of children, despite an absence of evidence confirming these crimes. Abetted by stories like *The Three Faces of Eve* and *Sybil*, the public became fascinated by the proliferation of "multiple personality disorder," where a single person could have hundreds, even thousands, of "alters." In retrospect, few experts now take these fads seriously, but Yalom was writing during the height of these fierce disputes, all the time casting a skeptical light. "We're so used to patients paying us to listen to their truth," Ernest's psychopharmacologist friend, Paul, tells him, "that we're probably naive about the possibility of lying" (216).

Lying on the couch also conjures up an erotic meaning, patient-therapist sex, perhaps the most forbidden—and common—transgression in psychotherapy. The 1990s saw an explosion of sexual malpractice suits against some of the most prominent psychotherapists in the country. Yalom was one of the first therapists to confront the growing problem of sexual boundary violations, a subject that had received little attention in professional journals. Yalom's novel shows the catastrophic consequences for patients and therapists alike who succumb to lying on the couch, an act that may be traced back to the unreality of transference love and countertransference love.

Seymour Trotter: Portrait of the Artist as a Con Artist?

Lying on the Couch opens with a thirty-three-page prologue, a description of the seventy-one-year-old psychiatrist Seymour Trotter, one of Yalom's finest fictional creations. Patriarch of the San Francisco psychiatric establishment and past president of the American Psychiatric Association, Trotter has vast experience and deep knowledge. There seems to be nothing about his profession that he doesn't know. Trotter not only voices Yalom's trenchant criticisms of contemporary psychotherapy, particularly the growing emphasis on psychopharmacology, but he also advocates a new existential psychotherapy based on authenticity and the therapeutic relationship.

Trotter tells Ernest that the first principle of psychiatric interviewing is to forge a warm, trusting relationship. Trotter recalls Carl Rogers's statement, "Don't waste your time training therapists—time is better spent in *selecting* them" (6). Like Yalom, Trotter argues for complete honesty in psychotherapy, recognizes the limitations of insight, and honors each patient's uniqueness. Like Yalom, Trotter believes that psychiatric labels do violence to patients. Like Yalom, Trotter praises Karen Horney, singling out her book *Neuroses and Human Growth* for its brilliance and lack of jargon. Like Yalom, Trotter laments the short shelf life of major psychiatric texts. The "fate of the leading theoreticians" is that their teachings "survive for about one generation" (13). Like Yalom, Trotter publishes books and articles about psychotherapy. Years earlier Trotter had written an article discussing Jung's belief that a new therapy language needs to be created for each patient. "I took it even further than Jung," Trotter boasts. "I suggested we invent a new therapy for each patient, that we take seriously the notion of the uniqueness of each patient and develop a unique psychotherapy for each one" (6). Echoing Nietzsche's belief that certainty is inversely proportional to knowledge,

Trotter comments that it's easier for therapists to make a diagnosis the first time they see a patient and harder after they learn more about a patient, an insight Yalom cites in *Love's Executioner*. Using Nietzschean language, Trotter exhorts Ernest to fulfill his destiny as a healer. Like Yalom, Trotter has little interest in psychiatric diagnosis and even less interest in rummaging, believing that, as his thirty-two-year-old patient Belle Felini puts it, "poking in the ashes of the past was just an excuse to evade personal responsibility for our actions." Yalom must have smiled ruefully at Trotter's next comment: "She had read my book on psychotherapy and cited me saying that very thing. I hate that. When patients resist by citing your own books, they got you by the balls" (8).

Like Yalom, Trotter abounds in psychological insights that he generously shares with others. He points out to Ernest, who began his career as a neurochemistry researcher without psychotherapy experience, that if you see a woman wearing long sleeves in the summer, "always think of wrist cutting and drug injections" (4). The first rule of good therapy, Trotter opines, is to abandon all technique, implying that a therapist should be more human and less mechanical. Arguing for boldness and creativity in psychotherapy, he is authoritative in all of his psychiatric judgments.

Perhaps most noteworthy of all, Trotter knows that a heightened awareness of death, occurring when people confront their own mortality, can lead to an increased appreciation for life. Patients waiting for the results of an HIV test, Trotter instructs Ernest, have a unique window of opportunity that a therapist may put to good advantage. "It's a time when you can help them to examine and reshuffle their priorities, to base their lives and their behavior on the things that really count. *Existential shock therapy*, I sometimes call it" (10).

Valuing intuition over textbook knowledge, therapeutic engagement over detachment, innovation over orthodoxy, Trotter reminds us of Yalom in nearly every way. Nor should we be surprised that the septuagenarian Trotter conveys the humor, wisdom, and worldly sophistication of Yalom, who was sixty-five when *Lying on the Couch* was published. Trotter seems to have come to terms with his own mortality, including his failing physical health. Momentarily forgetting Ernest's name, Trotter taps his temple and refers slyly to the four articles he has published on Alzheimer's disease: "naturally I forgot where, but in good journals" (3), one of the many examples of his droll wit. His speech is riddled with Yiddishisms, as when he says to Ernest, "Sit back, *boychik* [a Jewish term of endearment for a son] and I'll tell you a story" (4).

Nowhere is Trotter more like his creator than in his gift for storytelling. Indeed, of all Yalom's fictional protagonists, Trotter is a supreme wordsmith, a conjurer of illusions and spells. He holds Ernest's—and the reader's—rapt attention throughout the prologue. Trotter has the power to read Ernest's mind, anticipating his questions, sharpening his psychological acumen, leading him to past and present psychiatric research. Though Ernest has only one meeting with Trotter, the wizened psychiatrist's words and deeds irrevocably change the younger man's life. Trotter is in the twilight of his life: he walks with two canes, and his face, we learn, is being engulfed by its own wrinkles. Despite his physical decrepitude, his voice is captivating, self-confident, and exuberant. His sardonic speech recalls that of Saul Bellow, whose novels, like Yalom's, interrogate through penetrating humor and intelligence the inner and outer contradictions of contemporary life. In short, Trotter casts a magical spell over Ernest, verbal sorcery that nearly overcomes whatever resistance may arise from the darker implications of his story.

Combining psychiatric lecture, dramatic monologue, comedic solo, and cri de coeur, the prologue to *Lying on the Couch* is a tour de force. Trotter likens his interview with Ernest to Rilke's *Letters to a Young Poet*, but the reader may also be reminded of *Portnoy's Complaint*, where Philip Roth's benumbed hero, lying on the couch throughout the celebrated novel, never allows his psychoanalyst to interrupt the masturbatory confession until the end of the story, when the annoyed Spielvogel, finally able to speak, remonstrates, "So [said the doctor]. Now vee may perhaps to begin. Yes?"

The Therapist of Last Resort

A crucial difference between *Portnoy's Complaint* and *Lying on the Couch* is that whereas the patient sexually acts out in Roth's novel, the therapist acts out in the prologue to Yalom's novel. Trotter has been charged with sexual misconduct with Belle Felini, and he uses one argument after another to explain to Ernest, who has been appointed to serve on the Stanford Hospital Medical Ethics Committee that investigates the case, why he could not finally resist her sexual advances. Trotter's rationalizations are no less irresistible, and Ernest, like Dr. Spielvogel, can hardly get a word in edgewise.

Patient-therapist sex appears in countless novels and memoirs, nearly always with the rationalization that the latter is helping the former feel "special," but Yalom's fictional account has an ironic twist—several ironic twists. Born in Switzerland to wealthy parents, Belle has seen dozens of psychoanalysts, none of whom have been able to help her. Impulsive, action-oriented, not inclined to self-reflection or restraint, and endlessly seductive, she is sent to Trotter, one of the world's best analysts, the "therapist of last resort," as Yalom describes himself in *Love's Executioner*. But how can Trotter help her if she is so self-destructive, so resistant to observing boundaries in therapy? She is at first satisfied with an "avuncular" hug—the word means "uncle," Trotter patronizingly explains to Ernest—but she demands more and more. He remains unpersuaded by her arguments and firm in his professional behavior, all the while admitting to Ernest that he finds himself increasingly aroused by her. For every argument Trotter uses to discourage her sexual interest in him, Belle has a ready counterargument. To his statement that he is seventy and she thirty-four, she responds, "Chaplin, Kissinger, Picasso, Humbert Humbert and Lolita" (26), the latter two names demonstrating that she is a reader of serious literature, as he is. She might have also referred to Keats: her name identifies her as a Belle Dame sans Merci.

After what appears to be a therapeutic impasse, Belle makes an offer that Trotter finds difficult to refuse. If she agrees to "stay clean" for a year—no drugs, no sex pick-ups in bars, no cutting, no purging—will he reward her by taking her to Hawaii for a week? Taken aback, Trotter is initially dubious, but after concluding that there is no other solution to her problems, he negotiates a better deal. He will take her to San Francisco for a weekend if she promises to remain on good behavior for two years. She agrees, and the Faustian pact is sealed. She promises that she will take their secret to the grave. She makes spectacular progress during the following months, but Trotter panics as the end of the two years approaches. Nothing that he can say or do diminishes her ravenous desire for him, including his rapidly failing health. He reluctantly fulfills his part of the contract. They spend a weekend together as lovers, with no apparent ill effects. But the weekend has inevitably destroyed their therapeutic relationship, as Trotter suspected it would—he knows all about erotic transferences. Indeed, he penned the guidelines warning therapists against having post-therapy sexual relations.

The catastrophe Trotter has long predicted inevitably befalls him. Belle's husband files a medical malpractice lawsuit against him, using as evidence four photos of his wife and Trotter during their not-so-secret tryst. Trotter's wife leaves him, and both his career and reputation are forever ruined. Belle is awarded two million dollars, the limit of Trotter's medical malpractice coverage. Trotter tells Ernest that he never saw Belle again; he was forbidden by a court order to see or speak to her. He describes himself as suffering from "appropriate depression," confessing to Ernest that he is a "miserable, sad old man. Discouraged, lonely, full of self-doubts, ending my life in disgrace" (30).

A Cautionary Tale

Is Trotter's cautionary tale merely one more example of patient-therapist sex leading to predictable disaster for both parties? Ernest would have thought so were it not for a letter he unexpectedly received from Trotter, with no return address, a year later. Trotter thanks Ernest for his concern during the "demonizing witch hunt days" of the malpractice trial. The disgraced analyst declares that he is well and encloses a photo of Belle and himself, with her house in the background on a Caribbean island surrounded by a tropical sea. "Belle's come into a good bit of money," Trotter notes without elaboration at the end of the letter. The photo shows Trotter sitting in a wheelchair, with a "big, goofy, crooked smile" on his face while Belle, standing behind him, looks "forlorn and gaunt" (32).

What? Was Trotter's sexualized therapy with Belle nothing more than an ingenious scam to defraud his insurance company of two million dollars? Trotter has insisted that he has been acting toward Belle in good faith, but now everything he has said is open to question. Is he nothing more than a con artist? Ernest cannot stop looking at the photo. The reader shares his confusion. It seems from Belle's downcast eyes that she has received more than she bargained for. Is the prologue a guileful joke by a novelist who has revealed himself to be a cunning jokester?

Yalom characteristically leaves the Trotter affair ambiguous. Years later Ernest continues to think about the photo. When did Trotter and Belle decide to retreat to the island together? "Had Seymour decided at the very end to rescue her? Or had they schemed together much earlier? Perhaps from the very beginning?" (117). Ernest cannot answer these questions. Nor can we. There is no question in Ernest's mind, however, that Trotter's self-characterization as the therapist of last resort is a sign of hubris. The prologue turns out to be a mise en abyme, a play within a play, like "The Murder of Gonzago" in *Hamlet*, the scene that foreshadows the text's larger themes and meanings. Yalom exposes Ernest Lash to a similar experience with a highly seductive patient, with consequences that are far different from those of Seymour Trotter.

Trotter's first-person narration dominates the prologue, and only at the end do we discover that he has been conning Ernest and us. Trotter is one of Yalom's few unreliable narrators. Once Yalom begins the novel proper, he uses his more customary third-person narration, allowing us insight into the consciousness of his other characters. The cast of characters is varied. Ernest is the central protagonist, older and more experienced than he was in the prologue. Trotter's prediction that Ernest will make an excellent therapist has come true, but he is about to be tested in ways he cannot imagine. His experience with Trotter has taught him the importance of being *real*, but there are few words that are more elusive or ambiguous, and being real in therapy brings with it unique challenges.

The novel opens on a note of surprise, different from those seen in the prologue. Justin Astrid has been in treatment with Ernest for five years, three times a week, mainly because he requires help in extricating himself from a tormenting marriage, one of the worst Ernest has seen. Justin casually informs him that he has left his wife, Carol, variously described as a gorgon or demon, and their two young children. It was not psychotherapy that gave Justin the courage to leave his wife but his new, young girlfriend, Laura. Had Laura come along years earlier, Justin states, oblivious to the effect his words have on Ernest, he would not have wasted eighty thousand dollars in therapy fees. Ernest feels his face flushing: how can he avoid taking the statement personally?

Carol's response to her husband's abrupt departure is to go on a rampage, destroying all of his possessions, including his clothes, treasured ties, glass-covered beetle collection, high school and college diplomas, and porno video library. She vows revenge on both her husband and his therapist. She has never met Ernest, but she loathes him—and every other therapist. She has good reason to feel this way, we soon discover. When she was an undergraduate at Brown, her boyfriend of four years left her for another woman, and after she trashed his room in a rage, she went to the college mental health center, where she was treated by a psychiatrist, Ralph Cooke, who convinced her to have sex with him. "Touch is necessary for your healing, Carol."

For five months Cooke had sex with Carol, pronounced her "healed," and terminated treatment, presumably to begin having sex with another undergraduate. Enraged and humiliated, Carol decided at that moment to become a lawyer. In her senior year of college, a political science professor offered to write a letter for her for law school, but only if she would have sex with him. Finding herself once again falling into depression, she sought the assistance of a therapist in private practice, "Dr. Zweizung," who, like Cooke, began sexualizing treatment. "This time Carol knew what to do and immediately stalked out of the office, yelling at the top of her lungs, 'You scumbag!' That was the last time Carol had ever asked for help" (49).

Dr. Zweizung

Few readers of *Lying on the Couch* realize that Dr. Zweizung is based on a real psychotherapist. The Pulitzer Prize–winning poet Anne Sexton had a long sexual affair with her psychiatrist, who was pseudonymously called "Dr. Samuel Deitz," by the coeditors of *Anne Sexton: A Self-Portrait in Letters*. The affair began in 1964, when Sexton's trusted psychiatrist, Martin Orne, left Boston, where he had been treating her for years, to take a position at the University of Pennsylvania. She began seeing a new psychiatrist, who immediately sexualized therapy. Sexton started writing poems about her psychiatrist lover that were published in the posthumous collection *Words for Dr. Y*. Their affair lasted until 1969, when he abruptly terminated therapy. In an act long foreshadowed in her poetry, Sexton committed suicide in 1974 shortly before her forty-fifth birthday.

As Paul W. Mosher and I discuss in *Confidentiality and Its Discontents: Dilemmas of Privacy in Psychotherapy*, Sexton's biographer, Diane Wood Middlebrook, a Stanford English professor, referred to Sexton's transgressive psychiatrist as "Dr. Zweizung," a pseudonym that means "forked tongue" in German. "Details have been suppressed," Middlebrook notes tersely in the appendix of her 1991 biography, "to protect the doctor's anonymity" (431). Sexton saw the psychiatrist twice a week and paid for the therapy sessions. There was never any doubt that both patient and therapist knew that sex was destructive to the therapeutic relationship. "Sexton's coy phrase 'doctor-daddy,'" writes Middlebrook, "conveys how conscious she was of her own transgression in this relationship" (259). But most mental health professionals would place all of the responsibility and blame on the therapist, not on the patient. Patients are, after all, in need of help, and their judgment is inevitably impaired both by the nature of the psychological disorder that has brought them into therapy and also by transference love, which the transgressive therapist selfishly manipulates.

Sexton eventually became furious with the psychiatrist for his many broken promises to her. Shortly after he ended the affair, she fell down the stairs at her home on her birthday and broke her hip. In the hospital she "revenged herself on him," observes Middlebrook, by writing two sarcastic poems about their relationship. Sexton later conveyed her feelings toward him in a poem called "Speaking Bitterness"; she recalls the doctor kissing her "withered limbs" and promising to leave his wife and run away with her. "Oh, I remember the likes of him,/ his hand over my boots, up my skirts like a corkscrew" (*Complete Poems* 584).

Reviewing Middlebrook's biography in the *New York Times* on July 15, 1991, Alessandra Stanley was the first to disclose the identity of Sexton's psychiatrist, Frederick J. Duhl. The psychiatrist refused to speak to Stanley in a telephone interview about the biography's revelations other than to say, "You are dealing with an explosive subject; basically any doctor who has an affair with a patient loses his license in Massachusetts." In *Searching for Mercy Street*, a memoir about her tangled relationship with her mother, Linda Gray Sexton recalls her anger reading early drafts of Middlebrook's biography and learning about the destructiveness of Duhl's behavior: "however hurt and angry the rest of us might feel, Mother was the one who had taken the worst of the impact when Duhl curtailed the affair and the analysis" (274).

Both Middlebrook's biography and Stanley's review in the *New York Times* appeared five years before the publication of *Lying on the Couch*, but Yalom obviously preferred to use "Dr. Zweizung" as the name of the psychotherapist who invited Carol to have sex with him. Duhl died in 2010 at the age of eighty-one. Legal reasons might have prevented Yalom from using Duhl's real name—and the novelist doubtlessly appreciated the irony of "forked tongue." It's likely that Yalom knew many of the details of Duhl's sexual relationship with Sexton from Middlebrook *before* the publication of her biography. Yalom and Middlebrook were both Stanford colleagues; he warmly acknowledged her help in *When Nietzsche Wept*, and she wrote an admiring blurb that appears on the back cover of the paperback edition.

Understanding Duhl's calamitous sexual relationship with Anne Sexton helps us to appreciate Carol's rage toward the two psychotherapists who sexualized their treatment of her. In addition, we can understand why she despises *every* therapist, including her husband's therapist, whom she has never met. We can also understand Yalom's righteous anger toward therapists who betray their profession. Yalom feels compelled to identify other transgressive psychotherapists, including the early psychoanalytic pioneers, such as Carl Jung, Otto Rank, and Ernest Jones.

Another Fallen Idol: Jules Masserman

But therapist-patient sex remains a serious *contemporary* problem, as Yalom knows. Ernest's clinical supervisor, Marshal Streider, voices Yalom's horror over the case of Jules Masserman, who, like the fictional Trotter, was past president of the American Psychiatric Association, as well as past president of many other world psychiatric organizations. "Can you believe what he did?" Streider asks Ernest, "giving patients sodium pentothal and then having sex with them while they were unconscious? It's unthinkable!" (81). Masserman, author of the bestselling psychiatric textbook *Principles of Dynamic Psychiatry*, was described as the most prominent psychiatrist in the world. In the mid-1980s Barbara Noël came forward and stated that he had drugged and raped her over a period of nearly eighteen years while she was under the influence of sodium amytal, which produces prolonged sleep. Noël's assertion was supported by other Masserman patients, who offered evidence that they, too, were victimized by his sexual transgressions. The story appears in *You Must Be Dreaming*, coauthored by Noël and Kathryn Watterson. Paul Mosher and I discuss the case in the first volume of *Off the Tracks: Cautionary Tales About the Derailing of Mental Health Care*. Noël's malpractice suit, which Masserman's insurance company settled out of court, provoked national outrage, but the mental health community remained largely silent, too shocked and embarrassed to respond.

Yalom was one of the few therapists willing to voice outrage over the Masserman scandal. He offers several examples in *Lying on the Couch* of "fallen idols" to suggest why Carol's outrage must be taken seriously—and why Ernest is correct in saying that sex between patient and therapist sabotages treatment. In a later discussion between Ernest and Paul, the latter points out that there may not be enough scientific evidence to prove that sex in therapy is *always* destructive, but he quickly adds, "the question of therapist-patient sex is a moral question; there's no way science is going to prove to me that immorality is moral" (220).

A Revenge Plot

Carol's instincts incline her to murder her husband, but when her two colleagues offer practical objections, she imagines a more novel idea. What better way to destroy her husband than by destroying his therapist, Justin's "nipple"? Indeed, Carol resents paying for her husband's long and expensive treatment. "You don't know much about the therapy industry," she tells her two colleagues. "Some of the shrinks will keep you coming in perpetuity" (61).

The revenge plan is based on entrapment. Carol Astrid will enter treatment with Ernest without telling him she is Justin's wife (she calls herself "Carolyn Leftman"). After convincing Ernest that having sex with her psychiatrist in college was liberating and healing, Carol will then relentlessly sexualize therapy until he succumbs to her wiles. Afterward, she will sue the bastard for medical malpractice, thereby ruining his life and career. Her scheme is as devious as Trotter's but without any of his artful subterfuge. Carol does this at the worst possible time for Ernest, precisely when he has resolved to be as truthful, authentic, and self-revealing as possible, pushing therapist self-disclosure to the limits. It is a risky clinical experiment under the best of conditions—and perilous with a patient determined to destroy her therapist. Her slash-and-burn tactics make her a formidable opponent both in the courtroom and the analyst's office.

Yalom's central question in *Lying on the Couch* is whether a principled therapist's experiment with self-disclosure can withstand the test of a vindictive patient's relentless seductive advances. The novelist complicates the test by creating a psychotherapist who cannot anticipate the challenges inherent in the experiment. Ernest Lash is a work in progress, human, all too human. Ambitious and hardworking, he did not intend to become a psychotherapist. During his psychiatric residency he focused on the pharmacological treatment of mental illness, believing in the great promise of biological breakthroughs. He saw patients for twenty minutes, dispensing medications to them without talk therapy. Yalom's disapproval of purely psychopharmacological approaches to mental illness, the "siren call of biological psychiatry," could not be clearer. "Gradually, and here, Seymour Trotter played a role, Ernest realized the limitations, even the vulgarity, of treating all patients with drugs and, at the sacrifice of forty percent of his income, gradually shifted into a psychotherapy practice" (77). Receiving encouragement from a mentor like Trotter, however, is fraught with irony. Ernest still has much to learn as a psychotherapist, as Marshal Streider never fails to remind him.

Marshal Streider

Yalom uses Streider both as a narrative device and as a character involved in one of the novel's subplots. As a narrative device, Streider generally offers Ernest good clinical advice, such as always acting on the patient's behalf. Like Yalom, Streider is an absolutist when it comes to therapists avoiding having sex with present or past patients. Streider's criticism that Ernest is therapeutically "incontinent," too quick to offer interpretations, also reflects the novelist's judgment. Streider oversees Ernest's treatment of his patients, including Justin and Carol. Streider is Ernest's supervisor, not analyst, but the two roles can sometimes be blurred. "Supervision lay in the no-man's-land between therapy and education" (77–78). Some of Streider's advice to Ernest is questionable, however, or at least too conservative for the younger therapist bent on therapeutic authenticity. Streider advises Ernest not to reveal his countertransference feelings and fantasies to his patients, a position that Ernest will soon challenge. Streider hides behind analytic neutrality, refusing to reveal to his patients anything about himself. Insisting that the analyst's *only* role is to interpret, Streider misses the importance of the most powerful aspect of psychotherapy, the patient-therapist relationship.

Ernest's treatment of Carol is no laughing matter, but Yalom's talent as a satirist is evident when he describes Streider's involvement with psychoanalytic politics. Streider's quest to be the president of the Golden Gate Psychoanalytic Institute compels him to turn against his former training analyst, Seth Pande, one of only two living founding members of the institute. Pande has been accused of sexual and financial exploitation of his patients, but he refuses to resign as a training analyst. The anti-Semitic Pande, who has attacked Freudian theory because it reveals the "Jewish error," is modeled on the Pakistani-born analyst Masud Khan, whose anti-Semitic diatribes appalled the psychoanalytic community. (One of Pande's supporters is a Pakistani analyst named Mian Khan.) A maverick, Pande has theorized that men have an unconscious homosexual desire to merge with their fathers. Streider denounces the "womb-rectum" theory as a deviation from accepted psychoanalytic theory and then suggests that Pande's former male patients who have been harmed by this treatment return for a course of remedial psychotherapy. The institute places a formal notice of a "psychiatric Patient Recall" in the *San Francisco Chronicle*—"the first recall treatment case in psychiatric history" (210). Streider soon regrets his rash recommendation. One of Pande's ex-patients, Shelly Merriman, who has gambled away his family's money and in the process lost his wife (Carol's colleague), sees an opportunity to use the therapeutic recall to regain his wife and sharpen his poker skills. Streider is horrified when Shelly proposes to file a malpractice lawsuit against the institute, an idea that would lead to its bankruptcy and the end of Streider's hope to become the next president. Shelly agrees to drop the lawsuit only if Streider can help him figure out why he keeps losing in gambling, an agreement to which the analyst reluctantly agrees.

There is little to admire about Marshal Streider as a human being. Proud, vain, conceited, and materialistic, he is contemptuous of his wife, a gentle woman who, disappointed in both psychoanalysis and her psychoanalyst husband, has sought healing in ikebana, the ancient Japanese art of flower arrangement. Obsessed with money, the sixty-three-year-old Streider is guilty of serious nonsexual boundary violations with his patients. Streider rightly cautions Ernest against emotionally overinvesting himself with a patient, but he financially invests ninety thousand dollars with a con artist posing as a patient. The nonsexual boundary violation comes back to haunt him. Rage and the desire for revenge overcome Streider near the end of the story when he becomes the victim of a double swindle. He finds himself seeking legal advice and psychological comfort from a person who, also bent upon revenge, recognizes in him a dark double.

An Earnest Experiment with Therapist Self-Disclosure

If character is destiny, so might be a character's name. Yalom chose his protagonist's name after seeing a performance of Oscar Wilde's *The Importance of Being Earnest* in London. Ernest Lash's name offers insight into his own destiny. Those who are earnest are by definition serious, solemn, and grave. This is largely true of Ernest. Will he be a character who lashes, whips, or flagellates himself over real or imagined acts? Will he need to lash himself to the mast of reason, like Odysseus, when treating his new patient, Carol Leftman, and as Yalom does while treating Penny in *Love's Executioner*? Will Ernest's love for psychotherapy survive disillusionment? Is Yalom setting up his sometimes-clueless character to be a Humpty Dumpty, about to have a great fall?

An associate clinical professor of psychiatry at the University of California, San Francisco, Ernest is the author of a new book on bereavement, written in response to his wife's death in a car accident six years earlier. He yearns for a new relationship with a woman, one that will fulfill a deep need in him, but the yearning also creates a desire and vulnerability that Carol will attempt to exploit. Ernest's talk on spousal bereavement at a book-signing in Palo Alto faithfully reflects Yalom's point of view. Spousal bereavement is an opportunity for heightened existential awareness, Ernest declares, an occasion for renewed appreciation of the preciousness of life. Before he begins speaking, he gazes at an attractive woman who turns out to have been in a therapy group he had led ten years earlier. He fantasizes about having a sexual relationship with her but then berates himself because sex with a former patient is permanently off-limits. "Ernest hated his dark side," Yalom reminds us, hated thralldom to animal instinct. As it turns out, his former patient declines his offer to meet after the talk, but there is another woman in the audience, Carol, who is already plotting a relationship with him.

Carol enters therapy precisely at the time that Ernest resolves to practice a radically new egalitarian therapy based entirely on the here-and-now relationship between therapist and patient. He vows to reveal himself completely and avoid traditional psychotherapeutic approaches. "No historical reconstruction, no interpretations of the past, no explorations of psychosexual development" (102). In conducting this bold new therapy, Ernest will disregard what he has learned from his teachers and supervisors, including Marshal Streider. Ernest's new research project focuses on the "in-betweenness" of therapy, the space between patient and therapist, a topic on which he plans to write a journal article.

"Mutual Analysis"

Ernest is not the first to experiment with therapist self-disclosure. He and Paul discuss Sándor Ferenczi, the Hungarian analyst who was one of Freud's closest disciples and analysands before falling out of favor with the creator of psychoanalysis. "I just started to read the new Ferenczi clinical diaries," Paul tells Ernest. "Fascinating. Only Ferenczi of Freud's inner circle had the courage to develop more effective treatment" (101). Ernest is referring to *The Clinical Diary of Sándor Ferenczi*, published by Harvard University Press in 1988. In *The Yalom Reader* the novelist cites Ferenczi's "radical 1932 transparency experiment where he pushed therapist self-disclosure to the limit." Yalom considered using Ferenczi as a character in *Lying on the Couch*, alternating the action in the novel between 1932 and the present, but he abandoned the idea because he couldn't find a novelistic technique to meld the two eras together. "Finally I built Ferenczi's idea, not his person, into the plot by having my protagonist reenact Ferenczi's experiment in contemporary times" (415–416).

An intriguing character during the early history of psychoanalysis, Ferenczi overcame initial skepticism over what he called "mutual analysis," an idea suggested to him by a patient, R. N., who convinced him that their stalemated two-year-analysis could be saved only if it was based on reciprocity. Ferenczi experimented with double or contrasting sessions, where patient and analyst took turns being the analysand. "Can and should the analyst, analyzed in this way, be completely open, right from the beginning?" he asked on January 17, 1932. It did not take Ferenczi long to realize the limitations of mutual analysis, limitations that Ernest also realizes in *Lying on the Couch*. One problem is the loss of the analyst's confidentiality. "It would be like conducting analysis with the door open," Ferenczi observes on February 16 (34). Another problem is determining how much truth to reveal to the patient. What would an analysis look like, Ferenczi asks, if the analyst stated, "Basically I find you perfectly repulsive. I cannot stand your smell. Your face and your manners are awful" (35). Ferenczi sadly gave up mutual analysis because the experiment appeared too dangerous, an idea that many people, he concluded, would consider an act of "madness" (74). Yalom uses Ferenczi's idea of mutual analysis in *When Nietzsche Wept*, where both Breuer and Nietzsche take turns analyzing and being analyzed by the other. In *Lying on the Couch* Ernest Lash embodies Ferenczi's restless intellectual curiosity, honesty, clinical astuteness, self-criticism, and empathy.

Ernest doesn't give up the idea of therapist self-disclosure, but he learns to appreciate conventional wisdom. For the next 250 pages, Yalom contrasts Ernest's well-intentioned but increasingly exasperated statements to Carol with her cynical belief that he is merely setting her up to have sex with him. As she begins to praise him excessively, claiming he is the only therapist who can help her, he realizes that he must immediately qualify his naive belief in total therapist self-disclosure. He formulates the first of several principles for therapist self-disclosure. "*Reveal yourself only to the extent it will be helpful to the patient*" (105). What prevents *Lying on the Couch* from becoming a didactic study of therapist self-disclosure is the wry humor arising from Carol's misunderstanding of Ernest's statements. When he empathizes with her confession that she has been entrapped in a loveless marriage, she nods in rapt agreement while thinking, "*Oh, how brilliant . . . . Shall I genuflect?*" (109).

How can treatment succeed when therapist and patient have different agendas, the former committed to truth, the latter to duplicity? How can treatment succeed if one is out to manipulate and destroy the other? How can treatment succeed if there is so much lying on the couch? These questions dramatize the impossible distance existing between Ernest and Carol. Nowhere is the gulf between them wider than when Carol asserts that sex with her former psychiatrist saved her life. Everything Ernest has learned in school and discovered in his own practice prevents him from agreeing with Carol, but how can he disagree without contradicting and invalidating her experiences? He correctly reminds himself not to prejudge, to avoid being moralistic and judgmental, to enter the patient's own subjective world, which may be vastly different from his own world, but he cannot go against everything he believes. Unable to escape from this dilemma, all he can say truthfully is that he has never met a patient who was not harmed by sex in therapy. Unable to believe his sincerity, Carol redoubles her efforts to seduce him.

Midway through the novel Ernest learns that a patient he has been treating, Eva, a creative writing teacher struggling with advanced ovarian cancer, is near death. Accustomed to working with dying patients, Ernest races to her home to be with her. Yalom uses this event to describe one of Ernest's—and his own—therapeutic innovations. "With many of his patients, Ernest introduced the concept of regret into his therapy. He asked patients to examine regrets for their past conduct and urged them to avoid future regrets" (179). The use of anticipatory regret does not always succeed, we learn, but when it does, it enables patients like Eva to live more intensely, "sucking the marrow out of the bones of life" (180). Tellingly, Eva and Ernest had used his therapy office to confront the "terror of finitude." When she was too ill to see him at his office, he would telephone her and sometimes make home visits, never billing her for therapy. He fulfills his promise to be with her when she dies. Yalom avoids sentimentalizing the death when Ernest becomes furious at himself for experiencing unwelcome sexual arousal when he lies next to his dying patient.

Carol invents a persona for therapy, lest Ernest realize she is Justin's wife, but she nevertheless reveals the central problems in her life, so that she doesn't trip herself up. To her surprise and chagrin, she becomes emotionally engaged in talk therapy, regarding the process as beguiling. She still views Ernest with suspicion, but she begrudgingly admits to herself the accuracy of his interpretations. Using the technique of anticipatory regret, Ernest reminds her that it is not too late to transform her life. "The confrontation with death is a great catalyst for change," he gently tells her (202), an idea that appears in all of Yalom's writings.

Ernest quickly discovers that if his radical experiment with therapist self-disclosure is to succeed, he must be willing to reveal more about himself than he feels comfortable doing. Yalom delights in pushing his characters, therapists and patients alike, out of their comfort zones. When Carol asks him whether he is single or married—"The jacket of your book mentions no wife"—he discloses her death six years earlier. "Oh, I'm sorry," Carol replies with unexpected but heartfelt empathy. "That must have been hard" (204). Yalom has subtly shifted roles here, with the patient sounding like a therapist, the same technique the novelist uses throughout *When Nietzsche Wept*. Ernest's marriage was faltering and probably would have ended in divorce had his wife not been killed in an auto accident. Yet how can he reveal the details of his conflicted marriage without dangerously shifting the focus onto himself? To do so would be a disservice to the patient, who is paying for her own therapy, not the therapist's.

Ernest discovers another problem with therapist self-disclosure: the invasion of the therapist's privacy. The patient is guaranteed confidentiality; the therapist is not. Therapists' self-disclosures might become public knowledge, leading to their embarrassment or harm. On the other hand, Ernest doesn't want to abandon his experiment with therapist self-disclosure by retreating to the analyst's neutrality, a stance he regards as antithetical to authentic therapy. Asking himself what he should do, he reaches an important new rule in therapist self-disclosure: "*reveal yourself to the extent that it will be helpful to your patient; but if you want to stay in practice, have a care about how your self-disclosure will sound to other therapists*" (205). The desire for transparency does not force the therapist into reckless self-disclosure.

Yalom endorses all of Ernest's conclusions about therapist self-disclosure, but he also shows his protagonist's naivete regarding Carol's actions. Ernest tells Paul that her therapy hugs represent "agape, not lust" (221). The truth is that Carol's hugs are examples of neither agape nor lust but rage and revenge. Ernest's misreading of her is necessary for him to remain human, not omniscient; his misreading is also necessary to drive the novel's plot. Readers are interested in flawed human beings, not all-knowing characters.

Yalom complicates the plot when Carol's seductive behavior arouses Ernest. Should the therapist reveal that he is sexually aroused? If so, what effect would his confession have on therapy? He reaches another noteworthy conclusion about therapist self-disclosure. "Perhaps therapists should not share things about which they are heavily conflicted. Best that the therapist first work out those issues in personal therapy. Otherwise the patient gets saddled with the task of working on the therapist's problems" (227).

Carol's first breakthrough in therapy comes when Ernest raises an urgent question for which she is unprepared. If, as she has implied, her marital unhappiness is a replay of her mother's desperate situation, when her husband unexpectedly walked out of their marriage decades earlier, leaving her to raise the children alone, how can Carol break the vicious cycle so that the same grim fate does not befall her own daughter? Unnerved, the weeping Carol rushes out of Ernest's office. Far from seeing the significance of the question, an example of Ernest's clinical strategy of anticipatory regret, she thinks to herself, "*Goddamn him, he's done it again. Why am I letting the bastard get to me?*" (228). Ernest's question proves to be a turning point in her life. Without knowing it, Carol begins acting more compassionately to her children, who sense the change. She also begins thinking about her brother, from whom she has long been estranged. In addition, she becomes aware of a young man, Jess, who, like herself, is Ernest's patient but who holds the therapist in the highest regard.

Eroticized Transference

Carol is not yet ready, though, to give up her revenge plan. She intensifies her seductive behavior, and Ernest, who has studied the published literature on erotic transference, becomes increasingly uncomfortable. Reading one of Freud's essays about treating "women of an elemental passionateness," Ernest concludes that the creator of psychoanalysis had given up on the possibility of treating these patients. "Pessimistic about treating such patients, Freud claimed that the therapist had only two, unacceptable choices: returning the patient's love or being the target of the mortified woman's fury. In either case, Freud said, one must acknowledge failure and withdraw from the case" (251–252).

Ernest's comments are misleading, however, for Freud is not pessimistic about *all* cases of highly erotic transference, only those of a particular kind. Yalom doesn't refer to Freud's essay by name, but it is "Observations on Transference-Love," the last of six papers on technique written between 1911 and 1915. Insightful and masterfully written, the essay focuses on female patients who believe they have fallen in love with their therapist. Freud admits that analysts have not wanted to acknowledge the awkward and embarrassing nature of the problem. "But since we who laugh at other people's failings are not always free from them ourselves, we have not so far been precisely in a hurry to fulfill this task" (*SE*, vol. 12, 159). The six papers on technique were written mainly for psychoanalysts, not for patients or the general public. Freud was always reluctant to write about countertransference, fearing that acknowledging it would give more ammunition to the enemies of psychoanalysis. Freud's most noteworthy observation is that the analyst must guard against destructive countertransference when treating such patients. "He must recognize that the patient's falling in love is induced by the analytic setting and is not to be attributed to the charms of his own person; so that he has no grounds whatever for being proud of such a 'conquest,' as it would be called outside analysis" (160–161). The "outbreak of a passionate demand for love," Freud adds, is "largely the work of resistance" (162).

How should the psychoanalyst respond to a patient's transference love? Deploying his most haunting similes and metaphors, Freud argues that to urge the patient to renounce or repress these feelings would be useless, like using cunning spirits to summon up a spirit from the underworld and then failing to address a single question that might illuminate a dark mystery. But to gratify a patient's craving for love, on the other hand, would be disastrous for treatment. Instead, the analyst must steer between the Scylla of rejection and the Charybdis of gratification. "He must keep firm hold of the transference-love, but treat it as something unreal, as a situation which has to be gone through in the treatment and traced back to its unconscious origins and which must assist in bringing all that is most deeply hidden in the patient's erotic life into her consciousness and therefore under her control" (166).

Freud is confident that psychoanalysts can treat most patients who exhibit intense feelings of transference love, but there is "one class of women," he admits, who are not treatable. This is the class of patients to which Ernest Lash refers, "women of elemental passionateness who tolerate no surrogates." These "children of nature," according to Freud, refuse to "accept the psychical in place of the material" (166–167). Freud saw no hope for these patients. It's unclear how many women Freud believed fell into this category. Yalom has never written about a female patient who failed to be treated successfully because of a highly eroticized transference. Ernest fears that Carol might be one of these patients, but, we must point out, she is hardly a woman of elemental passionateness. Nor is she attracted to her analyst. Rather, sex is for her only a weapon in her arsenal to destroy her husband's—and his analyst's—life.

Wildcat Therapy

Torn between maintaining his professional integrity, which requires him to avoid sexualizing therapy, and continuing his experiment with therapist self-disclosure, which compels him to respond truthfully to Carol's increasingly personal questions about whether he is attracted to her, Ernest finds himself in a dilemma. How can he tell her that he would prefer to be her lover than her therapist? That he wears his best clothes for therapy sessions with her? That she has invaded his waking and sleeping life? Ernest is so troubled by the articles he reads on sexual boundary violations, warning against the therapist's unconscious collusion with the seductive patient, that he resumes a relationship with an acquaintance, an "old friend with whom he had a nonpassionate but sexually satisfying arrangement," in an effort to exorcise Carol from his thoughts. Yalom remarks in *The Gift of Therapy* that "*any* option, including visiting a prostitute, is preferable to the calamitous choice of acting out sexually with patients" (194). Ernest never wavers in his belief that although the desire for the truth has created his dilemma with Carol, the same desire for the truth will help him find a solution to the dilemma. He convinces her that one of her dreams, her revulsion over going to bed with "Baby Doc," the son of the former Haitian dictator Duvalier, represents her desire *not* to go to bed with her analyst.

As Carol begins to suspect that Ernest is more ethical than she thought, Marshal Streider becomes one of her clients. Yalom weaves together the two central strands of his plot, the major plot involving Carol's efforts to lure her patient into a sexual boundary violation and the subplot involving Streider's efforts to locate the con artist who led him into a nonsexual boundary violation. Streider consults a former patient, Julius Jarndyce, the senior partner in a San Francisco law firm. His name recalls the notoriously long court case *Jarndyce and Jarndyce* in Dickens's 1853 novel *Bleak House*. Streider is so distraught that he cannot wait a week to see his former patient. Instead, he is directed to Carol, to whom he unburdens himself, confessing every detail of the scam except his concern about professional ethics, which he is too ashamed to disclose. When Carol presses him on the ethics of therapist-patient financial boundaries, he concedes that "such rules are protective not only of the patient but of the therapist as well" (316). Realizing that her client is in a state of panic, Carol advises Streider to speak to a confidant, a friend or therapist. He has no friends, mistrusts therapists, despite being one himself, and so he enters into a quasi-therapeutic relationship with Carol, who soon guesses that he is Jess's ex-therapist and Ernest's former supervisor, a revelation she can share with no one because she is bound by her profession's rules of confidentiality. Carol makes one final halfhearted effort to seduce Ernest, and he responds with brutal honesty. "Hell will freeze over before I get involved sexually with you. Or with any of my patients!" (324). Only when he acknowledges that he is behaving in his own self-interest does she give up her revenge plan. The argument of self-interest often proves effective in Yalom's world: recall that Breuer uses this motive to convince Nietzsche to accept his proposal for reciprocal treatment.

It's odd that Ernest never thought to ask Carol whether she would violate her own profession's ban on sexual relations between lawyer and client. Lawyer-client sex, like therapist-patient sex, is unethical, mainly because of the inherently unequal power in the relationship, an inequality that makes it impossible for a vulnerable client, like a vulnerable patient, to give genuine consent. The reader cannot imagine Carol, driven to rage in her personal life but always acting on principle in her professional life, would to do anything to violate the ethics of her work.

Several unexpected developments occur in the penultimate session between Carol and Ernest. Ernest insists on speaking first, causing Carol to mumble to herself, "Whose therapy is this, anyway?" He announces that he has not been a good therapist for her; his self-disclosures about being sexually aroused have been countertherapeutic. He should have told her in advance, he adds, about his experimental treatment, which he now believes has failed. Carol objects to Ernest's self-lashing. Speaking both as a lawyer and patient, she rebuts his arguments. She is not yet ready to disclose her identity and her failed revenge plan, but she tells him that perhaps unconsciously she had been testing him throughout therapy, reassuring him that he passed the test. Without violating confidentiality, she asks his advice for treating her new therapist-client, who is burdened by feelings of arrogance, loneliness, and bitterness. Rising to the challenge, Ernest encourages her to help him seek a Nietzschean cosmic perspective. He also recommends existential shock therapy: Carol's client should project himself into the future, to the moment of his death and funeral, and imagine his epitaph. Her client's swindle, Ernest predicts, may prove to be his salvation. The nuanced chapter ends with Carol asking one final time for a paternal hug. "Settle for 'avuncular'?" asks Ernest affectionately, to which she responds, "What's 'avuncular'?"—the same word Trotter has defined for Ernest in the prologue.

The Wounded Healer

Carol is an effective "therapist" for Streider, but she cannot defuse his massive rage, and he is swindled out of another twenty-four thousand dollars by Peter Macondo. Carol doesn't give up on helping Streider, though, just as Ernest has not given up on her. She has several "psychotherapy" sessions with Streider that prove psychologically valuable to both of them. Aided by Ernest's recommendations, Carol functions as Streider's analyst. By catalyzing Streider's healing, she accelerates her own.

Early in *Lying on the Couch* Ernest and Paul discuss Jung's autobiographical *Memories, Dreams, Reflections*. Both characters are dismissive of Jung's concept of the wounded healer. Calling Jung's autobiography "bizarre" and "dishonest," Ernest asks incredulously, "The *patient* ministers to the therapist's wound?" to which Paul responds, "Just imagine the implications of that! It blows your fucking mind!" (98). The reader can reasonably conclude that Ernest and Paul represent Yalom's point of view. If one reads Jung's words carefully, however, the idea of the wounded healer becomes more convincing, particularly when he acknowledges that often the patient "is exactly the right plaster for the doctor's sore spot" (Jung 134). Carol is certainly a wounded patient, but in helping Streider, she functions as a wounded healer. Yalom brings to life in *When Nietzsche Wept* two wounded healers, a physician and a philosopher, each of whom ministers to the other's psychological wounds.

The End of the Novel

Yalom weaves together the various threads of the novel in the final chapter, which contains one surprise. Explaining to Carol his lifelong worry about money, Streider recalls his impoverished childhood, when his father struggled to make a living. "He had a tiny, six-by-six, grocery store on Fifth and R streets in Washington. We lived over the store" (359). It is the same description Yalom gives us in the "Autobiographical Note" about his own immigrant family's hardscrabble existence in a poor neighborhood in Washington, DC. Are Streider's anxieties over money a reflection of his creator's anxieties? We cannot answer this question solely on the basis of *Lying on the Couch*, but lest there be any doubt about the autobiographical connection, Streider relates how one day a customer came into his father's store asking for a pair of work gloves. Pointing to the back room, Streider's father told the customer it would take a few minutes to locate a pair, dashed out the back door, ran to an open market two blocks away, bought a pair of gloves for twelve cents, and then raced back to his store, where he sold the gloves to the customer for fifteen cents. The identical anecdote appears in "A Conversation with Irvin D. Yalom" at the end of *The Schopenhauer Cure*. Streider's preoccupation with money and status represents Yalom's shadow self, an insight that helps us to understand the novelist's ability to identify with all of his characters, including his least sympathetic ones. In *Becoming Myself* Yalom reveals other autobiographical sources of *Lying on the Couch*, including nearly being swindled out of a large amount of money to invest in a company that did not exist.

Carol has benefited from therapy in two ways, first, as Ernest's patient, and second, as Streider's "therapist." She is a changed person at the end of the novel. Grateful that she has been released from a chilling marriage, she is in a promising romantic relationship with a new man, Jess. Will the relationship culminate in remarriage? Yalom doesn't offer any clues, instead allowing his readers to reach their own conclusions. In the novel's last scene, Carol is finally ready for her confession to Ernest. Like Breuer at the end of *When Nietzsche Wept*, she has been holding back a terrible secret. Ernest, who has always suspected that she has concealed something significant from him, smiles "a little smugly" when she mentions she has a confession to make and then responds, in the last words of the novel, "always ready for the truth."

Ernest's experiment with therapist self-disclosure proves to be a resounding success at the end of *Lying on the Couch*. His love for psychotherapy has grown, as has his gratitude. He has faithfully followed Trotter's advice in the prologue to have an open channel to his "shadow," Jung's term for the dark side of the self. Carol has learned trust from her therapy with Ernest, and he has learned from her how to live with his shadow.

The Doctor of Desire

Any discussion of *Lying on the Couch* should mention at least briefly *The Doctor of Desire*, the 1987 novel by the distinguished psychoanalyst and creative writer Allen Wheelis. Like *Lying on the Couch*, *The Doctor of Desire* explores the catastrophic consequences of sexualized therapy, though the latter is a far darker novel than the former. Wheelis explored with unflinching honesty and courage the psychoanalyst's vulnerability to transgressive erotic desire, corrosive intellectual doubt, narcissistic injury, loneliness and isolation, and boredom. Few of Wheelis's colleagues dared to acknowledge in public the hazards of being a psychoanalyst. "Given that words are the bread and butter of psychoanalytic work," Daphne Merkin wrote in her laudatory obituary of Allen Wheelis published in the *New York Times Magazine* on December 30, 2007, "it would seem strange on the face of it that very few practitioners have written elegant or even lucid prose." Merkin cited only a handful of psychoanalysts who stand out in this "fallow field," including Irvin Yalom.

Yalom's Fictional Experiment

Lying on the Couch did not receive as many reviews as *When Nietzsche Wept*, but critics praised its intelligence and satirical wit. The novel is a "marvelous examination of how psychiatrists actually think," *Kirkus Reviews* enthused, "building to a vision of a community healthy and mature enough to confront its deepest and most persistent fears." The reviewer in *Publishers Weekly* commented that "as absorbing as it is, the novel presents the moral or professional blunders of the analysts as the acceptable price of doing business," a reading that is as incorrect as the spelling of the novelist's name: "Arvin D. Yalom." Jonathan Kirsch concludes his review in the *Los Angeles Times* with a coy disclaimer: "The rule of confidentiality that applies to book reviewers no less than psychotherapists prevents me from disclosing exactly how Yalom works out the cat's cradle of plots and subplots. But he manages it with such panache that all of his sleight of hand, as a novelist and a psychiatrist, will be forgiven." In its satirical wit, psychological acumen, and expert storytelling, *Lying on the Couch* demonstrates art's ability to instruct and delight. As Ruthellen Josselson observes, *Lying on the Couch* is Yalom's "most intricately plotted and least overtly pedagogical" novels, "but any student of psychotherapy finds much to challenge his or her thinking about the process" (97). Revenge tale, psychiatric case study, existential fable, and moral exemplum, *Lying on the Couch* is above all a love story about a therapist's devotion and gratitude to his profession. Repaying multiple readings, the novel appeals not only to young psychotherapists, the intended audience, but also to patients, students, educators, and the uncommon reader. It can be read anywhere: in an undergraduate literature, psychology, or ethics classroom; in a graduate psychotherapy program; or at home or in the office while lying on the couch.

Chapter 8

Momma and the Meaning of Life
The "Smoldering Inner Compost Heap" of Creativity

Published in 1999, a decade after *Love's Executioner*, *Momma and the Meaning of Life* returns to "tales of psychotherapy" but with a difference. The new collection, consisting of six stories, is darker and edgier, filled with mournful self-reproof, perhaps because Yalom is a decade older and more aware of life's inevitable disillusions. As in the earlier volume, irony and ambiguity characterize these stories. He never uses a formula in his psychotherapy tales, but he usually comes across as self-deprecating or even self-lacerating. He is almost always caught off guard, as is the reader. The stories reveal guilt over being an "overachiever," as he admits in *Staring at the Sun* (161), at the expense, he fears, of his commitment to family, friends, and patients. Life-affirming but not always heartwarming, some of the tales cast additional light on earlier and later writings, offering fascinating backstories or anticipating themes in later ones. Abounding in valuable therapeutic insights, the stories deserve a wide readership. Yalom presents vexing human dilemmas that cannot be resolved despite a wealth of clinical wisdom. Paradoxically, he appears more interested in his failures than successes, perhaps because the former represent cautionary tales fraught with moral ambiguity.

Whose Dream?
"Momma and the Meaning of Life"

The twelve-page title story opens and closes with the same dream. Dying in a hospital, the first-person narrator springs from bed, travels to an amusement park, and enters a House of Horrors. He sees his mother amid a group of onlookers, waves his arms, and, before being enveloped by the darkness, calls out to her, "Momma! How'd I do, Momma? How'd I do?"

Waking up from the dream, Yalom is transported back to his own childhood in Washington, DC, where he reflects on his conflicted relationship with his mother, who died ten years earlier. The son continues to yearn for his mother's approval despite his abiding anger toward her. "She was vain, controlling, intrusive, suspicious, spiteful, highly opinionated, and abysmally ignorant (but intelligent—even I could see that). Never, not once, do I remember sharing a warm moment with her. Never once did I take pride in her or think, I'm so glad she's my momma. She had a poisonous tongue and a spiteful word about everyone—except my father and sister" (3).

Questions abound. If Yalom is a reliable narrator, and if his relationship with his mother, his primary caregiver, was so problematic, how was he able to form more positive relationships with women later in life? Raised by a barely good-enough mother, how did he develop his extraordinary empathy and hopefulness? Why does he address her as "Momma" when there was so little genuine love in the relationship? Yalom's bitterness toward his mother—"How many times I prayed, Please, Dad, please, just this once, punch her out!"(4)—recalls his plea for his father to "pop" her in *Love's Executioner* (157). How was Yalom able to avoid becoming like his mother?

A Metaphor for Yalom's Creativity

More so than any of his earlier fictional or nonfictional books, "Momma and the Meaning of Life" reveals Yalom's fierce determination to become a writer, paying tribute to the philosopher who has had the greatest impact on him. "We need art, Nietzsche said, lest we perish from the truth. Hence I consider creativity as the golden path and have turned my entire life, all my experiences, all my imaginings, into some smoldering inner compost heap out of which I try to fashion, from time to time, something new and beautiful" (6).

And yet there's a disturbing irony here. The final story in *Love's Executioner* describes Yalom's efforts to fuse Marvin the man with the netherworld of his dreams, but an even greater distance between conscious and unconscious selves appears in "Momma and the Meaning of Life." Yalom has devoted his entire life, both as therapist and writer, to being a dream tinkerer. "I learned how to tame dreams, to take them apart, to put them together. I know how to squeeze out dream secrets" (6). Yalom's own dreams, however, suggest that he has unconsciously devoted himself to a different goal—"winning the approval of my dead momma" (6). Expert at fusing his patients' outer and inner worlds, he is himself in need of self-integration. His patients would be surprised to discover that he speaks from wrenching personal experience when he reveals that "abused children often find it hard to disentangle themselves from their dysfunctional families" (5).

There are other ironies in the story. Uneducated, Ruth Yalom could not understand her son's books, though she did appreciate them as material objects, his offspring. Losing her vision in old age, she nevertheless carried his books in a shopping bag, at one point removing them tenderly and fondling them. The proud mother makes a shrine of the books. The final irony occurs at the end of the story, when his mother tells him that he has misunderstood the dream in which he asks how he did in life, the same dream on which the story opens. How can she call into question *his* dream, Yalom indignantly wonders. She has the last words in the story. "That dream was *not* your dream, Sonny. It was *my* dream. Mothers get to have dreams too" (13). The joke is on Yalom, but what exactly is the meaning of the joke? That he has never imagined that his mother also had unfulfilled dreams? That the writer cannibalizes others' dreams and stories? These questions are part of the smoldering inner compost heap from which the writer fashions something new and beautiful.

Nancy Andreasen, who earned a PhD in English literature and was a professor of English at the University of Iowa for five years before changing careers and becoming a neuropsychiatrist, argues in her 2005 book *The Creating Brain: The Neuroscience of Genius* that creativity is highly intuitive, often arising from unconscious or dreamlike mental states (78). Andreasen's view is consistent with Yalom's. The smoldering inner compost heap is a vivid metaphor of Yalom's creativity, his ability to tap into early anxieties, fears, and desires, on both a conscious and unconscious level, which he then transmutes into artful stories. The need for maternal approval in this volume of psychotherapy tales compels him to acknowledge truths that oppose his lifelong efforts to distance himself from his primary caregiver. Like Philip Roth's Portnoy, Yalom confesses that his mother, whom he always thought was wrong in her judgments, was often right—and that she is, indeed, a central part of his existence.

Falling from Grace: "Travels with Paula"

"Travels with Paula" begins with a statement made by John Whitehorn, Yalom's mentor at Johns Hopkins, who urged his students to listen to and learn from their patients: "To grow wise you must remain a student" (15). Yalom then describes his lifelong efforts to follow that advice. Suffering from advanced cancer, Paula West is an exceptional patient and teacher, a woman who inspired Yalom to create a psychotherapy group for dying patients. The idea is well established now, but it was unprecedented in 1973. The group was remarkably successful, demonstrating that therapy improved both the quality and longevity of dying cancer patients' lives. The group succeeded by offering "presence" to the dying, allowing them to feel connected with others. Paula's grace touched Yalom's life, but then their relationship soured, and he fell from grace, leaving him saddened and bereft at the end, and leaving the reader to wonder whether he was right in concluding that he had acted in bad faith toward her.

Yalom captures Paula's special insights and courage, beginning with her opening statement to him: "I have terminal cancer. But *I am not a cancer patient*" (18). The two of them talked about life, death, spirituality, peace, and transcendence. Mostly they talked about death, Yalom notes, and then he presents us with an arresting sentence: "Each week four of us, not two, met in my office—Paula and I, her death and my own" (19). He credits her with learning to befriend and demythologize death, teaching him that what patients most fear is not dying but the isolation that accompanies it. One of her many insights is that physicians do not understand the importance of connection to their dying patients. "Why can't they realize that the very moment they have nothing else to offer is the moment they are most needed?" (20).

Paula also teaches Yalom how her deep religious faith has helped her to live with cancer. An Episcopal priest enabled her to escape despair and affirm a new purpose in life. "Familiar with the wise aphorism of Nietzsche, the Antichrist, 'He who has a "why" can put up with any "how,"'" the priest reframed her suffering. 'Your cancer is your cross,' he told her. 'Your suffering is your ministry'" (21). Yalom accepts without protest his assigned role in her divine plans: he was the object of her ministry, and he did everything he could to allow her to educate him, even if he could not share her religious faith. Paula's intense spirituality doesn't convert Yalom into a believer, but he is impressed with her belief that it is essential to prepare for death. Upon learning that her cancer had spread to her spine and that she had little time left, she wrote a farewell letter to her thirteen-year-old son that moved Yalom to tears. "In her final paragraph she reminded him that the lungs in the human fetus do not breathe, nor do its eyes see. Thus, the embryo is being prepared for an existence it cannot yet imagine. 'Are we not, too,' Paula suggested to her son, 'being prepared for an existence beyond our ken, beyond even our dreams?'" (23).

Paula is, along with Yalom, the driving force behind the creation of the psychotherapy group, which she aptly calls the "Bridge Group," and she appoints herself the group's spiritual consultant. She initiates important rituals, such as ending each meeting staring silently at a candle. "'Let's move closer together,' she said, stretching out her hands to the member on either side of her. 'Look at the candle and meditate for a few moments in silence'" (31). Yalom points out that he and Paula needed each other in ways that transcended a professional relationship. He remembers, "Paula filled me with light and . . . I was her rock, the haven for which she searched before we two were lucky enough to have found each another" (33).

In a footnote to his 1980 textbook *Existential Psychotherapy*, Yalom reports that a cancer patient recently remarked that Elisabeth Kübler-Ross's stage theory of dying was "skewed to a cachectic hospital population and overlooked the 'golden period' that occurs if a patient has time to assimilate his confrontation with death" (37). The patient, Yalom discloses in *Momma and the Meaning of Life*, was Paula. "She was deeply critical of Elizabeth [sic] Kübler-Ross, medicine's high priestess of death, who, failing to recognize the golden stage, had developed a negativistic clinical approach. Kübler-Ross's 'stages' of dying—anger, denial, bargaining, depression, acceptance—never failed to arouse Paula's ire. She insisted, and I am certain that she was correct, that such rigid categorizing of emotional responses leads to a dehumanization of both patient and doctor" (22).

Yalom, too, comes to arouse Paula's ire, though for different reasons. As the psychotherapy group for terminally ill breast cancer patients became well known in the Stanford community, Yalom was unable to spend as much time with Paula as before. Blaming himself for her disappointment, Yalom explains that he was "consumed with the goal of succeeding in the academic world, and my frenzied schedule of research, grant applications, lecturing, teaching, and writing limited my contact with Paula. Was I afraid of getting too close to her?" (31). Not necessarily, a reader might respond, but Yalom is not eager to absolve himself from guilt. In one of his pithiest sentences, he confesses that the success of the group was tied to his own professional success. "In short, it was time to promote it and to get promoted" (33). Paula was disappointed with Yalom when he applied for a grant that would evaluate the effectiveness of his approach to terminally ill breast cancer patients. Quick to indict himself, he calls attention to his use of first-person pronouns to describe a project that was inspired by Paula. Though he gave her full credit for her involvement with the group and made sure she was well compensated, his efforts to establish the psychotherapy group as a research project led to the corruption of their love.

The love was further eroded by a new and inexperienced female cotherapist whom Paula detested. Additionally, Paula resented a cancer specialist who belittled her comment, expressed during a two-day workshop mandated for federal funding of research projects, that "courage" and "spiritual depth" were accurate predictors of a person's psychological adjustment to cancer. Yalom found himself in an impossible dilemma, forced to choose between an inspiring but uncompromising patient, on the one hand, and his respected colleagues, on the other. Paula accused Yalom of "selling out to the bureaucracy" and soon disappeared from the group—and his life.

Yalom cannot stop thinking about Paula, however, and he wonders whether he could have done anything to repair their relationship. He has a number of surprises in store for the reader before ending the story, including the fact that Paula outlived all thirty members of the experimental Bridge Group and all eighty-six members of the control group. Several years pass, and when Yalom discovers that she is still alive but now suffering from lupus, he telephones her, and she invites him to lunch at her home. True to character, she now leads a lupus self-help group. Amid their reminiscences over the early months of the therapy group, a golden period for both of them, he is dismayed to hear that she has been "medically blacklisted" in the community because of her belief that all the cancer doctors who treated her were incompetent. She is also convinced that the medicine prescribed to her by her cancer doctors was responsible for her lupus. She now threatens to file malpractice suits against all of her cancer doctors.

Unable to believe her accusations, which strike him as signs of paranoia, Yalom once again finds himself in an impossible situation, forced to choose between her strong beliefs and his own. Empathizing with her dilemma, he urges her to write a "softer" letter to the medical board, "honest but softer," so that the physicians will receive only a reprimand rather than a license forfeiture. "All this, of course, was in bad faith. No medical board in the world was going to take her letter seriously" (49). She thanks him for his good advice, but he is struck by the irony that he has been acting in bad faith. Yalom's readers may disagree. The advice has been well intentioned, designed to preserve Paula's dignity while at the same time allowing her to do minimal damage to others.

In concluding that he could see only one way to respond to Paula, "to consider her a highly disturbed individual and treat her—'treat' in the dark, false sense of the word, in the sense of 'handling,'" Yalom recognizes that this was precisely the way he and his mother had interacted. "My mother and I, though loving one another [an admission he never makes in the preceding story] had never spoken directly, heart to heart, as two people reaching out with clean hands and clear minds. We had always 'treated' each other, spoken past each other, each of us fearing, controlling, deceiving the other" (48–50).

Yalom's relationship with Paula reminds us of the physician-philosopher relationship in *When Nietzsche Wept*. Like the fictional Nietzsche, Paula cannot compromise. Her insights into death and dying are breathtaking, almost Nietzschean, but she has many blind spots. Yalom has great admiration for Paula, but he must act guardedly toward her. Yalom and Paula demonstrate shifting roles and reciprocal healing, as we see in *When Nietzsche Wept*, and the importance of the clinical relationship, but therapist and patient have different agendas. They do everything they can to bridge the distance between them, but both feel betrayed and misunderstood by the other, as do Breuer and Nietzsche. All four characters speak past each other. And yet, more positively, Yalom and Paula make a difference in each other's life, as do the fictional Breuer and Nietzsche. One suspects that if Paula read the story, she would agree that Yalom was as fair in describing her point of view as he was in describing his own. Capturing her presence and luminosity, Yalom demonstrates, as his mentor John Whitehorn urged, his ability to learn from a patient.

"Makin' a Lot Out of Nuthin'": "Southern Comfort"

As Yalom waggishly notes in *Inpatient Group Psychotherapy*, many readers of his book mistake the title to be *im*patient group therapy (xii). We see Yalom's own impatience in "Southern Comfort," a story that conveys the limits of inpatient group psychotherapy and the perils of therapeutic hubris. We also see his remarkable ability, both as therapist and storyteller, for "makin' a lot out of nuthin," in the expressive words of Magnolia, an unkempt, obese seventy-year-old black woman who comes to life in this brief psychotherapy tale. The story demonstrates Yalom's belief that everything is grist for the therapist's mill, psychotherapy chaff winnowed into literary wheat.

Yalom establishes the tone and mood of "Southern Comfort" in the opening sentences of the story. "I put in my time. Five years," words that imply that he was in prison, either as an inmate or security guard. Only in the third sentence do we realize he describes a hospital setting. "For five years I led a daily therapy group on a psychiatric ward" (53). One can hardly imagine the author of an esteemed textbook on inpatient group psychotherapy expressing a more cynical judgment. Adding credibility to the story is that he offers an *insider's* perspective. Why would therapists subject themselves to the nightmarish landscape of inpatient groups—"the continual rapid turnover of members; the frequent psychotic outbursts; the conning, manipulative members; the patients burned out by twenty years of depression or schizophrenia who were never going to get better; the tangible level of despair in the room" (55). Yalom reserves the worst for the end. "But the real killer, the ball-breaker in this work, was the hospital and insurance industry bureaucracy" (55). After establishing the impossibility of the clinical situation, Yalom then asks how healers maintain their sanity. He has a simple answer: "Learn to cultivate hypocrisy" (57).

"Southern Comfort" is neither a feel-good psychotherapy tale nor a story that would be reassuring to a patient about to be hospitalized for a psychological disorder. If Yalom defined himself metaphorically in his first collection of psychotherapy tales as love's executioner, he seems ready in his second collection to wield a literal ax and decapitate everyone associated with inpatient group psychotherapy, including himself. Boredom, not rage, led to Yalom's decision to abandon inpatient group psychotherapy. But he didn't give it up entirely; every three months, when new psychiatric residents arrived, he would bicycle from his cozy book-lined office in the Stanford University Medical School to the hospital, a Dantesque House of Horrors, where for a few days he would impart his clinical expertise to a new crop of students.

Yalom's literary challenge is to depict the human stories of inpatient group psychotherapy in a lively, thoughtful, *honest* way. After noting the near-impossibility of the situation, he introduces five patients to the reader, allowing himself no more than a couple of descriptive sentences for each one. Martin is an elderly man confined to a wheelchair because of a muscle-wasting disease. Dorothy is a paraplegic as a result of a suicidal leap from a third-story window. Magnolia cannot move her legs for reasons that remain a medical mystery. Rosa and Carol are two anorexic young women who resemble concentration camp victims. The story focuses on a single therapy session. The therapeutic goal, Yalom informs the patients, is to help them identify aspects of their lives they wish to change. The emphasis will be on here-and-now therapy, which is what works best for group therapy. Yalom keeps reminding himself of his mantra, one that he will soon forget: "*small is beautiful. Small is beautiful*—small goals, small successes" (60).

Yalom's main focus is on Magnolia. "I was struck, when she introduced herself, by the way she held my gaze with her creamy brown eyes and by the dignity in her soft Southern drawl" (59–60). The title of the story obviously refers to Magnolia, but we know that Yalom is an ironist, and thus we cannot be sure whether therapy will be comforting or discomforting to her. Nor can we predict the nature of Yalom's relationship with her. How much Southern comfort will he experience? The few details we learn about Magnolia suggest that she is a devout Christian with a big heart and soul who would rather help others than ask for help herself. Yalom discovers from the nurses that although she is quiet and patient, she is often agitated, tearing at imaginary insects crawling on her skin. When Yalom asks her what she would like to learn from the group, she replies, "Ah'd like to learn to listen better in this group" (62), though she is already a good listener. Self-effacing to a fault, Magnolia deflects all compliments.

Magnolia entrances Yalom, evoking maternal feelings in him—more affirmative feelings than one might expect after reading "Momma and the Meaning of Life." Maternal loss pervades "Southern Comfort": his mother had died three weeks before the therapy session, and Magnolia reveals to the group that her own mother had died a year ago tomorrow. Yalom finds himself in need of "Magnolia-comfort," and he reflects on a line from a Judy Collins's song, "Pack up your sorrows and give them all to me" (68), an offer that he finds comforting. Suddenly we wonder, who comforts whom in this therapy session?

Like "Travels with Paula," "Southern Comfort" affirms the need for reciprocal healing, therapists and patients engaged in a mutual therapeutic process. Yalom is not exactly a wounded healer, but his mother's death has left him bereft, as his need for Magnolia-comfort indicates. He has mythologized her into an Earth Mother whom he invokes for protection and comfort. He is aware of this countertransference issue, however, and we assume that this awareness will allow him to control his own needs while attending to the group.

Magnolia has devoted her entire life to helping others, and Yalom's challenge is to find a way for the group to help her, a woman who has raised a son and fifteen foster children without assistance. Perhaps the other patients can help Magnolia learn to complain, Yalom states to the group. She resists the recommendation, though she admits that her own mother also felt that she, Magnolia, too often put herself last. Yalom urges her to practice complaining, and she complies by expressing bitter disappointment over never becoming a teacher. The other group members chime in, pointing out that although Magnolia never had an opportunity for an education, having to raise her seven brothers and sisters almost alone, she did, in effect, become a teacher to her son and foster children. Magnolia appreciates the group's support, and Yalom adds that she has indeed become a teacher after all. He then proudly glances at the psychiatry residents, pleased with his comment, which was a "gem." Pride cometh before fall, we think—and then disaster strikes.

Yalom's insistence on Magnolia's self-disclosure has opened a Pandora's Box of woeful complaints, releasing all of her demons. She unleashes a torrent of resentments and criticisms, including bad-mouthing for the first time in her life the husband who had deserted her. Yalom feels disoriented and alarmed by her weeping and scratching at invisible insects. He confesses that he had taken the lid off Magnolia's troubles, "but for once I did not want to look inside" (72). The therapy session ends positively, however, with Yalom praising the group members' hard work. They had done what Yalom wanted them to do, engaging with the discussion and making supportive comments of each other. Yalom praises Magnolia's hard work, and she accepts her compliment, replying, "Ah understan', Doctah. Ah understan' real good" (74).

Nevertheless, Yalom feels guilty and fraudulent because, nearly losing control of the session, he had been forced to improvise radically. He doubts whether his advice to encourage Magnolia to complain would help her. "Her symptoms—the inexplicable paralysis of her legs, the hallucinations of insects on her skin, her delusion that a conspiracy was behind the insect infestation of her home—were grave and far beyond the reach of psychotherapy" (76). He judges himself guilty of breaking a fundamental rule in psychotherapy: never strip patients of their defenses unless you can offer them something more positive. Magnolia had been a victim of his vanity, he concludes, mainly because of his desire for her to be his mother. Seduced by his therapeutic hubris, his grandiose rescue fantasy, and by his countertransference desire to crave motherly support, he had refused to have a "real encounter with Magnolia—the flesh-and-blood person, not the image I had imposed on her" (79).

"Southern Comfort" demonstrates Yalom's gift for making a lot out of nothing. Readers sympathize with the plight of a therapist who does his best under difficult circumstances and who is far more self-critical than most mental health professionals would be in his situation. He confesses to a litany of flaws—hungering for approval, feeling panic-stricken when Magnolia refuses to respond to his request to open up, and then becoming unnerved when she begins to wail and claw at her skin. Yalom is aware of the complexity of motivation, including the ways in which a character's confession of vanity may be a subtle manipulation of the reader's sympathy. He individualizes the five members of the group, conveying their vulnerability and dignity. The patients always strike us as human rather than a textbook compilation of symptoms. The contrast between Yalom's outer dialogue with the patients and psychiatry residents and inner dialogue with the readers highlights the public and private drama of inpatient group psychotherapy. And the story's evocative title captures Magnolia's soft Southern drawl, her magical spell over Yalom, her supportiveness of the group, and perhaps the legendary Southern liqueur—though it's gin, not Southern Comfort, that ruined Magnolia's marriage.

Reason versus Treason?
"Seven Advanced Lessons in the Therapy of Grief"

The longest and most emotionally charged story in *Momma and the Meaning of Life*, "Seven Advanced Lessons in the Therapy of Grief" is, as Yalom points out in the afterword to the Perennial edition, an "undistorted account of treatment (aside from omission of prosaic details and for disguised identity) containing a myriad of psychotherapy themes. The therapist as student and, conversely, the patient as teacher, a theme introduced in 'Travels with Paula,' is more fully developed in this story" (250). It is Yalom's most self-disclosing story in the volume. For readers who have lost a beloved spouse, "Seven Advanced Lessons in the Therapy of Grief" may be the only story that contradicts their own experiences of grief.

Irene is a surgeon with little respect for psychiatry, but after she discovers that her husband, Jack, has inoperable brain cancer, she requests to begin psychotherapy with Yalom. He's not eager; she's a close friend of two of his own closest friends, and he knows that boundaries would be messy. He warily accepts the case, partly because he and a colleague have recently finished three years of empirical research on spousal bereavement. "As a bereavement hotshot," Yalom quips, "how could I, in good conscience, withhold myself from Irene?" His vanity is further stoked when she tells him that she has followed his work and believes that he's the only one smart enough who can treat him. "The perfect plug for my socket of vanity" (85).

Seventy-one pages long, "Seven Advanced Lessons in the Therapy of Grief" contains so many fascinating clinical and biographical insights that one could easily write a commentary twice as long. The intensity of the patient's rage, bitterness, and guilt is greater than in any previous story, and Yalom senses that if she did not have a young daughter to care for, she would have committed suicide. The therapist-patient relationship is emotionally charged and constantly changing during the five-year, twice-a-week treatment.

Irene vows to form no more attachments after her brother's death, when she was twenty, lest she be hurt again; but she breaks the promise to marry her childhood boyfriend, Jack. After his death, which occurs at the end of the first year of therapy, when she is in her mid-forties, she once again vows to form no further attachments. Nor does she wish to form an emotional attachment to Yalom, since he, too, may die when she is in treatment, leaving her once again forsaken.

Yalom divides his story into seven lessons, each illustrating a clinical insight. Many of the lessons contain multiple insights, some advanced, others fundamental but worth repeating. Lesson One emphasizes that the therapist must embody the voice of reason. Throughout therapy Yalom confronts Irene's irrationality, marveling at her "dual nature," her extraordinary lucidity flanked by preposterous irrationality" (92). Lesson Two explores Irene's belief that only the bereaved can treat the bereaved, an idea that Yalom rejects. Lesson Three focuses on Irene's fury at Yalom for attempting to detach her from Jack and for presuming to understand her. Lesson Four looks at the "black ooze," Irene's metaphor for grief rage. She is convinced that each time Yalom approaches the black ooze, he will either abandon her or die. To demonstrate that the black ooze will not destroy him or their relationship, Yalom institutes a new therapy rule: whenever Irene explodes at him, they automatically schedule an extra session that week. Lesson Five, neatly summarized by the expression "reason versus treason," returns to the question of love and loss. "What I called rejoining life, she called betrayal of love. What I called detachment from the dead, she called abandoning of her love" (127). Lesson Six, which heralds a new stage of therapy occurring during the fourth year, affirms therapist and patient as fellow travelers, embarked on the same life journey. Lesson Seven involves the process of letting go, which may be particularly challenging when therapist and patient have worked closely together for several years.

A turning point occurs when Irene, vexed by Yalom's failure to understand her grief, asks him to read an article by the Russian poet Joseph Brodsky titled "On Grief and Reason" published in *The New Yorker*. Arguing that Robert Frost is a darker poet than most readers have recognized, Brodsky discusses a long narrative poem called "Home Burial" that depicts a farmer and his wife grieving differently over their son's death. The father upbraids his wife for clinging to grief, for mourning inconsolably. It's time to end grief, he says condescendingly to her. Enthralled by the poem, which he recognizes holds the key to Irene's inner life, Yalom concludes that "Home Burial" portrays the bitter parental clash that must have occurred in Irene's home after her brother's death. Yalom's misreading enrages Irene. "Her astonished stare was that of a teacher facing some dunderhead of a pupil as she wondered how he could ever have been promoted to her class" (124). Too stunned to speak, Irene finally hisses, "The farmer and the wife in that poem are not my mother and father. *They're us—you and me.*" Reeling from the mistake, Yalom quickly recovers. It's "*I*," he asks, "whose words continually give offense? And it is *I* who tries to force himself between you and your grief? And certainly *I* who blocks you at the door and tries to force grief medicine down your throat?" (125). Irene nods in agreement and begins to weep, the first time in three years of therapy that she has wept openly in his presence. "I handed her a tissue. And took one for myself. She reached out for my hand. We were back together again" (125).

Significantly, the therapeutic breakthrough is a result of a poem. Attuned as closely to the world of literature as he is to the world of therapy, Yalom immediately thinks of a Thomas Hardy poem he has cited earlier in his writings: "If a way to the Better there be, it exacts a full look at the Worst" (125–126). "Seven Advanced Lessons in the Therapy of Grief" offers Yalom's own full look at the worst, the paralyzing death anxiety that compels the bereaved to turn away from life. Yalom repeatedly cites poets, fiction writers, painters, and sculptors to elaborate on clinical insights. The references are second nature to Yalom, expressed easily and spontaneously.

There's no question where Yalom stands on the question of reason versus treason. Irene slowly learns to accept his advice, detach herself from her dead husband, and, at the end of the story, fall in love with another man, Kevin, whose wife had died a year earlier. Everything in "Seven Advanced Lessons in the Therapy of Grief" espouses this reasonable attitude toward grief. Yalom doesn't refer to himself in the story as love's executioner or disillusioner, perhaps because he doesn't wish to repeat himself. Instead, he reminds us of his own empirical research on bereavement. "I was taking a well-established, sound position, namely, that the work of mourning consists of gradually detaching oneself from the one who died and redirecting one's energy toward others" (96).

For additional support, Yalom cites Freud's 1917 essay "Mourning and Melancholy," which remains after a century the most influential theoretical statement about the mourner's need to detach himself or herself from the world of the dead in order to redirect attention to the world of the living. "Reality-testing has shown," writes Freud, in one of his most famous sentences, "that the loved object no longer exists, and it proceeds to demand that all libido shall be withdrawn ['decathected'] from its attachments to that object" (*SE*, vol. 14, 244).

The problem with the binary "reason versus treason" is not that bereavement is never-ending—grief diminishes over time for most people—but that it fails to suggest that the bereft may find ways to remain connected with the dead while forming new connections with the living. As J. William Worden observes in the third edition of *Grief Counseling and Grief Therapy*, "people do not decathect from the dead but find ways to develop 'continuing bonds' with the deceased" (35). One of the tasks of mourning, Worden adds, "is to find a place for the deceased that will enable the mourner to be connected with the deceased but in a way that will not preclude him or her from getting on with life. We need to find ways to memorialize the dead, that is, to remember the dead loved one—keeping them with us but still going on with life" (35).

The "continuing bonds" approach to grief is strikingly true in my own life. After the death of my first wife in 2004, I began teaching courses and writing books on love and loss, death education, end-of-life memoirs, and spousal-loss memoirs. I did not anticipate I would do this when Barbara was dying, but teaching and writing about death became my major way to deal with loss. Five years after her death, I began dating, and in 2011 I married a lovely woman whom I had known for several years, Julie. Photos of Barbara and Julie surround me in my office at the university and at home. Part of our home is a shrine to the deceased, both Barbara and Julie's parents, but Julie and I have not attempted to freeze time, as Yalom notes about Miss Havisham in *Great Expectations*.

I suspect Irene would have appreciated Phyllis R. Silverman's statement about the central paradox of bereavement: "We cannot live in the past or carry on as if the deceased is still a part of our life, but we cannot let go of the relationship, either—in a sense trying to act as if the past did not exist. The bereaved find ways to construct connections to their dead loved ones that are both comforting and sustaining" (38). Irene would have also appreciated a statement made by the playwright Robert Anderson that I quote in *Writing Widowhood*: "death ends a life, but it does not end a relationship, which struggles toward some resolution which it never finds." As I observe, "Widowhood memoirists continue their bonds with the deceased while simultaneously forging new bonds with the living" (7). Continuing bonds also helps to explain, as I suggest in *Dying in Character*, why dying authors feel compelled to write end-of-life memoirs: dying writers feel a need to forge a relational bond with readers that will survive the writer's death. Indeed, Irene tells Yalom near the end of "Seven Advanced Lessons in the Therapy of Grief" that she wants him to write about their therapy together. "You've learned from our work together," she remarks, "and *I don't want it to end with you.*" Noting Yalom's raised eyebrows in response to her words, she adds, "Yes, yes, I have finally gotten it. It's sunk in. You're not going to be around forever" (144). Writing captures the presence between therapist and patient, just as it does for authors of end-of-life memoirs.

Like the other stories in *Momma and the Meaning of Life*, "Seven Advanced Lessons in the Therapy of Grief" leaves us with questions. Would Irene's therapy have been less tumultuous if Yalom had affirmed a continuing bonds approach to her grief? Would he have been receptive to such an approach had he lost his beloved wife and tried to remain connected with her while forming new attachments? These questions do not diminish the power of the story. Yalom reveals the traps, tests, and minefields when treating the bereft, along with the black ooze that may tar patient and therapist alike. He succeeds in contrasting his own personality, that of an existential rationalist, with that of Irene, a grief-stricken romantic. As often as not, therapy sessions resembled a wrestling match, but both prevailed at the end, as did the unique therapy based on an egalitarian, mutually transparent relationship.

Unlike "Southern Comfort," where Yalom felt fraudulent for improvising in therapy, Irene convinces him that his willingness to improvise greatly helped her. "Lately I have found myself proclaiming, 'The good therapist must create a new therapy for each patient.' That is an extreme position, more radical than even Jung's suggestion, many years ago, that we create a new therapy *language* for each patient. But radical positions for these radical times" (151).

Overearnest Countertransference: "Double Exposure"

Following the Sturm und Drang of "Seven Advanced Lessons in the Therapy of Grief," Yalom closes *Momma and the Meaning of Life* with two lighter fictional stories involving Ernest Lash, the therapist who first appeared in *Lying on the Couch*. Yalom resurrects Ernest because he is a compelling persona, an iconoclastic existential psychiatrist like himself, committed to an authentic, mutually transparent therapist-patient relationship. Ernest continues to find himself in awkward or compromising situations that reveal the ironies and ambiguities of Yalom's approach to therapy.

Yalom calls "Double Exposure" a "what if story." As he explains in the afterword, years ago he routinely audiotaped the therapy sessions of a patient who had a two-hour commute to his office. She would receive the tape at the end of each session so that she could listen to it on the way to the next session. Once he forgot to give her the tape, and when she returned for it fifteen minutes later, the recording accidentally contained his therapy dictation of the hour. The dictation contained nothing unsettling, but what if it had revealed disturbing countertransference material that the therapist did not wish to disclose to the patient? "This 'what if' is the fictional scaffolding upon which the events and dreams of this tale are draped" (253).

Countertransference remains perhaps the trickiest problem in psychodynamic psychotherapy, particularly for therapists who may have trouble empathizing with a patient. Ernest find himself in this situation in "Double Exposure." He has been treating Myrna for four months, but he's frustrated by her lack of progress. She is also frustrated. Unlike her last two therapists, who listened to her in stony silence, distant and uninvolved, Ernest actively engages her, but she resists his efforts to focus on the here-and-now relationship. Despairing over her life and experiencing a midlife crisis at the age of thirty-five, she uses the therapy hour mainly to complain about her existence, including the $150 each therapy session costs her. She is not pleased when, in response to her repeated questions about how she can find a suitable man to date, Ernest impatiently makes a harsh and inappropriate comment: "Do you see 'Dating Bureau' on my T-shirt?" (161). Myrna's frustration turns into rage when she listens to his taped comments. "I feel demeaned," Ernest confesses to his tape recorder. "Nothing I do is good enough for her. Presses so many of my buttons that there's got to be something of my mother in this. Every time I ask her about our therapy relationship, she gives me that wary look as though I'm coming on to her. Am I? Not a whisper of it when I check into my feelings" (162). He then contradicts himself by referring to her "great-looking chest," imagining that he is "popping those buttons" but then worrying about staring at her breasts.

He also discloses other feelings that enrage Myrna, including her tendency toward whining and her lack of tenderness and softness.

Ernest had taped these comments to present the case to his countertransference seminar, during which Yalom satirizes contrasting classical and contemporary views of this crucial topic. On one end of the spectrum is Fritz Werner, an elderly orthodox psychoanalyst who was hired to chair the formerly leaderless seminar that has lately become contentious. Yalom reserves some of his most trenchant criticism for Werner, who is perceived by the younger therapists as arrogant and elitist, out of touch with the realities of contemporary therapy. Unlike the other therapists in the seminar, Werner sees wealthy patients for years, doesn't accept insurance, and therefore has no worries about the interference of managed care. In Ernest's felicitous words, Werner maintains the outdated position of "immaculate perception," the belief in the analyst's complete objectivity.

Ernest is at the other end of the countertransference spectrum. "Honesty above all. A devout skeptic in all other matters, Ernest believed with fundamentalist fervor in the healing power of honesty. His catechism called for honesty—but tempered, selective honesty" (164). Rejecting the classical position of analytic objectivity and neutrality, Ernest cites Yalom's favorite philosopher. "It's all interpretation. As Nietzsche knew a century ago" (175). Evoking Freud's *Totem and Taboo*, a world where mutinous sons rise up against the Oedipal father, Yalom suggests that the history of psychoanalysis is a history of implacable warfare. There is a glint in Werner's eye as he "relished the uprising, the spectacle of grown siblings suspending their rivalry and uniting in a joint patricidal campaign!" (175). Werner and Ernest may be on opposite ends of the countertransference spectrum, but Yalom never reduces either to caricature. Werner's criticisms of Ernest are largely accurate. Ernest has committed an egregious therapeutic error, one that will destroy therapy if left uncorrected. Werner faults Ernest not for having angry feelings but for therapeutic "incontinency," expressing those feelings through his sarcastic T-shirt comment.

Ernest finds himself in a compromising situation when Myrna hears on the audiotape his raw feelings about her. Listening to the tape while driving to her next therapy session, she screams out her response: "Asshole!" Myrna's fury reflects her feelings toward her former husband. Like Carol Astrid in *Lying on the Couch*, Myrna plots against her therapist, thinking: "The bastard!" Tellingly, four of Yalom's female patients—Carol, Irene in "Seven Advanced Lessons in the Therapy of Grief," Myrna in "Double Exposed," and, as we shall see, Pam in *The Schopenhauer Cure*—are all predisposed to rage, particularly toward their therapists. No one "does rage" better than Yalom—and no writer depicts more comically a female patient exacting revenge on a clueless male therapist.

The humor of "Double Exposure" arises from Myrna's decision to play back in therapy Ernest's countertransferential feelings without explaining the source of her knowledge. She suddenly develops a new assertiveness and directness, raising rhetorical questions to Ernest that feel like punches to his gut. "You really don't like me, do you?" (167). Insisting on mutual honesty, she asks him whether he finds her boring. Later she demands to know whether he regards her as *whining*, the word that appears on the therapy tape. Myrna's boldness continues in the next session. Ernest praises her therapeutic progress but feels defensive when she demands to know whether he regards her as attractive. "*I'm being crucified*, Ernest whimpered to himself. His worst nightmare about the here-and-now had come to pass" (186). Ernest finds himself in the same situation toward Myrna as his younger counterpart does in *Lying on the Couch*, forced to acknowledge sexual feelings toward a patient who is trying to wound him. In this case, however, Ernest has only himself to blame. Myrna enjoys seeing Ernest on the defensive, on the ropes, reeling from her verbal exchanges, yet she begrudgingly admits that he does his best to maintain an authentic relationship with her. She never reveals to him the secret of the dictation tape, but hearing about his countertransference proves to be a turning point in her therapy, allowing her to make important changes in her life.

"Geh Gesunter Heit": "The Hungarian Cat Curse"

The final psychotherapy tale in *Momma and the Meaning of Life*, "The Hungarian Cat Curse," is Yalom's most fantastical work, a story that begins realistically, with Ernest Lash trying to convince a patient not to terminate therapy, and then proceeds from dream to dream, to the point where reality and illusion become inseparable. Ernest is not particularly fond of Halston, the great-great-grandchild of fugitive slaves in Trinidad, yet he feels narcissistically injured when the patient tells him after only four therapy sessions that he is ending treatment. Ernest whispers to himself one of his mother's Yiddish expressions, "Geh Gesunter Heit," which means, affectionately, "go in good health," but which his mother used, mockingly, to imply, " 'Go away and stay away,' or 'God willing, it will be a long time before I ever see *you* again'" (202). As in "Double Exposure," Yalom links Ernest in "The Hungarian Cat Curse" to his own mother in the opening psychotherapy tale.

To understand why he is bored with Halston, Ernest asks him to recall in detail the events that led to a panic attack and a visit to a hospital's emergency room. Halston closes his eyes, and, after several minutes of silence, begins speaking, almost as if in a trance, about meeting a woman named Artemis, the goddess of chastity, virginity, and the hunt. Artemis is also, like her twin brother, Apollo, the bringer of sudden death and disease. Halston has glorious sex with Artemis, but she casts a spell over him, and he then dreams of being chased by a menacing cat, as big as a lion. Artemis turns into a robot with enormous breasts out of which streamed a radioactive liquid, a corrosive substance that begins to eat away at his feet and legs—not unlike the black ooze of "Double Exposure." Terrified, Halston wakes up, bolts out of bed, abandons the sleeping Artemis, and heads for the ER. What does the dream mean? Why does it have such an impact on Halston and Ernest? Curiously, fifteen years earlier Ernest had a similar experience when he spent a lovely evening with an old girlfriend, Judy, who mysteriously deserted him the following morning without leaving a trace. "He had been devastated. Psychotherapy had never entirely erased his pain, and even now, all these years later, the memory still stung" (213).

Obsessed with Artemis, whom he sees as an avatar of Judy, Ernest searches out Halston's dream-turned-into-a-nightmare woman, locates her in a combination bookstore-café, and engages in a prolonged discussion with her of twentieth-century German literature. He tells Artemis about his troubling experience with Judy, and she then relates a similar experience. "Really?" replies Ernest. "It's amazing how much we seem to have in common. Shouldn't we try to heal one another?" (220). Yalom exploits the dark humor of his deluded therapist's situation. "What are you doing?" Ernest asks himself. He realizes that he is being unethical by having a relationship with Artemis, hopelessly transgressing boundaries by pursuing the same woman who was involved with his patient. Ernest can imagine the judgment of his clinical supervisor, Marshal Streider. "Dr. Lash is a fine and ethical clinician except when he occasionally lapses into thinking with his small head" (220).

The story becomes more surreal when Ernest has the identical experience with Artemis that Halston did. Is history repeating itself? Thoughts of the past overcome Ernest at the beginning of the evening, and, caught up in reverie, he recalls early sexual fantasies, including making love to his Aunt Hannah, riding the roller-coaster at Glen Echo Amusement Park, and playing chess with his father. "The Hungarian Cat Curse" seems to be another version of the "House of Horrors" that Yalom describes in "Momma and the Meaning of Life," implying that the volume has come full circle. Ernest has sex with the enchanting Artemis, falls asleep, and then experiences Halston's nightmare, menaced by a giant cat and victimized by a poisonous liquid gushing from Artemis's monstrous breasts. He tries to scream, "'Momma! Momma! Help me, Momma!' But no words came" (223). He then wakes up and abandons Artemis, as Halston had done. Yalom then introduces the most inspired character in the story, the rapacious cat Merges, whose name means "rageful" in Hungarian. Ernest's efforts to defuse Merges of his murderous rage and convince him to give up his revenge against a woman who has drowned him in an earlier life recall the therapist's similar relationship with Carol in *Lying on the Couch*. The story ends with Merges unexpectedly blessing Ernest and Artemis, urging them to make the most of their lives.

"The Hungarian Cat Curse" is Yalom's most experimental short story, evoking elements of a Grimm Brothers' fairy tale, fabulism, and magical realism. Yalom regards the story as his most imaginative and comic work. The story combines all of the themes in *Momma and the Meaning of Life*, as Yalom observes in the afterword, including the "therapist's delight when a taxing and unpleasant patient decides to terminate, his boredom with a particular patient and the subsequent use of that boredom as a guide in therapy, the therapist's chagrin at the damage his patient has inflicted on another, his yearning to redress that wrong, lapses in which he loses sight of his patient's best interests, his grandiose rescue fantasies, his lustful fascination with a character in a patient's life, his dilemma about whether healers are ever off duty." All of these foibles and others, Yalom adds, are taken from his personal experience (255).

Critical Praise

Momma and the Meaning of Life never became a bestseller, like *Love's Executioner*, but it received widespread praise. The *Kirkus Reviews* regarded the volume as a "worthy sequel" to *Love's Executioner*, a conclusion shared by *Booklist*: "Yalom absorbingly recounts the resilience some patients bring to the task of healing themselves." The *Times Literary Supplement (London)* praised the book's literary and psychological strengths. "Unlike most psychotherapists, Yalom can tell a story and tell it so well that it is easy to forget what one is reading is a distillation of weeks, months, even years of therapeutic work. . . . And Yalom does it with enviable openness and style."

Chapter 9

The Gift of Therapy
The Hazards and Privileges of Being a Therapist

"My patients worry about my health," Yalom admits in the beginning of *The Gift of Therapy*. "Will I be there for the long haul of therapy? When I leave for vacation, they fear I will never return. They imagine my funeral or visiting my grave" (xiii). It is an unusual way to begin a book, especially one devoted to therapy. Disclosing his patients' anxiety over his mortality reveals his own anxiety. One senses that the therapist is a wounded healer, wounded, as everyone is, by approaching death. Yalom has spent his entire life writing about death anxiety, and it is appropriate for him to mention his patients' concerns about his mortality now that he has become a septuagenarian.

Published in 2002, when Yalom was seventy-one, *The Gift of Therapy* is, along with *Love's Executioner* and *When Nietzsche Wept*, one of his most popular works. The book opens on an elegiac tone as he recalls his forty-five-year career as a psychotherapist and reflects on how his profession has drastically changed over the years. Many of these changes, he laments, do not bode well for the future. Psychotherapy is now in a crisis as a result of the intrusiveness of managed care, the siren call of psychopharmacology, and the misguided belief that only EVT, empirically validated therapy, is legitimate. Yalom is rightly worried about psychotherapy's future, worried "about how it may be deformed by economic pressures and impoverished by radically abbreviated training programs" (xv). Subtitled *An Open Letter to a New Generation of Therapists and Their Patients*, *The Gift of Therapy* is partly a how-to book for therapists and partly a distillation of the major themes of his earlier writings. The book conveys Yalom's passionate belief in the healing power of psychotherapy and the hope that his beloved profession will weather the present storm.

Yalom recalls in the introduction the precise moment of the book's inception. While walking through the Huntington Library's exhibit of best-selling books from the Renaissance in Great Britain, he noticed that three volumes were books of numbered "tips"—recommendations that "attracted the attention of the multitudes," such as advice on animal husbandry, sewing, and gardening. The idea of writing a book of tips suddenly became appealing. Shortly before this experience he had reread Rainer Maria Rilke's *Letters to a Young Poet*. Feeling the ghost of Rilke hovering over him, Yalom consciously attempted to raise himself to Rilke's standards of "honesty, inclusiveness, and generosity of spirit" (xix).

The five sections in *The Gift of Therapy* cover a wide range of topics, beginning with the therapist-patient relationship, which constitutes forty of the eighty-five brief chapters. (The chapters average three pages long, but some are only a page.) Among the topics included in the therapist-patient relationship are avoiding diagnosis (except for insurance), viewing the therapist and patient as fellow travelers, teaching empathy, acknowledging errors, affirming the here-and-now, and giving feedback. The second section moves from the process of therapy to content, including death, meaning in life (not *the* meaning of life), and freedom. The third section addresses a variety of issues, such as note-taking, weeping patients, home visits, touching patients nonsexually, and exploring previous therapies. The fourth section deals with dreams in therapy, including using dreams pragmatically, paying attention to the patient's first dream, and attending carefully to dreams about the therapist. The final section focuses on the "hazards and privileges" of being a therapist. Most of the chapters highlight aspects of therapy that Yalom has examined in his earlier writings, but he considers other topics for the first time. In the chapter called "Freud Was Not Always Wrong," he discusses his shifting relationship to psychoanalysis and provides detailed information about a subject seldom discussed: the therapist's own experience in therapy. Yalom also discusses how patients have responded to his writings, a topic on which he elaborates in greater detail, as we will, in his next nonfiction book, *Staring at the Sun*.

Aging writers, regardless of their academic fields or disciplines, worry about whether, after their deaths, their books will be read. Yalom is no exception. Early in *The Gift of Therapy* he refers to the pioneering psychoanalytic author Karen Horney. "Her name is unfamiliar to most young therapists. Because the shelf life of eminent theorists in our field has grown so short, I shall, from time to time, lapse into reminiscence" (2). He remains silent over whether his own books will have a short shelf life. Tellingly, Yalom does his best to resurrect psychotherapists who may be unfamiliar to his readers: Karen Horney, Erich Fromm, Carl Rogers, D. W. Winnicott, Sándor Ferenczi, Rollo May, Harry Stack Sullivan, Melanie Klein, and Allen Wheelis.

Feedback

Yalom uses the word *feedback*, not criticism, to help patients learn more about themselves. "A goal of therapy is to increase reality testing and to help individuals see themselves as others see them. It is through the agency of feedback that the *blind self* grows appreciably smaller" (113). Feedback must always be applied gently to be effective. One of Yalom's favorite expressions is to "strike when the iron is cold" (120), that is, giving feedback when a patient is emotionally receptive to it. Feedback may also involve a therapist's acknowledgment of mistakes: "an open admission of error is good model-setting for patients and another sign that they matter to you" (32). "Age states" is another feedback technique. "Sometimes I experience a patient as being in one age state, sometimes another, and I try to find an acceptable way to share this with the patient, usually commenting upon it when I experience the patient in an age-appropriate state" (122–123).

Yalom offers four recommendations about feedback that he dramatizes in his novel about group psychotherapy, *The Schopenhauer Cure*: (1) "It stems from here-and-now observations"; (2) "It follows the generating event as closely as possible"; (3) "It focuses on the specific observations and feelings generated in the listener rather than guesses or interpretations about the speaker's motivation"; (4) "The recipient checks out the feedback with other members to obtain consensual validation" (114).

Therapist Self-Disclosure

Some of Yalom's new readers in *The Gift of Therapy* may be surprised by a statement he makes in a chapter about the need for caution when therapists reveal aspects of their lives to patients—surprised more by the second sentence than the first. "If therapist disclosure were to be graded on a continuum, I am certain that I would be placed on the high end. Yet I have never had the experience of disclosing too much. On the contrary, I have always facilitated therapy when I have shared some facet of myself" (90). Yalom never regretted a self-disclosure in therapy, not because patients have always responded positively to learning about an aspect of his personal life, but because a negative patient response can be helpful if a therapist focuses on the here-and-now. All therapist self-disclosure must pass one test: "Is this disclosure in the best interests of the patient?" (87).

As an example, Yalom cites a disclosure several years earlier to his outpatient therapy group about his conflicted relationship with his mother, who had recently died. Some of his patients wanted to know the details of her death and funeral. "I answered all with great candor and told them, for example, of my fractious relationship with my mother and how I had chosen to live in California partly in order to put three thousand miles between my mother and me. She had been a dragon in many ways, but she had lost her fangs as she had aged and in the last several years our relationship had grown much closer and I had been a dutiful son" (91). Yalom explored this contentious relationship in the title story of *Momma and the Meaning of Life*, but he reveals new information in *The Gift of Therapy* about the therapeutic value of writing about his mother. "The crisis of meaning depicted in the dream [about the House of Horrors] prompted me to explore my life in a different manner. In a story I wrote directly after the dream, I engaged in a conversation with my mother's ghost in order to heal the breach between us and to understand how our life meanings both intertwined and conflicted with one another" (134).

To appreciate how far Yalom has traveled in his attitude toward therapist self-disclosure, we need to look at his first therapy dream, which is still fresh in his mind after forty years. He cites the dream not mainly to illustrate his changed attitude toward self-disclosure but to demonstrate the unusual importance of a patient's first dream in therapy, before the "dream-weaver" within the patient's unconscious becomes unduly guarded as a result of analytic investigation. "I am lying on a doctor's examining table. The sheet is too small to cover me properly. I can see a nurse inserting a needle into my leg—my shin. Suddenly there's an explosive hissing, gurgling sound—WHOOOOSH." He then interprets the dream for us. "The meaning of the dream—the loud whoosh—was instantly clear to me." As a boy Yalom suffered from chronic sinusitis, and every winter his mother took him to a physician who drained and flushed his sinuses. Yalom hated the procedure. "I remembered my observing the quivering, disgusting contents of the chrome semicircular drainage pan and thinking that some of my brains had been washed out along with the pus and mucus." The dream disclosed all of Yalom's fears of being exposed and penetrated by the upcoming analysis. He was particularly afraid that he would lose his "mind, be brainwashed, and suffer a grievous injury to a long, firm body part (depicted as a shinbone)" (244–245).

The Touching of Hands

Yalom discloses in *The Gift of Therapy* one consequential detail omitted from "Travels with Paula" in *Momma and the Meaning of Life*. Paula surprised him at the close of one therapy session by stating, "Let's move closer together," and she then asked everyone to hold hands as they looked at a burning candle and meditated in silence for a few moments. Paula's suggestion went against Yalom's medical training, and he was uncomfortable, but he soon recognized that it was a momentous act. He elaborates on this in *The Gift of Therapy*, commenting that he had never held hands before with a patient but felt that he had no choice in this situation. "I joined in and immediately felt, like all the members, that it was an inspired way to end our meetings, and for several years we closed each session in this manner" (188).

The touching of hands evokes the Christian practice of the laying on of hands, associated with the receiving of the Holy Spirit. For Yalom the act is similarly holy but in a secular way, implying that human connection is a therapeutic force against fear and isolation. The touching of hands symbolizes the intimacy of the therapist-patient relationship, the inviolable trust that arises from the giving and receiving of the gift of therapy. Paula's suggestion of moving closer together convinced Yalom to end each therapy session by shaking a patient's hand or clasping his or her shoulder.

The Therapist's Therapy

The Gift of Therapy glosses earlier writings, filling in details to stories that had already been told, but there is one subject that Yalom elaborates on in far greater depth than he had done previously: the different types of therapy he experienced during different stages of his life:

> My own odyssey of therapy, over my forty-five-year career, is as follows: a 750 hour, five-time-a-week orthodox Freudian psychoanalysis in my psychiatric residency (with a training analyst in the conservative Baltimore Washington School), a year's analysis with Charles Rycroft (an analyst in the "middle school" of the

British Psychoanalytic Institute), two years with Pat Baumgartner (a gestalt therapist), three years of psychotherapy with Rollo May (an interpersonally and existentially oriented analyst of the William Alanson White Institute), and numerous briefer stints with therapists from a variety of disciplines, including behavioral therapy, bioenergetics, Rolfing, marital-couples work, an ongoing ten-year (at this writing) leaderless support group of male therapists, and, in the 1960s, encounter groups of a whole rainbow of flavors, including a nude marathon group. (41)

Yalom observes in *The Gift of Therapy* that choosing not to enter a psychoanalytic institute was one of the best decisions of his career, but he admits that his feelings toward psychoanalysis have dramatically changed. "Perhaps I am unduly alarmist but it seems to me that, in these days of relentless attack on the field of psychotherapy, the analytic institutes may become the last bastion, the repository of collected psychoanalytic wisdom, in much the same way the church for centuries was the repository of philosophical wisdom and the only realm where serious existential questions—life purpose, values, ethics, responsibility, freedom, death, community, connectedness—were discussed" (221). Two of the most positive developments in recent psychoanalysis have been an emphasis on intersubjectivity and two-person psychology, developments that Yalom has long championed before they became accepted elsewhere. He has also affirmed the role of empathy in therapy, as well as elaborating on Jung's idea of the wounded healer.

Yalom never implies that a therapist should seek treatment from a patient, but he admits that part of the unexpected gift of therapy lies in the therapeutic nature of helping others. "I know that I have, countless times, begun a therapy hour in a state of personal disquiet and ended the hour feeling considerably better without commenting explicitly on my inner state" (107). Yalom doesn't give an example of being in a state of personal disquiet and ending the hour feeling considerably better about himself, but we can readily offer one. Imagine an existential psychiatrist who is dying of cancer and who wishes to spend his remaining months of health doing what he has always done, helping his patients. Imagine the therapist reflecting on his successes and failures, seeking a final understanding of the mystery of therapy. Yalom imagined such a situation in his next novel, *The Schopenhauer Cure*, a fictionalized account of the gift of therapy.

Chapter 10

The Schopenhauer Cure

Searching for an Antidote

Yalom's starting point in his 2005 novel *The Schopenhauer Cure* was not the development of a particular plot, character, or place but a cluster of ideas centering around four topics: "1) How group therapy works; 2) How philosophy in general, and the philosophy of Arthur Schopenhauer in particular, might influence the practice of psychotherapy; 3) How Schopenhauer's strange life history and his significant personal pathology influenced his philosophical conclusions; and 4) How the awareness of death influences one's life conduct" ("Writing *The Schopenhauer Cure*" 10). To explore one of these topics in a novel is challenging; to explore all four is daunting.

Complicating Yalom's story is that Schopenhauer was one of the world's most misanthropic philosophers. Notorious for his pessimistic philosophy, vitriolic comments about women, and extreme suspicion of human relationships, Schopenhauer may have been the most dislikable thinker of all time. In one of his most infamous metaphors, humans, or "bipeds," as he disdainfully called them, are nothing more than porcupines who, crowded together to save themselves from freezing, cannot help driving their sharp spines into each other. The prickly early nineteenth-century German philosopher was one of the world's most strident naysayers, a man who would have opted not to come into existence had he been given a choice. Compared to Schopenhauer, Nietzsche, despite being his greatest disciple, was a wooly-eyed optimist.

Imagine, then, creating a fictional character, Philip Slate, who, modeling himself on Schopenhauer, feels contempt for everyone. How can such a person aspire to be a clinical philosopher? How can the members of a therapy group tolerate him, particularly a woman who, when she was a freshman in college, was seduced and then discarded by him when he was her teaching assistant? Is such an odious character capable of having a convincing change of heart? Why title a novel the "Schopenhauer Cure" when the cure itself is so flawed? Can an existential psychiatrist, Julius Hertzfeld, with the help of the members of his therapy group, provide a life-saving antidote to a flawed philosophical cure?

Yalom describes *The Schopenhauer Cure* as an "odd amalgam of fiction, psychobiography and psychotherapy pedagogy" (vii). The description hardly does the novel justice. Combining psychology, philosophy, biography, and thanatology, *The Schopenhauer Cure* offers life lessons in the form of a rousing story.

An Existential Psychiatrist

To meet Julius Hertzfeld is to recall Ernest Lash of *Lying on the Couch*. Julius is twenty years older than Ernest, more clinically experienced, tested by the vicissitudes of life, but essentially the same person. Sixty-five years old, "Julius had reigned over the psychiatric community for thirty years. In his position as professor of psychiatry at the University of California he had trained scores of students and, five years before, had been president of the American Psychiatric Association" (3). Change University of California to Stanford, omit the presidency of the APA—Yalom has no interest in professional politics—and you have a portrait of an older Ernest Lash—and of the novelist who created both characters.

Like Ernest and Yalom, Julius loves his profession. "I've always regarded therapy more as a calling than a profession, a way of life for people who care about others," he tells Philip early in the story (61). Julius repeatedly affirms his commitment to the members of his therapy group—to *every* group he has taught in the past quarter of a century. "The group was more than a clump of people; it had a life of its own, an enduring personality" (94). Julius feels a nontransgressive love for the members of the group, respecting each person's individuality.

Like Yalom, Julius recognizes that his cherished profession is under siege from all sides. These external threats and internal doubts never prevent Julius from doing his job well. He has the reputation of being a "no-bullshit doctor's doctor," a "therapist of last resort, a canny wizard willing to do anything to help his patient" (3). Seymour Trotter was also known as a therapist of last resort, and the two psychiatrists have more than a little in common. Born in the Bronx, Julius was more interested as an adolescent in gambling than in schoolwork. He "dumbed himself down," got into trouble, fell from grace, and found himself "role locked," a phenomenon in which no one could appreciate or relate to the new person he had decided to become. Moving at age fifteen with his family to Washington, DC, where his father struggled to make a living, Julius reinvented himself after the move, when, with "raw chutzpah," he nearly was elected president of his high school class. Julius never doubted the wisdom of becoming first a physician and then a psychiatrist. Like Socrates, he believes that the wisest are those who acknowledge humbly the limitations of their knowledge. He also respects professional boundaries, unlike Yalom's earlier therapist of last resort.

A Psychiatrist Who Writes

Julius loves clinical work, like Yalom, but his greater passion, unfulfilled, is to become a creative writer. He succeeds modestly as a psychiatric researcher and clinician. "He was a good, contributing professional writer (he had published two books and a hundred articles in the psychiatric literature), but Julius yearned to write literature and for decades had collected plots for short stories from his imagination and his practice. Though he had started several, he never found the time, nor the courage, to finish and submit a story for publication" (253). Creative writers will not be surprised by Yalom's use of the word *courage* here: the blank page can be paralyzing. Julius's decision not to undertake the "great unfulfilled project in his life: to be a real writer" is his only failure of nerve.

Julius's failure to write fiction, however, does not prevent him from writing about the subject he knows best, psychiatry. He knows that good writing can arise even from an experiment's failure. The writer is an opportunist: everything is grist for the writer's mill, including failure. Julius's three-year treatment of Philip twenty years earlier was not a success, but it was "marvelously facilitative for Julius's writing, and many ideas emerging from the sessions found their way into his celebrated article 'The Therapist and the Will' and into his book *Wishing, Willing, and Acting*" (24).

What kinds of plots does Julius imagine for fiction? In a file in his computer titled "Short Story Plots," he has two ideas for a list of plots on "Victims confront their enemies." The first confrontation occurs on a luxury ship cruising off the Turkish coast. "A psychiatrist enters the ship's casino and there across the smoke-filled room sees an ex-patient, a con man who had once swindled him out of seventy-five thousand dollars" (253). The plot, as readers of *Lying on the Couch* will quickly discern, is a continuation of Marshal Streider's efforts to take revenge on his former patient who cheated him out of tens of thousands of dollars. Julius's second confrontation plot involves a female attorney "who was assigned a pro bono case to defend an accused rapist. On her first jail interview with him she suspects he is the man who raped her ten years before." This plot reminds us of another character in *Lying on the Couch*, Carol Astrid, a lawyer whose rage is exceeded only by her desire for justice. Of the two revenge plots, Yalom uses the latter in *The Schopenhauer Cure*, showing how the Berkeley literature professor Pam Swanvil confronts her massive rage when she discovers to her horror that Philip, her former teacher, has entered the therapy group.

And Who Also Reads

Julius may not be a novelist, as Yalom is, but he is a lover of literature and philosophy. The opening paragraph of *The Schopenhauer Cure* reveals Julius's familiarity with the life-and-death homilies of the pre-Socratic philosophers. "He agreed with the Stoics, who said, 'As soon as we are born we begin to die,' and with Epicurus, who reasoned, 'Where I am, death is not and where death is, I am not. Hence why fear death?'" (1). Julius has recited these consolations to his dying patients, and now he applies them to his own life.

Julius's favorite philosopher is, no surprise, Nietzsche, whose writings he quotes with academic authority. Julius knows not only Nietzsche's words but also their ambiguities. Julius has highlighted two passages from his dog-eared copy of *Thus Spake Zarathustra*, the book he had used decades earlier when he was writing an article about Nietzsche's unacknowledged influence on Freud. One passage is "Consummate your life"; the other is "Die at the right time." Julius knows that Nietzsche's ambiguous language is capable of multiple interpretations. "Julius often likened Nietzsche's words to a Rorschach exam; they offered so many opposing viewpoints, that the readers' state of mind determined what they took from them" (11). Julius returns to Nietzsche near the end of the story, reflecting on the parallels between Nietzsche and Zarathustra. "Following Zarathustra's path, he had shared his ripeness, transcended himself by reaching out to others, and lived in a manner that he would be willing to repeat perpetually throughout eternity" (282).

Other details confirm Julius's love for literature. He has a stack of unread novels on his bedside table that, regrettably, he won't have time to read. Years earlier Pam had given him a copy of John Gardner's *Grendel,* a novel that he read and quoted from to another patient, Rebecca, who later tells him how much the story has meant to her. Philip is also a great reader of literature and philosophy, though unlike Julius, he parades his knowledge. Philip points out, pedantically, that long before Gardner, Heidegger suggested that death is the *"impossibility of further possibility"* (197). Julius recalls hearing, forty years earlier, when he was a student, the psychoanalyst Erich Fromm invoke the ancient Roman poet Terence's words: "I am human, and nothing human is alien to me" (180). Julius's favorite writers are those who, unlike Schopenhauer, affirm connection and engagement, such as Camus and Sartre. Tellingly, Julius's daughter is a literature professor, and his son is a Johns Hopkins neurobiological researcher, suggesting the family's commitment to both the arts and sciences, Yalom's twin passions.

Other Authorial Qualities

Julius embodies Yalom's mistrust of religion, despising the "tools by which religions strip their followers of reason and freedom" (9). Admitting to the group that he envies a father confessor's power to dispense forgiveness to worshipers, Julius reassures himself that he lives "according to principles of reason" and does not infantilize his patients by "representing mythology as reality" (201). And yet despite his rejection of supernatural religion, Julius is not afraid to acknowledge the lessons from sacred writings, as when he thinks about the Talmudic observation "to redeem one person is to save the whole world" (284), an injunction that is his raison d'etre for being a therapist.

Julius's unflinching awareness of death heightens his appreciation of life. "To live in despair because life is finite or because life has no higher purpose or embedded design is crass ingratitude" (10). He embraces Spinoza's and Einstein's response to death: "simply bow one's head, tip one's hat to the elegant laws and mystery of nature, and go about the business of living" (10). Death is the opposite of life, but dying is not the opposite of living: It's a part of living. Julius's temperament resembles Yalom's. "Julius was congenitally trusting of his patients. He was one of those optimistic souls who was greatly destabilized by duplicity" (217). Optimism is neither naivete nor shallowness; Julius is trusting but not foolish. Self-disciplined, running three miles a day to remain fit, he believes in moderation, like the ancient Greeks, balancing work and pleasure. "Too much of life's show is missed if we never take off our coats and join in the fun" (10).

A Group Psychotherapist

The Schopenhauer Cure enacts many of the major recommendations that Yalom offers in *The Theory and Practice of Group Psychotherapy*. Julius's first lesson to Philip is that patients most value the therapeutic relationship. "They rarely remember an important insight their therapist offered but generally fondly recall their personal relationship with the therapist" (62–63). Julius insists on three ground rules for the members of the group: (1) confidentiality—speaking to no one about the members of the group; (2) self-disclosure—striving to reveal as much about oneself as possible to the other members of the group; and (3) group cohesiveness—informing the group of any contact between members outside of the ninety-minute-long psychotherapy session.

One of Julius's central assumptions is that a good group therapist can show how a patient's here-and-now conflicts reveal problems in the patient's past or present life. "I make the assumption," he tells Philip, "that group members will manifest the same behavior in the group that has created difficulties for them in their social life. And I further assume that ultimately they will generalize what they learn about their group relationships to their relationships outside" (67). Additionally, Julius advises Philip to avoid dual relationships with patients, including romantic and business relationships. Julius puts these recommendations into practice. He explains, as Yalom does in his textbooks, the difference between vertical and horizontal self-disclosures. He demonstrates that risk-taking in self-disclosure should be encouraged. Therapy, whether it is individual or group, always involves reciprocity. Julius invokes Martin Buber's I-Thou relationship as enabling intimate and reciprocal self-disclosures.

Yalom endows his fictional psychiatrist with many of his own professional experiences. Like Yalom, Julius in his early career has led a therapy group of breast cancer patients, an experience that proved transformative for them and himself. Sadly, the patients learned how to live "only after their bodies were riddled with cancer" (251).

Death Discovery Day

Julius receives his own death sentence early in the novel when a dermatologist informs him that he has an ulcerated melanoma, with probably only a year of good health left. Yalom's language paradoxically comes alive at the thought of cancer devouring his character's body. "How startling it was to realize that suddenly he was no longer the supreme life form. Instead he was a host; he was nourishment, food for a fitter organism whose gobbling cells divided at a dizzying pace, an organism that blitzkrieged and annexed adjacent protoplasm and was now undoubtedly outfitting clusters of cells for cruises into the bloodstream and colonization of distant organs, perhaps the sweet friable feeding grounds of his liver or the spongy grassy meadows of his lungs" (8). No matter how horrifying the idea of death may be to Yalom, the ability to express in metaphorical language the deadly process of metastasis provides a degree of aesthetic pleasure to him. Death remains Yalom's muse, as his language demonstrates.

Death is no stranger to Julius, for ten years earlier his beloved wife, Miriam, whom he had known since high school, died in a car accident. It's significant that the two central psychiatrists in *Lying on the Couch* and *The Schopenhauer Cure* are both widowers. Yalom has been fortunate to have a long and deeply fulfilling marriage, but he can imagine how a man in Julius's situation must feel after the loss of his wife. Yalom offers two observations that carry the ring of truth. "Though he had loved Miriam from the moment he laid eyes on her in the tenth grade, he simultaneously resented her as an obstacle blocking him from the multitude of women he felt entitled to enjoy." The most happily married husband or wife is likely to understand the truth of this remark. Yalom also recognizes the element of idealization that envelopes the dead. "In the ten years since the car crash took her from him, he had cherished her more than while she was alive" (93).

After discovering he has terminal cancer, Julius thinks about writing a personal article for the *Journal of the American Psychiatric Association* on "The Psychiatrist Confronts Mortality" or perhaps something for the *Sunday Times Magazine* or maybe even a book, possibly called *Autobiography of a Demise*. Part of the reason for such writing, Julius realizes, is counterphobic motivation. He never writes the article or book, for lack of time, and perhaps for lack of courage, but one senses that Yalom would have found both the time and courage to write.

Beginning with "DDD," death discovery day, Julius throws himself into his work, the therapy group he is leading. Work has always been Julius's supreme pleasure. Work is not only therapeutic for Julius but also *redemptive*. Nowhere in Yalom's stories do we see a more striking illustration of a *wounded healer*. "So caught up was he by the drama of the meeting that for an hour and a half he forgot his own despair. That was not unusual. All group therapists know about the wonderfully healing qualities inherent in the atmosphere of the working group" (39). Julius intends to make the most of his remaining time by throwing himself into his work, believing that he will help himself by helping others. Work is his entire life; not for a moment does he consider abandoning his patients. He intends to die in harness, working to the end, devoting himself to others. Part of his challenge as a therapist is to be honest about his feelings of approaching death without burdening patients with his own fears and thus sabotaging their therapy. Instead of feeling good about the patients he has helped, however, Julius reflects on those who, despite his best efforts, he failed to help. And so he decides to get in touch with his most conspicuous failure.

A Prickly Biped

Julius's telephone call to Philip Slate, after the passing of twenty-two years, sets into motion the novel's plot. Philip is as disagreeable as Julius remembered him. When Philip invites him into his office, Julius is astonished to learn that his former patient is now a clinical philosopher. How can a person with no interpersonal skills be a therapist? Julius is further startled when Philip asks him to be his supervisor. Philip has no problem being supervised by a therapist who failed to help him in individual therapy. "Research shows that therapy, in any hands, is unsuccessful for about a third of patients. Besides, there's no doubt I played a significant role in the failure—my stubbornness, my rigidity. Your only error was to choose the wrong type of therapy for me, and then persist in it far too long" (60). Philip speaks to Julius here and elsewhere in a hectoring, often supercilious tone, distancing himself from his former therapist as much as possible. How can Julius connect with a person whose entire life demands disconnection?

Philip Slate is hard, cold, and unfeeling, a blank slate in his absence of emotions. A metamorphic rock composed of clay or volcanic ash, slate is often used for gravestones. Philip's emotions are entombed in his hard though brittle exterior. Yalom chooses his two protagonists' names carefully. Philip is aware of the appropriateness of his name. "Perhaps there's no hope for me," he declares near the end of the story. "My slate of relationships, past and present, is blank" (334). Philip's slate of relationships may be blank, but he is not quite a tabula rasa, as the eighteenth-century Swiss philosopher and novelist Jean-Jacques Rousseau declared. Philip continues to struggle against an instinctual life force that drives him apart from all human contact. Julius Hertzfeld's name is also suggestive. The "Hertz" sounds like *Herz*, which means "heart" in German. Hertz is also a homonym for "hurts," suggesting the existential pain arising from Julius's terminal illness.

Julius is not looking for pity when he explains over the telephone that he has health problems and is considering retirement, but Philip never expresses sympathy or concern, not even later when the two men meet in person. To this extent Philip resembles Irene at the beginning of her therapy in *Momma and the Meaning of Life*, unwilling to see Yalom as a real person with a narrative, a story of his own. Consulting his therapy notes in 1980, when Philip first entered therapy, Julius recalls his patient's chief complaint: "I am driven against my will by sexual impulses" (14). Yalom uses summary rather than scenic narration to describe Philip's "complaint," a word that scarcely does justice to his sexual addiction. Twenty-six years old at the time he begins therapy, Philip makes no attempt to deny his conflicts, as Julius's clinical notes of the first session reveal: "PRESENT ILLNESS—*Sexually driven since thirteen—compulsive masturbation throughout adolescence continuing till present day—sometimes four, five times daily—obsessed with sex continually, masturbates to give himself peace. Huge hunk of life spent on obsessing about sex—he says 'the time I've wasted chasing women—I could have gotten Ph.D.s in philosophy, Mandarin Chinese, and astrophysics'*" (19).

One of the few details Philip remembers about his therapy is a question Julius asked him, one Julius used when he reached an impasse with patients: What epitaph would you like written on your tombstone? Philip's silence compels Julius to supply his own answer: "He liked to fuck." Julius's harsh statement had little impact on his patient at the time, but Philip made use of it ten years later—a "time-delayed intervention," Julius later dryly observes—when he resolved to change his life.

Philip's agonized question at the time he began therapy—"Why can't I do what I truly want to do?"—poses an intellectual challenge to Julius. He continues to think about the question long after his patient terminated treatment. Will-paralysis is a question for the psychotherapist, philosopher, and novelist—a perfect subject for a writer like Yalom.

Philip is the only character in a Yalom novel to suffer from a sexual addiction. Philip may remind us of Merges in *Momma and the Meaning of Life*, though the feral creature is acting "naturally." Preferring one-night stands to sustained relationships, Philip rarely sees a woman for more than a month. Usually the woman breaks up with him, but it doesn't matter, since he avoids all entangling alliances. Keeping a score card of his sexual conquests, he informs Julius with flat affect, feeling neither pleasure nor shame, that in the previous year he slept with ninety different women. He had no interest in any of them. Nor does he have interest in his job as a chemist developing pesticides, a detail that is entirely consistent with his belief that most living creatures are pestilential. Philip would agree with Sartre's sardonic observation in *No Exit*: "Hell is other people." Philip's father, an investment banker who was chronically depressed, committed suicide when Philip was thirteen, and Philip had no relationship with his mother (or his stepfather), from whom he had been estranged for twenty years. He did not even attend her funeral.

Analytical but lacking in warmth or empathy, Philip is a striking example of a person who scores high on intellectual intelligence but abysmally low on emotional intelligence. Friendless, he cannot look anyone in the eye. His explanation—"Meeting the gaze of the other distracts me from searching for the answer the other might wish to hear" (162)—is largely a rationalization for his failure to connect with people. Three years of therapy did nothing to alleviate his symptoms, broaden his perspective, or change his behavior.

Much in Philip's life has changed, however, since the end of his therapy with Julius. A small inheritance allowed him to quit his job and enter graduate school. He earned a PhD in philosophy from Columbia University; teaches at a small California college, though his few students appear bored with his lectures; and started a career in philosophical counseling, a movement, rooted in the Socratic tradition, that began in California in the 1980s to help clients discover a philosophical understanding of their lives.

The novel's antagonist, Philip often reveals Yalom's own point of view. This is not unusual: novelists typically project themselves into many different characters, all of whom may embody aspects of their creators' lives. Philip functions authorially when he informs the group of the assumptions behind philosophical counseling. "At best there exists only a vague boundary between education and therapy. The Greeks—Socrates, Plato, Aristotle, the Stoics, and Epicureans—all believed that education and reason were the tools needed to combat human suffering. Most philosophical counselors consider education to be the foundation of therapy. Almost all ascribe to Leibniz's motto, *Caritas sapientis* meaning 'wisdom and care'" (261–262). Yalom, too, believes in philosophical counseling, using the wisdom of philosophy to enrich psychotherapy. Existential psychiatry has its roots in the great philosophers of the distant and immediate past.

Yalom cites in the acknowledgments page of *The Schopenhauer Cure* Peter B. Raabe, a philosophy professor at Simon Fraser University and the first person in Canada to be awarded a doctorate based on his theoretical and practical work in philosophical counseling. Raabe points out in his 2002 book *Issues in Philosophical Counseling* that philosophical counseling is not psychotherapy because it does not "pretend to understand the unconscious (if such a thing exists) or to be able to interpret it, and therefore to know people better than they know themselves." What philosophical counseling can do, Raabe states, is to teach clients "those philosophical abilities and dispositions that will help them avoid or prevent problems in the future" (16).

Philip can use all the help he can get from philosophical counseling and psychotherapy. What is mainly responsible for Philip's transformation since Julius last saw him? Years earlier he had entered treatment with another "therapist," Arthur Schopenhauer, whose bracing writings have changed Philip's life both for better and for worse.

Buddenbrooks

Philip invites Julius to hear him deliver a lecture on the importance of Schopenhauer's philosophy, a talk that Philip has prepared mainly for his former therapist's benefit. The lecture focuses on Thomas Mann's novel *Buddenbrooks*, published in 1901 when the future Nobel laureate was only twenty-six years old. Depressed over the inevitability of death, the forty-eight-year-old paterfamilias, Thomas Buddenbrooks, temporarily finds comfort when by chance he picks up a volume of philosophy he had bought years earlier at a used bookstore. Mann never names the author of the volume, but he gives readers the title: "On Death and Its Relation to Our Personal Immortality." The author is Arthur Schopenhauer.

Despite receiving his doctorate in philosophy from Columbia, one of the nation's greatest universities, Philip knows nothing about good teaching. He drones on in a boring, lifeless voice, making no effort to involve his students in discussion. It's true that he lectures in a large classroom, in which there are only about thirty listless students, along with a few sleeping homeless people, but he makes no effort to conceal his contempt for his audience. His disdain is not limited to his students, whom he refers to as "clods who attend this pigsty of a university" (52). His teaching may be characterized as the pedagogy of humiliation. "If I appear desultory," he sneers, "I ask your forbearance"—and then he commands a student to walk to the blackboard and spell out "desultory," "forbearance," and another word, "debut," a pedagogical strategy designed to belittle his listeners. Philip gains his students' attention only by mentioning that a philosopher he has just mentioned, Kant, will be on the final examination. The content of Philip's lecture is not offensive, but his condescension is unforgivable. His oracular voice betrays his lack of wisdom.

Philip's teaching is mind-numbing, and during the lecture the students slowly exit the room, unreceptive to their professor's remarks. Julius is caught off guard during the lecture when Philip addresses him by name, recommending Mann's novel to "anyone intending to die." One of the passages from *Buddenbrooks* that Philip chooses to read aloud foreshadows questions that remain implicit throughout *The Schopenhauer Cure*. What is a parent's legacy to a child? What is a therapist's legacy to patients? By the time Philip reads a passage in which Thomas Buddenbrooks silently muses on his life, everyone has fled the classroom except for Julius.

In entering into a dialogue with two of the world's greatest writers, Schopenhauer and Mann, Yalom raises the age-old question: What do the dying pass on to the living? The specter of the absent father looms throughout *The Schopenhauer Cure*. Arthur Schopenhauer's father committed suicide, as did Philip's father. What is the dark legacy of suicide—and how does a wounded son avoid sharing his father's fate? Yalom is not ready to answer these questions, but his explanation will involve, in part, strengthening each group member's capacity for interpersonal relationships.

Philip reads Thomas Mann's novel selectively, not carefully. It's true that Schopenhauer's words initially intoxicate Thomas Buddenbrooks. Enraptured by Schopenhauer's idea of the will, Buddenbrooks believes that "[d]eath was a joy, so great, so deep that it could be dreamed of only in moments of revelation like the present. It was the return from an unspeakably painful wandering, the correction of a grave mistake, the loosening of chains, the opening of doors—it put right again a lamentable mischance" (Mann 526). Philip fails to mention, however, that the next day Buddenbrooks wakes with a feeling of "shame at the emotional extravagances of the night," unable to find comfort in the idea that he will be merged with the universe" (528). Nor is Julius impressed with Schopenhauer's consolation. The "idea of rejoining the universal oneness without any persistence of me and my memories and unique consciousness," he writes in his journal after Philip's lecture on Schopenhauer, "is the coldest of comfort. No, it's no comfort at all" (54).

Striking a Bargain

Julius and Philip are in different stages of their lives, but each needs the other. Julius wants to know how Philip transformed his life with Schopenhauer's help. Why did Philip succeed with Schopenhauer after failing with Julius? Philip has completed his course work in a counseling program but needs two hundred hours of professional supervision to receive a state counseling license. There are deeper reasons, however, to explain why each needs the other. Julius believes that Philip is presently incapable of being an effective therapist. By being a patient in Julius's group psychotherapy class, Philip may learn something important about therapy. Philip believes that Julius may learn something essential about himself, and about dying and death, from Schopenhauer's philosophy. And so Philip proposes a unique supervision-tutoring swap, with each man benefiting from the other. The proposed swap reminds us of Yalom's first novel, where Breuer and Nietzsche took turns healing and being healed by the other. Unlike Breuer, whose relationship with Nietzsche is complicated by a terrible secret he cannot disclose to the philosopher, Julius's relationship with Philip is not compromised in this way. Julius does have a dark secret he has never confessed to anyone, however, one that establishes an unexpected connection to Philip.

Yalom may have considered using the "swap" technique again in *The Schopenhauer Cure*, but he decided against it for several reasons. First, the novelist had no desire to repeat himself, using the same aesthetic technique twice. Second, Philip's lecture did nothing to pique Julius's interest in learning more about Schopenhauer's life or work. Third, a therapist should avoid dual relationships with patients, including teacher and student, which is what a supervision-tutoring swap would be. Finally, Julius knows that Philip is not ready to see patients and be supervised. Philip needs "remedial work" (69), a euphemism for learning to be human.

And so Julius makes a counteroffer. He agrees to be Philip's clinical supervisor only if Philip spends six months as a patient in Julius's psychotherapy group. The counterproposal alarms Philip. "How will it profit me to hear others describe their lives and problems en masse? The very idea of such a chorus of misery appalls me, although, as Schopenhauer points out, there is always pleasure in learning that others suffer more than you" (66). Philip's connection between Schopenhauer and schadenfreude, the pleasure derived from another person's suffering and misfortune, betrays the philosopher's cynical view of human nature. How can a clinical philosophy succeed if it is based on schadenfreude? Will Julius's agreement with Philip turn out to be a devil's pact? Philip's statement reveals how much he needs to learn before he can become a person, much less a therapist. He accepts the proposal under one condition: if Julius is willing to credit the group therapy sessions as supervisory hours. Both men take a risk by agreeing to the proposal. Julius knows he is making a questionable ethical decision. Philip will be a reluctant, perhaps hostile patient, and his resistance may harm the group. He has spent a lifetime constructing a hard character armor, and therapy will require loosening if not abandoning the self-imprisoning shield. Each man agrees to work with the other despite serious misgivings. Their evolving relationship is one of the triumphs of the novel.

Criticizing the Excesses of His Profession

Yalom casts a skeptical eye on the excesses of his profession. He may not mention the name of a particular author or book that he believes has had a dangerous impact on psychotherapy, but one can often infer the object of his criticism. During Philip's first group meeting, Gill feels an urgent need to speak about how a therapist gave his wife, Rose, a book about child sexual abuse that convinced her that she was sexually molested in her childhood. Rose now has, in Gill's words, "an idea feexed," which prompts Philip's immediate correction: "An idée fixe." With her therapist's approval, Rose jumps to the conclusion, without any evidence, that her father sexually abused her in childhood. Mortified by the accusation, Rose's father agrees to attend her therapy session, traveling hundreds of miles to get there. Rose asks Gill to also attend—"for protection."

Yalom knows as a psychiatrist that sexual abuse, particularly against a helpless child, is a serious problem with far-reaching psychological consequences. As a novelist, he would never take the crime lightly. But during Rose's therapy session, her accusations against her father grow wilder and wilder, as Gill recounts to his own therapy group. "Accusing him of everything, even inviting his neighbors, his poker chums, his coworkers at the fire department—he was a fireman back then—to have sex with her when she was a child" (80). Another member of the group, Rebecca, asks Gill how Rose's father responded to the accusations. "He behaved like a mensch," Gill says. "He's a nice old man, about seventy years old, kindly, sweet. This is the first time I met him. He was amazing—God, I wish I had a father like that. Just sat there and took it and told Rose that, if she had all that anger, it was probably best to let it out. He just kept gently denying all her crazy charges and took a guess—a good one, I think—that what she is really angry about is his walking out on the family when she was twelve" (81).

The book that Rose's therapist swears by is almost certainly *The Courage to Heal*, by Ellen Bass and her former student Laura Davis. First published in 1988 and now in its fourth edition, *The Courage to Heal* remains the bestselling self-help book of all time. The book served as a battle cry for women who believed they were sexually abused in childhood, sometimes during the first year or two of life, but then had no memory of the experience until they entered therapy decades later. *The Courage to Heal* triggered the recovered memory (and the satanic ritual abuse) phenomenon that roiled psychology and psychotherapy for two decades.

Memory researchers have demonstrated that memory is not like a tape recorder or camera, faithfully reproducing a sound or image, but an ongoing process that involves constant change, revision, and often distortion. In *The Myth of Repressed Memory*, Elizabeth Loftus and Katherine Ketcham showed, in a classic experiment called "Lost in the Mall," that it is easy to create false memories in children. Memory is malleable, not only unreliable but also easily manipulated. As the Cambridge researcher Frederic Bartlett observed nearly a century ago, remembering is an "imaginative reconstruction, or construction, built out of the relation of our attitude towards a whole active mass of organized past reactions or experience. . . . It is thus hardly ever really exact" (qtd. by Oliver Sacks, *Hallucinations*, 154, n.7). Therapists can plant, deliberately or not, an idea in a patient, thus creating an idée fixe, as seemed likely in Rose. Julius wisely avoids giving Gill advice about how to respond to his wife's situation. And Yalom wisely reminds his readers that psychotherapy has had its share of fads and false cures that, in retrospect, damage patients.

Julius's worst fears about Philip appear confirmed during the early group meetings. The tensions between the two are palpable. Philip upstages Julius by informing the group about his terminal diagnosis. "I feel preempted, I feel like I had a big news story to tell you and I've been scooped," Julius complains, "scooped on my own life story—or death story" (97). Julius thus experiences a double narcissistic injury, first when he receives his terminal diagnosis, then when he is deprived of the opportunity to narrate it in his own words. Julius needs to tell his own story, not have someone tell it for him. Even when Philip tries to be helpful, citing Spinoza's Latin phrase *sub specie aeternitatis*, the need to take a cosmic-eye view of life, Julius finds the advice unhelpful, the wrong kind of medicine he needs. Julius's medicine for dealing with the dark thoughts assailing him night and day, reminding him that he has no future, is the intense life he experiences in his therapy group, a medicine that Philip finds toxic. The other group members are quick to perceive the hostility between Julius and Philip. Asked why he has chosen to invite Philip to the group, Julius uncharacteristically responds, "I frankly don't know my motives" (102). Julius believes that what he most needs now is to shore up his attachments, while Philip believes, like Schopenhauer, that the more attachments one has, the more burdensome life becomes. Their contrasting attitudes point to the double entendre in the novel's title, as Ruthellen Josselson suggests: " 'The Schopenhauer Cure' refers both to the cure that Schopenhauer provides and to the cure that Schopenhauer needs" (91).

"A New Life-Form"

The group members are so baffled by Philip that they regard him as a "new species, a new life-form" (167). Tony, a college dropout who has spent time in jail for assault, accuses him of intellectual "preening" by offering "snappy, deep-sounding slogans," efforts, Tony adds, that are a form of seduction. Philip impersonally rejects the charge. There's something fascinating and offputting about Philip even when he quotes Schopenhauer's belief, expressed late in life after he had received the fame he had long craved, that, as *fellow sufferers*, "we stand in need of tolerance and love from our neighbors in life" (168). Yalom is particularly fond of Schopenhauer's term, suggesting in *The Gift of Therapy* that the expression abolishes distinctions between patients and therapists, "between 'them' (the afflicted) and 'us' (the healers)" (8). Yet when Philip uses "fellow sufferers" early in the story, he still intellectualizes, unable to *feel* the truth of Schopenhauer's term.

Readers cannot help wondering whether this new species or life-form called Philip Slate is entirely devoid of emotions, a tabula rasa lacking the capacity to understand the affective nature of life, or whether he has repressed his emotions to the degree where they have become permanently inaccessible. Philip is Yalom's most unusual character, one who refers to himself in the third person, fails to look at other people or address them by name, speaks in a disembodied voice, emanates an otherworldly untouchability, and appears to inhabit a different planet.

Arthur Schopenhauer

Philip does not believe in reincarnation, but if he could go back in time, he would want to be Arthur Schopenhauer. Believing Schopenhauer has saved his life, Philip is convinced the philosopher can save others' lives. Quickly losing interest in teaching because no student was good enough for him, a statement Schopenhauer felt was true about his own brief, unsatisfying stint as a professor, Philip now turns to philosophical counseling. Since philosophy had healed him, he tells the group, so might it heal others. *Healing* is an ambiguous word, and the limitations of the Schopenhauer cure are immediately evident.

Nevertheless, Philip is correct that reading Schopenhauer's writings enabled him to overcome a serious sexual addiction, a fact that Julius regards as remarkable. "Most therapists today would say it's not possible to overcome a severe sex addiction on your own." Whatever Schopenhauerian techniques Philip used were undeniably effective—"better than anything I offered," Julius admits, "even though I gave it my best shot" (329).

Unlike *When Nietzsche Wept*, which takes place in 1882, a decisive year in the life of Yalom's two major characters, *The Schopenhauer Cure* is set in the present, 2005, 145 years after the historical philosopher's death at the age of seventy-two. Since few of Yalom's readers are likely to know much about Schopenhauer, the novelist decided to narrate two parallel stories of self-discovery and self-transformation. Philip Slate's first intellectual and psychological breakthrough occurs when he reads Schopenhauer's writings in graduate school and, with the philosopher's help, breaks a self-destructive addiction. A second and more noteworthy breakthrough occurs when Philip learns, as a member of Julius's therapy group, the importance of human relationships. To help us understand Philip's first cure, Yalom shows us Schopenhauer's growth as a person and thinker.

Sixteen of the forty-two chapters in *The Schopenhauer Cure* focus on the life and work of the historical philosopher. The chapters illuminate the many parallels between Philip and Schopenhauer. "To know Schopenhauer is to know me," Philip apprises the members of the therapy group. "We are inseparable, twin-brained" (169). Like Philip, Schopenhauer experienced a "love-bereft childhood" that ineluctably shaped his life and philosophy. Schopenhauer's father was a businessman who committed suicide when his son was still an adolescent. Schopenhauer was often enraged with his mother, whom he held accountable for his father's suicide. In a reference to an influential theory proposed by the psychoanalyst Erik Erikson, Yalom observes that children deprived of a maternal bond "fail to develop the basic trust necessary to love themselves, to believe that others will love them, or to love being alive. In adulthood they become estranged, withdraw into themselves, and often live in an adversarial relationship with others. Such was the psychological landscape that would ultimately inform Arthur's worldview" (42)—and Philip's. Being deprived of maternal love is difficult enough, but being deprived of a father through suicide creates a double whammy.

A Father's Suicide

Yalom has much to say about the impact of Heinrich Schopenhauer's suicide, at age sixty-five, on his teenage son's life. "Every suicide leaves a wave of shock, guilt, and anger in the survivors," the novelist points out, "and Arthur experienced all these sentiments." One positive consequence of Heinrich's suicide was that it allowed his only son to pursue his passion to become a philosopher, a career choice of which his father would surely have disapproved. In this sense, Yalom observes, Schopenhauer benefited from his father's early death, as did Nietzsche and Sartre, who also lost their own fathers in early life. "Could Nietzsche have become the Antichrist," Yalom rhetorically asks, "if his father, a Lutheran minister, had not died when Nietzsche was a child?" (108).

The darker side of Schopenhauer's liberation was his fear that he may have contributed to his father's suicide. Relief is often accompanied by guilt, then anger, which can be both internalized and externalized. No death is more difficult to mourn and work through than suicide, which creates a lifelong legacy, or illegacy, of dark emotions. Schopenhauer came to believe that his mother was responsible for his father's suicide, resulting in the son's "vicious criticism of his mother's behavior toward his father" (124). Yalom might have pointed out that, like Schopenhauer, Ernest Hemingway blamed his mother for his father's suicide, an accusation that is played out in his most autobiographical novel, *For Whom the Bell Tolls*. The lifelong misogyny expressed throughout Schopenhauer's and Hemingway's writings may be understood, in part, as a response to the conviction that the writer's mother was responsible for the suicide of the father. Philip struggles with the same problem of a father's suicide.

Yalom prefaces forty-one of the forty-two chapters with apt epigraphs by Schopenhauer. Yalom helpfully offers bibliographical citations that enable readers to find key passages in Schopenhauer's writings for further study. Sometimes the passage is paradoxical or koanlike: "Life is a miserable thing. I have decided to spend my life thinking about it" (23). Sometimes the passage reveals a startlingly new definition of genius, as when the philosopher writes, "Talent is like a marksman who hits a target which others reach; genius is like a marksman who hits a target which others cannot see" (31). Schopenhauer is on target here; the aphorism itself is a work of genius. Sometimes the passage foreshadows orthodox Freudian theory, with all of its deterministic rigidity: "The solid foundations of our view of the world and thus its depth or shallowness are formed in the years of childhood. Such a view is subsequently elaborated and perfected, yet essentially it is not altered" (41).

Some of the passages are cautionary tales, as when Schopenhauer observes that a "person of high, rare gifts who is forced into a job which is merely useful is like a valuable vase decorated with the most beautiful painting and then used as a kitchen pot" (107). Often the quote reflects the theme of the chapter, as the preceding one does, describing Schopenhauer's narrow escape from his father's efforts to make him into a merchant. Some of the passages affirm the importance of the here-and-now, a frequent Yalom theme, as well as the need for self-fulfillment. Some of the passages bespeak enduring insights into mortality that one can appreciate only on the brink of death. "The cheerfulness and buoyancy of our youth are due partly to the fact that we are climbing the hill of life and do not see death that lies at the foot of the other side" (171). And some of Schopenhauer's statements appeal equally to Yalom: both are people of the book. "The monuments, the ideas left behind by beings like me are my greatest pleasure in life. Without books I would long ago have been in despair" (261). Other Schopenhauer passages betoken a cynicism that Yalom pointedly rejects. "He is a happy man who can once and for all avoid having to do with a great many of his fellow creatures" (175).

This is the statement that guides Philip's life. Yalom uses as chapter epigraphs Schopenhauer pronouncements that characterize Philip's misspent life, both the orgiastic heights and the self-loathing depths of sexual addiction. Some passages are insufferably arrogant, as Philip is for most of the novel. "By the time I was thirty I was heartily sick and tired of having to regard as my equals creatures who were not really so at all. As long as a cat is young it plays with paper pellets because it regards these as alive and as something similar to itself. It has been the same for me with human bipeds" (207). Other passages reveal, if not humility, the recognition that we are all imperfect, deserving of patience and forgiveness, an insight Philip achieves by novel's end. "We should treat with indulgence every human folly, failing, and vice, bearing in mind that what we have before us are simply our own failings, follies, and vices" (309).

Some passages inspire hope and determination to acquire wisdom only to show the futility and delusion of such an effort. "The greatest wisdom is to make the enjoyment of the present the supreme object of life because that is the only reality, all else being the play of thought. But we could just as well call it our greatest folly because that which exists only a moment and vanishes as a dream can never be worth a serious effort" (73). Other passages evoke an aha moment, an epiphany. "Great sufferings render lesser ones quite incapable of being felt, and conversely, in the absence of great sufferings even the smallest vexations and annoyances torment us" (129). One parable reveals the unpredictable consequences of self-disclosure. "If I maintain silence about my secret it is my prisoner; if I let it slip from my tongue, I am its prisoner. On the tree of silence hangs the fruits of peace" (191). The novel's final epigraph reads like Schopenhauer's valedictory summing up to the world. "Mankind has learned a few things from me which it will never forget" (343).

Only one chapter epigraph does not come from Schopenhauer. Yalom instead uses a statement by Nietzsche: "Some cannot loosen their own chains yet can nonetheless liberate their friends" (321). Reading Schopenhauer helped loosen Nietzsche's own chains, but he then needed liberation from his former mentor.

Yalom points out the extensive pathology in Schopenhauer without pathologizing him. The novelist combines insight and empathy in his psychobiographical portrait. Yalom's prefaces and psychobiographical narrative allow Schopenhauer to come alive to his readers. Yalom is, as both a teacher and storyteller, the opposite of the narrowminded Philip. Yalom casts much light on the connections between Schopenhauer's life and work, and the novelist's interpretations are always thoughtful and provocative. The Schopenhauer passages that serve as chapter epigraphs in the novel reveal the depth and breadth of Yalom's knowledge of the philosopher. Most of the passages come from Schopenhauer's first and greatest book, the work by which he is most remembered, *The World as Will and Representation*. Some passages come from his late book, *Parerga and Paralipomena*, which, despite its unwieldy title, achieved unexpected popularity and catapulted the philosopher to fame. Some passages, according to the notes, indicate that Yalom modified the English translation with the help of Walter Sokel, a distinguished professor of German and translator who died in 2014 at the age of ninety-six. In short, Yalom has scoured the entire Schopenhauer corpus for pithy sayings. And Philip, of course, can hardly utter an expression in the story without quoting his master.

Confessions of a Philosopher

Yalom acknowledges many sources for his understanding of Schopenhauer's life and philosophy, singling out two scholars for special praise. His greatest debt is to Rüdiger Safranski, the author of *Schopenhauer and the Wild Years of Philosophy*, published in English in 1991. Yalom also cites Bryan Magee for his 1999 study *Confessions of a Philosopher*, which gave him the idea of bibliotherapy, "curing oneself through reading the entire corpus of philosophy" (viii). Magee's book is of particular interest to us because, like *The Schopenhauer Cure*, it is highly personal, showing how philosophy can help one suffering from the illness called life. Born in 1930, one year before Yalom, Magee is a prominent British philosopher who has also been a Member of Parliament, radio and television producer, and music and theater critic. Magee is in many ways a kindred spirit of Yalom. The two share many of the same philosophical and artistic beliefs, including an abiding interest in Schopenhauer. Magee's experience of bibliotherapy with Schopenhauer is different from Philip's experience, however, and it is instructive to compare their stories.

Magee suffered in his middle and late thirties a midlife crisis of "cataclysmic force." Despite having everything in life he wanted, including fulfilling relationships, professional success, and an adventurous life, he was overwhelmed by a "hyper-vivid and preternaturally powerful" feeling of mortality. How could life have meaning, Magee wondered, in the face of death? Like Yalom, Magee could find no comfort in God. He remains intellectually agnostic, concluding that the most important questions are unknowable. Magee's midlife crisis, when he came close to a breakdown, was less intellectual than existential, and beyond the ability of language to describe. He was not suicidal during this period because he lacked the agency to end his life. He was certain he was going to die, however, like a fire that goes out when it runs out of fuel. Instead of dying, Magee discovered a philosopher who changed his life, or rather *re*discovered a philosopher, since Magee had read the thinker's work a half-dozen years earlier, without much benefit. It took a midlife crisis to convince Magee of the philosopher's importance. The philosopher was Schopenhauer. "He showed me what was implicit, ungrasped, in much of my own experience" (267).

Unlike Philip, who sought and received Schopenhauer's help for curing a sexual addiction, Magee finds in the philosopher's writings the most plausible answer to the question "What is life?" When Magee began reading Patrick Gardner's 1997 critical study *Schopenhauer*, a book Yalom also read, the words leaped at him off the page in a way that he had never experienced before or since. "When I read the words the 'solution of the riddle of the world is only possible through the proper connection of outer with inner experience' it was as if someone had switched a light on inside my head" (353). Once he finished reading Gardner's book, Magee rushed out to read all of Schopenhauer's works. Rereading *The World as Will and Representation*, Magee found the experience life-transforming. "It was as if my hearing had been restored. Never have I had the feeling of being so directly and vividly in personal contact with an author: Arthur Schopenhauer was in the room there with me, sitting in front of me, talking to me, his hand on my arm or my knee, coining each new-minted phrase as he uttered it" (356).

Yalom would not agree with all of Magee's observations in *Confessions of a Philosopher*, including the following statement: "Of the religions I studied, the one I found least worthy of intellectual respect was Judaism. I have no desire to offend any of my readers, but the truth is that while reading foundational Jewish texts I often found myself thinking: "How could anyone possibly believe this?" When Magee made this comment to his "Jewish friends," they often said, "no intelligent Jew did" (347). Magee's statement is not only offensive but also wrong. One wonders how Magee and his friends could fail to appreciate, to cite only one Jewish philosopher and theologian, Martin Buber, whose writings Yalom quotes extensively throughout *The Schopenhauer Cure*. Moreover, Yalom demonstrates in his last novel, *The Spinoza Problem*, the Dutch philosopher's contributions to Jewish secularism.

Schopenhauer and Art

Schopenhauer was the first great philosopher to grant the highest value in life to art, the aesthetic impulse. Unlike Plato, arguably the world's greatest philosopher, highly suspicious of art, Schopenhauer became, as Safranski points out, "*the* artist's philosopher," influencing Friedrich Nietzsche, Richard Wagner, Thomas Mann, Marcel Proust, Franz Kafka, and Samuel

Beckett, among others (219). Both the philosopher and the artist gaze into the "ultimate nature of things, the ultimate mystery of existence," observes Magee. "As Schopenhauer put it, the philosopher is doing *in abstracto* what the artist is doing *in concreto*." Magee then quotes a philosophically trained novelist. "When Iris Murdoch said, 'For better and worse art goes deeper than philosophy,' she was right to imply that there are some respects in which philosophy surpasses art, and also right to imply that it comes short of it overall" (24).

Schopenhauer and Literature

Some of Yalom's most insightful observations focus on Schopenhauer's influence on literary writers, an influence not always acknowledged by literary scholars. Early in the novel Philip instructs Julius on Schopenhauer's influence on Sartre. "Schopenhauer believed 'Homo homini lupus'—*man is a wolf to man*; I'm certain that he was the inspiration of Sartre's *No Exit*" (64). Later, during a group session Pam refers to a passage in Nabokov's 1951 memoir *Speak, Memory*, which describes, in her words, life as a "spark between two identical pools of darkness, the darkness before we were born and the darkness after we die" (246). She has in mind the stunning opening sentence of Nabokov's memoir: "The cradle rocks above an abyss, and common sense tells us that our existence is but a brief crack between the two eternities of darkness" (Nabokov 5). Pam becomes irate when Philip points out that Nabokov "undoubtedly lifted" the passage from Schopenhauer. "You think Schopenhauer once said something vaguely similar. Big fucking deal!" Closing his eyes for greater concentration, but also because of his fraught relationship with her, Philip recites the entire passage from Schopenhauer's essay "Additional Remarks on the Doctrine of the Vanity of Existence," which Yalom then documents in the notes at the end of the novel: "A man finds himself, to his great astonishment, suddenly existing after thousands and thousands of years of non-existence; he lives for a little while; and then, again, comes an equally long period when he must exist no more" (246).

Pam is still furious at Philip for his sexual exploitation of her when she was his student; otherwise, one might expect her, as a literature professor, to appreciate his literary acumen. Though she may fail to see the relevance of his remark, Yalom's readers grasp that it helps to authenticate Philip's intimate knowledge of Schopenhauer and the skillful way in which Yalom incorporates the philosopher's writings into the novel. Schopenhauer's words are important for another reason. If he is right that existence after death is identical with existence before life, mortality loses much of its sting.

The Will

Schopenhauer's major work, *The World as Will and Representation*, first published in 1818 and subsequently revised, argues that a blind, irresistible, savage, malignant will drives human existence. Schopenhauer believed that we are bound to the "wheel of the will" and that we are constantly hovering over the abyss. Developing a metaphysics of the body, he localized the workings of the will in the genitals. As a rule, Safranski suggests, Schopenhauer believed that "we do not stand a chance against our sexuality" (137). In his unsatisfactory relationships with women, "Arthur Schopenhauer very personally experienced sexuality as the humiliation of his supreme autonomy" (137), an experience Philip well understands. Indeed, he embodied this brutish will twenty-five years earlier. "I was predatory, I was driven, I was insatiable, I thought of little else. My whole being was caught up in the pursuit of women—new women, always new women, because once I bedded a woman I rapidly lost interest in her" (265). Philip would agree completely with an early poem Schopenhauer wrote that evokes the nightmare of lust: "O lust, o hell/ O senses, o love,/ Not to be assuaged/ From heights of heaven/ You dragged me/ And flung me down/ Into the dust of this earth:/ Here I lie in fetters" (qtd. in Safranski 66).

The Psychological Schopenhauer

Yalom's major interest in Schopenhauer lies in his influence on psychotherapy, a profession that did not exist in the early nineteenth century. Yalom uses Philip to educate the members of the therapy group on Schopenhauer's impact on psychological thought. He was the first philosopher to "look at impulses and feelings from the *inside*," Philip remarks, "and for the rest of his career he wrote extensively about interior human concerns: sex, love, death, dreams, suffering, religion, suicide, relations with others, vanity, self-esteem. More than any other philosopher, he addressed those dark impulses deep within that we cannot bear to know and, hence, must repress" (286). Without Schopenhauer, there would be no Nietzsche or Freud, at least not as we know each thinker. Observing that he wrote his doctoral dissertation on

Schopenhauer's influence on Freud, paralleling Julius's article on Nietzsche's unacknowledged influence on Freud, Philip remarks that he is indebted to Schopenhauer because the philosopher normalized his sexuality. Philip also points out that Schopenhauer was the first major European figure to introduce Eastern thinking into Western philosophy. It is precisely for this reason that Pam has journeyed to India to attend a spiritual retreat in the hope of letting go of her anger toward the men who have failed her in her life. Her pilgrimage doesn't succeed, revealing Yalom's skepticism of a life based on renunciation and the absence of attachments.

Schopenhauer contra Nietzsche

Much of the opposition between Philip and Julius reflects the larger tension between Schopenhauer and Nietzsche. Julius spends almost as much time quoting from Nietzsche as Philip spends quoting from Schopenhauer. Julius seems to have memorized *Thus Spake Zarathustra*, from which he quotes repeatedly. Philip has also read the same philosopher, observing that Nietzsche "once said something to the effect that when we wake discouraged in the middle of the night, enemies that we had defeated long ago come back to haunt us" (130). Even when Philip quotes from Nietzsche, however, he cannot help adding that he "looted the works of Schopenhauer" (83). Julius has an ally in Pam, who loves Nietzsche as much as he does. Her favorite literary aphorism comes from *Thus Spake Zarathustra*: "One must have chaos in oneself to give birth to a dancing star" (152). Near the end of the novel Pam concedes that "Schopenhauer was a brilliant stylist and wrote the best prose of any philosopher. Except for Nietzsche, of course—no one wrote better than Nietzsche" (331).

Nietzsche began as Schopenhauer's disciple, but he evolved a philosophy that was the opposite of his mentor's. Nietzsche rejected Schopenhauer's pessimism and insisted on a life-affirming philosophy, a celebration of life. Schopenhauer was philosophy's most famous naysayer, Nietzsche, the most famous yea-sayer. Schopenhauer's destructive will became in Nietzsche's philosophy the "will to power," the courage to take charge of one's life by becoming all that one is capable of being. Unlike Schopenhauer, Nietzsche had little interest in Eastern spirituality.

And yet despite their differences, Schopenhauer and Nietzsche had much in common. Yalom's statement about Schopenhauer—"How disquieting to encounter a thinker so gifted yet so socially challenged, so prescient yet so blinded" (210)—is equally true of Nietzsche. Both philosophers were isolated and lonely for most of their adult lives, great geniuses who were strikingly deficient in their interpersonal skills. Yalom's observation that Freud's "unacknowledged co-revolutionary was Arthur Schopenhauer, who, long before Freud's birth, had posited that we are governed by deep biological forces and then delude ourselves into thinking that we consciously choose our activities" (190)—is also true of Nietzsche. Both rejected formal religion, which they believed enslaved worshipers. Both philosophers insisted on the subjective nature of truth, arguing that the interpreter is inseparable from the interpretation. And both philosophers were in agreement, as Yalom observes, that "death-anxiety is least where self-realization is most" (340). Julius shares all of these beliefs, as does Yalom.

Pam Swanvil

Apart from Julius and Philip, Pam Swanvil is the most interesting and outspoken character in the novel. Cut from the same cloth as Carol Astrid in *Lying on the Couch*, Pam is highly educated, accomplished, and articulate. She is also enraged most of the time. She feels betrayed by all the men in her life, beginning with Philip and his sexual exploitation of her. She had an affair with her gynecologist, Earl, twenty-seven years her senior, whom she later married. Impressed at first by Earl's literary sensibility, she discovers later that his mastery of great literature derived from Cliffs Notes, which he read to impress others. Pam left him after she learned he was sleeping with his patients. She then had a relationship with a fellow Berkeley English professor, John, who promised to leave his wife but then changed his mind. "Hour upon hour she oscillated between hating him, loving and desiring him, and wishing him dead" (146).

The early chapters in *The Schopenhauer Cure* offer insight into Pam's pursuit of Eastern enlightenment and the reasons she returned home largely unchanged. Yalom masterfully evokes the details of her expedition to India, including the exotic ancient erotic carvings of the *Kama Sutra*, the aroma of cinnamon and cardamom in the crowded streets, and her involvement in a ten-day festival of Ganesha in Bombay. Pam's guide, Vijay Pande, initiates her into the iconography of Lord Ganesha, who preached the cutting of all bonds of attachments. Yalom evokes in a few pages the cultural divide between the East and West. As Pam reveals that she stumbled upon the retreat by accident and was told that she should enter it with an open mind, Vijay begins shaking his head, and when she asks him if he disagrees with what she said, he replies, "Ah, remember that Indians shake their heads from side to side when they agree and up and down when they disagree—the reverse of the American custom" (119). Details like this lend credibility to the novel.

Pam's experience at the Vipassana meditation, taught by the guru Goenka, leaves something to be desired. She cannot free herself of desire, or attachments, and though she is a dedicated student, always giving her teachers the benefit of the doubt, she finds herself disappointed and disillusioned. She endures ten days of silence, which does have a cleaning effect on her mind, but she finds the idea of equanimity, or what one of the teachers calls *equipoise*, deadening to her imagination. None of the literary geniuses she most admires—Kafka, Dostoevsky, Woolf, Hardy, Camus, Plath, or Poe—would have been able to write in such a state of mind. Nor, we might add, would a novelist like Yalom be able to thrive in such an atmosphere.

Pam doesn't return to the therapy group until the second half of the novel, but her opening words, on seeing the new member, are memorable. "'Oh, it's Slate?' said Pam, pointedly not looking at Philip. 'Not Philip Sleaze? Or Slimeball? She glanced at the floor. 'Julius, I don't know if I can stay in the room with this asshole!'" (175). Her words energize the group. Yalom's two angry female characters, Carol Astrid and Pan Swanvil, one a lawyer, the other an English professor, are masters of invective, and their vernacular expressions, filled with salty language, enliven *Lying on the Couch* and *The Schopenhauer Cure*, respectively. Yalom is sympathetic to Pam's rage toward Philip, and he allows her to vent her feelings. Julius knows that he must find a way to help Pam overcome her anger toward Philip, lest she achieve a pyrrhic victory, destroying her adversary and herself in the process. Part of Julius's challenge is that, just as he is skeptical of the recovered memory movement, he is skeptical of the "forgiveness industry," with its simplistic platitudes and formulas. Julius is not eager to jump on the forgiveness bandwagon. Just as Julius, as a therapist, must find a way to help both Pam and Philip overcome their mutual mistrust of each other, Yalom, as a novelist, must allow both to remain in character while at the same time expanding their point of view.

Pam and Philip prove to be worthy antagonists, two professors who are equally gifted in citing intellectual authorities to support their positions. Pam has no trouble explaining to the group how, in Martin Buber's words, Philip exploited her in the past. Yalom reveals through Pam his talent for capturing, without reducing, the complexity of a scholar's writings. "Buber's a German-Jewish philosopher, died about fifty years ago, whose work explores the true encounter between two beings—the 'I-thou,' fully present, caring relationship—as opposed to the 'I-it' encounter that neglects the 'I-ness' of the other and uses rather than relates. The idea has come up a lot here—what Philip did to me years ago was to use me as an it" (222).

Risky—and Reciprocal—Self-Disclosures

Pam's reference to Buber is part of a longer discussion of risky self-revealing disclosures. Gill startles everyone by admitting he is an alcoholic, drinking himself to oblivion every night. Julius's shock turns into dismay when he realizes that Gill has never admitted this in either group therapy or in two years of individual therapy. Julius at first feels deceived, but he quickly recognizes that Gill should be praised, not condemned for his self-disclosure, however belated: "risk taking must always be supported and reinforced" (218). Gill's confession gives Philip an opportunity to ask Julius whether he is willing to share one of his own secrets. Taken aback, Julius waits until the next session to disclose a secret he has never confided to anyone except a close friend several years earlier, shortly after Miriam's death, when his grief took a "bizarre turn." Experiencing a "tremendous surge in sexual energy," he became obsessed by sex and had affairs with married and unmarried women, including a relative of Miriam's.

Significantly, Julius has followed Yalom's advice about therapist self-disclosure, which has been one of his enduring contributions to both individual and group psychotherapy. "The therapist has no more potent method to build behavior norms than personal modeling," Yalom points out in *The Gift of Therapy* (77). A few pages later he adds, "All comments must pass one test: Is this disclosure in the best interest of the patient?" (87). One of Julius's motives in making this confession is to express his identification with Philip. Another motive is to encourage the group to deidealize him, to realize that he is human, all too human.

Startled by Julius's confession, the members of the group remain silent, unsure what to say, but when they regain their voices, they respond empathically, asking him vertical questions about how these women reacted to his sexualized behavior. He doesn't hesitate to respond. "There was a lot of awkwardness. And a lot of shame" (239). Julius then raises a horizontal question. How do the group members feel about his self-disclosure? Having modeled the kind of self-disclosure he expects from the others, Julius initiates a valuable discussion. Tony asks Julius why he made the self-disclosure and answers his own question. "Is it because you made a bargain with Philip?" Julius then makes a prophetic comment. "Good question, Tony. I appreciate your getting me started. A few minutes ago I was wishing I had a cotherapist here to help me, and then you come along and do the job. You're good at this. Therapy could have been a good career for you" (240). Later reflecting on his self-disclosure, Julius realizes that, as a result of his terminal diagnosis, he has grown as a person and therapist. He has become a wounded healer.

Julius's self-disclosure catalyzes Pam's and Philip's equally risky self-disclosures. With only six more meetings left, Pam suddenly announces that she has been having an affair with Tony, who is unprepared for her announcement. Julius reminds her that she has broken one of the group's contracts. "The danger of an out-of-group relationship is that it *jeopardizes the therapy work*. How does it do that? *Because people in a tight relationship will often value that relationship more than the therapy work*" (300). Pam, so judgmental of others—she is referred to as the group's "chief justice"—has difficulty defending her actions, falling back on one rationalization after another, including acting on "automatic pilot," a metaphor that allows Philip to respond, softly, "As did I, long ago" (313). Finally she concedes that she made a mistake and apologizes for using and humiliating Tony. She also admits that she has learned something important from the group. "I do believe, now, it's possible to forgive the person but not the act. I think I might be capable of forgiving a changed Philip. *But he hasn't changed*" (316)—to which Philip responds that he too has changed. "My life has been very different—I have been with no woman in twelve years" (317). As if this bombshell self-disclosure is not explosive enough, Philip adds several key details, revealing anguish for the first time in the novel. He found the strength to change, he confesses, because life had become unbearable. Julius's epitaph comment helped Philip realize that he would spin forever on the wheel of torment unless he found a way to escape from it. By patterning his life after Schopenhauer's, Philip found a cure that worked—until his participation in the therapy group, when he realized that the denial of emotions and rejection of human connection created serious, even life-threatening side effects.

Seeing Pam in the therapy group reminded Philip of the frenzied emotions he felt toward her years earlier, when she was his student, and now. "Philip was prepared to hold nothing back, not his raw jealousy, not the caveman mentality of possessing Pam, not even the image of Tony with the Popeye forearms, but he was now overcome by a massive diaphoresis, which soaked him to the skin" (319). Yalom uses a rare technical word without defining it, but he allows readers to infer its meaning from the context of the passage: excessive sweating, usually caused by disease or extreme stress. Philip runs out of the room, and a few minutes later, when he returns with Tony, the emotionally intense chapter ends, with Philip utterly drained.

The penultimate meeting of the group is filled with surprises. Pam begins the meeting with a quote by Epictetus about the importance of taking part in civic life, learning to put up with insults, and tolerating other people. She accuses Philip of selectively picking and choosing only those passages that support his own positions. Pam and Philip then debate over whether Schopenhauer, who was chronically depressed for much of his adult life, should be taken seriously when he opined that most people would choose never to have been born. Philip predictably agrees with Schopenhauer that life consists of suffering from start to finish. Pam's motive in bringing up two of his favorite philosophers, Epictetus and Schopenhauer, Philip charges, was to "trap and confound" him. When pressed, Philip acknowledges that he didn't want to insult Pam, who may have been trying to help him. Using a word that is not part of his everyday vocabulary, and sounding like a lawyer in cross-examination, Tony advises Philip to make his intentions and behavior *congruent*. Philip unexpectedly agrees and then admits he needs therapy. Seeing everyone pretend to be shocked, he grins—for the first time in the novel. Tony, who despite a lack of formal education has the intuitive understanding of a therapist, expresses the theme of the novel: "Schopenhauer has cured you, but now you need to be saved from the Schopenhauer cure" (330).

Selectivity Error

Philip offers Pam a heartfelt apology for the years of suffering he has inadvertently caused her. He is not ready to renounce Schopenhauer's despairing vision of life, but he listens intently to Julius, who discloses how reading *Thus Spake Zarathustra* helped him come to terms with his terminal diagnosis. Pam, too, adores the novel and cites her favorite passage. "It's when Zarathustra says, '*Was that life? Well, then, once again!*' I love people who embrace life and get turned off by those who shrink away from it." Yalom uses the literature professor to offer his own view of Schopenhauer. "I'm teaching a course on biography," Pam says, "and in my reading last week I ran across an amazing passage in Erik Erikson's biography of Martin Luther.

It goes something like this: '*Luther elevated his own neurosis to that of a universal patient-hood and then tried to solve for the world what he could not solve for himself.*' I believe that Schopenhauer, like Luther, seriously fell into this error and that you've followed his lead" (332). Pam might have cited a related insight in *Young Man Luther* that applies to both Schopenhauer and Philip Slate. "Some day, maybe, there will exist a well-informed, well-considered, and yet fervent public conviction that the most deadly of all possible sins is the mutilation of a child's spirit; for such mutilation undercuts the life principle of trust, without which every human act, may it feel ever so good and seem ever so right, is prone to perversion by destructive forms of conscientiousness" (70).

Like Schopenhauer, Philip has fallen into a selectivity error by not allowing himself to see that life is a tragedy filled with joy. Yalom describes other selectivity errors as well, including one made by Pam. Bonnie observes that the Buddhist retreats Pam attended emphasize "loving kindness and connectivity—not solitude." Julius remarks that many of the ancient Greek philosophers quoted by Philip also affirm friendship. Philip still feels besieged, but Julius reminds him that he must enter the social world if he intends to become a counselor. Looking directly into Julius's eyes, Philip characterizes himself in the worst possible way, a creature incapable of loving or being loved. Beginning to sob, Philip bolts from the room, followed by Julius, who urges him to return. "You must go back, my boy," the therapist tells him. "This is what you came for, this very moment, and you mustn't squander it. You've worked well today—exactly the way you have to work to become a therapist. Only a couple of minutes left in the meeting. Just come back with me and sit in the room with the others. I'll watch out for you" (335). Both men then return together to the group. "Philip reached around and briefly, just for a moment, put his hand atop Julius's hand, then raised himself erect and walked alongside Julius back to the group" (335).

Yalom allows his readers to draw their own conclusions about the meaning of the novel's climactic scene. Recall that Philip's biological father committed suicide. We can't help wondering how the suicide affected the son's life. Yalom's statement about Schopenhauer's reaction to his father's death—"Every suicide leaves a wake of shock, guilt, and anger in the survivors"—almost certainly applies to Philip's reaction to his own father's death. To what extent does Philip's self-loathing, his belief that he is monstrous, unfit to live, represent an identification with a father who took his own life? The novel never explores the reasons behind Philip's sexual addiction, but might his behavior have been an expression of anger toward his mother, whom he may have blamed for his father's suicide, thus paralleling Schopenhauer's life? Might Philip's sexual compulsivity be a response to feelings of depersonalization, numbness, and emptiness that sometimes arise from trauma, as M. F. Schwartz and colleagues have theorized? Philip has overcome his sexual addiction by breaking *all* attachments, a response that has been helpful in some ways and harmful in others.

The father symbolism surrounding Julius in this scene is striking. Julius rarely thinks about his children, but surely he must reflect on the question old Thomas Buddenbrooks asks in Mann's novel: "Have I hoped to live on in my son?" (49). Julius's terminal illness further complicates the situation, and Philip is again losing a vital figure in his life, one who has functioned as a lifeline. Julius promises to watch out for Philip once they return to the therapy group, but both men know that the therapist won't be around much longer to watch out for anyone.

Julius's therapy group is his most sustaining family, and by the end of the novel he has earned the trust and love of his wayward son. Philip knows for the first time the depth of Julius's feelings for him. He has internalized Julius's love, and soon he will be following in the therapist's footsteps. Julius is asked how he feels after he and Philip return to the group. "I'm feeling wonderful in my head, I'm so swept away, so admiring of the work this group has done—I'm so glad to have been a part of this. Physically, yes, I have to admit I am ailing, and weary. But I have more than enough juice left for our last meeting next week" (335–336). Not much else is left to be said in this chapter—except that the group never meets again. The next day Julius is stricken by severe headaches, lapses into a coma, and expires three days later.

Dying in Harness

"Die at the right time," Nietzsche exhorts his readers, and Julius follows the philosopher's sage advice, dying in character by working to the end of his life. Julius has few regrets about his life. We recall his statement that those who live fulfilling lives have fewer fears about death than those who remain unfulfilled. Julius dies offstage, but if we had access to his final thoughts, we would bear witness to a man who doubtlessly affirms the joy of having been alive. "I cannot pretend I am without fear. But my predominant feeling is one of gratitude. I have loved and been loved; I have been given much and I have given something in return; I have read and traveled and thought and written. I have had an intercourse with the world, the special intercourse of writers and readers."

These are not Julius's words but Oliver Sacks's upon learning that he has terminal cancer—metastatic melanoma. In his brief article "My Own Life," published in the *New York Times* on February 19, 2015, Sacks described how he felt entering the final chapter of his life. He had much in common with the dying Julius and even more in common with his exact contemporary, Irvin Yalom. The famed British neurologist and writer was born in 1933, two years after Yalom, and authored several bestselling case studies, one of which became an iconic film, *Awakenings*, starring Robin Williams and Robert De Niro. A professor of neurology and psychiatry, Sacks sought, like Yalom, to integrate the arts and sciences. The *New York Times* described Sacks as a "poet laureate of contemporary medicine" and "one of the great clinical writers of the 20th century," statements that could also be made about Yalom.

Reading "My Own Life," one is struck by how many of Sacks's statements could have been made by Yalom or his surrogate, Julius. "It is up to me now to choose how to live out the months that remain to me," Sacks writes. "I have to live in the richest, deepest, most productive way I can." He cites one of his favorite philosophers, David Hume, who, upon learning that he was mortally ill at age sixty-five, wrote a short autobiography in a single day, titled "My Own Life." Sacks continued writing after his terminal diagnosis, completing his autobiography and a book titled *Gratitude*. If Julius had more time after the final session of group therapy, it's likely that his last words would have been close in spirit to Sacks's. "Over the last few days, I have been able to see my life as from a great altitude, as a sort of landscape, and with a deepening sense of the connection of all its parts. This does not mean I am finished with life. On the contrary, I feel intensely alive, and I want and hope in the time that remains to deepen my friendships, to say farewell to those I love, to write more, to travel if I have the strength, to achieve new levels of understanding and insight." Sacks died six months later.[1] Why does Yalom kill off Julius before the final group therapy session? Julius's terminal diagnosis is an essential component of the novel, affecting all of the group members, but it is not the story's primary focus: finding an antidote to the Schopenhauer cure. Yalom dramatizes

---

1. "I never met Sacks," Yalom wrote in response to this paragraph, "but I admired his work and so loved his memoir that I wrote a fan letter to him a few days before he died. His assistant wrote me that she read my letter aloud to him."

Philip's breakthrough in the penultimate therapy session; showing rather than telling us about Julius's death might have been anticlimactic. Yalom has always been more interested in how characters live with the idea of death than with the moment of death itself. A curt two-sentence account avoids a sentimentalized or idealized death scene that is all too common in literature. (Oscar Wilde jeered that one must have a "heart of stone" to read the death of Dickens's Little Nell in *The Old Curiosity Shop* without laughing.)

Yalom was not interested in rewriting *The Death of Ivan Ilych*, showing a character in the final throes of death. Rather, Yalom wanted to imagine events with which he was intimately familiar. As a psychiatrist, he had worked with many dying patients, but he has never *shown* a person dying (apart from a brief account of Eva Galsworth's death in *Lying on the Couch*), perhaps because it would take him too far away from his stated purposes in writing fiction.

Many of Julius's statements about death early in the novel take on special significance at the end of the novel. "No one practices endings," Julius tells the group. "They only happen once. No textbooks are written about this situation—so everything is improvisation" (135). Without disagreeing with Julius, one may point out that writing about dying and death may be considered an example of practicing an ending, a dress rehearsal for an event that comes whether one is ready or not.

Death is the single event in life that novelists can only imagine rather than know, as the literary critic Garrett Stewart has pointed out. "Despite its brutal factuality at the close of life, dying is by nature the one inevitably fictional matter in prose fiction. Death for the self exists only as nonexistence, is not a topic so much as a voiding event, has no vocabulary native to it, would leave us mute before its impenetrable fact" (4). Julius has spent a lifetime preparing for death, reading everything he could on the subject, teaching others not to fear it, while simultaneously living to the fullest. A brief, offstage death suggests that Julius was as prepared as he could be.

The last two chapters of *The Schopenhauer Cure* bring the novel's two interrelated stories to an end. Schopenhauer, facing death with lucidity, achieved in the final years of life the recognition and fame for which he long searched. His death was brief and painless: one moment he was reading on his sofa, the next moment he succumbed to a pulmonary embolus. Schopenhauer wrote in his will that he wanted only his name on his gravestone, in his own words, "nothing more, no date, no year, no syllable." In Yalom's own words, "The man lying under this modest headstone wanted his work to speak for him" (342). Many have spoken eloquently for Schopenhauer, including Yalom. The final chapter in *The Schopenhauer Cure* takes place three years later. Pam, Philip, and Tony have become friends, and Pam kisses each of them on the forehead, exclaiming, "Remember Julius loved you both. And I do too." She wishes them good luck on this special day. An hour later the two cotherapists begin leading their first therapy group together. Seven members file into Philip's office and sit down on what used to be Julius's chairs. "Philip had wept twice as an adult: once during that last meeting of Julius's therapy group and again upon learning that Julius had bequeathed him these nine chairs" (344).

Perhaps the major question at the end of the novel involves the depth and breadth of Philip's transformation. Can a person who has never known how to relate in a healthy way to others grasp the error of his ways, learn to value human connection, and become an empathic therapist? Another question involves the tidy resolution at the end of the novel. All of the patients make significant progress and work as hard as possible to solve their interpersonal difficulties while Julius is still alive. Is their remarkable therapeutic progress realistic—or dictated by the aesthetic demand for closure?

Arousers and Fulfillers

The dying have much to teach the living. No one knows this better than Yalom, whose fictional and nonfictional writings are meditations on mortality. Death is never far from Julius's group therapy sessions, and he has much to accomplish in the one healthy year he has left.

In her 1994 novel *The Good Husband*, Gail Godwin likens a fictional character's dying to a final examination. Magda Danvers, a fifty-eight-year-old English professor, is dying from ovarian cancer, and she wonders what her final words will be. Taking stock of her life, she makes a distinction between *arousers* and *fulfillers*. Magda is an arouser. She has shown her students and readers "some pointers toward the wholeness, led them on day-trips toward it, but," she notes, "I haven't provided the wholeness myself. That is art's purpose. It may be the only way we can get what we strive for in this life. The human condition is notorious for its lack of wholeness" (168). By contrast, Julius and his creator are fulfillers, allowing us to see the beauty and wholeness of life.

"I can bear the thought that in a short time worms will eat away my body," Schopenhauer scoffed, "but the idea of philosophy professors nibbling at my philosophy makes me shudder" (337). Yalom uses this remark as an epigraph to the novel's penultimate chapter. Schopenhauer was unusually thin-skinned, dismissing the work of most of his contemporary fellow philosophers, whose writings he judged inferior. It is not likely that Yalom, who is always generous in his comments about fellow psychiatrists and novelists, will fear literary critics eviscerating his novels. *The Schopenhauer Cure* remains a riveting story about the inner workings of a psychotherapy group in which a dying therapist, in the tradition of the great philosophers, psychologists, theologians, and literary writers preceding him, can minister to human despair.

Widespread Praise

The Schopenhauer Cure generated largely positive reviews in several interdisciplinary journals and newspapers. Joan-Dianne Smith began her discussion of the novel in the *International Journal of Group Psychotherapy* with a sentence with which many of the other reviewers agreed: "Arguably the most realistic, honest, and poignant portrayal of the experience of group therapy in fiction, this intriguing page-turner will appeal to anyone interested in philosophy, psychotherapy, and the human struggle for meaning." Andrew Barley called *The Schopenhauer Cure* in the bimonthly publication *Philosophy Now* a "very poignant and personal book," a "fine testament to the author's belief that we should aspire 'to create beyond oneself.'" Merle Rubin characterized the novel in the *Los Angeles Times* as a highly distinct brand of fiction. "Unlike novelists who disclaim any extra-literary motives in writing, Yalom's aims are unabashedly educational. Contrary to a widely held misconception, 'educational' can mean interesting. Yalom's enthusiasm is contagious, and his knack for presenting complex ideas and theories in clear, engaging prose makes him a popularizer in the finest sense. And he certainly knows how to tell a page-turning story."

Most of the criticisms of *The Schopenhauer Cure* appeared in reviews that were largely positive. Glen O. Gabbard argued in the *American Journal of Psychiatry* that the plot developments were driven more by the novel's themes than by the psychological dimensions of the characters. Some reviewers expressed frustration by the juxtaposition of the psychotherapy sessions and the life of a dead philosopher, the same narrative structure Yalom uses in his next novel, *The Spinoza Problem*. "Yalom's braid doesn't hold together," Skye K. Moody lamented in the *Seattle Times*, "because the reader inevitably regrets jumping back from one fascinating story to the next and back again.

And yet, in its unraveling, the sending up of Hertzfeld reveals Yalom's brilliance as a storyteller."

Two Endings

We don't ordinarily think of scientists or physicians recommending revisions to a novel's ending, but an article published in the *Journal of Oncological Science* does precisely that. The author, Nalan Akgül Babacan, recalls meeting Yalom when she was a young medical student. "At that time, I was under black wings of a deep depression." Reading Yalom's books was transformative. "I read one book after another, and I am sure Irvin Yalom also contributed to the insight and life energy that I had gained when my therapy was completed. I continued to read his new books throughout my medical career and I became a part of a different philosopher's life with each work." Now an oncologist in Istanbul, Babacan speculates that Julius probably fell into a coma and died as a result of a brain metastasis. Until the 2010s, the expectancy for a patient with metastatic melanoma was six to nine months; now, however, as a result of revolutionary new anti-tumor drugs, the prognosis is much brighter. The new treatments for melanoma raise for Babacan an intriguing question: "Will we have a new ending for Irvin Yalom's famous book? Who knows, maybe the master of literature would have to choose another tumor with poorer survival or maybe Julius, although he had brain metastasis, would have benefited from a long and sustained response to his treatment and with this prolonged survival, he would have gently touched the lives of more people with the existential book that fed his soul upon diagnosis. Who knows?"

Even without this revision, Yalom has achieved by novel's close his four stated goals, showing us how group therapy works, how philosophy might influence the practice of psychotherapy, how Schopenhauer's life influenced his thinking, and how an awareness of death influences one's life. Yalom has fulfilled another implicit goal, showing us how education is the foundation of therapy. Education and psychotherapy both demonstrate, in Philip's words, wisdom and care. *The Schopenhauer Cure* also explores the nature of legacy, the gifts the dying bestow on the living. Legacy is an expression of gratitude for the priceless gift of sheer existence. No one is more grateful at the end of the story than Julius, grateful for the opportunity to consummate his life. It may be an exaggeration to say that as a result of Julius's legacy, Philip has an endowed chair, nine of them, the sign of a distinguished professor, but it is true that Philip will gladly teach what he has learned from his mentor. One does not need to believe in God or an afterlife to realize that Julius's spirit dwells in those whose lives he has touched. He remains a master teacher-therapist who instructs his patient-students how to live and die. Yalom never tells us what Julius wanted on his headstone, but Henry Adams's words come to mind: "A teacher affects eternity; he can never tell where his influence stops" (300).

Chapter 11

Staring at the Sun
Novel Healing

Yalom was seventy-five when he penned *Staring at the Sun*, and he reveals the many reasons he continues to write about death, beginning with the need to confront his own death anxiety. Believing in the importance of transparency, he suggests that writing is a process of desensitization. "I guess we can get used to anything, even death" (178). Yet there are other reasons to write about death, including the desire to teach others. "I've learned a great deal about tempering death anxiety and wish to transmit what I can to others while I'm still alive, still intellectually intact" (178). Yalom dryly notes that when his friends ask him what he is currently writing about, they don't know how to respond to his answer that he is working on a book about overcoming the terror of death. "With only a few exceptions, no one asks a follow-up question, and before long we are on a different topic" (276).

Yalom's title comes from a maxim (cited on the title page) by the seventeenth-century French writer François de La Rochefoucauld: "You cannot stare straight into the face of the sun, or death." Yalom offers an unflinching glimpse into the role of death anxiety in psychotherapy patients. "It's not easy to live every moment wholly aware of death," he concedes. "It's like trying to stare the sun in the face: you can stand only so much of it" (5). All of Yalom's writings demonstrate his acute awareness of death, but *Staring at the Sun* is his most personal book to date. He never shies away from offering personal examples of death anxiety. One way Yalom stares at the sun is to describe his patients' death anxiety; another way is to describe being with his teachers and mentors at the end of their lives; still another way is to describe his near-paralyzing anxiety while awaiting medical results of a potentially life-threatening lesion detected on an X-ray.

Perhaps the most unusual way Yalom stares at the sun is to reread his own fiction, which results in novel healing.

The power of *Staring at the Sun* rests on Yalom's authority both as a psychiatrist who has devoted his entire life to treating patients suffering from death anxiety and as an author who views patients and therapists alike as fellow travelers. "I feel strongly—as a man who will himself die one day in the not-too-distant future and as a psychiatrist who has spent decades dealing with death anxiety—that confronting death allows us, not to open some noisome Pandora's box, but to reenter life in a richer, more compassionate manner" (9). The reference to the "not-too-distant future" establishes the urgency of the book, which at times reads like an end-of-life memoir.

The seven chapters in *Staring at the Sun* explore different aspects of death anxiety. Chapter 1, "The Mortal Wound," serves as an introduction. Yalom's most influential mentors have not been the great psychologists but the classical philosophers, particularly Epicurus, whom he views as a proto-existential psychotherapist. Although Epicurus is best known for his enjoyment of sensuous pleasure, particularly food and drink, he is also associated with the goal of attaining tranquility, ataraxia, an idea Yalom develops in his next and last novel, *The Spinoza Problem*.

Chapter 2, "Recognizing Death Anxiety," suggests that the fear of death is not a symptom of or stand-in for something else but bedrock anxiety. The fear of death pervaded the lives of the patients Freud and Breuer wrote about in *Studies on Hysteria*. Two of the ways people attempt to overcome death anxiety are through supernatural religion, which promises life after death, and through their children, who for many parents represent their "immortality project" (25).

Chapter 3, "The Awakening Experience," offers a number of clinical vignettes illustrating how a confrontation with death can heighten one's appreciation of life. Yalom might have called his book "Awakenings" had not Oliver Sacks used the same word for the title of his 1973 book. Yalom cites Heidegger's distinction between two modes of reality, everyday reality, "how things are," where we are absorbed with quotidian reality, and ontological reality, "that things are," the miracle of being. Chapter 4, "The Power of Ideas," focuses on the philosophers, therapists, and literary writers who explored ways of coping with death anxiety while staring at the sun. Yalom devotes much of the chapter to a discussion of Epicurus, who anticipated our contemporary view of the unconscious, including the idea that death anxiety is hidden to most people and must be inferred by disguised manifestations. Yalom discusses other philosophers as well, including Nietzsche, showing how the philosopher's two granite statements, "become who you are" and "that which does not kill me makes me stronger," can be helpful to psychotherapy patients.

Chapter 5, "Overcoming Death Terror Through Connection," affirms the therapeutic power of presence. Yalom contrasts two types of loneliness, everyday loneliness and existential loneliness, the latter of which is more profound. Empathy is the most powerful tool to overcome both everyday and existential loneliness. Yalom is not the first therapist to affirm empathy. Carl Rogers was an early advocate of empathy, and Heinz Kohut formed a new psychological movement based on empathy. No therapist, however, has written about empathy more eloquently, over a longer period of time, than Yalom.

Chapter 6, "Death Awareness: A Memoir," is the most intriguing, deepening our understanding of the ways in which Yalom transmutes personal experiences into his fiction. He writes for the first time about his early experiences with death; discusses some of the poems and stories that have had the greatest impact on his life, including E. E. Cummings's "Mister Death," a poem that was so stunning that he memorized it on the spot; and interprets some of his most haunting death dreams. He also explains why he feels compelled to write about death.

The final chapter, "Addressing Death Anxiety: Advice for Therapists," is the longest in the book, appealing mainly to readers unfamiliar with Yalom's existential approach to psychotherapy. He focuses on several patients in this chapter. Asked by one patient how he deals with his own fear of death, Yalom responds, "I have my three A.M. bouts with anxiety about dying, too, but they occur far less now, and, as I grow older, gazing at death has some positive results: I feel more poignancy, more vitality, in my life; death makes me live more in each moment—valuing and appreciating the sheer pleasure of awareness, of being alive" (209). Perhaps the most important word in Yalom's answer is *too*, which, not unlike Olive Smith's expression, "that seems to be the way *we're* built," suggests the therapist's connection with his patient.

There are no new theoretical breakthroughs or shocking disclosures in *Staring at the Sun*, nothing that will stun Yalom's longtime readers. But, as with his earlier nonfiction works, there are surprises in his new book. A highlight is Yalom's discussion of how the experience of being with his dying mentor, Rollo May, led to a vivid dream that he used in a novel. Another highlight is how he comforted himself while waiting for the results of an MRI. Death continues to be Yalom's muse, as *Staring at the Sun* demonstrates.

The Use of Therapist Self-Disclosure

One of the revelations in *Staring at the Sun* is the number of therapies Yalom has personally experienced, including Rolfing, a form of deep-tissue bodywork popular in the 1970s. Rolfing eventually lost popularity because it was physically and emotionally painful. "My bête noir is bizarre belief," Yalom admits in *Staring at the Sun*: "aura therapy; semi-deified gurus; hands-on healers; prophets; untested healing claims of various nutritionists; aroma therapy; homeopathy; and zany ideas about such things as astral traveling, healing power of crystals, religious miracles, angels, feng shui, channeling, remote viewing, meditational levitation, psychokinesis, poltergeists, past lives therapy, and UFOs and extraterrestrials who inspired early civilizations, designed patterns in wheat fields, and built the Egyptian pyramids" (245).

Few of Yalom's suggestions to therapists are more disturbing than therapist self-disclosure. "It sets their teeth on edge. It evokes the specter of a patient invading their personal life" (241). Yalom has always used therapist self-disclosure to facilitate patient self-disclosure, but he has been careful not to share information about his family with his patients or readers. Now, however, for the first time he breaks this rule to demonstrate his knowledge that parents worry, sometimes excessively, about their children. The self-disclosure was not anticipated. Susan was distraught over the recent arrest of her son for a drug-related crime, and when Yalom scheduled an appointment with her during the early morning, a time that was usually reserved for writing, she asked why he was breaking his pattern. He told her that he would be traveling part of the next week to attend his son's wedding. Wanting to contribute something that might be helpful, Yalom added, "It's my son's second marriage, Susan, and I remember going through a bad period at the time of his divorce—it's awful to feel helpless as a parent. So I know from experience how dreadful you've been feeling. The desire to help our kids is hardwired into us." Susan later told him, during their last session, that this was the most valuable moment of her therapy. Significantly, it was not any of Yalom's interpretations of Susan's situation, or her own insights, that represented a turning point in her therapy, but his decision to share something about himself, a confirmation of the overwhelming importance of the therapist-patient relationship.

The Awakening Experience

Those who refuse to stare at the sun may console themselves that, to cite Ecclesiastes, there is nothing new under the sun. Some of Yalom's expressions are new, though not the ideas behind them. He uses the term *awakening experience* to describe how an urgent or irreversible event may jolt a person from an everyday state of mind into intense ontological awareness. A close encounter with death is a quintessential awakening experience. Yalom cites several literary examples of awakening experiences, such as Scrooge's epiphany arising from the visit of the Ghost of Christmas Yet to Come in *A Christmas Carol*, and Pierre's last-moment reprieve from a firing squad in *War and Peace*. The most famous example of a mortality awakening experience is *The Death of Ivan Ilych*, where the dying protagonist discovers near the end of his life that he has lived by the wrong values. Tolstoy conveys this epiphany in the sentence "In place of death there was light." Some readers have interpreted this as a Christian awakening: Ivan Ilych's final silent words, "It is finished," were the historical Jesus's last words. The secular Yalom does not present this reading. Instead, he affirms the dying protagonist's preternatural clarity arising from his explosive insight into the truth of existence, which is to live simply without hurting others.

Yalom has long believed that grief can be an awakening experience. Literature abounds in awakening experiences, and for this reason they can be helpful to psychotherapy patients. When one of his patients, Alice, describes the pain of giving away all the items in her household to move to a retirement home, he reads to her an apt passage from *Anna Karenina* depicting the abyss lurking below the bare scaffolding of life. The Tolstoy passage helped Alice, notes Yalom, "partly because her experience was named and thereby imbued with a sense of familiarity and control, and partly because of its implications for our relationship—namely, my having taken the time and effort to locate the passage containing some of my favorite Tolstoy lines" (43).

What's unusual about Yalom's relationship with Alice was that it lasted—"Hold on to your chairs, all of you younger readers familiar with the contemporary brief therapy model" (37–38)—for thirty years! She first began seeing him when she was fifty, for problems associated with her son as well as several friends and customers, and over the years she returned to therapy several times for other reasons, including her husband's death. Alice was not receptive to all of Yalom's ideas; sometimes she left curt messages on his answering machines telling him that his statements "felt like a slap in the face" (129). Their relationship, which was based on Yalom's willingness to assure her that he would never abandon or shun her, weathered these storms. Yalom offers us an unexpected coda to Alice's story. Two days after her move into a retirement community, she began a therapy session with the words "I'm happy." In an allusion to the title of an extended essay by Virginia Woolf, Yalom tells us that for the first time in Alice's life she had a room of her own.

Another patient, a cerebral forty-nine-year-old lawyer, Will, had an awakening experience largely as a result of Yalom's systematized clinical notes. Yalom vaguely remembered an earlier therapy session when Will had choked up with tears, but Yalom checked his notes when the patient could not remember anything about the moment. "I walked over to my computer, did a word search on 'tears' in his file, and after a minute sat back down. 'It *was* about your father. You were saying, sorrowfully, that you regretted never really talking personally to him, and suddenly you teared up'" (64). Will is impressed that Yalom remembered the tears in his eyes from an earlier session. The reader is impressed as well. In later sessions Will broke down repeatedly because of his new awareness of his hidden fears of his father's death as well as his own. Yalom doesn't make the connection for his readers, but he may have made extensive clinical notes so that he could later write about the case. If this is true, then Will's decision to allow Yalom to write about his story may have been responsible for the therapeutic breakthrough.

The Rippling Effect

One of Yalom's most powerful ideas in *Staring at the Sun* is the *rippling* effect,

> concentric circles of influence that may affect others for years, even for generations. That is, the effect we have on other people is in turn passed on to others, much as the ripples in a pond go on and on until they're no longer visible but continuing at a nano level. The idea that we can leave something of ourselves, even beyond our knowing, offers a potent answer to those who claim that meaninglessness inevitably flows from one's finiteness and transiency. (83)

As far as I know, Yalom is the first psychotherapist to refer to rippling. Used honorifically, the rippling effect is a legacy, a gift that is handed down to others. Yalom offers many examples of rippling, including leaving something of yourself behind for others, such as guidance, wisdom, or virtue. Making a contribution to society, science, or the arts is another way to create a rippling effect. "I feel blessed to be a therapist: watching others open up to life is extraordinarily satisfying. Therapy offers opportunities *par excellence* for rippling. In every hour of work, I am able to pass along parts of myself, parts of what I have learned about life" (165). Yalom's supreme rippler is Julius in *The Schopenhauer Cure*, passing along the gift of therapy to his patients, who will benefit from his help. He, in turn, has benefited from them: their trust, insights, and good will.

Ars moriendi: Yalom and Morrie Schwartz

Yalom's metaphor of the rippling effect, concentric circles of influence, recalls an allegory cited by Morris Schwartz in his 1996 book *Letting Go: Morrie's Reflections on Living While Dying*. A Brandeis sociology professor, Schwartz, who inspired Mitch Albom's 1997 bestseller, *Tuesdays with Morrie*, recounts a story told to him by his meditation teacher about a male wave who is terrified about crashing into the shore and perishing. "You don't understand," a female wave says to him reassuringly, "You're not a wave; you're part of the ocean" (127). Yalom doesn't cite either Schwartz or Albom, but Yalom would be sympathetic to the idea that the dying are part of a larger whole, connected to those who precede and follow them. Schwartz died of amyotrophic lateral sclerosis (ALS), Lou Gehrig's disease, in 1995 at the age of seventy-eight. There are passages in *Tuesdays with Morrie*, such as making death one's final research project, which the dying Julius in *The Schopenhauer Cure* would have appreciated and perhaps shared with his patients. "Since everyone was going to die," Schwartz observed, "he could be of great value, right? He could be research. A human textbook. *Study me in my slow and patient demise. Watch what happens to me. Learn with me*" (10).

Like Yalom, Schwartz knows that the worst aspect of dying is isolation. "Am I going to withdraw from the world, like most people do," Schwartz asked Ted Koppel on ABC's *Nightline*, "or am I going to live?" Schwartz then answered his own question in a way that Julius and Yalom would certainly endorse. "I decided I'm going to live—or at least try to live—the way I want, with dignity, with courage, with humor, with composure" (21). Many of Schwartz's life lessons are similar to those that appear in *Staring at the Sun*. "The way you get meaning into your life is to devote yourself to loving others, devote yourself to your community around you, and devote yourself to creating something that gives you purpose and meaning" (43). Schwartz's chief lesson, "Once you learn how to die, you learn how to live" (82), is the theme of *Staring at the Sun*. All of Yalom's books affirm the paradoxical belief that although the physicality of death destroys us, the idea of death saves us. One can imagine Yalom inscribing the words Schwartz selects for his own tombstone: "A Teacher to the Last."

Yalom and Schwartz both write from the point of view of participant-observer, a perspective the latter developed during the five years he worked at Chestnut Lodge, a psychiatric institution in Rockville, Maryland. *Staring at the Sun* and *Letting Go* are both inspirational without being platitudinous, an observation that cannot be said about the sentimental *Tuesdays with Morrie*. *Staring at the Sun* and *Letting Go* are both contemporary examples of *ars moriendi*, the art of dying. Yalom and Schwartz often refer to similar philosophers and poets, including Martin Buber and W. H. Auden. Yalom's comment that the dying often learn too late to appreciate life recalls Schwartz's droll observation in *Tuesdays with Morrie*: "Now that I'm dying, I've become much more interesting to people" (32). Schwartz coauthored three books early in his career and regretted near the end of his life that he hadn't written more, a regret that the highly prolific Yalom does not have.

Staring at the Sun is a more scholarly work than either Schwartz's *Letting Go* or Albom's *Tuesdays with Morrie*. Written from both an existential and psychodynamic perspective, *Staring at the Sun* is filled with the compassion, wisdom, and humor that both the common and uncommon reader will appreciate. Didactic without being dogmatic, Yalom has the rare ability to write upliftingly about grim topics.

Gratitude

Nothing sends off more ripples than gratitude. Yalom explored the darker implications of gratitude in *When Nietzsche Wept*, in which the philosopher refuses to be beholden to Breuer, fearing to be under anyone's power. In *Staring at the Sun* Yalom emphasizes only the positive side of gratitude, its ability to forge enduring relationships. He mentions using the "gratitude visit," one of the exercises devised by Martin Seligman, the founder of the positive psychology movement. Yalom asks his patients to undertake a gratitude visit. "Think of someone still living toward whom you feel great gratitude that you have never expressed. Spend ten minutes writing that person a gratitude letter and then pair up with someone here, and each of you read your letter to the other. The final step is that you pay a personal visit to that person sometime in the near future and read that letter aloud" (135). I have used a version of the gratitude visit in several of my writing courses, inviting students to express their gratitude to anyone, including those who are no longer alive. Yalom offers a personal example of the rippling nature of gratitude, demonstrating that gratitude is a gift that enriches both benefactor and recipient. "As a paterfamilias, I always pick up the check when my family dines at a restaurant. My four children always thank me graciously (after offering only feeble resistance), and I always say to them, 'Thank your grandfather Ben Yalom. I'm only a vessel passing on his generosity. He always picked up the check for me.' (And I, by the way, also offered only feeble resistance.)" (136).

Patients Reading Their Therapist's Books

Several of Yalom's examples of the rippling effect involve patients who have read his books. He reveals in both *The Gift of Therapy* and *Staring at the Sun* how his patients responded to him as a therapist-writer. "Most of my patients have read some of my books," Yalom states in *The Gift of Therapy*, "and their responses to my writing constitute a rich source of material. Some are intimidated by my having written so much. Some express concern that they will not prove interesting to me. One patient told me that he read a book of mine in snatches in the bookstore and didn't want to buy it, since he had 'already given a donation at the office.' Others, who make the assumption of an economy of scarcity, hate the books because my descriptions of close relationships to other patients suggest that there will be little love left for them" (51).

Yalom declares a few pages later that after the publication of *Love's Executioner*, he assumed that patients would be wary of being treated by a therapist who writes about psychotherapy. For this reason, he routinely assures new patients that he has never written about patients without first receiving their permission, and without using deep identity disguise. He implies that his patients do not worry that he will write about them without permission and without heavy disguise. Nor do they worry that he will regard them only as potential subjects for a psychiatric case study. What do they worry about? They are less concerned "with being written about than with not being interesting enough to be selected" (73).

In a 2015 interview with Terence Clarke published in the *Huffington Post*, Yalom admits that his reputation as a well-known writer has dramatically altered his practice as a psychotherapist, an issue he would "love" to write about in the future. "Now, literally every patient I see has come to me because of something I've written, and that does have a significant impact upon the course of the therapy. It makes me into a bit of a larger-than-life figure for the people I see, and maybe potentially it even gives me more power to do good, as long as ultimately I can get past their need to see me as a special sort of figure. I don't want to be idealized by a patient because of what I've written."

Not everyone shares Yalom's belief in the value of therapists writing about patients even with their permission and the use of deep identity disguise. Two articles appearing in the *New York Times* in 2015 and 2016 take a dim view of this practice. In "Why I Never Wrote About My Patients," Lisa Gornick, a psychoanalyst and author of two novels about therapy, begins by acknowledging that it is professionally acceptable to write about patients if they have given consent and have their identities disguised. The practice makes her uncomfortable, nevertheless, and she maintains that therapists who write about their own patients are exploiting them. She argues that patients, feeling psychologically coerced, are no more able to give therapists permission to write about them than children are able to give consent to sexual encounters with adults. Gornick believes that the therapeutic encounter should be a "sanctuary where, in the quiet company of an abstinent therapist, a patient can examine his or her most troubling thoughts and feelings." She also suggests that she would not be able to "maintain the hovering attention that the therapeutic work required if in the back of my mind I was foraging for something I might write."

Gary Greenberg reaches a similar conclusion in "Should Therapists Write About Patients?" though for a different reason. Like Gornick, he believes that patients feel subtly manipulated into giving permission if only because of the need to please their therapist. Greenberg describes his astonishment when his lawyer told him that the question isn't whether readers will recognize patients' identities in a published case study but whether patients will recognize themselves. Greenberg's inclination was to dismiss the warning. "After all, hasn't the world benefited from the beautifully rendered case studies by such masters of the craft as Sigmund Freud and Irvin Yalom?" Greenberg changed his mind when an irate patient who had given consent came to his office, book in hand, and angrily asserted, "I know this is me. I can't believe you would do this." Greenberg was dumbfounded. "Buried in the page, like a telltale heart, was that person's story. I knew it, the patient knew it, and we both knew in that moment that I had caused a wound beyond healing. I had used the patient for my own purposes. Our relationship was over."

In *Confidentiality and Its Discontents: Dilemmas of Privacy in Psychotherapy*, Paul W. Mosher and I discuss the many horror stories of patients discovering that their therapists have written about them without permission. Judy Leopold Kantrowitz argues in *Writing About Patients* (2006) that the use of heavy disguise without a patient's consent is acceptable, but her position has been challenged by Glen O. Gabbard (in "Disguise or Consent"), Peter L. Rudnytsky, and others. Elyn R. Saks and Shahrokh Golshan report in *Informed Consent in Psychoanalysis* (2013) that, based on an empirical study of sixty-two psychoanalysts who participated in their study, only a small percentage of analysts disclosed to their patients the possibility that they intended to write about them—an alarming conclusion.

Yalom avoids these problems by showing his patients *in advance* how he intends to write about them. He is thus in a unique position to discuss the impact of such writing in therapy. He offers several reasons in *Staring at the Sun* why patients may wish a therapist to write about them in a case study. Patients can reread a case study to remind themselves what they learned in therapy. They can read how far they have grown and developed since therapy—or, in some cases, how far they still may need to travel. They can read how their lives resemble those of other patients. They can read what their therapists learned as a result of the patients' stories. And they can read how they have made a difference in their therapists' lives or in those of their readers. Some of these reasons admittedly may be narcissistic, the pleasure of seeing how a therapist's world revolved around a patient's life, if only temporarily, but other reasons may be both educational and therapeutic. There's another reason patients may want their therapist to write about them: to remain connected with him after his (and their own) death. As Irene admits in "Seven Advanced Lessons in the Therapy of Grief," "*I don't want it to end with you.*"

Yalom never comes across as either self-serving or defensive about using his patients' stories in his writings. He allows his patients to speak for themselves in *Staring at the Sun* about how they feel reading their therapy stories:

> In *The Gift of Therapy*, I describe an incident where a patient who had lost her hair because of radiotherapy had felt extreme discomfort about her appearance and was fearful that someone

would see her without her wig. When she took a risk by removing her wig in my office, I responded by gently running my fingers through her few remaining wisps of hair. Years later, I saw her again for a brief course of therapy, and she told me that she had recently reread the passage about her in my book and felt joy that I had recorded this piece of her and passed it on to other therapists and patients. It gave her pleasure, she said, to learn that her experience might in some way benefit others even those unknown to her. (87)

Therapists who are themselves patients may find comfort appearing in a published case study. Jeff, a psychiatrist and longtime member of a leaderless support group in which Yalom was involved for the past fifteen years, was dying of cancer, and following his terminal diagnosis a few months earlier, he had been serving as a guide for all the other members on "how to face death in a direct, thoughtful, and courageous manner" (181). Despite a confidentiality rule, Jeff gave Yalom permission to record his feelings about the dying man's ordeal and his impact on the group. "A wave of sadness swept over me," Yalom writes. "There must be a way to save it. If only this group had been filmed and then shown over some total earth channel watched by all living humans, it would change the world forever." Yalom did not tape the group's meetings, but he realized there was another way to capture its essence: by writing about it. "Yes, that's the ticket—save, preserve, combat oblivion. Am I not addicted to preservation? Isn't that why I write books? Why am I writing this note? Isn't it some futile effort to record and preserve?" (184) There is a coda to the story. "Two weeks later, when we met in Jeff's home as he neared death, I again asked his permission to publish these notes and also whether he would prefer that I refer to him with a fictitious name or his real one. He asked that I use his real name" (185). Yalom invokes the rippling effect to explain the "sliver of comfort" Jeff experienced from the knowledge that his real name and clinical vignette would appear in *Staring at the Sun*. A related explanation for the sliver of comfort Jeff as well as Yalom experienced is what I call in *Dying in Character* the writer's creation of a *posterity self*. "The desire to create a posterity self is one of the main motives for writing about death. We write not only for the present but also for the future, a future in which we will no longer be alive" (16). There were probably other reasons Jeff wanted his real name used: to authenticate Yalom's clinical vignette, to convey his gratitude to Yalom for recording the event, and to help Yalom's readers come to terms with their own death anxiety.

Fiction Imitating Life

Like *Momma and the Meaning of Life*, *Staring at the Sun* illuminates Yalom's earlier writings by showing the ways in which he used life experiences in his novels. As an example of remaining connected with the dying, he tells us that decades ago a patient asked him, as he was saying good-bye to her for the final time, to lie next to him in her bed. "I did as she requested and, I believe, offered her comfort. Sheer presence is the greatest gift you can offer anyone facing death (or a physically healthy person in a death panic)" (130). Yalom fictionalized the scene in *Lying on the Couch*, when Ernest Lash lies next to his patient Eva Galsworth. It is one of the most memorable passages in the novel. Ernest was ashamed of momentarily becoming sexually aroused, but he "managed to banish it and to devote himself to hugging Eva in a loving fashion" (181). Eva soon lapsed into a coma and died a few hours later, with Ernest and her sister at her side. Yalom never tells us, nor is there reason to ask, which details in this scene are real and which are imagined. The scene demonstrates the connection between the living and the dying, the power of presence in the face of absence.

Another example of art arising from life is Ernest's Smokey the Bear dream in *Lying on the Couch*. Ernest interprets the dream as a response to dressing Eva's body in preparation for cremation—"Smokey the Bear representing cremation!" (183). Yalom discloses in *Staring at the Sun* that he had the Smokey the Bear dream immediately after helping to prepare the body of his therapist and mentor, Rollo May, for cremation. In the dream he is wearing a nightshirt bearing the smiling face of Smokey the Bear, but the face becomes brighter and brighter. "The dream woke me, not so much from terror, but from the brilliance of the blazing emblem on the nightshirt" (175). The dream signified Yalom's efforts to diminish the terror of death.

Three Mentors

The Smokey the Bear dream appears in chapter 6, "Death Awareness: A Memoir," in which Yalom discusses how death affected three of his mentors: Jerome Frank, John Whitehorn, and Rollo May. Yalom had a memorable encounter with death as a result of being with them near the end of their lives. Frank, one of Yalom's former professors at Johns Hopkins and the author of *Persuasion & Healing*, developed dementia in his nineties. At first Frank couldn't remember him and apologized for his memory loss. "Every morning my memory, the whole slate, is wiped clean." At last came a flicker of recognition. Reaching out to Yalom, Frank implied that life can still be good despite losing everything. "I treasure that gift," Yalom reports, "a final, end-of-life act of generosity by an extraordinary mentor" (167).

Whitehorn, another legendary professor of psychiatry at Hopkins, had a massive stroke that left him paralyzed. Yalom never figured out why his dying mentor requested to see him. "That he reached out to me, a student whom he had not seen in ten years, and with whom he never shared what I considered an intimate moment, indicates not so much any specialness on my part but rather his tragic lack of connectedness with people whom he cared for and who cared for him" (171). Yalom writes about Whitehorn with a combination of sympathy and criticism, not always easy to do when writing about the dead. The Latin phrase *De mortuis nihil nisi bonum*, "of the dead, nothing unless good," suggests the superstitious fear of speaking ill of the dead lest ill words come back to haunt the speaker.

Of the three mentors, Rollo May had the greatest impact on Yalom's life, important as a mentor, therapist, and friend. May's 1958 coedited book, *Existence: A New Dimension in Psychiatry and Psychology*, published during the second year of Yalom's psychiatric residency, profoundly influenced Yalom's development as an existential psychotherapist. As a result of reading the book, he enrolled in an undergraduate survey course in the history of Western philosophy, a decision that was probably as momentous as going to medical school. "Ever since, I have continued reading and auditing courses in philosophy and found there more wisdom and guidance in my work than in the professional literature of my field" (172–173). Many of the essays in the volume *Existential Therapy* (2012), edited by Laura Barnett and Greg Madison, celebrate Rollo May's contributions.

One can see why Yalom was so impressed with Rollo May. Rejecting all forms of scientific orthodoxy, which he calls "methodolatry," May demonstrates how scientific rigidity became a "Procrustean bed on which the empirical facts were stretched to fit a preconceived pattern" (22). Yalom must have been struck by May's definition of anxiety. "It is not a peripheral threat which I can take or leave, for example, or a reaction which may be classified beside other reactions; it is always a threat to the foundation, the center of my existence. Anxiety is the *experience of the threat of imminent non-being*" (50). And Yalom must have been intrigued by May's therapeutic techniques, one of which includes the following question. "I often have found myself having the impulse to ask, when the patient comes in and sits down, not '*How are you?*' but '*Where are you?*'" The "where," May continues, includes "whether he is detached or fully present, whether his direction is toward me and toward his problems or away from both," and "whether he is running for anxiety" (85).

Years later, when he began experiencing intense death anxiety as a result of working with terminally ill patients, Yalom entered into therapy with Rollo May, seeing him weekly for three years. Yalom makes no effort to minimize the severity of his anxiety during this time. "It was the isolation accompanying death that most haunted me; and, at one point, when I was experiencing great nighttime anxiety during lecture trips, I arranged to spend the night at an isolated motel not far from his office and to have sessions with him before and after that night" (173). The two of them "colluded," Yalom admits drolly, in "never staring at the sun," but the therapy was still valuable, and after it ended the two of them became close friends. Yalom concludes from the end-of-life experiences of his three mentors that to overcome death anxiety, one must maintain a connection with other people, a connection he feels with his patients and readers.

Undoing Death

Yalom is one of the few theorists in any discipline who reveals how his life experiences have influenced the construction of his theory. The childhood event that stands out to him most starkly was the reassurance he received from the family physician, Dr. Manchester, who was summoned when Yalom's father suffered a near-fatal heart attack. The physician held his stethoscope to the father's chest and allowed the fourteen-year-old son to listen. "See, ticking away, regular as a clock. He's going to be all right." The entire evening was a life-transforming event for Yalom, partly because of the terror arising from his father's close encounter with death, partly because of his mother's accusation, "You've killed him," and partly because of the physician's comforting words. "Then and there I decided to be like him, to be a physician and to pass on to others the comfort he had given me" (154). Yalom doesn't elaborate, but we can infer that counterphobic motivation lay behind the decision to become a physician, a way to keep his demons at bay.

Yalom recalls two momentous events surrounding his mother's death, at age ninety-three. The first event demonstrates that the unconscious sometimes works in strange and comic ways. Yalom decided, on the night before her funeral, to honor his mother's memory by baking a batch of her wonderful kichel, a popular Jewish pastry. "But the pastries were a failure," he bemoans. "It's the only time that ever happened. I forgot to put in the sugar! Perhaps that was a symbolic message from me to myself that I had focused too much on my mother's dourness. It's as though my unconscious was nudging me: 'You see, you've forgotten the good parts—her caring; her endless, often unspoken, devotion'" (156). Yalom's interpretation is true to his character, criticizing himself for his failure to appreciate his mother's hidden qualities. A less self-critical interpretation is that, apart from her baking, his mother was simply not a sweet person. The other noteworthy event involved a dream he had the night after his mother's funeral. The dream opens with his mother screeching his name, and as he hurries down the path to his childhood home, he opens the front door and sees all the members of his extended family, all of whom were in reality dead, sitting on the stairway, row after row, with sweet expressions on their faces. Yalom interprets this as a "death-defying" dream, an effort to undo death. The dream has another meaning, closely related to the first meaning, the need to remember the dead. "My mother called my name to tell me, 'Remember me, remember all of us, don't let us perish.' And so I have" (157).

"Remember Me"

Immediately after using the phrase "Remember me," Yalom recalls a startling example of forgetting. While writing *When Nietzsche Wept*, he composed a "few lines of doggerel" that his fictional philosopher recites in a cemetery: "till stone is laid on stone/ and though none can hear/ and none can see/ each sobs softly: remember me, remember me." Yalom composed these lines "in a flash" and was delighted at the opportunity to be a published poet, even if the lines were for a novel. About a year later his secretary came across in his office a large sealed envelope, yellowed with age, and when he opened it, he discovered that it contained a lost packet of poems he had written in his childhood and adolescence. "Among the verses were the identical lines, word for word, that I thought I had freshly composed for the novel. I had actually written them decades earlier, at the time of my fiancée's father's death. I had plagiarized myself!" (158).

Life Imitating Fiction

Remembering is at the heart of *Staring at the Sun*, and perhaps the most moving moment in the book occurs when Yalom writes about how he was able to cope with near-paralyzing death anxiety. Experiencing severe pain in his hip a few years earlier, he went to an orthopedic surgeon who ordered an X-ray and then was "foolish and insensitive" enough to point to a small spot on the X-ray and comment in a "matter-of-fact, doctor-to-doctor" tone that it might be a metastatic lesion—"in other words, a death sentence." During the next three days, while waiting for an MRI, Yalom was flooded with death anxiety. Of the different ways he found comfort, the most effective turned out to be reading a novel, his own recently completed *The Schopenhauer Cure*, where his dying protagonist, Julius, begins rereading *Thus Spake Zarathustra* and considers Nietzsche's idea of the eternal return. Julius ponders Nietzsche's challenge, Yalom tells us in *Staring at the Sun*, and realizes that, yes, he would live his life over in the same way if he could, with no regrets. "Reading my own words provided the comfort I had been seeking. *Consummate your life. Fulfill your potential.* Now I understood Nietzsche's counsel more fully. My own character, Julius, had shown me the way—a potent and unusual instance of life imitating fiction" (161).

Chapter 12

The Spinoza Problem

"A Sedative for My Passions"

The Spinoza Problem was published in 2012 when Yalom was eighty-one, an age when most novelists have stopped writing. (Turning eighty, Philip Roth declared that he had no further desire to write fiction.) *The Spinoza Problem* is Yalom's most ambitious and expansive novel, offering a glimpse into one of the world's most elusive philosophers. Many biographical studies have been written about Schopenhauer and Nietzsche. The two philosophers' extensive writings and correspondence shed light on their inner lives. By contrast, we know almost nothing about Spinoza's personal life.

Yalom noted in a 2012 interview with Gary Presley that *The Spinoza Problem* was his most difficult writing project, taking four years from start to finish. "When formulating the plot, it did not dawn on me that a novel, taking place in two time periods, would double research time. Most of my research was done from reading and with the help of colleagues in the philosophy department at Stanford and colleagues elsewhere in the United States, Holland and Germany."

Philosophy's supreme rationalist, Spinoza argued that the best way to achieve well-being and fulfillment is to overcome what we would call identity and selfhood, adopting instead an attitude of *sub specie aeternitatis*, viewing oneself from the aspect of eternity. But how does a novelist capture eternity? How can one embrace the vastness of the universe without losing a sense of being human? How can a novelist begin to imagine the inner life of a character who insisted, as Spinoza did, that all the personal references in his letters be stricken after his death? In short, how was Spinoza able to detach himself from the world of emotions and dwell in the empyrean world of pure reason?

Little is known about Spinoza's day-to-day existence in seventeenth-century Holland apart from the fact that he was excommunicated from the Dutch Jewish community, survived an assassination attempt, retreated from public view, embraced solitude, supported himself as a lens grinder, and continued to write incendiary texts until the end of his life, dying suddenly in 1677 at the age of forty-four. And yet without knowing much about Spinoza's private life, Yalom found himself drawn to him, partly because Spinoza was a great philosopher who heralded the Enlightenment and the modern age, and partly because he was an astute psychologist who prefigured Schopenhauer, Nietzsche, and Freud. The Dutch philosopher was a hero to Albert Einstein, who, visiting the Spinoza Museum on November 2, 1920, fell in love with the thinker, famously declaring himself to be a disciple. Einstein was in turn one of Yalom's early heroes. Another reason I suspect Yalom was drawn to Spinoza was because of the philosopher's affirmation of "nobility" (also translated as high-mindedness), the "desire by which each one strives, solely from the dictate of reason, to aid other men and join them to him in friendship" (*Spinoza Reader* 187).

A Mysterious Philosopher

The challenge of writing a novel about Spinoza was that, to cite Winston Churchill's words in a different context, he was a "riddle, wrapped in a mystery, inside an enigma." Scholars continue to debate the meaning of Spinoza's radical theological views. Was he, as he stated repeatedly, a deeply religious thinker who believed that "Nature is God, God is Nature"? Or was he, as his opponents maintained, a disingenuous atheist and secret mystic?

Spinoza's beliefs were so heretical that, at the age of twenty-three, he was excommunicated permanently from the Jewish community, forbidden to have contact with any Jew: his family, friends, business customers, *anyone*. Rejected by Jews and mistrusted by Christians, Spinoza redefined his existence while living in voluntary exile and accepted the ban with characteristic equanimity, believing that the excommunication, unprecedented in its duration and severity, was for the best. Yet if Spinoza felt no conflict over lifelong banishment from the world in which he grew up, and if he was so guarded about exposing his inner life, how can a novelist write about him? Conflict is necessary for a story; without conflict, there is no art. As Yalom admits ruefully, for years he was stumped by the challenge of writing about a man who sought to refine himself out of his philosophical writings.

Clearly, on one level, *The Spinoza Problem* is about *Yalom's* difficulty creating the characterization and plot necessary for a novel.

Reichsleiter Alfred Rosenberg

Yalom ruminated over the philosopher until a visit to the Spinoza Museum in Rijnsburg, a small village outside of Leiden in the Netherlands, where Spinoza lived from 1660 to 1663, led to an epiphany. Initially disappointed that the 159 volumes of Spinoza's own library were only replicas—all of the philosopher's possessions were auctioned off after his death—Yalom was told by his host that early during World War II German ERR troops had confiscated everything in the museum, including Spinoza's books. His curiosity piqued, Yalom asked what the letters stood for. "Einsatzstab Reichsleiter Rosenberg. The taskforce of Reich leader Rosenberg—that's Alfred Rosenberg, the major Nazi anti-Semitic ideologue" (xiii).

Strangely, the Nazis did not burn the books, all of which were miraculously returned to the Spinoza Museum after the war. But why did the Nazis take the trouble to steal Spinoza's books when they could have seized far more valuable objects, such as Rembrandt paintings? "The ERR had some mysterious interest in Spinoza," Yalom's host explained. "In his official report, Rosenberg's officer, the Nazi who did the hands-on looting of the library, added a tantalizing sentence: 'They contain valuable early works of great importance for the exploration of the Spinoza problem'" (xiii). Yalom could not stop thinking about the Spinoza problem—and shortly thereafter began writing.

Yalom never found any historical evidence linking Rosenberg and Spinoza. Every passage in the novel connecting the two men, Yalom explains in "Fact or Fiction? Setting the Record Straight," is fictional, including Rosenberg's two visits to the Rijnsburg Spinoza Museum in the Netherlands. The plot of *The Spinoza Problem* is so carefully constructed that it is easy for the reader to believe that these two visits are historically accurate—as *I* assumed, I admit, with embarrassment, until Yalom gently pointed out my misreading.

Devising a solution to the Spinoza problem was no easy task, for it meant that Yalom had to imagine the inner life of a cryptic Dutch philosopher and a Nazi ideologue guilty of appalling crimes against humanity. Rosenberg is Yalom's most sinister character. To understand such a figure requires both insight and empathy. Since *The Spinoza Problem* is a therapy novel, about the content and process of therapy, Yalom needed to create a character whose capacity for destructiveness exceeded that of any figure the novelist had yet imagined but who was still believable and potentially treatable. *The Spinoza Problem* is Yalom's bleakest novel, a story where the talking cure is powerless against evil.

In planning the novel, Yalom connected two historical characters who were separated by three hundred years. The seventeenth century was the Age of Inquisition, when thousands of Jews in Spain and Portugal were forced to convert to Christianity or flee from their homes and cultures. Those who did neither suffered the fate of martyrdom, burned at the stake. The new converts, or *conversos*, as they were called, lived under constant suspicion, fear, and surveillance. Any converted Christian who betrayed signs of lapsing back into Judaism could be punished by death. Many Jews from the Iberian Peninsula fled to Amsterdam, Europe's most tolerant city, but they too had to be careful, for the price of acceptance meant that they could make no statement that would be perceived as undermining the belief in God, the sanctity of the Bible, or the existence of an afterlife.

Jews who challenged rabbinic orthodoxy, like Spinoza, were excommunicated. Spinoza's ban, which occurs midway through the novel, and which Yalom quotes accurately, could not be more unnerving.

> By decree of the angels and by the command of the holy men, we excommunicate, expel, curse, and damn Baruch Spinoza with the consent of God, Blessed be He, and with the consent of the entire holy congregation, and in front of these holy scrolls with the 613 precepts which are written therein; cursing him with the excommunication with which Joshua banned Jericho and with the curse which Elisha cursed the boys and with all the castigations which are written in the Book of the Law. (145–146)

The seeds of Hitler's final solution of the Jews were planted in the Inquisition and the language of excommunication. The seventeenth-century Spanish-Portuguese Inquisition was a catastrophe exceeded only by the unimaginable calamity of the twentieth-century Holocaust.

Two Invented Characters

Writing a novel that *could* have happened, Yalom observes in "Fact or Fiction? Setting the Record Straight," he invented two important characters in the story, Franco Benitez and Friedrich Pfister, to serve as "gateways to the psyche of my protagonists" (318). According to early biographers, the historical Spinoza was betrayed by two unnamed men, called in the novel Franco Benitez and his cousin Jacob Mendoza, both of whom engage the young philosopher in religious discussion for the purpose of disclosing his heretical views to Amsterdam's chief religious authority, Rabbi Saul Levi Mortera. Unlike his cousin, who soon drops out of the story, Franco is a reluctant spy, and after Spinoza's excommunication, he remains secretly devoted to the philosopher. Their relationship develops into a warm, trusting friendship that is fully realized.

Spinoza plays the role of teacher, friend, and psychologist to Franco, but as in other Yalom novels, the principle of reciprocity appears: teachers and students, mentors and mentees, and therapists and patients often exchange roles. The historical Spinoza, so revolutionary in his ideas about religion, philosophy, and democracy, had traditional views about women, who, he believed, lack men's intelligence and therefore should not enjoy men's rights and privileges. To understand Spinoza's inner life and his affective world, Yalom uses Franco to uncover the philosopher's blind spots. Unable to change Bento's mind, Franco embodies a more progressive attitude, anticipating feminism and reform Judaism. Spinoza's relationship with Franco allows Yalom to explore the therapeutic uses of the philosopher's writings, much as Schopenhauer's writings serve as philosophical counseling to Philip Slate. Unlike Slate, who must receive an antidote to the Schopenhauer cure, Franco is never harmed by Spinoza's counseling, but he is mystified by some of the philosopher's axiomatic beliefs. Spinoza's views are not Franco's, and Yalom highlights their differences at the end of the story.

To understand Rosenberg's inner life, something that no novelist has attempted to do, Yalom creates his second notable character, a German psychoanalyst, Friedrich Pfister, who elicits the future Nazi's feelings on a wide range of subjects. (It's possible that the Oskar Pfister Award that Yalom received from the American Psychiatric Association in 2000 inspired the fictional analyst's last name.[1]) In the beginning of the story Friedrich is a young medical student who is a friend of Alfred Rosenberg's older brother. Friedrich first sees Alfred Rosenberg when he is an angry and confused young man, searching for an identity, before his involvement with the Nazi Party. Later Friedrich attempts to understand Rosenberg's tortured relationship with Hitler and deep narcissistic injuries. Throughout the novel Friedrich remains a sympathetic character, practicing an early form of existential psychiatry.

---

1. "Interesting speculation," Yalom wrote to me. "That never occurred to me."

Though he is later conscripted by the Nazis to serve as a Wehrmacht physician, Friedrich is repelled by anti-Semitism, but he is forced to obey orders and "treat" Rosenberg when he becomes severely depressed. Friedrich has a good understanding of Rosenberg's twisted psychology, but how would a therapist treat an anti-Semitic patient who knows that the creator of the talking cure was a hated Jew? And why would a Nazi be obsessed with a seventeenth-century philosopher who was a despicable Jew? These questions drive the plot of the novel.

Integrating the Two Stories

Spinoza wrote a number of books, including *Theological-Political Treatise*, a readable account of his views on religion and political philosophy. Spinoza was ahead of his time in arguing for a strict separation between church and state. His most influential work is the puzzling *Ethics*, written in the form of a Euclidean proof. Completed in 1674 and published posthumously in 1677, the *Ethics* is as much a statement about metaphysics as about moral philosophy. Yalom relies on both foundational Spinoza texts. It was largely on the basis of the *Ethics* that Bertrand Russell called Spinoza the "noblest and most lovable of the great philosophers. Intellectually, some others have surpassed him, but ethically he is supreme" (552).

Yalom always goes out of his way to acknowledge his sources, and the scholar to whom he is most indebted is Rebecca Goldstein, author of *Betraying Spinoza*, published in 2006. A philosopher, novelist, and recipient of a MacArthur "Genius" Award, Goldstein offers a highly personal account of Spinoza's greatness. She doesn't try to capture Spinoza's inner life, as Yalom does, but she does seek out the "pounding pulse of subjectivity within the crystalline structure of radical objectivity," a project that amounts to what she apologetically calls "betraying Spinoza" (66). Like Yalom, Goldstein is a paradoxicalist, and she captures a salient aspect of Spinoza's life and work. Trying to "think of himself as outside of the awful dilemmas of Jewish identity," Goldstein writes, Spinoza is, "paradoxically, Jewish at the core, a core that necessitated, for him, the denial of such a thing as a Jewish core" (178). Scholars are only now beginning to explore Spinoza's Jewish identity. Citing Yosef H. Yerushalmi's observation that Spinoza is the "first great culture-hero of modern secular Jews," Daniel B. Schwartz adds that Spinoza is "still the most oft-mentioned candidate for the title of first modern secular Jew" (2).

Yalom doesn't mention Antonio Damasio's *Looking for Spinoza* (2003), a penetrating study of the philosopher's theory of affects. Damasio, one of the world's foremost neurologists, sees Spinoza as a protobiologist, formulating a system of ethics based on the need to preserve one's own life while at the same time furthering other lives. Like Einstein before him and Yalom after him, Damasio writes about his pilgrimage to Rijnsburg to learn more about Spinoza's life. Damasio, too, fell in love with the philosopher, whom he sees as a forerunner of modern biological thinking, though he concludes in frustration: "something in him never yields to scrutiny and the strangeness about him never abates" (264).

Much more is known about Alfred Rosenberg. The author of *The Myth of the Twentieth Century*, which became a huge bestseller in Nazi Germany, second only to Hitler's *Mein Kampf*, Rosenberg authored several other books, including his *Memoirs*. *The Spinoza Problem* is a gripping account of the rise and fall of not only Alfred Rosenberg but also the malevolent ideology that he created, embodied, and disseminated. Many books have been written about Hitler, but even though Rosenberg is sometimes mentioned in these studies, no one has attempted to offer an inside analysis of his life.

As in *The Schopenhauer Cure*, *The Spinoza Problem* juxtaposes the story of a controversial philosopher's growth and development with that of an individual who, living in a much later historical period, seeks to find out more about the philosopher's life. Striking differences exist between Golden Age Amsterdam and Nazi Germany, but Spinoza's writings triggered violent denunciations in both historical periods. Though written in Latin, Spinoza's books were placed on the Catholic Church's *Index of Forbidden Books* and banned by Dutch authorities. One of the paradoxes of Spinoza's life was that the author of these controversial writings was neither polemical nor contentious in his private life.

The Spinoza Problem consists of thirty-three chapters, a chapter on Spinoza always followed by another on Rosenberg. The constant juxtaposition between the seventeenth and twentieth centuries forces the reader to track the interrelationships between the two stories. Although stories are "best told," Franco explains to Bento, "from the beginning rather than from the end backward" (278), stories may be best *explained* when they are told separately rather than simultaneously. Consequently, I'll first examine the Spinoza story and then turn to the Rosenberg counterstory. Many of the subtle intersections between the two stories become apparent only on a second reading. The novel presents us with a double history and biography, showing how Spinoza and Rosenberg lived in parallel but at times colliding universes. Both characters confront similar problems of early maternal loss but chose different psychological solutions that changed their lives and the course of history.

Covering three hundred years of turbulent political and cultural history, Yalom's novel reveals how Spinoza has remained deeply problematic for different reasons. To his contemporaries, he was a heretic; to Goethe and other German writers of the Enlightenment, he was the deep thinker who discovered a sedative for the passions; to Rosenberg, he was an impossibility, a Jewish genius; and to our century, he remains a mystery, a man who serenely investigated the uncharted waters of reason, a voyage that continues to produce affective shock waves for his readers. Yalom's novel demonstrates what Spinozistic therapy might look like. The novelist first shows us the evolution of Spinoza's half-born ideas, conveying the high drama of intellectual birth, including a depiction of the forces that nearly succeed in aborting the new creation. Yalom then suggests, near the end of the story, how Friedrich seeks to involve his ambivalent analysand in philosophical counseling. There is never any doubt that Friedrich will fail in his therapeutic efforts, but what's singular about the story is the extent to which Spinozistic therapy anticipates so many contemporary ideas of healing.

What's in a Name?

Spinoza did not choose his given name or surname, but no philosopher had a more apt moniker. His Hebrew name, Baruch, means "blessed," which is also conveyed through his Portuguese and Latin names, Bento and Benedictus, respectively. It is a perfect name, for the aim of life, in his view, is the search for blessedness, perfection. Yalom calls his protagonist "Bento," as I will, reserving "Spinoza" for the historical philosopher. The name de Spinoza, which derives from the Portuguese (D'espinhosa), means "from a thorny place." Perhaps no philosopher since Socrates has been more of a thorn in the side of religious and civil authorities, who banned his writings and placed him under surveillance. Spinoza scholars continue to debate the meaning of his work, the "Spinoza problem." As Goldstein remarks, "The name Spinoza strangely suits. Spinoza, as a Jew, presents himself to us adorned in a crown of eternally thorny questions" (16).

Readers found Spinoza's writings anything but blessed. In his introduction to *Theological-Political Treatise* (also translated as *Tractatus Theologico-Politicus*), Brad S. Gregory calls attention to the hostility and even revulsion the book engendered immediately after its publication in 1669 or 1670. Published in Latin instead of Dutch, mainly because Spinoza feared that it would be officially prohibited if it appeared in the vernacular language, the book provoked "some of the most violent reactions to any published work in the seventeenth century" (27).

Rosenberg's name also has significance, though of a different type. Early in the story he makes an anti-Semitic high school campaign speech that offends Headmaster Epstein. No anti-Semite, Epstein remarks that he and his wife are "pure German" despite their Jewish-sounding name. Rosenberg receives a stern rebuke from the headmaster, who explains that, as a result of the government passing laws late in the eighteenth century to transform Jews into German citizens, one can never be sure about the religious or ethnic identity of a name. If Jews refused to pay for a traditional name, they would receive a ridiculous-sounding appellation, such as "Schmutzfinger" or "Drecklecker." Epstein informs the morose student that "Rosenberg" is an old German name, but for the past century it has also become a common Jewish name in the country. "I assure you," the headmaster warns Rosenberg, "that if, or when, you make the trip to the Fatherland, you will see glances and smirks, and you will hear rumors about Jewish ancestors in your bloodline" (8).

Yalom's Spinoza

Yalom generally avoids speculating on Spinoza's childhood and adolescence, partly because almost nothing is known about this obscure period in the philosopher's life, and partly because of Yalom's belief that one's existence in the here-and-now offers valuable clues to one's past. Most of the Spinoza story in the novel centers around 1656, the fateful year of his excommunication from the Jewish community and banishment from Amsterdam. As the novel opens, Bento has a foreboding of danger. Cautious by nature, he realizes that in the "curious duel between reason and emotion," the former is always overmatched (12). He has vowed to conduct his life in a holy way without lying, a decision that flies in the face of prudence.

Yalom's Spinoza has an ability seen in neither his fictional Schopenhauer nor Nietzsche, the power to detach himself from his feelings through meditation. The first time this occurs is after a troubling conversation with his brother, Gabriel, about the internal contradictions and inconsistencies in the Hebrew Bible. "He had lately been practicing a meditation wherein he disconnected himself from his flow of thought and viewed his mind as a theater and himself as a member of the audience watching the passing show" (41). Spinoza's meditation never takes the form of a trance, mystical communion, or self-hypnosis. His ability cannot be reduced to a psychoanalytic defense mechanism, such as denial, or a form of compartmentalization. There is no evidence that Spinoza acquired this self-detachment from a study of Eastern spiritualism. Rather, the meditation or mindfulness is a self-soothing technique that allows him to achieve inner tranquility.

Spinoza's mindfulness gives him a maturity that neither Schopenhauer nor Nietzsche experienced even at much older ages. Forewarned by his future Latin and classics teacher, the ex-Jesuit Franciscus van den Enden, that the rabbinical authorities may be setting a trap for him, Bento disregards the friendly paternal warning when Jacob, in the presence of his cousin, asks him a series of incriminating questions testing his religious orthodoxy. Jacob does most of the talking; Franco is visibly anxious, unhappy to be complicit in the interrogation. "Franco has lost his faith," Jacob tells Bento. "He doubts everything. All religious ritual. Prayer. Even the presence of God. He is frightened all the time. He doesn't sleep. He talks of killing himself" (3). Jacob's explanation is mainly a pretext. The real reason Jacob and his cousin engage Bento is because he has offended their autocratic uncle, Duarte Rodriguez, by filing a lawsuit in a Dutch civil court rather than in a local Jewish court, as was customary during the time. Unless Jacob and Franco agree to help the unscrupulous Rodriguez, he will do everything in his power to have the cousins' family in Portugal hunted down by the Inquisition and killed, as Franco's father was killed.

An Early Psychologist

Ironically, Franco *is* anxious, depressed, and frightened, largely because of his gnawing doubts over religion. Realizing that Jacob has not allowed his cousin to speak, Bento asks Franco the reason for his agitation. "Because of doubt and feelings. . . . Feelings so strong that I fear to describe them. Even to you." Bento responds like an empathic therapist. "Trust me to understand your feelings and not to judge them" (44). Bento calms Franco, first, by guaranteeing complete confidentiality, second, by reminding him that there is no Inquisition in Holland, and finally, by convincing him that he must learn to understand the part of consciousness that remains hidden and beyond reason. "[S]ome part of your mind, not under your control, continues to behave as though there is great immediate danger. Is it not remarkable how our minds are divided? How our reason, the highest part of our mind, is subdued by our emotions?" (44).

Yalom's Spinoza, like the historical philosopher, has a striking insight into the Freudian unconscious, the repository of subterranean emotions containing the power to overwhelm reason. And yet both the fictional and historical Spinoza retain their faith in the force of reason to subdue the irrational, unruly side of existence. Thus, when Franco remarks that terror prevents him from speaking, Bento responds that *nothing* is too terrifying to withstand the light of reason. "Courage!" he exclaims, an exhortation that emboldens Franco to confess his paralyzing spiritual and existential crisis, his growing skepticism over the Jewish and Christian rituals in which he has been forced to participate.

Spinoza's psychological insights are best seen in the *Ethics*, which Yalom has read carefully and integrated into the story. In part 1, "Of God," Spinoza propounds a startlingly psychoanalytic theory of psychological determinism. "[M]en think themselves free, because they are conscious of their volitions and their appetite, and do not think, even in their dreams, of the causes by which they are disposed to wanting and willing, because they are ignorant of [those causes]" (110). In part 2, "Of the Nature and Origin of the Mind," Spinoza advances a theory of multiple causation, similar to what Freud called "overdeterminism," where there is a complex causative network. "*In the mind there is no absolute, or free, will, but the mind is determined to will this or that by a cause which is also determined by another, and this again by another, and so to infinity*" (146). Freedom for Spinoza lies in knowing why we act as we do so that we can gain control over our actions. Part 3 of the *Ethics*, "Of the Origin and Nature of the Affects," contains Spinoza's affective theory. He recognizes that both the past and future can shape the present. Spinoza's emphasis on reciprocal love and gratitude characterizes Bento's relationship with Franco. This "*reciprocal love, and consequent . . . striving to benefit one who loves us, and strives . . . to benefit us,* is called *thankfulness, or gratitude*" (176). Significantly, Spinoza's affirmation of gratitude is never subverted by the existence of resentment, which Schopenhauer, Nietzsche, and Freud later associated with the shadowy side of thankfulness.

Spinoza champions love, but he has much to say about hate, including a statement that summarizes Alfred Rosenberg's life: "*If someone imagines that someone like himself is affected with hate toward a thing like himself which he loves, he will hate [that person]*" (177). Other Spinozistic insights into hate apply to the paranoid Rosenberg. "*He who imagines he is hated by someone, and believes he has given the other no cause for hate, will hate the other in return"* (175).

Spinoza's psychological ideas, no less than his theological and philosophical ideas, proved troublesome to readers across the centuries. He knew his writings would not be well received. He includes in part 4 of the *Ethics*, appropriately titled "Of Human Bondage, or the Powers of the Affects," a statement from Ecclesiastes: "He who increases knowledge increases sorrow" (208). Like Freud, who had great respect for him, Spinoza was one of the disturbers of the world's peace. The two revolutionary thinkers had much in common, as Yirmiyahu Yovel points out in *Spinoza and Other Heretics*. "Freud is the greatest Jewish heretic of our century. Spinoza, three centuries earlier, was his foremost 'brother in nonfaith' (a term coined by Heine and used by Freud)." Yovel calls Spinoza and Freud, along with Nietzsche, "philosophers of the dark enlightenment" (136), offering insights that continue to be unsettling.

Yalom's Spinoza has a quality that was not abundant in Freud: empathy. Bento realizes that insight without empathy is of little use in helping people change their lives. Knowledge may be power, as both Socrates and Freud asserted, but empathy, the ability to understand another's thoughts and feelings, is essential for the patient-therapist relationship. Yalom's Spinoza has an intuitive grasp of contemporary narcissism theory, including a knowledge of Kohutian self-psychology, and he appreciates the value of empathic mirroring, a gift that Friedrich Pfister also has. Bento discerns Franco's fears and uncertainties, and, no less important, he is able to forgive Franco for betraying him to Duarte Rodriguez. Franco's psychic healing is made possible through his developing relationship with Bento, who never disappoints him.

A Critic of Supernatural Religion

Franco is furious at God for allowing injustices to occur. Why cannot God effect miracles during their own age, as he did in biblical times? Franco demands of both Jacob and Bento. "Has the mighty, all-powerful God gone to sleep? Where was that God when my father was burned at the stake? And for what reason?" (47). Franco's timely and timeless questions are as much about the Holocaust as the Inquisition. *The Spinoza Problem* is the first novel in which Yalom confronts the harrowing questions raised by the Holocaust. Bento does not hesitate to respond to the questions, but his answers are not the ones Franco desires or expects. "I believe the problem has its root in a fundamental and massive error, the error of assuming that God is a living, thinking being, a being in our image, a being who thinks *like* us, a being who thinks *about* us" (47). Bento's criticisms of the Jewish Bible never feel like a dry theological discussion. His belief that Jews are not the "chosen people" and that men, not God, wrote the Bible evoke knee-jerk denials from Jacob, whose constant interruptions anticipate the objections to Spinoza's thinking that have been raised in the last three centuries. Additionally, Jacob's interruptions allow readers time to reflect on Spinoza's methods of reasoning and conclusions. Yalom's presentation of theology and philosophy is always in the service of the story. Jacob is predictably outraged by Bento's heretical answer, though secretly pleased that he has gathered the incriminating information Duarte Rodriguez demands. Bento gives Jacob even more self-damning testimony in the next chapters of the story as Yalom skillfully presents the historical Spinoza's radical theology.

As he demonstrated in *When Nietzsche Wept* and *The Schopenhauer Cure*, Yalom presents complex and often tortuously expressed philosophical ideas in clear, succinct prose. Bento's critique of religion is smoothly transmuted into convincing dialogue. The three characters never become authorial mouthpieces. Readers are aware of several ironies in these chapters. Both Bento and Jacob sense that each may be the victim of the other's traps. Bento is wary of having his words used against him, as indeed happens, and Jacob is wary of having his entire faith undermined by dispassionate reason. Bento's words have opposite effects on the two cousins. The close-minded Jacob, reflective of the orthodox Jewish community, is outraged by what he hears. Unable to bring himself to question his religious training, he supplies the information that leads to Bento's excommunication. Jacob functions as a Judas figure, betraying a man of indomitable faith. By contrast, the open-minded Franco, struggling with the question of God's existence, is transformed by Bento's theological discussion and, as a result, has his faith strengthened. There is never a doubt where Yalom's sympathies lie, yet he is aware of the survival value of orthodox thinking, and he knows the dangers of intellectual rebellion. He also knows that belief in supernatural religion will continue to exist despite the rational arguments of thinkers like Spinoza.

In urging Jacob and Franco to use their God-given reason, Yalom's Spinoza reflects the novelist's own point of view. To begin with, Bento insists that the Bible can be understood only in the historical context in which it was written. Bento challenges the central tenets of his religious upbringing. The Jews may be the chosen people, as the Old Testament repeatedly claims, but Bento recites many biblical passages indicating that the ancient Jews were no different from others. "Sadly there is much evidence in the Torah that when the Israelites had power, they were as cruel and as pitiless as any other nation. They were not morally superior, more righteous or more intelligent than any other ancient nations" (59). Additionally, the Bible speaks in metaphors, Bento calmly tells the cousins. "God's words" are the prophets' words. Yalom succeeds in conveying Bento's exhilaration in bursting the "shackles of silence" (61). We feel his passion in offering his radical critique of supernatural religion. Jacob is horrified, but Franco is comforted. "You help my sanity," he tells Bento. "I was losing my bearings, and your clear thought, the way you take nothing on the basis of authority, is—is like nothing I have ever heard" (62).

Yalom's Jewishness is evident throughout *The Spinoza Problem*. He remains fiercely proud of being a secular Jew, attuned to the ancient history of Jewish persecution and survival. He celebrates the great Jewish philosophers, theologians, scientists, psychologists, and creative writers, earning a right to be included in their distinguished company. He is keenly aware that Jews have been called the "people of the book," and he is part of that tradition, but he has little patience for Kabbalistic authors who find hidden supernatural or messianic meaning in words. As Bento later complains, the "Jews everywhere worshipped not golden idols but idols of paper and ink" (163). Part of being a secular Jew for Yalom means having the right, indeed, the responsibility to question every aspect of existence, and to hold the process of disputation *sacred*. In a word, Yalom is Spinozistic.

The next chapter in Bento's story takes place at the van den Enden academy, where the historical philosopher studied with other young men, including the German student Dirk Kerckrinck, who like himself developed a crush on van den Enden's fetching daughter, Clara Maria. Bento learns about the Greek notion of *eudemonia*, well-being. Bento is a fast learner, absorbing Plato's belief in the *harmony of the soul*. Bento also learns about Aristotle and a philosopher closer to Yalom's heart, Epicurus, who wrote about *ataraxia*, tranquility or freedom from anxiety. Bento has already displayed his ability to free Franco from anxiety, but now he learns about the long philosophical tradition of ataraxia dating back to the ancient Greeks. Epicurus anticipates three of Yalom's signature ideas: we should strive for earthly happiness because there is no afterlife; the fear of death is a major source of anxiety; and an understanding of philosophy helps to diminish the dread of death.

A Passion for Education

Yalom conveys van den Enden's and his own passion for teaching. The novelist creates a lively dialogue among the teacher and his students, each contributing to the discussion of Epicurus. Dirk, who is studying to be a doctor, asks a pertinent question. "Does he mention service to others and one's community or love?" "An apt question from a future physician," van den Ended enthusiastically responds and then offers an extended account of Epicurus, who considered himself a medical philosopher. In van den Enden's words, Epicurus believed that the "behemoth of anxieties underlying and feeding all the other worries is the fear of death and the afterlife."

Like many teachers, van den Enden offers an answer that does not entirely address his student's question. Again like most teachers, van den Enden has forgotten part of his student's question. *Unlike* most teachers, van den Enden good-naturedly asks his student to repeat the question. The conversation then focuses on a single word. Before repeating his question, Dirk asks what the word *behemoth* means. "Good question," responds the teacher. "Who here knows that word?" Only Bento raises his hand. "Monstrous beast," Bento declares. "From the Hebrew *b'hëmah* that appears in Genesis and also in Job." Van den Enden is grateful for the knowledge. "Job, eh. I didn't know that myself. Thank you. Now, back to your question, Dirk" (78). Like Epicurus, Yalom is a medical philosopher, and his passion for education reveals his pedagogical love, the nontransgressive love that teachers and students feel for each other. Chaucer's statement in *The Canterbury Tales* characterizes both the historical and fictional Spinoza as well as Yalom himself: "gladly would he learn and gladly teach."

The discussion of Epicurus, however, is not yet over. Like many classroom conversations that involve class participation, the deliberation veers in an unexpected and potentially hazardous direction. A Catholic student named Edward, whose uncle had been the bishop of Antwerp, inquires whether Epicurus ever spoke about God. Van den Enden praises the question and acknowledges that the Greek philosopher placed no emphasis on the supernatural. Edward provocatively asks whether Epicurus believed in God, and van den Enden gently points out that the question should be whether the philosopher believed in the *gods*, since ancient Greece was, like most cultures at the time, polytheistic. The teacher's correction does not deter Edward from asking whether Epicurus denied the divine, to which van den Ended responds, with an implicit warning to Bento, who has remained conspicuously quiet during the discussion, "No, he was bold, but not foolhardy. He was born about sixty years after Socrates had been executed for heresy, and he knew that disbelief in the gods would have been bad for one's health" (79). Unable to accept a non-Christian God, Edward interjects that he cannot imagine a God who "sacrificed His own son did not intend for us to live in a particular holy manner." Believing that the Christian God is more difficult to accept than the Old Testament God, Bento retorts, "There are many conceptions of gods invented by many cultures." The two students engage in a heated exchange, and neither is mollified when van den Enden ends class by endorsing Epicurus's advice that his followers "participate serenely in all community activities, including religious ceremonies" (79).

Alarmed by Bento's refusal to be silent about his heretical religious beliefs, van den Enden tries to make light of the situation, pointing out that a truth-telling merchant is an oxymoron and will have no customers. Bento fails to appreciate the wry warning, reminding van den Enden of something he has observed about his student: Bento has no sense of humor, a serious limitation in Yalom's world. The chapter continues with Bento affirming his desire to live in a community that is not in thrall to false beliefs, an impossibility, according to van den Enden, who then offers the reason for his passion for teaching. "As long as there is ignorance, there will be adherence to superstition. Dispelling ignorance is the only solution. That is why I teach" (81). Yalom respects both the student's commitment to uncompromising truth and the teacher's recommendation for caution and pragmatism. The chapter ends portentously with Spinoza's realization that discretion is no longer possible.

Blessed Reunion

Bento continues his assault on supernatural religion the next time he meets Jacob and Franco. Jacob has not yet accumulated enough damaging evidence, and Yalom has not yet finished with his critique of supernatural religion. Acting as a barely disguised inquisitor, Jacob plies Bento with questions. Bento does not hesitate to point out one Biblical contradiction after another, reaching an unshakeable conclusion. "*The Bible was put together by human hands*" (93). Contending that the Torah contains two kinds of law, moral law and civil law, Bento maintains that only the former should be taken seriously, such as the statement in Isaiah: "Cease to do evil, learn to do well; seek judgment, relieve the oppressed" (97). Jacob tries to trap Bento into counseling Franco to disregard ceremonial laws, but Bento, taking a lesson from van den Enden and Epicurus, responds prudently. "I do not negate the importance of civic tranquility, but I do differentiate it from blessedness." He is unequivocal in his rejection of the supernatural element of religion. "The world to come, immortal life, blissful afterlife—I repeat, all such phrases are the inventions of rabbis" (98).

The most poignant moment in the chapter occurs when the distraught Franco asks whether he must give up the hope of being reunited with his beloved martyred father. Bento's answer is Yalom's. "I have given up these childish hopes and have replaced them by the certain knowledge that I hold my father inside me—his face, his love, his wisdom—and in this manner I am already united with him. Blessed reunion must occur in this life because this life is all we have" (99). Bento does not use the word *internalization* to describe this process, a word that would not be coined until the twentieth century, but that is what he means. Bento's notion of the blessed reunion anticipates contemporary grief theory, where mourners take in and adopt as an integral part of themselves the memory of a lost loved one while moving forward with their lives.

Spinoza was intimately familiar with loss. His mother died shortly before his sixth birthday; his stepmother died when he was nineteen; and his father died when he was twenty-one. In addition, his oldest brother died when he was seventeen, a half sister died when he was sixteen, and his sister Miriam died when he was eighteen. Spinoza's statement in the *Ethics* suggests that a life based on reason eliminates the fear of death: "*A free man thinks nothing less than of death, and his wisdom is a meditation on life, not on death*" (235). How is it possible, we wonder, to live without pondering and perhaps brooding over mortality? How does one live without the fear of loss? How was Spinoza able to overcome the death anxiety pervasive in Yalom's world? The novelist will soon return to these questions. Bento makes one more comment before the chapter ends, one of the historical Spinoza's most problematic statements: "God is Nature. Nature is God" (100), a shorthand formula for a complex theology.

Rabbi Mortera

After dramatizing Spinoza's iconoclastic religious beliefs, Yalom next shows how Rabbi Mortera deals with the developing crisis. Bento is summoned to Amsterdam's Talmud Torah Synagogue over which Mortera presided for thirty-seven years. Yalom presents us in this chapter with a condensed history of the persecution of European Jews. Mortera functions as an authorial history teacher, a rabbinical authority, and a credible character struggling to make the best decision for the embattled Amsterdam Jewish community. After noting that when the Jews came to Spain a thousand years ago they lived peacefully with the Moors and Catholics for centuries, Mortera describes how Jews were eventually driven out of one country after another. Enduring a pogrom in Mainz in 1096, they were persecuted for blood libels and forced in 1391 to convert to Christianity. The Spanish Inquisition in 1492 began the conversion or expulsion of every Jew, a process that occurred in neighboring Portugal in 1536.

Many readers of *The Spinoza Problem* probably know about the Christian persecution of European Jews, but they may not know, as Rabbi Mortera tells Bento, that in many cases monks led the persecutions. "Whenever Jews are slaughtered, the men of the cross are to be found at the head of the pack" (111). Nor may readers know about the large numbers of Jews who preferred martyrdom to conversion, a fact that Bento cannot understand or accept. Yalom endorses the truth of Rabbi Mortera's history of the European persecution of Jewry; the rabbi's voice is apocalyptic, foreshadowing the twentieth-century annihilation of six million Jews. Rabbi Mortera also reminds Bento of the Jews' precarious existence in Amsterdam. Jews began seeking safety in Amsterdam in 1579, when the Netherlands declared independence from Spain. Jewish freedom depended upon the agreement not to undermine Christian orthodoxy.

Bento is aware of most of this history. His parents were descendants of Portuguese Marranos, Sephardic Jews who were banished from Spain in 1492 and fled to Portugal, where they were forced to convert to Catholicism in 1536 but secretly retained their Jewish faith. The word *marranos* has the connotation of "swine," indicating the contempt that many Gentiles had for the Jews who converted to Catholicism. Near the end of the sixteenth century, Spinoza's family moved to Amsterdam, where they resumed the practice of Judaism. Spinoza had a rigorous Jewish education under the guidance of Rabbi Mortera. Yalom's Mortera is shocked to learn about Spinoza's heretical beliefs, but it's likely that these ideas developed slowly as a result of his voracious reading and prodigious memory rather than as a consequence of a sudden revelation. Bento has difficulty remaining quiet during Mortera's history lesson, and the novelist succeeds in conjuring up the past as living history. We can understand Mortera's belief that Jewish civilization is now imperiled, and we can also understand Bento's disbelief that the coming of the Messiah is imminent, as his rabbi maintains. Yalom evokes the generational, philosophical, and temperamental differences between the two men. The novelist never reduces either to a stereotype or caricature.

Mortera gives Bento every chance to avoid banishment, telling him that although Jacob Mendoza and Franco Benitez bore damaging witness against him to the parnassim, which has issued a pending *cherem*, Mortera will do everything he can to support Bento if the two cousins have lied. Bento remains inflexible. "They did not lie, Rabbi," he replies calmly, and then, casting discretion to the winds, he proclaims that rabbinical authority is based on generations of superstitious scholars. Mortera is thunderstruck, and all efforts at a compromise fail.

A Quiet Revolutionary

Understanding and accepting his fate, Bento never feels sorry for himself, nor does he view himself as a martyr. Yalom's Spinoza contains a humility that could not be more different from other characters in history or literature who engage in heroic rebellions against church or state. Stephen Dedalus, the Bildungsroman figure in James Joyce's *Portrait of the Artist as a Young Man*, views himself at the end of the novel as a promethean figure, embarking on a momentous journey that will change the course of Irish history. "I go to encounter for the millionth time the reality of experience and to forge in the smithy of my soul the uncreated conscience of my race" (252–253). By contrast, Spinoza, one of the greatest intellectual rebels in history, quietly slipped out of Amsterdam, seeking nothing more than a room where he would be able to write. Flaubert's statement characterizes both the historical and fictional Spinoza: "Be regularly and orderly in your life like a bourgeois, so that you may be violent and original in your work." Spinoza lived more like an ascetic than a Dutch burgher, but no thinker was more revolutionary.

It is remarkable how little the personal affects Spinoza's judgment. Yalom captures Bento's refusal to allow his emotions to influence his reasoning. The young man might have made an effort to thank Mortera for his efforts to reach a compromise or reconciliation, or to acknowledge the older man's dismay, but then again, this might have been out of character. There's one odd moment in their exchange when Bento offers to spare Mortera the ordeal of writing the ban. "You have been my Hebrew teacher, and you have taught me well. Allow me to repay you by composing the *cherem* for you. You once showed me some of the most brutal *cherems* issued by the Venetian community, and I remember every word of them" (116). Is this a generous offer to spare the old man unnecessary pain, or an act of overweening arrogance? Spinoza is not usually an ironist, and Bento's offer seems straightforward, with no hint of sarcasm. We admire him throughout the novel, but at times it's an admiration that we might reserve for a higher species.

A more human side of Bento emerges when he alerts his brother, Gabriel, and sister, Rebekah, to the impending *cherem*. The chapter begins with Bento wandering through the section of Amsterdam, where most of the Sephardic Jews like himself lived, trying to absorb for the final time the sights of the city that he must soon leave. Cameras had not yet been invented, but he attempts to store each picture in his mind so that he can recall it in the future. "He stared at each image for a long time, as if to imbue it with permanence, so it might be called back again in the future, even though the voice of reason murmured that all will evaporate and life must be lived in the present" (125). Yalom fuses the psychological and philosophical into a single poignant sentence.

Early Maternal Loss

Bento gives a full account of his meeting with Mortera, refusing to rationalize or minimize his role in the *cherem*. His brother is so overcome by grief that he can hardly speak, apart from imploring his brother to change his mind, but his sister is livid. Bento struggles with his emotions in this chapter, straining to keep his voice calm. He can do nothing to mollify Rebekah, whose words inflame the chapter. She comes across as angry and shrill, preoccupied more with her own precarious situation than with Bento's.

Rebekah makes two significant observations that cast light on Spinoza's problem. The first is a reference to the life of another Jewish heretic, Uriel da Costa, who challenged Jewish law; received a *cherem* from Mortera's teacher; was expelled from Jewish communities in the Netherlands, Germany, and Italy; begged for mercy; was forgiven; again banished for heretical statements; and finally committed suicide in 1640. "That's what happens," Rebekah ominously warns Bento. "There is no life outside the community." Da Costa's madness and suicide remain a cautionary tale, though perhaps more for Rebekah than for Bento. The biographer Steven Nadler observes that there may have been a close link between the Da Costas and the Spinozas, both prominent Jewish families. There was no doubt, according to Nadler, that Spinoza, like all the members of the Amsterdam Jewish community, was familiar with Da Costa's subversive beliefs; "he probably meditated long and hard over them" (66). Rebekah's second observation is that Bento never recovered from their mother's death. In her view, Bento was so "scorched" by his mother's death that he never got over it, which may explain his refusal to risk loving another woman or indeed risk any type of emotional loss.

Rebekah doesn't mention additional losses that may have affected Spinoza, the details of which appear in Nadler's biography. Michael Spinoza's first wife, Rachel, died in 1627, when he was thirty-eight, only a few years after their marriage. His second wife, Hannah, the mother of Rebekah, Baruch, and Gabriel, died in 1638. He thus lost both wives after only a few years of marriage. Shortly after the death of his second wife Michael Spinoza married a third time; his new wife, Esther, raised Baruch from the time he was eight until her death in 1653, when he was twenty. Michael Spinoza had to bury three wives: how could his grief not affect his son? It's little wonder that Spinoza equated love with loss, leading to the conclusion that emotional attachments were dangerous.

Rebekah's theory of the role of early and repeated loss in her brother's life deserves serious consideration. It's interesting that Rebekah advances this theory of loss rather than Yalom himself as the story's narrator. Rebekah is wrong when she asserts that no one matters to Bento, but she may be right when she suggests that, as a consequence of maternal loss, he has tried to detach himself from the affective world. This would be an understandable response to grief. Ideas can certainly be dangerous, as *The Spinoza Problem* demonstrates, but emotions can be more perilous and unruly. Gabriel rejects his sister's interpretation by pointing out that he has lived in the same family, suffered the same deaths, and yet doesn't think or act like his brother, but this ignores the fact that people respond to the same events differently. Yalom quotes Spinoza's prescient observation in the *Ethics*: "*Different men can be affected differently by one and the same object; and one and the same man can be affected differently at different times by one and the same object*" (*Spinoza Problem* 266; *Ethics* 180). Yalom's suggestion of the decisive role of early loss in the philosopher's life is one of his most impressive insights in *The Spinoza Problem*. Nadler, the author of the first major biography of Spinoza to appear in any language, never hints at this possibility, nor do the other Spinoza scholars who have written about the development of his ideas.

Cherem

After dramatizing Bento's fraught farewell to his family, Yalom wisely chooses restraint to describe the *cherem*, which was issued on July 27, 1656. In the absence of historical information, Yalom takes us into the Talmud Torah Synagogue, where nearly three hundred congregation members cram the temple. Why the massive turnout? "The frenzy was fueled by the same thrill, the same horror and dark fascination that, through the ages, had inflamed crowds to witness crucifixions, hangings, beheadings, and autos-da-fé" (143–144). Bento is not present to hear Rabbi Mortera read aloud in a booming voice the *cherem* in Hebrew, followed by another rabbi's translation into Portuguese. The congregation is stunned by its unprecedented severity. Yalom quotes most of the language of the historical document. There is no need for the novelist to embellish the language, which is chilling enough. Yalom devotes only four pages to the delivery of the *cherem*, unlike the nine pages devoted to Bento's wrenching farewell to his family.

The low-keyed portrayal of the issuance of the *cherem* differs from many of the earlier portrayals of the event. Will Durant, for example, depicts Spinoza in *The Story of Philosophy* (1926) as a martyr who found himself "bitterly and pitilessly alone" following the excommunication (170). There's no evidence that Spinoza was bitter, and despite his solitude, he was never without friends or supporters. Sometimes Durant gets the facts wrong, as when he implies that, following the ban, Spinoza's father, "who had looked forward to his son's preeminence in Hebrew learning, sent him away" (171). Michael Spinoza died in 1654, two years *before* the *cherem*.

Yalom's portrayal of the excommunication is largely consistent with the most recent research about the historical event. Richard Popkin observes that, in contrast to earlier accounts of the excommunication, most of which were ideologically driven, Spinoza apparently did not regard the event as momentous. He chose to remain silent about the *cherem*, and the announcement of the ban did not take place in a synagogue, as Yalom shows, but in a private chamber. There was thus no public drama surrounding the event. Popkin debunks other legends associated with the ban. "From what we know now, I think it safe to say that his excommunication was not one of the traumatic events of the seventeenth century or a decisive turning point in the struggle between orthodoxy and modernity. It seems to have been a minor local event in the Amsterdam community, one that was never discussed later on" (275). There is no question, though, as Nadler points out, that the text of Spinoza's *cherem* exceeded all the others "in its vehemence and fury" (127). As a novelist, Yalom is permitted, even required, to imagine the event, or nonevent, and his only embroidery, as far as we can tell, is the depiction of the congregants as morbidly fascinated by the pronouncement. This detail foreshadows the more diabolic public denunciations of heretical ideas and heretical Jews three centuries later.

An Assassination Attempt and Exile

Avoiding overstatement and understatement, Yalom shows how the ache of modernism affects Bento. He accepts his destiny and even sees the positive implications. "I am no longer a Jew," he reminds himself repeatedly. One cannot change one's identity so easily, however, and his inner life remains largely the same despite the outward changes of his existence. He accepts without judgment Franco's confession of having betrayed him, and in return Bento confides one of his own secrets: in some ways he *welcomed* the *cherem* because he knows it will be easier to live among Gentiles as an excommunicated Jew than to conceal his thoughts from his own people. There's another reason he welcomed the ban. "I plan eventually to write, and it may be that there is a better chance the world at large will read the work of an excommunicated Jew than a member of the Jewish community" (180). Franco is so devoted to Bento that he expresses the wish to be his student or disciple, but the latter softly turns him down, resolving to avoid future attachments.

One of the stranger aspects of Spinoza's life was that not long after the excommunication, a fanatical Jew tried to murder him outside the synagogue, slashing him twice in the abdomen while yelling the word *herege* (heretic). With the help of Dirk, who grapples with the attacker, Bento survives the attempted assassination. Seriously wounded, Spinoza kept the slashed, blood-stained coat, though no one knows why, perhaps as a memento mori, a reminder of his close call with death. Dirk and Clara later comfort Bento. He feels no hatred for his would-be assassin, though he does feel that emotion, for the first and only time in the novel, along with jealousy, when he discovers that Dirk and Clara have fallen in love with each other, thus ending the possibility that Bento might have a romantic relationship with her. "If you want to flourish," Bento counsels himself, "you must overcome your passions by anchoring your feelings to something unchangeable, something eternally enduring" (199). Once again, the affective world proves heartbreaking to Bento and, in this case, fickle and treacherous, highlighting the danger of intense emotional attachments.

Friendship

Bento's major role in the rest of the Spinoza story is as a therapist to Franco, who continues to grapple with the question of God. Bento engages in the kind of philosophical counseling we have seen in *When Nietzsche Wept* and *The Schopenhauer Cure*. He quotes from Yalom's familiar pantheon of philosophers, including Epicurus and Seneca. Bento is also counseled by Franco, affirming Yalom's belief in reciprocity. Bento confides his distress over Clara's tender feelings for Dirk, which allows Franco to jolt him out of his tormented jealousy by pointing out the irrationality of yearning for a Catholic woman who is deeply committed to the supernatural element of religion he detests. Bento and Franco's reciprocal and heartfelt friendship is a hallmark in Yalom's fiction.

In 1662 Franco travels to Rijnsburg, the small Dutch village in which Spinoza lived. Franco and Bento rejoice in each other's contentment and self-fulfillment. Bento lives alone and supports himself by grinding lenses, spending the rest of his time thinking, reading, and writing. The metaphor of lens grinding is salutary, for Yalom examines his character with the precision and clarity of a magnifying glass, helping us to understand his quest for blessedness. Bento enjoys his privacy and feels no jealousy or regrets. Franco has married, has a child, and now pursues rabbinical studies at Spinoza's old school. Franco has even been granted a generous stipend by Rabbi Mortera. Like an expert pianist, Yalom knows how to play silence. Franco correctly infers from the awkward stillness during their conversation that their relationship has changed. Bento agrees and articulates the unexpected dissonance in their friendship. "Before, it was *I* who was the teacher and *you* the student who agreed with my views and wanted to spend his life in exile with me. Now it's all changed" (245).

Talking allows the two men to understand and overcome their tension. They realize that they can still remain connected despite the fact that their lives have gone in different directions. The conversation ranges across a wide variety of subjects: their different views of stories, the value of Talmudic study, and Bento's admiration for Euclid, a transformative influence on Spinoza's writing of the *Ethics*. They also discuss Bento's favorite Talmud story, when a heathen approached Rabbi Hillel and promised to convert to Judaism if the rabbi could teach him the whole Torah while standing on one foot. "Hillel replied, 'What is hateful to you, do not do to your neighbor. That is the whole Torah—all the rest is commentary. Go and study it'" (249). These are the Torah stories that Spinoza and Yalom admire. Bento discloses one more aspect of his life to Franco, his commitment to a different kind of love, an intellectual love, what he calls in Latin *amor dei intellectualis*, intellectual love of God. The idea is central to Spinoza's theology and philosophy. Franco seeks to grasp the nature of this radical new vision of God, asking several questions, including whether Bento deifies Nature or naturalizes God. Bento promises to answer the question the next time they meet.

Understanding Spinoza's Deprecation of Women

The final two Spinoza chapters take place in 1666 in Voorburg, the village near The Hague in which the philosopher was affectionately called the "Sage of Voorburg." The year 1666, we learn, was numerologically awash with outlandish predictions, including the belief held by many Jews of the time that the Messiah had arrived in the form of Sabbatai Zevi. The "Messiah insanity," as Bento calls it, ended badly for Sabbatai Zevi: when he was arrested by the Ottoman sultan and given the choice of martyrdom or conversion to Islam, he chose the latter.

Franco's rabbi was a messianist, and as a result of Franco's skepticism, he expects a *cherem* will be issued against him. Picking up on Franco's light-heartedness in narrating the story of his restricted freedom, Bento learns that Franco and his family will soon be moving to the Dutch island of Curaçao in the New World, where he will have his own synagogue. The conversation then turns to the subject of women, who are, in Bento's view, inferior to men, accurately reflecting the historical Spinoza's attitude. Unlike Bento, Franco admires women's intelligence, perhaps because he is married to an intelligent woman. Using Spinozistic language and logic, Franco demonstrates the irrationality of the philosopher's disdain for women. Their discussion is interrupted, but it continues in the final Spinoza chapter, where Franco offers Yalom's explanation of why Spinoza held women in such low esteem. "I've had a very loving relationship with my mother and now with my wife and daughter, and my guess is that your attitudes toward women are *necessarily* negative because of your previous contact with them" (306). Bento, however, cannot change his mind about women. Franco's explanation of Bento's suspicion of women deepens our understanding of the historical Spinoza. Yalom observes in "Fact or Fiction? Setting the Record Straight" that in showing how Franco was far ahead of his time in his enlightened attitude toward women, the novelist had in mind Mordecai Kaplan, a "twentieth-century pioneer in the modernization and secularization of Judaism" (319).

Thorny Spinoza

The final Spinoza chapter explores the thorniest aspects of his theological and philosophical beliefs. Some of these views are strikingly different from Yalom's, and as he has done earlier, he allows readers to reach their own conclusions. He begins by introducing two central Spinozistic terms, *conatus*—the desire to flourish, similar in some ways to Schopenhauer's will, Nietzsche's will to power, and Freud's id—and *sub specie aeternitatis*. Bento then elaborates on the need to cast off one's identity, that is, overcome the boundaries between self and other. Once this happens, he explains to Franco, "a great calmness floods in," but this joyful experience betokens a loss of separation rather than of connection. "So you see there is a difference—the difference between men huddling together for warmth and safety versus men who together share an enlightened joyous view of Nature or God" (302). Bento's image of men huddling together to keep warm evokes Yalom's preceding novel, where Schopenhauer's porcupines, crowding together to keep themselves from freezing, cannot help driving their sharp spines into each other. Bento's image is not one of prickly human nature but the possibility of uniting with divine perfection. Franco cannot grasp Spinoza's unorthodox beliefs, and he notes wryly that thinking about loss of personal identity gives him a headache.

What exactly does Spinoza have in mind when he talks about viewing the world from the point of view of eternity? Is the great rationalist suggesting *mysticism*? Is Spinoza's notion of mindlessness a transcendent experience? If so, how do we reconcile this with his belief in an imminent God? Does the intellectual love of God lead to immortality? The lifelong foe of supernatural religion, Spinoza made a number of statements in the *Ethics* that hint at a belief in immortality. The precise details of Spinoza's doctrine of immortality, Heidi M. Ravven concedes, are "notoriously elliptical" (188). No less mystifying is Spinoza's statement that God and Nature are one and the same. Agreeing with Chekhov's critical dictum, Yalom presents these questions without resolving them.

Appreciating Stories

One of Spinoza's surprising blind spots is his failure to appreciate stories, a serious problem from the point of view of Yalom the storyteller. By contrast, Franco delights in stories, and he recites the following account of

Rabbi Yohanon: "The story of his curing another rabbi by giving his hand to him, and then when he himself fell ill, he was visited by another rabbi, who asked, 'Are these sufferings acceptable to you?' And Rabbi Yohanon responded, 'No, neither they nor their reward.' The other rabbi then cured Rabbi Yohanon by giving him his hand'" (246). The Talmud story is a variant of Jung's idea of the wounded healer that Yalom discusses in *The Schopenhauer Cure*. Bento has heard of Rabbi Yohanon's story, and he quickly summarizes its theme: "the prisoner cannot free himself and the reward of suffering lies in the world to come" (246). Yalom implies that only the first part of Bento's statement is correct. In Yalom's view, the story doesn't endorse an afterworld but rather emphasizes that teachers and students, therapists and patients, authors and readers can heal and be healed by each other. Yalom's sympathies here are entirely with Franco, not Bento. "Why forsake the pleasure of a good story," Franco asks, "a pleasure that seems so benign, so universal? What culture doesn't have stories?" Students will always be interested in stories, Franco adds, "whereas there will never be a long line of students eager to learn about Euclid and geometry" (249). Franco is not afraid to call attention to Bento's narrow-mindedness on certain issues, recalling Nietzsche's observation that one repays a teacher badly by remaining a pupil.

Human Spinoza

Yalom succeeds throughout *The Spinoza Problem* in humanizing history's most enigmatic philosopher, showing that, contrary to inferences gleaned from his writings, he was not a cold, cerebral rationalist. Yalom's Spinoza treasures human love, though he must keep himself safely distant from others. Bento sometimes comes across as saintly, but he is far from perfect. Yalom's Spinoza understands that love begets love and that those who hate are usually victims of their passions. At the heart of Spinoza's theology and philosophy lies a profoundly ethical vision, the belief in tolerance and benevolence. He maintained that blessedness is not the reward of virtue but virtue itself, a belief he put into practice in his own life. Spinoza's hope for a universal religion is as elusive now as it was in the seventeenth century, but he does everything possible to make the dream into a reality. Franco calls this vision of paradise "still a thousand years away," to which Bento responds, "I don't doubt it takes effort. All things excellent are as difficult as they are rare" (302), a statement that echoes the last line of the *Ethics* (265).

As the Spinoza chapters close, Bento and Franco lovingly part ways, the latter off to the New World with his family, where they presumably will flourish, the former to continue his radical thinking and writing. Franco urges Bento to be cautious and not put his name on the new book he is writing. "I believe what you say, but it will not be listened to in a reasonable way. Not now, not in our lifetime" (308). The novel ends with Bento returning to his world of "solitude," the final word of the story, but Franco's warning foreshadows the counterstory of Alfred Rosenberg, who becomes obsessed by the Spinoza problem.

Gazing into the Future: *The Myth of the Twentieth Century*

The counterstory begins in chapter 2 of *The Spinoza Problem*, which takes place in Reval, Estonia, on May 3, 1910. The sixteen-year-old future Nazi ideologue "looks like everyone and no one," in Yalom's menacing words. The novelist then gazes into the future, resolving whatever uncertainty the reader may have over Alfred Rosenberg's fate:

> In nine years he will hear a stirring speech at a meeting of the German Workers' Party by a new prospect, a veteran of World War I named Adolf Hitler, and Alfred will join the party shortly after Hitler. In twenty years he will lay down his pen and grin triumphantly as he finishes the last page of his book, *The Myth of the Twentieth Century*. Destined to become a million-copy best seller, it will provide much of the ideological foundation of the Nazi Party and offer a justification for the destruction of European Jews. In thirty years his troops will storm into a small Dutch museum in Rijnsburg and confiscate Spinoza's personal library of one hundred and fifty-one volumes. And in thirty-six years his dark-circled eyes will appear bewildered and he will shake his head no when asked by the American hangman at Nuremberg, "Do you have any last words?" (5)

One might expect a million-copy bestseller published in 1930 to be readily available, but when I requested a copy of *The Myth of the Twentieth Century* from my university's interlibrary loan service, I was informed that no participating university library owned the book. It was the first time in my long teaching career at the University at Albany that I was unable to receive a copy of a requested book. I then turned to the internet, where a copy was available from Amazon. The copy I received, crudely printed and difficult to read (paragraphs are not indented), did not have the usual Library of Congress cataloging information. The words "Made in the USA" appeared on the last page of the book, followed by "Middletown, DE," along with the date: "20 July 2016"—the date I ordered the book. The book cover is a photo of Hitler saluting tens of thousands of German soldiers, all standing in military formation. The back cover offers a sympathetic summary of Rosenberg's ideology without mentioning his inglorious ending.

The Myth of the Twentieth Century is a thoroughly despicable book, 381 pages of hatred and bigotry masquerading as cultural history. The book idealizes "Aryanism," which it equates with the "nordic people of northern Europe," and demonizes other cultures that have been "corrupted by Semitic influences." I had intended to read the book carefully as part of my research for *The Spinoza Problem*, as Yalom doubtlessly did, but I hadn't anticipated that the book would literally sicken me. Page after page spews racial venom. "Jewishness" is for Rosenberg a virulent disease that must be eradicated for Aryan survival.

Memoirs

Yalom also cites Rosenberg's *Memoirs*, written while he was awaiting trial for war crimes. My copy of Rosenberg's *Memoirs*, which I acquired through interlibrary loan, was published by a small independent press I had never heard of, Ostara Publications. The anonymous introduction leaves no doubt that the publisher is a Holocaust denier who takes a pro-Rosenberg stance. "At the end of the war, he was arrested along with other major leaders of the Third Reich, and put on trial in Nuremberg. There he denied any knowledge of the alleged 'holocaust,' telling the court that he had only heard of the claims at Nuremberg but that he didn't believe them" (vi).

Rosenberg offers in his *Memoirs* a sanitized view of *The Myth of the Twentieth Century*, a self-justification echoed by the anonymous editor. We learn in a footnote that Rosenberg's "no-holds-barred depiction of the history of Christianity earned it the accusation that it was anti-Christian, and that controversy overshadowed the most interesting sections of the book which deal with the world racial situation and the demand for racially homogeneous states as the only method to preserve individual world cultures" (58,

n. 47). The editor thus advances an insidious argument, defending racism to preserve international diversity. Rosenberg's *Memoirs* reveals little about his inner life, but occasionally his insecurity breaks through, as when he observes that Hitler "esteemed me highly, but he did not love me" (130). He closes *Memoirs* with the belief that the defeated Third Reich will one day be resurrected. "As other great ideas knew heights and depths, so National Socialism too will be reborn someday in a new generation steeled by sorrow, and will create in a new form a new Reich for the Germans" (201). Yalom quotes the same sentence in *The Spinoza Problem* (316).

The Rosenberg Problem

Reading *The Myth of the Twentieth Century* evoked so much bile in me that I couldn't finish the book. I *was* able to complete Rosenberg's *Memoirs* but only because it was shorter and slightly less vituperative. Who would want to publish these vile books, I couldn't help wondering. And who would want to read them apart from researchers like myself? Seeking an answer to "the Rosenberg problem," I Googled Ostara Publications and confirmed what I had suspected. According to its website, "Ostara Publications intends to be the world's primary Eurocentric resource. Developed in response to anti-white discrimination the world over, the study and expansion of the Eurocentric worldview is vital to the continued existence of our people and civilisation." In an article published by the Southern Poverty Law Center, Leah Nelson characterizes Arthur Kemp, the publisher of Ostara (and presumably the anonymous editor of Rosenberg's *Memoirs*), as a "notorious South African white supremacist" who not only writes for white supremacist publications but also has opened an online bookshop featuring reprints of "previously impossible-to-find racist tracts from times gone by."

The best that can be said about the historical Alfred Rosenberg is that, unlike his fellow Nazi officers, he was hanged mainly for writing a book, *The Myth of the Twentieth Century*. As his *Memoirs* demonstrates, he never acknowledged his complicity in the catastrophe wrought by the Nazis. Few novelists would have the insight and empathy to create a fictional character like Rosenberg, and few therapists would be able to treat such a venomous patient. Yet this is precisely what Yalom does in *The Spinoza Problem*. The reader doesn't turn away from the fictional Rosenberg, which makes the novel more impressive.

An Assignment on Goethe

The early chapters of *The Spinoza Problem* introduce an insolent high school student who spouts social Darwinism, "survival of the fittest," and the racist theories of Houston Stewart Chamberlain (1855–1927), an English historian who married Richard Wagner's daughter. Rosenberg proclaims Chamberlain's *Foundations of the Nineteenth Century* a "noble book."

Rosenberg's teacher, Herr Schäfer, and Headmaster Epstein devise an unusual academic assignment in an attempt to free him from anti-Semitism. The headmaster asks Rosenberg to name his greatest hero, the person he admires above all others. "Goethe," the student replies immediately, extolling him as the greatest of all Germans. The teacher and headmaster then ask Rosenberg to read the two chapters in Goethe's *Autobiography* wherein he expresses his deepest admiration for Spinoza, then make three copies of everything Goethe says about the philosopher. Rosenberg has never heard of Spinoza, and when he complains that the assignment will be too much work, he is told that a student who called a headmaster unfit for his position because he is Jewish would be expelled from any school in Estonia or in Germany. Rosenberg begrudgingly agrees to the assignment. Rosenberg has difficulty completing his homework, however, because it's not always clear when Goethe is speaking about Spinoza, and so the teacher now requires his student only to memorize a shortened passage from the *Autobiography*. During their next meeting, Rosenberg mechanically recites a key passage suggesting why Goethe is so indebted to the philosopher: "The mind which worked so decisively upon me and had so great an influence on my whole manner of thinking was Spinoza. After I had looked about throughout the world in vain for a means of cultivating my strange nature, I came at last upon the Ethics of this man. I here found a sedative for my passions; there seemed to open for me a wide and free view over the material and mortal world" (35).

Rosenberg can recite from memory the passages in which his beloved Goethe affirms Spinoza's calming influence on his troubled mind, but he cannot fathom why Goethe believed he was Spinoza's "most decided worshiper." Rosenberg admits, looking at his notes, that contrary to what Spinoza's enemies claimed, Goethe did not believe the Dutch philosopher was an atheist. Goethe admired Spinoza, Rosenberg slowly concedes, because Spinoza was "good and lived a life pleasing to God" (37). Goethe was so impressed with Spinoza, the headmaster points out, that he carried a copy of Spinoza's *Ethics* in his pocket for an entire year, a detail that does not appear in the *Autobiography*.

Goethe recalls in the *Autobiography*, in a passage not quoted in Yalom's novel, the "peace of mind and clearness of ideas" that came over him when he first began reading Spinoza's posthumous writings. These are the same qualities that Franco experiences in Bento's presence. Rosenberg became obsessed with Spinoza's writings, Yalom suggests, because of the hope that he too could experience psychic healing, a sedative for his passions, through bibliotherapy.

Two other great German writers, the headmaster informs Rosenberg, also admired Spinoza, Lessing and Heine, both of whom reported a "clarity and calmness" from reading the *Ethics*. The headmaster makes Rosenberg promise that he will read the entire *Ethics* before his twenty-first birthday. Finally, the headmaster discloses to the flabbergasted Rosenberg that Spinoza was a Jew. The headmaster then lists other great German Jews, some of whom were forced to convert to Christianity, such as Felix Mendelssohn and Gustav Mahler, as well as the English prime minister Benjamin Disraeli and the French composer Jacob Offenbach. "So many geniuses," the headmaster muses. "What is your explanation?" (39). Rosenberg doesn't have an explanation except to agree with Chamberlain's claim that Spinoza, like Jesus, may have been of the Jewish culture but didn't have a drop of Jewish blood.

Doubleness

The double plot and double biography of *The Spinoza Problem* allow us to see, though perhaps not on a first reading, that Yalom's two characters find themselves in similar situations. Both are thorns in the sides of their teachers; both are criticized for being "insolent" students and threatened with banishment or expulsion; both write books that are condemned as heresies or abominations. Both are critics of traditional religion, which they seek to reverse or overthrow in favor of their own radical religious vision. Both appeal to reason, Spinoza to what he calls the truth of God's eternal reason, Rosenberg to what Hitler grotesquely calls in the novel "rational anti-Semitism" (138). Both seek to "turn reason into passion," as Bento observes to Franco (208), and as Friedrich observes to Karl Abraham about Rosenberg (213). Both lived in centuries dominated for a time by a religious or political Inquisition in which countless people were slain for their beliefs. Both men suffer early maternal loss that have lifelong effects on their character. Finally, both lived in solitude, one voluntarily to devote himself to the life of the mind and the pursuit of perfection, the other involuntarily in an attempt to receive love and recognition from the century's most monstrous person.

The Beginning of "Treatment"

Yalom summarizes briefly the years between Rosenberg's graduation from high school and his encounter with Friedrich Pfister in Estonia in 1918. Rosenberg tries to honor his promise to read the *Ethics* before his twenty-first birthday, but he can't get beyond the first page. The *Ethics* remains one of the most formidable philosophical texts, composed in a Euclidean style that betokens Spinoza's affinity for masks and disguises, which he used perhaps in an effort to mislead the censors. The Euclidean form of the *Ethics* compelled Heinrich Heine to call Goethe the "Spinoza of poetry" (Yovel 58), an insight that is lost on Rosenberg. Nevertheless, he cannot quite part with Spinoza's book.

Like his historical counterpart, Yalom's Rosenberg began his studies at the Polytechnic Institute in Riga, Latvia, and then moved with the rest of the students to Moscow in 1915 when German troops threatened the Baltic countries. Returning home in 1918, he meets Pfister—and that's when Yalom begins his examination of Rosenberg's inner life. Yalom's challenge is to create a plot that allows Rosenberg's developing friendship with Friedrich Pfister to evolve naturally into a trusting relationship. Friedrich's closest friend is Eugen Rosenberg, six years older than Alfred; Friedrich has often heard Eugen speak about his estranged brother.

As Alfred Rosenberg's casual friendship with Friedrich deepens into the beginning of a therapeutic relationship, we notice that our feelings toward the former become more positive, despite our condemnation of the historical figure. It is easier to empathize with the fictional Alfred Rosenberg, partly because we see his vulnerability, partly because we have a greater understanding of his life, and partly because we strive to reach the kind of enlightened judgment that the novelist himself reaches. We abhor the historical Rosenberg as soon as we read *The Myth of the Twentieth Century* and *Memoirs*, but we see other sides of him when we read *The Spinoza Problem*. To cite one small but meaningful difference, I often find myself referring to the historical figure as "Rosenberg" and the fictional character as "Alfred." Some readers may not want a humanized portrait of Rosenberg, preferring to demonize him, but it is to Yalom's credit that he attempts to understand and, at times, sympathize with him.

"Timing Is Everything"

Friedrich discloses that he has completed his psychiatric training, which helps Alfred understand how his new friend can almost read his mind. Friedrich also reveals that he is beginning psychoanalysis in Berlin with Karl Abraham, a member of Freud's inner circle. To Alfred's question—Why involve yourself in a Jewish field?—Friedrich plausibly answers, "It *will* be a Jewish field unless we Germans step in. Or put in another way: "It's too good to be left to the Jews" (85). Friedrich then challenges Alfred to begin a Spinozistic inquiry into the sources of his anti-Semitism. "Sometimes I think our field really began with Spinoza, who believed that everything, even emotion and thought, has a cause that can be discovered with proper investigation" (86). Alfred instantly becomes defensive, and Friedrich realizes that he has been too aggressive. He recalls the frequent admonishments of his clinical supervisor, Eugen Bleuler: "Young man, psychoanalysis is not a battering ram: we do not just hammer away until exhausted egos raise tattered white flags of surrender. Patience, patience. Win the patient's confidence. Analyze and understand resistance—sooner or later resistance will melt away and the road to the truth will open up" (87).

As a therapy novel, *The Spinoza Problem* foregrounds Friedrich's many clinical mistakes, one of which is to tell a patient more than he wishes to hear. Friedrich's *impatience* compels him to disclose to Alfred something Friedrich was told by Eugen Rosenberg years earlier: their great-grandmother was a Russian Jew. There's no historical evidence to suggest this, but it *could* have been true. Moreover, Headmaster Epstein has prepared us for this detail. Alfred furiously denies the statement, and once again Friedrich is reminded of Bleuler's sober advice to him. "You do not have to say everything you think, Doctor Pfister. Therapy is not a place for you to feel better by discharging troublesome thoughts. Learn to hold them in. Learn to be a vehicle for unruly thoughts. Timing is everything" (89).

Yalom sustains throughout the novel a double focus, showing how Spinoza's struggle in the aftermath of the Inquisition parallels the rise of the world's most horrific inquisition, National Socialism. Alfred retains his copy of the *Ethics*, and Friedrich promises to be his guide. On Friedrich's recommendation, Alfred begins reading the *Ethics* and is stunned by Spinoza's critique of religion, which coincides with his own. Experiencing cognitive dissonance, he suddenly realizes why his great heroes like Goethe revere Spinoza. But perhaps they didn't realize, Alfred convinces himself, that as result of the "new science of race," tainted blood is dangerous to the nation, a rationalization that his friendship with Hitler reinforces. Still haunted by the philosopher, Alfred journeys twice to Rijnsburg to visit the Spinoza Museum. The first time occurs in 1922, when he comes across a copy of the poem Einstein wrote after spending an entire day at the Spinoza library. Alfred makes the mistake of telling the museum guide that he is determined to find out the origin of Spinoza's ideas. "You're not here to learn more about Spinoza," the guide sputters. "You're here to destroy him. To prove he stole his ideas." Humiliated when he is ordered out of the museum, "Alfred had seen the face of hell: A Jewish guard with authority over an Aryan, Jews blocking access to non-Jews. . . . He would never forget this day" (157).

And he doesn't. Much happens in the novel between his ejection from the Spinoza Museum in 1922 and his triumphant return in 1941 as Reichsleiter Rosenberg. He travels to Berlin to meet Friedrich, who has become a consultant in the outpatient department for nervous and mental disorders. Alfred updates his life, including his enthusiasm over discovering a book that confirms his anti-Semitic feelings, the notorious *The Protocols of the Elders of Zion*, later exposed as a hoax. Friedrich has been in psychoanalysis for the past three years, and he has become a better listener. He recalls his promise to help Alfred understand Spinoza's devilishly perplexing *Ethics*.

Genuinely interested in helping Alfred, Friedrich also sees him, less altruistically, as a potential case study. He has known Alfred for a quarter of a century, from the time he tried to give him a piggyback ride when he was a young boy. Friedrich has also known Alfred's father, brother, surrogate mother, and doctor. Alfred continues to be the same worried boy incapable of having fun that he was twenty-five years earlier. "The lifelong persistence of such traits fascinated Friedrich. What a rare opportunity to study the genesis of personality formation! This might be a major professional breakthrough" (189). The lifelong persistence of such traits also fascinates Yalom, as his novels demonstrate. If Yalom doesn't fully succeed in making Friedrich into a three-dimensional character, the young German psychiatrist's altruism, ambition, and growing wariness combine to make him believable. So, too, is Friedrich's dialogue with Alfred convincing, except for the repeated use of the Yiddish word *schmoozing*.

Friedrich's psychological insights are also credible, and the first official therapy session goes well. Admitting that his colleagues call him a "sphinx," Alfred follows Friedrich's request to free associate on the image. "Sphinx . . . desert, huge, mysterious, powerful, enigmatic, keeps its own counsel . . . dangerous—the sphinx strangled those who did not answer his riddle" (191). With Friedrich's help, Alfred sees that his sphinxlike behavior has both advantages and disadvantages. Alfred then begins admitting his unrequited love for Hitler, an idealized father figure from whom he desires the love denied to him by his own father. "I think he likes me, but he doesn't love me" (193), Alfred confesses, using nearly the same language, we recall, that appears in Rosenberg's *Memoirs*.

Like Yalom, Friedrich believes in here-and-now therapy, avoiding a long and probably futile search into his patient's distant past. In his 1977 biography *The Psychopathic God: Adolf Hitler*, Robert Waite emphasizes Hitler's unresolved Oedipal issues, his flawed defense mechanisms, and his use of projection to demonize his enemies, culminating in toxic anti-Semitism, but Waite's psychobiographical approach is not Yalom's. The novelist focuses mainly on Rosenberg's personal and interpersonal problems, along with the ways in which these problems manifest themselves in the therapist-patient relationship.

"Hate in the Counter-Transference"

Unbeknownst to Alfred, Friedrich has been talking about him to Karl Abraham. Friedrich is horrified by a letter he has received from Alfred stating the publication in his newspaper of *The Protocols of the Elders of Zion*, a book that inspired the Russian tsar to order a series of deadly pogroms. How can Friedrich be a therapist to a patient who commits such vile acts? This is one of Yalom's major therapy questions in the novel. "I know he is dangerous," Friedrich admits. "How do I handle my countertransference?" (211). Abraham raises a related issue: the *supervisor's* countertransference. "Being a Jew makes it impossible for me personally to treat this lethal, anti-Semitic individual" (211). Abraham warns Friedrich that he will never be able to analyze a man who refuses to understand his past. The question becomes for Abraham—and Yalom—*why* Friedrich wishes to help a sociopath. Is it because, Abraham wonders, Friedrich is trying to get in touch with his own early childhood, perhaps to reverse the process of time? If so, Alexander responds, the effort is fruitless. "*Seeing Alfred Rosenberg can do nothing for your inner conflicts*" (212). Agreeing with his supervisor's judgment, Friedrich nevertheless believes that he may be able to transform Rosenberg into a moral person. Abraham can scarcely conceal his skepticism. "Ah, if you could successfully analyze anti-Semitism, you'd get the Nobel Prize that has, so far, eluded Freud's grasp" (212).

Friedrich's question to Abraham recalls D. W. Winnicott's classic 1949 essay "Hate in the Counter-Transference," where he discusses the difficulty of treating psychotic patients. Winnicott did not have in mind sociopathic patients like Rosenberg, but much of what the British analyst says applies to Yalom's character. Winnicott seeks to understand the analyst's "objective" countertransference. To understand hate in the countertransference, an analyst must first be able to create what Winnicott calls a "holding environment," a safe therapeutic setting. Friedrich cannot do this. Nor does he have the time to help his patient normalize his feelings of hate. Friedrich's "analysis" of Rosenberg takes place in the 1920s and 1930s, when psychoanalysis had a narrow view of countertransference, which Freud perceived as an impediment to therapy. A wider vision developed decades later, when countertransference began to be seen as a therapeutic tool, cocreated between analyst and patient, which could be a vital source of information to both. Even with a wider view of countertransference, however, Friedrich can never disclose the objective hate he feels for Rosenberg, who will soon be his political superior, armed with the power to destroy his career as a physician.

Three years pass before Rosenberg's next meeting with Friedrich. During this time Hitler led a failed putsch in Munich, was arrested and imprisoned for treason, and in his absence appointed Rosenberg as party leader. Pardoned after only thirteen months, Hitler emerges more despotic than ever, insisting that everyone call him Führer, and publicly humiliating Rosenberg. Why does Hitler refuse to praise his most loyal follower? Friedrich turns Rosenberg's agonized question around. "Why does his love for you mean so very much?" (233). True to Abraham's prediction, the nonanalyzable Rosenberg breaks off therapy and issues a veiled threat: "I'll make sure these Jew thoughts will leave Europe along with the Jews" (238).

The last meeting occurs in Berlin in 1936, when Friedrich, now a Wehrmacht physician, is summoned to treat the severely depressed Reichsleiter Rosenberg. The historical Rosenberg had at least two prolonged psychiatric hospitalizations for "agitated depression," so it's in the realm of possibility that he had some form of psychotherapy. Rosenberg has been crushed by the scathing reviews of *The Myth of the Twentieth Century* and by Hitler's coldness toward him. Both rejections have resulted in a devastating narcissistic injury. Realizing that he must be careful, for the welfare of his wife and two sons is at stake, Friedrich insists at the beginning of the meeting that each must respect the other's privacy: confidentiality goes both ways. Alfred agrees, and he then brings up Goethe's admiration for Spinoza. "I want what Goethe got from Spinoza. I need all these things. I want a sedative for my passions" (265).

Spinozistic Therapy

Yalom has adroitly prepared us for Friedrich's Spinozistic treatment of Rosenberg. Throughout the story we gaze into Friedrich's (and Yalom's) therapeutic bag of tricks, which contains questions to explore the therapist-patient relationship. He challenges Alfred to ask himself the following questions: "Do I have any regrets about my talk with Friedrich? Were there important issues I did not raise?" (175). Another question is, "Tell me, what would be the perfect thing for me to say?" (232). These questions not only help Alfred begin talking about his life but also develop and sustain suspense in the story. The narrative questions drive both Rosenberg's therapy and Yalom's novel.

Friedrich's therapeutic strategy is based on Spinoza's belief that everything we do is determined by internal and external forces. If we become aware of this causative network, we will be in a position to understand our lives. Friedrich's treatment plan is to help Rosenberg free himself from his masochistic dependence on the sadistic Hitler's approval. One's self-love should be dependent on something eternal and immutable, Spinoza suggests, namely, on God's perfect love, not on an imperfect person, and certainly not on a cruel and destructive person. Part of the difficulty of Spinozistic therapy, Friedrich realizes, is that there is no single or simple technique in the philosopher's system, nothing like confession in Catholicism or catharsis in psychotherapy. This is what makes Spinozistic therapy more challenging than other forms of philosophical counseling—and why Yalom's task in this novel was more formidable than in *When Nietzsche Wept* or *The Schopenhauer Cure*.

As before, therapy fails, this time because of the unexpected arrival of Hitler, who announces to the Reich leader that he has been nominated to receive the newly created German National Prize for Arts and Science. Now validated by the only person whose approval means anything to him, Rosenberg has no further use for Friedrich, confiding to Hitler, "I don't think I can get the Jew out of him. We should watch him. He may need some rehabilitation" (272). Rosenberg's betrayal of confidentiality ends his relationship with Pfister, the only person who could have helped him resist his fatal attraction to Hitler. Pfister disappears from the novel, left to ponder the limitations of the talking cure. Friedrich's attempts to treat Rosenberg, the novelist observes near the end of "Fact or Fiction? Setting the Record Straight," are based on how Yalom himself would have treated him. Some readers may wonder how the compassionate Wehrmacht psychiatrist could continue to serve the Nazi cause, but many good people find themselves involved, voluntarily or not, in destructive movements. Another novelist might have shown Friedrich trying actively to oppose German militarism, but this would have been counter to Yalom's intentions in his teaching novels, where therapy is always in the service of healing.

The final Rosenberg chapter describes his second visit to the Spinoza Museum in 1941, an event that proves to be no more successful than the first visit nearly two decades earlier. Obsessing over a quote he had come across by Albert Einstein, "The secret to creativity is knowing how to hide your sources" (290), Rosenberg is convinced he can expose Spinoza's sources and thus unmask him as a Jewish hoax. He confiscates the books in the Spinoza library, but when he returns to Berlin, he realizes he can't read any of them, since they are written in Greek and Latin, languages Rosenberg doesn't understand. He never finds the evidence to support his belief that Spinoza had stolen all of his ideas from other thinkers. Nor does Rosenberg find the Spinozistic sedative for his passions that had such a profoundly calming effect on Goethe.

The Best and Worst of Human Nature

The Spinoza Problem leaves us with two startlingly different historical characters whose lives come together in fascinating ways. "Spinoza lived his philosophy," Yalom remarks in the epilogue; "he attained *Amor dei intellectualis*, freed himself from the bondage of disturbing passions, and faced the end of his life with serenity" (309). Spinoza's writings continue to be controversial. Spinoza's portrait appeared on the Dutch thousand-guilder note, and in 1956, the three-hundredth anniversary of his excommunication, David Ben-Gurion, the prime minister of Israel, supported a new Dutch memorial plaque at the church where the philosopher was buried. Nevertheless, some of the orthodox members of the Israeli Knesset were outraged by Ben-Gurion's praise of a heretic; they continued to believe that the 1656 *cherem* was justified. Alfred Rosenberg never repudiated Hitler or Nazi ideology, and, along with other high-ranking officers, he was hanged in 1946. In an act of poetic justice, his body was burned in the Dachau crematorium. Rosenberg's death has not put an end to his writings, which continue to be published by those who are enthralled by Aryan purity.

Yalom offers in *The Spinoza Problem* a stunning contrast between good and evil. He captures the unworldly aspect of Spinoza's character, his unearthliness, without sacrificing the philosopher's human side. Baruch Spinoza becomes a flesh-and-blood character, perhaps for the first time in modern literature. Cautious in temperament but revolutionary in spirit, Yalom's Spinoza demonstrates that quiet lives can be extraordinary. Fusing fact and fiction, memory and myth, the novel presents us with a cogent psychological explanation for Spinoza's efforts to subdue unruly emotions, a sedative for his passions. Yalom reveals how the philosopher's sedative never dulls his capacity for joy and wonder. We see Spinoza's powerful impact on Goethe, and we understand why he carried a copy of the *Ethics* in his pocket for a year, a source of inspiration and psychic healing. So, too, is *The Spinoza Problem* a source of inspiration and psychic healing, an example of artistic truth built upon historical truth.

In showing how Alfred Rosenberg was a slave to his desire for Hitler's approval, Yalom captures his character's obsessive ruminations, the contrast between his smug superiority and his abject self-loathing, and his idealization of Hitler. Suffering from a deep narcissistic injury that he can never acknowledge, Alfred experiences a precarious and unstable inner world. His tragedy, in Yalom's view, was that he could never understand Spinoza's vision of blessedness. Alfred dies unable to solve the Spinoza problem, a failure that Yalom has transmuted into a deeply moving novel abounding in philosophical and psychological wisdom.

Misreading Einstein's statement, Alfred Rosenberg never realizes that every genius uses ideas of others to discover new and original truths. Yalom has hidden his own sources, psychiatric, philosophic, and literary, which he has spent a lifetime pursuing. Much of the success of *The Spinoza Problem* lies in its many different authentic voices. Righteous without being self-righteous, Bento de Spinoza comes across as gentle but fearless, suspicious of emotions yet deeply passionate about ideas, a visionary who continues to inspire those who study his writings. Franco Benitez is a devoted student who becomes an enlightened teacher, unafraid to point out his mentor's blind spots and pursue his own vision of God. Rabbi Mortera echoes the severe voice of the Orthodox Jewish community, burdened by the treacherous forces of history. The character who is closest to Yalom himself, Friedrich Pfister is unfailingly thoughtful and empathic, knowing, however, that neither is a match for evil. Alfred Rosenberg remains for most of the novel caught between two worlds, one dead to him, the other powerless to be born. He makes his fateful choice and is forced to live with the consequences. Yalom's own voice is equally strong, that of a master psychiatrist and novelist who gives us unflinching insight into the best and worst of human nature.

A Novelist at the Height of His Powers

One cannot read *Staring at the Sun* or, as we shall see, *Creatures of a Day*, without being reminded of the author's advanced age. If one knew nothing about the author of *The Spinoza Problem*, however, one would not guess the novel was written by an octogenarian. The story demonstrates the storyteller at the height of his imaginative power, the conjurer's magic never more convincing. Michael Johnson found *The Spinoza Problem* to be Yalom's greatest fictional achievement. Other reviewers agreed. "Irvin Yalom is the most significant writer of psychological fiction in the world today," Martin Seligman blurbed. "I didn't think he could top *When Nietzsche Wept* or *The Schopenhauer Cure*, but he has. *The Spinoza Problem* is a masterpiece."

In the final haunting scene in *The Spinoza Problem*, Yalom does not merely tell us that the bodies of Rosenberg and nine other Nazis were burned in the Dachau crematorium. Yalom's glance lingers to the end of their misbegotten histories, tales of men who worshiped a false messiah. "Sixty pounds of ash, all that remained of the Nazi leaders, were scattered into a stream and soon drifted into the Isar River, which flows through Munich, where this saddest and darkest of all stories had begun" (317).

Chapter 13

Creatures of a Day

Anticipating Endings

Creatures of a Day and Other Tales of Psychotherapy, published in 2015, offers us a glimpse into the mid-octogenarian's life as both psychiatrist and writer. Yalom does his writing between seven and ten in the morning, a time he ordinarily holds "inviolable," but he is willing to forego his writing to meet with a patient who desperately needs help. He readily acknowledges that, like his patients, he struggles to come to terms with death anxiety. "You're facing what all of us must sooner or later confront," he advises a nurse with melanoma, "I have no specific malady, but my hoary age forces me to think about the end of my life all the time" (120).

Yalom's title comes from the *Meditations* by the second-century Roman emperor-philosopher Marcus Aurelius. "All of us are creatures of a day; the rememberer and the remembered alike. All is ephemeral—both memory and the object of memory. The time is at hand when you will have forgotten everything; and the time is at hand when all will have forgotten you. Always reflect that soon you will be no one, and nowhere." Yalom uses the darkly brooding passage for the book's epigraph and the title of the tenth and final vignette. Marcus Aurelius was an excellent choice for Yalom's thematic focus. As classical scholar R. B. Rutherford points out in his introduction to Marcus Aurelius's work, "the *Meditations* show more clearly than almost any ancient text how important a role philosophy might play in the life of an educated man" (xviii). The mood of *Creatures of a Day* is less funereal than elegiac, and as with his earlier volumes of psychotherapy tales, the emphasis is not on death but life. Carpe diem, Yalom exhorts his readers, seize the day; but remember that an awareness of death heightens the appreciation of life.

The tales in *Creatures of a Day* are not extended therapies but brief, evocative therapeutic sketches, sometimes based on only one or two sessions. The tales resemble portrait miniatures, where every detail is meticulously depicted. Each vignette raises knotty questions. How can Yalom help an elderly man who has requested a single consultation to discuss a writer's block that has lasted for sixty years? How can he comfort a young man who has experienced multiple losses in his life including the suicide of his employer? How can he console a sixty-nine-year-old Russian ballerina who lives in the past? How can he make sense of a bungled case years earlier with a Stanford radiologist when, at a recent chance meeting, the patient's wife states that she owes her present life to Yalom? How does he treat a seventy-seven-year-old former CEO who regards therapy as a competition and refuses to acknowledge insights that he secretly knows are true? How does he respond when he discovers that a nurse's "priceless gift" to a severely ill patient was motivated by cruelty, not compassion? How can he convince a patient who wants to be a writer to share her stories with him when she has spent her entire life concealing them from everyone? How does he pay tribute to a patient who has been a "pioneer of dying" when he could not fulfill his pledge to be with her at her death? How can he respond to a woman who suddenly sees the past changing before her eyes? How does he offer wisdom from philosophers when their ideas often fail to comfort?

In each vignette Yalom appears to be as bemused and humbled by his therapeutic sorcery as his patients. The psychotherapy vignettes reveal patients who are often in extremis, suffering not from diagnosable disorders but from problems with existence pain. The characters in the vignettes are creatures of a day, each the rememberer and the remembered. Yalom's challenge is to improvise a therapy for each patient, transmuting a suffering life into a tale of reclamation. *Creatures of a Day* demonstrates the gift of therapy, with each patient being the recipient and benefactor of therapeutic gratitude.

Needing a Witness: "The Crooked Cure"

Yalom is the first to acknowledge that, as he has grown older, he has become more careful about the patients he sees. "I have set up an invisible shield around myself now through selection," he told Simmy Richman in a 2015 interview. "Certainly, I'm seeing a very literate group and a group of people who are interested in the kind of things I am writing about." Most of the patients in *Creatures of the Day* enter therapy with Yalom because they have read one or more of his books.

Yalom's patients do not fear that he will write about them without permission, but not all of them are enthralled with his writings. Paul Andrews, the wizened eighty-four-year-old patient in the opening story, "The Crooked Cure," offers backhanded praise of *When Nietzsche Wept*. "A bit slow-going at first, but it gathered steam. Despite the stilted language and the stylized, improbable dialogue, it was, overall, not an unengrossing read" (4). Yalom must have chuckled when he heard the evaluation: everyone's a literary critic! Although it is never clear what Paul seeks in a single consultation, it appears that he has suffered from chronic unresolved grief. He has had a forty-five-year correspondence with his dissertation director, Claude Mueller, the author of a Nietzsche biography that Yalom admires. Professor Mueller's death twelve years earlier, in 2002, is a loss that Paul continues to grieve. Yalom senses that Paul now seeks a relationship with another eminent scholar, "trolling for another dance partner!" (8). The best that Yalom can do is to bear witness to the depth of Paul's grief. "I wonder if that painful loss still lingers and *that* is the reason you desired a relationship" (12). Yalom feels flummoxed by Paul's cryptic evasiveness, but he earns his patient's respect by commenting on the deep love that existed in Paul's relationship with Mueller. Given the choice between unreflective living and Socratic self-examination, Paul chooses the former, thanks Yalom for the "exceedingly helpful" consultation, and leaves, forcing the therapist and reader to ponder the many riddles of the patient's existence.

Therapeutic v. Truthful Endings: "On Being Real"

Throughout *Creatures of a Day* Yalom bears witness to his patients' and his own death anxiety. His patients are keenly aware of his age and the possibility that he might not be around to help them in the near future. Their fears over his health show up in many of the stories. "*Of course* my age concerns you," Yalom tells Charles in "On Being Real." Charles still grieves the death of his father many years earlier and the recent death of his employer and mentor, James. Yalom openly expresses his patients' fears. "We both know that at my age, at eighty-one, I'm approaching the end of my life. You're now grieving for James and also for your father, and it's only natural that you're worried about losing me as well" (27).

After Charles admits that he's worried about Yalom's death, the therapist decides to disclose his own fears as well, describing, like the protagonist in Samuel Beckett's play *Krapp's Last Tape*, a fantasy that fortunately has not come true.

> I saw my dead wife turning toward me with a large smile, beckoning to me. As I watched her, I was flooded with poignancy and unimaginable grief. Then suddenly it all vanished, and I snapped back to the present, and there she was, alive, radiant, in the flesh, flashing her beautiful September smile. A warm flush of joy washed over me. I felt grateful that she and I were still alive, and I rushed to embrace her and to begin our evening walk. (28)

Yalom and Charles both tear up, and the latter correctly infers from hearing the fantasy that one must count one's blessings. "Yes, exactly," affirms Yalom, "I'm saying that anticipated endings may encourage us to grasp the present with greater reality." Both glance at the clock and realize they have run out of time—an apt detail to include.

Like all of the stories in *Creatures of a Day*, "On Being Real" ends surprisingly. Charles is "wiped out" by the exhausting session, adding, empathically, "You've got to be tired too," to which Yalom responds energetically, "Not at all. Actually, a deep and true session like this one enlivens me." A perfect ending, right? Wrong. A few seconds after Charles leaves his office, Yalom slaps himself on the forehead, silently muses that he must be more truthful, opens the door, and confesses, "Charles, I just slipped back into an old mode and did exactly what I don't want to do. The truth is I *am* tired from that hard deep work, a bit wiped out in fact, and I'm grateful I have no one else on my schedule today." Yalom looks at Charles, unsure how he'll respond to the truth. "Oh Irv, I knew that. I know you better than you think I do. I know when you're just trying to be therapeutic" (29).

The reader marvels at the appropriateness of contrasting "therapeutic truth" with real truth in a story titled "On Being Real." Real truth is harder to achieve both in therapy and writing, for one must go counter to conventional wisdom. What would have happened if Yalom did not open the door and agree he was wiped out? It's likely that Charles would have still benefited from the session, perhaps having his fears of Yalom's health momentarily allayed, but the therapy session would have been less authentic. Therapy both enlivens and exhausts the venerable therapist. Yalom's ending is perfect, and it may be that a truthful ending is, paradoxically, therapeutic as well. Real truth involves, in this case, Yalom's decision to admit his limits, his physical and mental exhaustion as he ages. Acknowledging he doesn't have much time left shows us, rather than merely tells us, that one must grasp the present with greater vitality—even as vitality inevitably diminishes.

The Mirage of Love: "Arabesque"

Natasha, a former ballerina, remains obsessed with her first husband, Sergei, a world-famous dancer, even though she was so furious with him when he abandoned her that she slashed his face with a broken bottle. Yalom tries to convince her in two therapy sessions that she is in love not with her ex-husband but with her magical youth, when she was a prima ballerina at La Scala. The humor of "Arabesque" derives from Natasha's many criticisms of Yalom, all of which he accepts good-naturedly. Calling Sergei the "love of my life," she qualifies herself. "The love of my life doesn't necessarily mean my *conscious* life. You, a famous psychiatrist, should appreciate that." "Mea culpa," he confesses. "I found her soft jabs rather charming and enlivening" (38). A moment later she berates him for "not listening" to her, for failing to grasp that Sergei was a "god" who soared above everyone in the clouds. Finding Yalom's words about Sergei cruel, she asks whether he speaks like this to all of his patients. "Please consider it a compliment," he remarks, "to the strength I see in you" (42).

Familiar with his books, Natasha calls Yalom love's executioner. It's not love he stalks, he counters. "My prey is the mirage of love." He then invokes a passage from Schopenhauer to compare obsessional love with the blinding sun. "When it dims in later years, we suddenly become aware of the wondrous starry heavens that had been obscured, or hidden, by the sun" (48). Natasha appreciates his honesty, but she can't help quipping that a "few more healing sessions like this, and I'll need to go home by ambulance." The session ends with Natasha asking if she can get back to him by email or Skype if she has further questions. "Of course," he answers. "But remember: I'm aging. So don't wait too long" (50).

The Uncertainty Principle: "Thank You, Molly"

The Uncertainty Principle, also known as the Indeterminacy Principle, asserts that in quantum mechanics the position and velocity of an object cannot both be measured exactly at the same time. One does not usually think of the Uncertainty Principle governing psychotherapy—unless one reads "Thank You, Molly." Everything about the story is indeterminate. Molly was Yalom's long-term housekeeper and Jack-of-all-trades. She was also a "major thorn" in his life. He fired her four times, only to rehire her each time, confirming the truth of her claim that she was "indispensable" to him. One can only imagine Yalom's exasperation with and dependence on her.

The story opens with Yalom attending Molly's funeral service. He is surprised to see so many of his Stanford colleagues in attendance. He recalls that Molly had her own rigorous confidentiality code, never revealing the names of her other clients. As the service ends, a stately man approaches him. "I'm Alvin Cross, and this is my wife, Monica. I saw you for therapy half a lifetime ago" (52). Mortified that he cannot recognize his former patient's name or face, Yalom stalls for time. The mystery deepens when Monica expresses her pleasure in finally meeting Yalom, declaring that she owes her marriage and two wonderful children to him. Returning home, Yalom rifles through his patients' files and comes across extensive therapy notes even though he saw Alvin only for twelve hours. Yalom then recreates the 1982 case, which he "bungled" in every way. Alvin had entered therapy for several reasons: the recent death of his brother, from whom he had long been estranged; his isolation from men and women; and his compulsive masturbation, about which he was deeply ashamed. Perhaps the main reason Alvin entered therapy was because he had heard Yalom give a presentation at medical grand rounds about his psychotherapy work with terminally ill cancer patients. "I'm the guy who writes those death sentences," Alvin, a radiologist, admits. "I've been writing those kind of reports for a long time, for five years, yet your talk brought the job home to me in a different way" (55). Understanding how his patients feel when they read his death sentences has stirred up Alvin's own death anxiety.

The early therapy sessions are helpful, and Alvin speaks openly about his life. Yalom's medical training has taught him how to take a history of a patient's present illness followed by an examination of the patient's family, education, and development. His self-taught literary education allows him to capture in a few paragraphs the essence of a person's story.

Desiring a wife and children, Alvin had dated several women over the years, but each woman ended a possible relationship with him after visiting his home. Why? Alvin's refusal to explain creates another mystery. Soon he hits a wall in therapy and decides to end treatment. "It's not you, Irv; it's me. Look, there are just some things I'm not ready to discuss." The mystery intensifies. Yalom cannot accept Alvin's decision to terminate therapy and demands to know the reasons for his intense resistance. "I was almost battering my patient, but I couldn't stop. My curiosity was aflame and had taken on a life of its own" (74). The reader's curiosity is also aflame. What was Alvin holding back from Yalom? What was Alvin's relationship to Molly? The story becomes curiouser and curiouser when Yalom makes an unusual proposal to hold the next therapy session at Alvin's home. Unnerved, Alvin asks for time to consider the suggestion. The next morning he telephones Yalom with the decision to end therapy. Yalom wears him down, forces him to agree to a home visit, and later that evening enters Alvin's home, where he sees the patient facing a window, too mortified to face him.

The mystery turns out to be that Alvin is a hoarder. His house is so crammed with old telephone books, yellowed newspapers, dusty books, medical charts, and X-rays that Yalom can hardly clear a path to reach him. Hoarding was not a familiar topic in psychiatry in the early 1980s, Yalom reminds us, and when he offers to help Alvin, who is now "roiling with humiliation and anger," the patient turns him down. Yalom is so upset with himself for pushing Alvin too hard that he consults with a psychiatrist friend to help him understand his own dismay. The story about the radiologist-hoarder seems to end.

The tale unexpectedly continues, however, at Molly's funeral service, when Yalom sees Alvin for the first time in decades. How was he able to turn around his life? The two men agree to meet for a cup of coffee, and Alvin is surprised that Yalom cannot recall the recommendation that changed the radiologist's life. Yalom had called Alvin a day or two after the final therapy session to give him the name of a person to get his house—and life—back in order. Molly worked for Alvin for thirty years, until her death, taking care of his home, bills, and taxes. "You turned my life around," Alvin gratefully tells Yalom. "You gave me so much. But, most of all, you gave me Molly" (80).

The Prison of Retirement: "Don't Fence Me In"

Rick Evans, the septuagenarian ex-CEO in "Don't Fence Me In," begins therapy with an exclamation. "That book of yours, *Staring at the Sun: Overcoming the Terror of Death* is strong, very strong. Especially for someone my age.

That book is why I'm here" (84). Like Paul Andrews, Rick knows how to be subtly dismissive. In an effort to accelerate therapy, since they are meeting for only one session, Yalom decides to share a self-disclosing experience with him about the ravages of aging, visiting an ophthalmologist for failing eyesight at age forty and being told, "Well, young man, you're right on schedule. Presbyopia" (88). " 'Nice story,' Rick replied. 'I read it somewhere in one of your books. I get your point, but actually it's not really *my* point" (88).

Rick finds himself having "severe and persistent adjustment problems" now that he has retired and moved to a retirement home. He rejects as farfetched Yalom's suggestion that giving up his former spontaneity to live in a highly structured retirement home brings the idea of death close to home. "I could see him shaking his head ever so slightly. 'I've never thought of it as a prison. It's run damn well, and I can leave anytime I choose' " (101).

Several of the stories in *Creatures of a Day* give Yalom the opportunity to write about himself, including his life as a writer. Rick accuses Yalom of ignoring the importance of spontaneity, but the therapist disagrees, happy to acknowledge how much he values spontaneity in his own life. "I personally treasure spontaneity. I rely on it when I write. I value being pulled by something unexpected and going off into unpredictable directions. In fact, I love it" (100). Rick's problem, Yalom suggests, is not his devotion to spontaneity but his refusal to face his mortality of which his life in a retirement home is a daily reminder. The therapy sessions appear to Yalom like a contest, and Rick terminates, apparently without having received much help. Four months later Yalom receives an email from him acknowledging the insights acquired from therapy. Rick encloses the song lyrics of "Don't Fence Me In," including a line about a sheriff who said, "I'm sending you to jail" (102).

Deeds Not Thoughts: "Show Some Class for Your Kids"

"Show Some Class for Your Kids" reveals the startling differences that may arise over a single expression. The story begins with Yalom's discussion of Astrid, for whom he served as a therapist and supervisor for over a decade. Yalom helped her work through the deaths first of her brother and then her sixteen-year-old son. He visited Astrid at home when she became ill from serious autoimmune liver disease. Astrid attributed her recovery both to a liver transplant and to a nurse who, practicing tough love, whispered in her ear, "Show some class for your kids," advice that Astrid felt was the turning point in her life. Surviving the liver transplant, she abruptly died from an aneurism. Yalom attends the funeral and, while leaving, is approached by Justine, Astrid's nurse, who informs him that Astrid had given her a copy of *The Schopenhauer Cure*. "Are you still taking patients?" Annoyed by the adverb, which reminds him of his age, he agrees to see her, wondering whether she was the one who had befriended Astrid.

During the third and final therapy session, Yalom decides to break confidentiality by asking Justine whether she was the nurse who had whispered the life-transforming statement in Astrid's ear. Stunned by the question, Justine replies, after a long silence, "Yes," and Yalom then explains why her words were a "priceless gift" to Astrid. "She said it immediately, miraculously, brought her out of herself, that it made her think of others, that it gave her a sense of meaning, that it told her that, even if she were dying, she *still* had something to offer her family—she could model how to face death" (127). Justine is speechless. "Good God," she finally says, "This is the cruelest joke." She hadn't *whispered* the words into Astrid's ear; she had *hissed* them. Why? Because of Justine's envy of Astrid's wealth and large family. "She was pitiful. I was spiteful, viciously envious, and totally exasperated by her" (127).

How would a therapist respond to Justine's confession? How would *anyone* respond? Part of the power of *Creatures of a Day* is that in each story readers wonder how they would react in Yalom's situation. Many of the therapy stories pose vexing psycho-moral questions. What can Yalom say to Justine that will be empathic and honest? How can he avoid making her feel worse about herself? Each psychotherapy tale challenges readers to second-guess Yalom's decisions.

Yalom reminds Justine that despite her ambivalence toward Astrid, she nevertheless brought great comfort to Astrid's life. "In the end *it is deeds not thoughts that really count*" (127). He also asks her to do a thought experiment, remembering the many patients she has aided in her life. Yalom then imagines all of the people whose lives she helped, perhaps transformed. Justine silently nods her head in agreement. The story ends with Yalom's willingness to be a therapeutic guide in Justine's future, an invitation he hopes she will accept.

Sifting Through Dark Pages: "You Must Give Up the Hope for a Better Past"

The next story, "You Must Give Up the Hope for a Better Past," offers insight into the lives of two writers, Yalom's patient and himself. Sally, a physics technician, was in therapy with Yalom six years earlier, for only four sessions, to help her grieve her father's death. She did not mention during that time her desire to become a writer. Now, however, approaching her sixtieth birthday, she wants to retire from her present job and pursue a lifelong dream. "I've made the decision to put my writing first" (132). She has been secretly writing poems and stories her entire life, but she has been too afraid to show them to anyone. She received a literary prize for new writers when she was eighteen, but she always felt undeserving of the award, a fraud. She keeps all of her writings in two boxes, one sealed and stored out of sight, containing all of her old writings, from adolescence to about fifteen years ago; the other, where she stores her recent work, is "open for business" under her desk. Yalom can barely restrain his enthusiasm over reading her writings. He warns himself, though, to be careful: "Don't over-identify." Sally began writing poems and stories when she was an adolescent. Discovering at the age of fourteen that her father had snooped through her room and seized some of her writings, which he then concealed in a drawer containing his sweaters, she burned all of her poems. "Such violence toward yourself!" Yalom bemoans. He discloses to her, in an effort to discourage her from destroying another old packet of poems written to her demon lover Austin, that he has a large folder entitled "Cuts" that contains all of the material deleted from his novels and stories. There's no evidence that Yalom suffers from hoarding disorder, as Alvin Cross previously did, but he cannot part with the material that failed to make the final cut of his published books.

Sally is afraid to reread her stories, particularly the autobiographical "Riding on the Bus," which describes the day she spent contemplating suicide when she was thirteen. She fears that rereading this story and her other gloomy writings will suck her back into the past, but Yalom promises that he will safely anchor her in the present. She unseals the box containing her old writings and reads a poem written in 1980. His eyes welling up with tears, Yalom is uncharacteristically at a loss for words for a moment and then declares that he loves it. "What an honor to share such pivotal and precious moments! And listening to her read her poetry was such a treat. I'm tone deaf and never appreciate concerts or opera but have always delighted in the spoken word—theater and, above all, poetry readings. And here, today, I am being paid to be present at this extraordinary drama and to listen to exquisite lines of poetry" (141).

To convince Sally that she should not feel fraudulent because the poems she had written to Austin were based on a torrid affair that soon fell apart,

Yalom offers his insights into artistic creativity. "I told her the transformation of dung into beauty is artistic triumph, and that if it weren't for errant passion, death, despair, and loss, the great bulk of art would never have been born" (142). It would be hard to find another passage about artistic creativity, expressed by either an artist or theorist, that compresses more meaning into a single sentence. Yalom persuades Sally not to destroy her poems to Austin, and, deservedly, he feels like a "hero who had rescued a precious ancient manuscript from the flames" (142). Yalom is heroic, or at least creative, in another way: he has written a story about Sally, transforming her errant passion and despair into a moving tale. Yalom's story ends with a twist. Sally rereads "Riding on the Bus" to him, not the original story, which she could not locate, but a new story, written the previous day. The compassionate bus driver buys Sally a Coke in the revised ending, invites her to sit near him by the heater in the front, where she accompanies him for the rest of the day, and unknowingly saves her life. "Pretty impressive route you've taken," Yalom proclaims. The last line of *Yalom's* story, spoken by Sally, conveys one of the loveliest compliments he has received. "It's not so hard if you've got a kind bus driver" (145).

A Pioneer of Dying:
"Get Your Own Damn Fatal Illness: Homage to Ellie"

Yalom has written much about how his twin passions, existential psychotherapy and writing, synergistically complement each other, but he has never implied a conflict of interest between being a therapist and writer. That's why "Get Your Own Damn Fatal Illness: Homage to Ellie" is so gripping. The story opens with Yalom receiving, while on a month-long writing retreat in Hawaii, a "farewell" email from Ellie, announcing her decision to hasten death by refusing to eat and drink. He knew she was going to die; five months earlier, when she saw him for the first time, she told him that she was suffering from ovarian cancer and had less than a year to live. The email nevertheless stunned him.

A science writer and editor, Ellie is a gifted prose stylist, as was evident when she wrote him requesting a few therapy sessions. Yalom readily agreed to work with her, but there was one problem: she could not afford his fee. He made the same offer to her that he had made to Ginny Elkin forty years earlier. He was willing to waive a fee if she agreed to write a summary of each session, as he would do; each would then email the summary to the other before the next meeting. The proposal delighted Ellie, and she immediately accepted his proposal. He also agreed to her request to meet with her until she died, a bold request that he had never received before. Disappointingly, their summaries for the six therapy sessions struck Yalom as "stilted and uninspired"—hers perhaps because of her growing fatigue and "repetitive expressions" of gratitude to him for treating her without a fee, his because it was apparent she had "little energy for engagement." He feared it would be inappropriate to comment on her summaries when she was so close to death. During this time, he was "consumed" with finishing *The Spinoza Problem*. Additionally, he felt guilty for not making an effort to visit her at her home when she was too ill to travel.

Another therapist-writer might not have written about Ellie or simply ended the vignette with her farewell email to him, suggestive of her heartfelt gratitude. Yalom surprises us, first, by stating that before her death he put his novel on hold to reread her writings, and second, by confessing his failure to appreciate her writings on a first reading. Deciding to use her writings for the present book, he telephoned her for permission. She was pleased and had only one request, the same that the dying psychiatrist Jeff had in *Staring at the Sun*: to use her real name rather than a pseudonym. She is the only patient in *Creatures of a Day* whose name he has not changed. Yalom's vignette of Ellie is more of a remembrance of her than a distillation of their therapy together. He quotes from several of her writings, including the following example from her fourth summary: "I hate having to explain my situation to people who are novices to dying. Irv puts me at ease and he's not afraid to go into the darkness with me. . . . I need people who can look straight into my eyes. Irv is good at that. He doesn't look away" (162).

Staring into the eyes of a dying person recalls La Rochefoucauld's metaphor of staring at the sun. There is a poignant irony here, as Yalom points out. Ellie was grateful for his willingness to work with her, pro bono, and his presence helped her. Nevertheless, he believes that he *did* turn away from her because of his own death anxiety. He failed to appreciate her words at first not because they were stilted and uninspiring, as he believed, but because of the power of denial—his *own* denial. He had falsely blamed her for a lack of intimacy in therapy when, in fact, he was to blame. "I was the problem. I was protecting myself." And yet, paradoxically, his denial allowed him to complete his own work. There's another irony in the story. Reflecting on his own fears of death, Yalom realizes that not once during his prolonged analysis with Olive Smith did the topic of death anxiety arise. "Incredible! My ultimate perishing—the most terrifying fact of my life—had never surfaced, never once spoken of, in that long personal analysis" (163). Yalom speculates that Olive Smith, in her seventies during that time, may have been protecting herself from her own fears of mortality. Equally surprising, Yalom is convinced that he made Rollo May anxious during therapy.

Seeing Past a Label: "Three Cries"

Only eight pages long, the shortest tale in *Creatures of a Day*, "Three Cries" is a protest against lost individuality as a result of a psychiatric diagnosis or an impersonal expression of love. Helena saw Yalom only once for a single consultation years ago, but she made a lasting impression on him. The week before the consultation, she had achieved a symbolic milestone in her life, passing her state exams and becoming a licensed clinical psychologist. Milestones are not always good, she sadly remarks to Yalom, and then explains why she is filled with regret.

Involved in a fifteen-year "bourgeois marriage," Helena cannot stop thinking about a former lover, Billy, who had died three months earlier of brain cancer. He was not exactly the demon lover Austin, whom Sally transmuted into romantic poetry, but Billy and Helena shared many passionate moments together. Gazing at her favorite photo of Billy with her new "therapist's eyes," Helena suddenly realizes that he might have been bipolar and that their "craziness" together was "nothing but. . . ." Unable to complete the sentence, she begins crying. She cries for a second time when describing her disillusionment over receiving an email from Billy, shortly before his death, expressing how much she meant to him. The email had been sent to 113 people, thus calling into question the specialness of their friendship. A few moments later she breaks down for the third time when she tells Yalom that she and Billy were born only a few hours apart. "It's just chance that I'm here and he's dead. It could have been the other way around" (176).

Yalom might have titled this therapy tale "Love's Executioner" had he not used it elsewhere, but he goes in a new direction here, arguing against psychiatric labeling. "I can appreciate how destabilized you must feel now, Helena. All these years you saw your life one way, and now suddenly you're faced with a new and different version of reality" (179–180). Yalom's insight comforts Helena, for she feels understood. The stories in *Creatures of a Day* demonstrate the yawning gaps that prevent people from understanding each other and even themselves, but Yalom's clarifying insight has narrowed the gap with Helena. She is also comforted by his observation that Billy probably felt isolated and desperate when he realized he was dying; his effort to contact everyone he knew was not intended to destroy his unique relationship with her. Billy returns to his "former complexity and exuberance"—the last words in the story.

Messages to One's Everyday Self: "Creatures of a Day"

The title story in a volume of psychotherapy tales is usually exceptional, as "Creatures of a Day" demonstrates. A philosophy major in college and now a dermatologist, Jarod Halsey seeks out Yalom because he has read the therapist's novels. Jarod is no Philip Slate, driven by insatiable sexuality, but he regards himself as a "prick" because he is considering ending a relationship with a woman, Marie, who has recently had a mastectomy. Jarod cannot decide whether he wishes to make a commitment to Marie or another woman, Alicia. Each woman believes he intends to marry her, when, in fact, he is not sure he wants to be with either of them.

Like Philip, Jarod prefers to involve his therapist in abstract philosophical debates rather than engage in rigorous self-examination. Jarod admits that he is reluctant to say anything in therapy that would tarnish Yalom's view of him. He idealizes Yalom and wants the therapist to regard him as brilliant, with a promising future ahead of him. How can Jarod benefit from therapy, Yalom wonders, if he is unwilling to express what's troubling him?

To address this question, Yalom decides on an unorthodox strategy, reading a passage from Marcus Aurelius's *Meditations* to convince him to disregard others' perceptions of oneself. The ancient philosopher knew that only one's own perceptions can be harmful. Yalom uses this strategy successfully with another patient he is seeing at the same time, Andrew. But Jarod doesn't see how the philosophical passage applies to his own life. Instead, to embellish his image with Yalom, Jarod recites a question he had asked his Dartmouth professor about Marcus Aurelius's intended audience. How annoying, Yalom silently muses, upset that Jarod is still trying to impress him. Nevertheless, Yalom responds to Jarod's question. "As far as I know, the scholars have felt that Marcus Aurelius was repeating these phrases to himself primarily as a daily exercise to bolster his resolve and to exhort himself to live a good life" (192).

Yalom's explanation, however, does little to facilitate therapy, and he blames himself for the failed strategy. "He came to see me in extremis, and I responded by becoming professorial and pompous and reading him arcane passages from a second-century philosopher. What an amateurish error! What was I expecting? That simply reading Marcus Aurelius's words would, presto, magically enlighten and change him?" (196). The characters and situations are vastly different, but Yalom's statement may remind us of Friedrich Pfister's failed strategy in hoping that Alfred Rosenberg might benefit from reading Spinoza's philosophy. As always, Yalom accepts full responsibility for a failure in therapy, more responsibility than a reader may believe is warranted. Increasingly frustrated, Yalom asks Jarod to ponder for the next session the connection between not knowing what he wants for himself and his craving for Yalom's approval.

Yalom's question jolts Jarod into a breakthrough, the discovery that he has been looking at the therapist rather than at himself to figure out what he wants in life. He then opens a folder and shows Yalom several passages from the *Meditations* that relate to his life. Jarod reads these passages to Yalom, who realizes that this session is the mirror image of the last one: "today he the reader and I the listener" (204). Jarod resists Yalom's question to explain specifically how the passages have affected him, but he makes a perceptive observation about Marcus Aurelius's daily practice of self-scrutiny. "Last week I raised the question, 'To whom was he writing?' I understand now. It is obvious that his meditations are messages to his everyday self from that deep part of himself committed to live a good life. I think you implied that. Well, now *I* want to be able to do that. I admire him tremendously. What else can I say?" (204–205). There's much more that Jarod could say, beginning with the observation that his characterization of Marcus Aurelius is equally true of Yalom himself. One cannot imagine a person more fully engaged in the daily practice of self-scrutiny than Yalom. Yalom's meditative writings are messages to both his everyday self, from that deep part of himself committed to live a good life, *and* to his readers, therapists and nontherapists alike.

The Therapist's Pleasure

Yalom's wisdom is also imbued with joy: joy of being both a psychotherapist and a writer. All of Yalom's psychotherapy stories reflect his love for being a therapist. What makes Yalom's delight remarkable is that, as Michael

Shulman points out in an article published in a 2016 issue of the *Journal of the American Psychoanalytic Association*, analysts have often described their work as "depriving, painful and hard to endure, while its pleasures have been the subject of little commentary" (697). In a far-ranging study that casts light on psychoanalysis from its Freudian inception through the present, Shulman concludes that many, perhaps most, "routine accounts of analysts' experience of the work and its woes might well lead to the conclusion that ours is an unusually painful vocation, that analysts' workdays are typically difficult to endure, and that burnout would be common" (698).

A glance at *Creatures of a Day* reveals Yalom's supreme pleasure working with patients. He rejoices in aha moments, subtle epiphanies, as when he discovers that instead of interviewing Paul Edwards in "The Crooked Cure," the patient has been subtly interviewing him. Yalom is captivated by Paul, whereas other therapists might be merely frustrated, angered, or annoyed. Yalom relishes sharing his life with Charles in "On Being Real," allowing the therapist to connect with another person, resulting in an authentic, life-affirming encounter. Yalom loves engaging in repartee with Natasha in "Arabesque," reveling in jokes to match her droll humor. Despite his therapeutic errors in "Thank You, Molly," Yalom delights in helping Alvin Cross. In "Don't Fence Me In" Yalom confides to Rick Evans, "I feel blessed to be of help to others, especially others who are facing the issues I'm dealing with—aging, retirement, dealing with the death of a spouse or friends, contemplating my own death" (91). Justine Casey may not have intended the words she whispered, or hissed, into Astrid's ear to be a priceless gift in "Show Some Class for Your Kids," but Yalom's story provides pleasure to many people, including Yalom himself. He is so elated hearing Sally read her poems and stories to him in "You Must Give Up the Hope for a Better Past" that he feels guilty for enjoying the session with her. He ends "Get Your Own Damn Fatal Illness: Homage to Ellie" by regretting that he did not have more therapy encounters with a "great-souled woman." In "Three Cries" Yalom reminds Helena that he is moved and engaged by her words. Both of his aha experiences in "Creatures of a Day," the first with Andrew, the second with Jarod, leave him "full of humility and wonder."

Yalom shows in these stories that a therapist's intimacy with a patient need not be transgressive. Nor must a therapist's desire to write about a patient be exploitative or exhibitionistic. Yalom not only proclaims his love for psychotherapy but he also *shows* it in every story. Therapy is an adventure for him, abounding in intellectual and emotional challenges. Every adventure involves dangers, and psychotherapy is no exception. Some of Yalom's therapeutic strategies are risky, but there are more successes than failures, and even the failures are themselves learning experiences.

Conclusion

Yalom's Cure and *Becoming Myself*

Yalom's Cure, a 2014 documentary, and *Becoming Myself*, a 2017 memoir, offer intimate glimpses of the therapist's life as a mid-octogenarian. The documentary, directed by Sabine Gisiger, opens and closes with ships and sailboats slowly traveling past Manhattan, with Edvard Grieg's lilting Peer Gynt Suite playing in the background, followed by Yalom's provocative therapy question: If you draw a line that begins with your life and ends with your death, where are you now? The question may be shocking, Yalom concedes, but it emphasizes the "schedule" to one's life. He raises another intriguing therapy question. Many people are filled with regrets. If we were to meet again a year from now, what would you do differently during that time to live a regret-free life?

The Swiss-born Sabine Gisiger remarked in an interview with Sunita Sehmi that she wanted to make a film that affects viewers in the same cathartic way that the reading of Yalom's books moved her, a film that "inspires the audience to think about themselves and their own existence." Filled with sadness and grief over the death of her father and her divorce, Gisiger came across *Love's Executioner*, which inspired the idea for her documentary. Reading Yalom's therapy tales "helped me to understand others and, more importantly, myself. I wanted to pass on the comfort I felt to others, and thus began the process." *Yalom's Cure* is a tender homage to the therapist's work and life, an autumnal portrait revealing the ripeness of existence.

The documentary shows the therapist sitting in his studio, nestled in the trees in picturesque Palo Alto, California, engaged in his two great passions, working with psychotherapy patients and writing. We see him sitting at his writing desk, his bookcases crammed with volumes on clinical psychiatry and philosophy. We see him bicycling slowly around Stanford and Palo Alto, a dapper elderly man wearing his signature khaki Alpine hat. We see him snorkeling gracefully in Hawaii while on a writing retreat. We see archival footage of immigrants entering the United States a century ago, suggestive of his parents' passage through Ellis Island. We see home videos of his mother and father and the area in Washington, DC, where they lived above a small grocery store. We see photographs of the young Irv Yalom and Marilyn Koenick, who was only fourteen when they began dating, and photographs of the happy bride and groom in 1954, when they were married. We see him giving a bottle to an infant while his wife contentedly watches him, removing a cigarette from his mouth. And we see him on vacation with his wife, four children, and five grandchildren in Ménerbes, a quaint walled village in southeastern France.

The seventy-four-minute documentary explores several aspects of Yalom's life: his conflicted relationship with his parents, his decision to become a psychiatrist mainly because it was the best way to pursue his dream of becoming a writer, his relationship with his wife and children, his continued commitment to psychotherapy and writing, and his thoughts on aging and death. *Yalom's Cure* sometimes resembles a therapy session or philosophy class; the documentary's meditative quality will appeal mainly to those who wish to learn more about Yalom's life, though they will learn little about his distinctive contributions to psychotherapy, fiction, or creative nonfiction.

A Lack of Foundation

Yalom affirms a here-and-now approach in therapy, but when asked a question at a large conference about the "interesting twists to the storyline of your own life," he returns to his origins. "You know, I get a lot of applause and a lot of honor, but there's a part of me for which this is very unreal." Photographs of his parents, Benjamin and Ruth Yalom, show up on the screen as he speaks. "My parents were uneducated entirely, so I always feel I don't have any foundation behind me. It's a little destabilizing. And no matter how much success I have, or how popular my books are, there's always a little uneasiness. Is this really me? Have I really done this?"

Yalom returns to the absence of nurturing parents later in the documentary, revealing the gains and losses of a lack of foundation. "There's a sense of taking a lot of pride in the fact that you've been your own creator, your own father, your own mentor. That can give you a lot of satisfaction. On the other hand, there's this longing, maybe a kind of early-life longing, for a mentor or parent who would have guided you and taken you along all this way." Lacking a guide in his own early life continues to fill him with sadness, but he plays that role to his patients. "I'm a guide on this voyage of self-exploration. And I'm a guide because I've been there before."

The portrait that emerges from the documentary is consistent with what Yalom has conveyed about himself in his books. He acknowledges candidly his problematic relationship with his parents, particularly with his mother. Despite his disappointment over their relationship, Yalom admits that he cannot get her out of his mind—as his dreams reveal in *Momma and the Meaning of Life*. He then tells us that grief is more difficult for people who have unfinished business. Asking himself, in retrospect, whether there was anything he could have done to make his mother's life happier, he says, "I probably should have been talking to her those two years."

The Beginning of a Lifelong Relationship

Yalom did not want to have the same kind of marriage his parents had. "I didn't want to repeat the cycle of the passive father and overly aggressive mother.... Marilyn is someone who has her own mind, but there's no attempt to overpower me."

Gisiger's documentary juxtaposes past and present footage of Irv and Marilyn's long life together. The film captures their delight being with each other, a joy that has only increased over time. Of the two, Irv Yalom is more laid back and reserved, Marilyn Yalom more spontaneous, playful, and daring. We watch them sitting naked in a hot tub, relaxing and enjoying themselves. To avoid being in a dry, academic documentary, Marilyn says, grinning, they should allow viewers to see that he is a real flesh-and-blood person. "I think you're an exhibitionist," he quips, in his best diagnostician's voice, to which she responds, teasingly, as she moves toward him, "Well, maybe, maybe it's possible. If I don't have an audience, what's the point?"

The documentary offers new information about the early years of the Yaloms' marriage. "It was not his looks I fell in love with," Marilyn Yalom explains, "but his personality: he was interesting." In an interview with Terence Clarke in the *Huffington Post*, Yalom stated that his friendship with Marilyn began because they both loved to read. They liked the same authors, Dostoevsky, Dickens, and Steinbeck. He was certain that she was the right woman for him: "At 16, I already bet a friend that I would marry her." Some of the girls thought he was a "bit of a nerd," Marilyn observes, adding that the word wasn't used at midcentury. "His other strong point was that he liked me. And he seemed very safe." He was more infatuated with her during this time than she was with him. He went "steady" with her throughout high school, but he wasn't sure she went steady with him.

The challenge during the early years of their relationship was negotiating the differences in their personalities. She was more outgoing, social, and self-confident; he was consumed by his academic studies. The photos and videos of their teenage years show him looking intense and serious, a young man impatient to make his mark on life, while she looks flirtatious with a winsome smile. In one photo she teases him, sticking out her tongue. She was eager to date other men when she was an undergraduate at Wellesley. Reading from what appears to be an old letter to him, she remarks, "we met when we were very, very young, and regardless of what you think, I should now regret it very much if during the past six years, I had not known and enjoyed other males." Her dating experience in college gave her the assurance that she could handle herself with other men. He couldn't understand, however, her need to be with other men. "Unfortunately, you couldn't see that my enjoyment of others did not in any way lessen my feelings for you. The fact of the matter is that I can enjoy and benefit from my relationships with others while you do not." Though she credits her feminism to her daughter, Eve, the young Marilyn already seemed to have a protofeminist sensibility in the 1950s.

Irv Yalom intimates that his fierce drive for academic success precluded other activities. "I studied all the time. College and medical school were horrors for me. Medical schools would only take five percent of their class for Jews, so that meant I had to have a very good record to get in."

Yalom has written about experiencing intense periods of anxiety during certain periods of his life, and his wife confirms this in the film. "I think there are some people who have a stream of anxiety inside of them. In Irv's case, it probably expressed itself in being impatient or in a feeling somehow that he had to prove himself in life. There wasn't a great deal of ease in him." He agrees with her comments. "When I started medical school I was in a tremendous hurry—to get through, get married, nail down this nice-looking woman that I met."

Marilyn Yalom

A year younger than her husband, Marilyn Yalom studied at Wellesley, the Sorbonne, and Harvard. She earned a PhD in comparative literature from Johns Hopkins, was a professor of French in the California State College system, and is now a senior scholar at the Clayman Institute for Gender Research at Stanford, having served as its director from 1984 to 1985. The Yaloms team taught a course together at Stanford in 1975 on "Death in Literature and Psychology." A cultural historian, Marilyn Yalom is the author of twelve books that have been translated into twenty languages. She was presented with a Certificate of Recognition from the California State Assembly "honoring extraordinary leadership in the literary arts and continued commitment to ensuring the quality of reading" for her 2008 book, *The American Resting Place: Four Hundred Years of History Through Our Cemeteries and Burial Grounds*, with photos by Reid Yalom. She was decorated as an Officier des Palmes Académiques by the French government in 1991. Her 2012 book *How the French Invented Love* was short-listed for the Phi Beta Kappa Gauss Literary Award and for the American Library in Paris Book Award. Her 2015 book *The Social Sex* adopts a cultural-historical approach to female friendship in the Western world.

How the French Invented Love is sophisticated cultural history, and it also highlights Marilyn Yalom's irrepressible humor. She recalls a conversation with the bestselling writer Elisabeth Badinter shortly after her husband, Robert, was elected to the French Senate following a long government career. When Marilyn Yalom "thoughtlessly" inquired the age of her husband, Elisabeth Badinter cut her short with a smile: "He's sixty-eight and handsome as a god." Amazed by her "open expression of sensual love," Marilyn Yalom rejoined, "An American woman would not have said what you just said." Asked how an American would respond, she replied impishly, "More likely, he's sixty-eight and a pain in the ass," to which both women then broke into laughter (45).

Marilyn Yalom speaks several times about her own marriage in *How the French Invented Love*, but she also discloses two of her romantic relationships before marriage. She recalls visiting a church in Tours, France, with a Catholic boyfriend when they were both studying abroad during her junior year in college, adding, parenthetically, "a friendly priest took us for two sweethearts seeking premarital counsel!" (238). Near the end of the book she remembers a love affair in France with a Norwegian when she was twenty, mentioning a telephone call forty years later when they immediately recognized each other.

Marilyn Yalom points out a crucial difference between French and American psychotherapy. The French conviction that love and sex should remain mysterious limits what couples confide to a therapist. She cites a Parisian family therapist expressing horror over the idea of a frank discussion of these subjects. "He is quoted as saying: 'Mystery is an essential ingredient in maintaining interest in our partner over time. To keep my marriage enlivened, I must feel there's always more to my wife than what I already know'" (47). The therapist portrayed marriage as two intersecting circles that do not completely overlap. "'In France,' he said, 'when we think about 'the relationship,' there's rarely more than one-third of each circle that overlaps. Married people here are not only entitled to their privacy, they *must* have private lives to remain interesting and alluring to each other'" (47).

The Yaloms have many shared intellectual interests, but they have moved in different directions from their early academic training. "I went through a period in which I was very interested in Irv's field. I was writing a psychoanalytic interpretation of Joyce's *Ulysses*, and then I made a switch from teaching literature to women's studies. I don't say that psychotherapy is inadvisable for other people when you have a good therapist. But for me, maybe I had so much already in my private life that that's not what I needed." Following this observation, we see her taking a yoga lesson, her preferred form of stress-reduction, with her teacher telling her, "Be as sensitive to the world around you as to your body."

Marilyn Yalom's deep psychological insights enrich her feminist and cultural scholarship, as can be seen in the distinction she makes between "love-as-sickness" and "lovesickness" in her discussion of Proust in *How the French Invented Love*:

> Love-as-sickness is more dangerous than lovesickness. The lovesick person languishes from the absence or indifference of the loved one, but usually gets over it, either by winning the beloved or by moving on to another love. As opposed to lovesickness, love-as-sickness implies that the lover is beyond hope. He or she will always suffer while in love and never reach a "healthy" state of loving, which would demand, minimally, some concern for the other person's well-being. Proust's characters are too immersed in their own internal misery to be able to care for another in any mature fashion. (271)

Conclusion

A Legendary Marriage

It's no surprise that the Yaloms have enjoyed a long and close marriage. One infers this from their acknowledgment of each other's help in their many books. Irv Yalom refers to his wife in *Love's Executioner* as "always my toughest critic and staunchest supporter." He elaborates on this in *When Nietzsche Wept*. "My wife, who has always been my first, most thorough, and most merciless critic, surpassed herself in this book—providing not only the continuous critiques from first to the final draft, but also suggesting the book's title." He dedicated *The Gift of Therapy* to "Marilyn, soulmate for over fifty years. Still counting." The counting happily continued in *Creatures of a Day*, dedicated to "my wife of sixty years, yet not long enough."

Marilyn Yalom's citations, dedications, and acknowledgments are no less heartfelt. In her 1985 book *Maternity, Mortality, and the Literature of Madness*, she quotes her husband in the chapter on Sylvia Plath. "As the psychiatrist I. Yalom has written, 'The loss of a parent brings us in touch with our own vulnerability; if our parents could not save themselves, who will save us?'" (18). The dedication in her 1997 book *A History of the Breast* is alluringly alliterative: "For Irv, For ever." She concludes her 2001 book *A History of the Wife* with a wry acknowledgment: "As always, I counted on my husband, Irvin Yalom, Emeritus Professor of the Stanford psychiatry department, for a close reading of the text and spirited discussions when we disagreed. Married to him for forty-six years, I have come to know the plethora of meanings hidden in the little word 'wife.'" Dedicating *How the French Invented Love* to her husband, she uses a medieval expression, "Ni vous sans moi, ni moi sans vous": "Neither you without me, nor I without you."

The Yaloms are both distinguished writers, each the other's soul mate, but they are preoccupied with different subjects. Marilyn Yalom has written a book on cemeteries and burial grounds, but she is best known for her books on love. Irvin Yalom is best known for his books on existential psychotherapy, his role as love's executioner, and his emphasis on death anxiety. The Yaloms' marriage thus appears to be a serendipitous union of opposites: a marriage of Eros and Thanatos, love and death.

The documentary does not idealize the Yaloms' marriage. One senses that there were dangerous times when the marriage was imperiled. "I'm sure there were moments in the course of marriage where I would have walked out," Marilyn Yalom admits. "I mean, there are always those moments. But in the end, the tie to Irv, and the tie to the children, and the tie to the family always proved stronger. So I never moved out." He speaks in the same way. "There were times that I might have fallen in love or be prey to that, and that was a great feeling to have, but it was always very, very temporary. And I have always had this attachment to Marilyn that was rock solid for me." Both emphasize, in Marilyn Yalom's words, that for a marriage to work, "your primary commitment is to the other person. That's something that one has to remind oneself of all the time, you know, over and over again."

Cultural and Gender Differences in Love

Marilyn Yalom is keenly aware of the cultural influences on love and the differences between French and American visions of marriage. She first became aware of these cultural differences when she studied at the Sorbonne in Paris. In an interview with Royal Young on the 2012 publication of *How the French Invented Love*, she speaks about the intensity of love in the French experience. "More than anything, there is a belief that love has its own justification, that it should be experienced as passionately as possible. The French have a wonderful expression, *amour passion*, which is the ultimate. If you've lived in France long enough, one day someone will tell you about their *amour passion*, the passionate love of their life, or they will ask you if you've ever had an *amour passion*." What happens if one has not had this type of love? "Well, then they look at you rather sadly. For a French person, lack of desire in someone is really seen as a defect."

The French have a nine-hundred-year tradition of romantic love, Marilyn Yalom points out in the interview, going back to the troubadours and minstrels. "You have gallantry at the highest level. In *Madame Bovary*, when she's at the nun's school, what's hanging on the wall? A picture of the mistress of the king of France. [laughs] So it's in their unconscious that love counts, that sex counts, that love is embedded in the flesh."

Marilyn Yalom never offers a judgment of love outside of marriage, but she states that it's increasingly difficult to have an enduring relationship with another person, whether that person is one's spouse or not. Her comments in the interview on her own marriage resemble those in the documentary. "Having been married for 57 years to the same person, not without enormous strains and difficulties at times, I have to say I appreciate the longevity of our marriage and the fact that we have a shared history and still want the best for each other. That is very precious."

Irvin and Marilyn Yalom both acknowledge the power of "falling in love," *amour passion*, but they write about the phenomenon differently. He is more suspicious of *falling* in love, regarding it, clinically, as an obsession or infatuation that not only does not last but can lead to serious conflicts. "The idea is that you stand in love, not fall in love." She writes about passionate love from a cultural perspective, observing that in some cultures marital and extramarital love coexist simultaneously. She cites Simone de Beauvoir and Jean-Paul Sartre for advocating a primary relationship outside of marriage. "That is, you were free in your love and sexual relationships. Freedom was the password." Irv and Marilyn Yalom both affirm undying love and have worked hard to make the ideal into reality, but she has a keener appreciation of the French view that love and passion have their own reasons for existence.

The only moment in *Yalom's Cure* when wife and husband spiritedly disagree with each other occurs over whether men and women love differently. As a feminist scholar, Marilyn Yalom believes there are significant gender differences in love. She refers in the documentary to the story of Héloïse and Abelard, which she discusses in both *A History of the Wife* and *How the French Invented Love*. "She had held on to her love for Abelard long after he had withdrawn from her. And so they come down historically as the prototype of the male who is driven primarily by lust, and the woman, whose sense of attachment is much longer." Irv Yalom objects to his wife's generalization. "Well, no, wait a minute. All women—is that so men don't go through this, too? I mean, I've seen men by the dozen sitting there pining by the dozen for this old lover that they've had. This happens to men too. This is not—this is not an absolute gender issue." Holding her ground, Marilyn Yalom cites a contemporary researcher for support. "Well, I'm thinking in particular of the book by the neuropsychiatrist Louann Brizendine. She says that 'a man has two and a half times as much brain space devoted to sexual pursuit as a woman, while the female brain's empathy system is considerably more active than the male's.'" Irv Yalom remains unconvinced. "It's almost saying that men can't have real love for women or want to be with them or want to send them away. I wouldn't think of sending you away." "That's true!" Marilyn remarks, smiling.

Without taking sides on the controversial issue of the gendered nature of love, one can note that Louann Brizendine has changed her mind about this subject. A neuropsychiatrist who holds an endowed chair in psychiatry at the University of California, San Francisco, Brizendine is the author of the bestselling books *The Female Brain* (2006) and *The Male Brain* (2010). She argues in the former that "girls arrive already wired as girls, and boys arrive already wired as boys. Their brains are different by the time they're born, and their brains are what drive their impulses, values, and their very reality." She admits that in writing *The Female Brain* she "struggled with two voices in my head—one is the scientific truth, the other is political correctness. I have chosen to emphasize scientific truth over political correctness even though scientific truths may not always be welcome" (161–162). She must have rued that remark, for in a 2014 interview with Alina Tugend, Brizendine concedes that she might have "let the pendulum swing too far the other way" when emphasizing the innate differences in the sexes. "Males and females are more alike than they're different," she now maintains. "After all, we are the same species."

Are there gender differences in Yalom's novels? Yalom's male characters are more sexually driven than his female characters, but that may be because the central protagonists in the four novels are all males: Breuer and Nietzsche, Ernest Lash in *Lying on the Couch*, Schopenhauer and Philip Slate, and Spinoza and Alfred Rosenberg. Breuer is sexually obsessed with his patient Anna O., a grim obsession that does not lift until the end of the novel. Nietzsche appears to be obsessed by the idea of Lou Salomé's betrayal of him, not by her sexuality. Seymour Trotter succumbs to Belle Felini's sexual advances in *Lying on the Couch*, but it's hard to know where transference and countertransference love end and a desire to defraud an insurance company begins. Carol Astrid's pursuit of Ernest is motivated not by lust but revenge: her husband has left her for a younger woman. Philip Slate is the embodiment of voracious sexual appetite, the best example of Marilyn Yalom's thesis that men are driven by lust, women by attachment.

Yalom's female characters sometimes find themselves in the throes of obsessional love, as we see with Thelma in *Love's Executioner*. But after completing the story, readers may remember more vividly *Yalom's* confession of being tormented by obsessional love: his acknowledgment in the same story that he had encountered a woman at a conference who "invaded my mind, my thoughts, my dreams." The obsession was gratifying at first but eventually required him to reenter therapy where, after several months of hard work, his mind was his own again. A close reading of Yalom's novels and psychotherapy tales suggests that his male characters are more driven by lust than his female characters—and more tormented by sexual obsessions. Or to use Marilyn Yalom's terms, her husband's male characters demonstrate, as did Proust, love-as-sickness, a more dangerous condition than lovesickness.

Tellingly, Yalom's male characters don't show the same attachment bonds as his female characters. We don't see any male characters in Yalom's novels or psychotherapy tales suffer from *prolonged* grief over a child's or spouse's death, but we do see Penny grief-stricken over her daughter's death in *Love's Executioner* and Irene devastated over her husband's death in *Momma and the Meaning of Life*. Natasha remains obsessed with her ex-husband in *Creatures of a Day*, though Yalom attributes this mainly to her desire to regain her magical youth. A complicating factor in discussing gender differences in the three volumes of psychotherapy tales is that Yalom sometimes changes a character's gender to protect a patient's identity.

Anticipated Endings

Yalom's 2015 interview with Simmy Richman evokes a valedictory mood. The interview ends with living a regret-free life, much as *Yalom's Cure* opens. "I always wanted to be a writer," Yalom tells Richman. "Maybe, had I been brought up in another generation, I might have just gone into writing rather than medicine—which is not to say that I didn't also have a great attraction towards the idea of being a healer. Fortunately, I've been able to combine the two in ways I could never possibly have imagined."

Yalom's Cure closes with two quotes, Thomas Hardy's observation, "If a way to the Better there be, it exacts a full look at the worst," and Schopenhauer's insight that when the sun dims in later years, we suddenly become aware of the wondrous starry heavens. Yalom implies that in some ways life as an octogenarian is better than as a septuagenarian. "In the 70s all these things go wrong to your body and you can't do the things you want to. Many people suffer from terminal despair, but it's been the opposite for me. I'm freer and not anxious about things and I feel very creative and very excited about my work. So I just want to say that to the younger people, there may be even better days ahead. . . . Right now, I'm enjoying the night sky."

Writing Good-Bye: *Becoming Myself*

Yalom continues to savor the night sky in his memoir *Becoming Myself*, published when he was eighty-six. The title alludes to Nietzsche's injunction, "Become who you are." The last chapter in the memoir, "A Novice at

Growing Old," is the most moving, perhaps because, like Prospero in *The Tempest*, Shakespeare's final play, Yalom announces that he is burying his magic wand. He continues to write for three to four hours each morning, six or seven days weekly, but he is convinced that *Becoming Myself* is his last book. "My friends and colleagues groan when they hear me say this. They've heard it many times before. But I fear this time is different" (342).

Yalom doesn't offer in *Becoming Myself* a final evaluation of his career as a literary writer, but he does in *Staring at the Sun*, where he expresses delight in the carpentry of the writing process: "finding the perfect word, sanding and burnishing rough sentences, tinkering with the tick-tocks of phrase and sentence cadence" (196). Yalom has never tired of the aesthetic pleasure of writing, the craft of prose. "As a writer, I know I lack the poetic imagery of the great contemporary writers like Roth, Bellow, Ozick, McEwan, Banville, Mitchell, and countless other writers whose work I have read with awe, but I have actualized what gifts I have. I'm a fairly good storyteller; I have written both fiction and nonfiction; and have had far more readers and acclaim than I had ever dreamed possible" (160–161).

Yalom never compares himself to other writers of psychotherapy tales, but apart from Freud, the greatest writer of psychological case studies, Yalom stands out as first among equals of those authors who combine therapeutic insights and masterful storytelling. The highest literary praise Yalom received, he declares in *Becoming Myself*, was Rollo May's statement about *Love's Executioner*: "Yalom writes like an angel about the devils that besiege us" (191). Yalom's gift for storytelling earned him the title "Scheherazade in the Consulting Room," as Laura Miller colorfully characterized him in an article published in the *New York Times* in 2003. She was referring to *Love's Executioner*, which contains, in her words, "startling revelations, hard-won transformations and the weirdest of moral quandaries," but the title is equally appropriate for all of Yalom's psychotherapy tales. In *Lying on the Couch* Seymour Trotter laments the short shelf life of major psychiatric texts, lasting for about only one generation; Yalom's fictional and nonfictional books will last much longer than that, taking their place among the classics in their field.

How does Yalom bring to a close a writing career spanning a half century? By citing Nietzsche's words from *Thus Spake Zarathustra*: "Was *that* life? Well then once again." It is the same statement Pam Swanvil quotes near the end of *The Schopenhauer Cure*. In ending a book on Irvin Yalom, one can do no better than to cite Nietzsche's sentence *preceding* his life-affirming injunction in *Thus Spake Zarathustra*, a sentence that conveys the essence of Yalom's work as a psychiatrist and writer: "Courage . . . is the best slayer, courage which attacketh: it slayeth even death itself" (173).

Works Cited

Adams, Henry. *The Education of Henry Adams.* Boston: Houghton Mifflin, 1918.
Albom, Mitch. *Tuesdays with Morrie: An Old Man, a Young Man, and Life's Greatest Lesson.* New York: Broadway Books, 1997.
Andreasen, Nancy C. *The Creating Brain: The Neuroscience of Genius.* New York: Dana Press, 2005.
Antoninus, Marcus Aurelius. *The Meditations,* trans. A. S. L. Farquharson, and *selection from The Letters of Marcus and Fronto,* trans. R. B. Rutherford, with introduction and notes by R. B. Rutherford. Oxford: Oxford University Press, 1989.
Babacan, Nalan Akgül. "Will We Have a New Ending for Irvin Yalom's Novel? A Medical Oncologist View." *Journal of Oncological Science* 2 (2016): 5–6.
Barley, Andrew. "Review of *The Schopenhauer Cure.*" *Philosophy Now* 52 (2005). Https://philosophynow.org/issues/52/The_Schopenhauer_Cure_by_Irvin_Yalom. Accessed November 9, 2016.
Barnett, Laura, and Greg Madison, eds. *Existential Therapy: Legacy, Vibrancy and Dialogue.* East Sussex, UK: Routledge, 2012.
Bass, Ellen, and Laura Davis. *The Courage to Heal: A Guide for Women Survivors of Child Sexual Abuse.* New York: Harper & Row, 1988.
Berman, Jeffrey. *Dying in Character: Memoirs on the End of Life.* Amherst: University of Massachusetts Press, 2012.
———. "Remediable and Irremediable Suffering: Allen Wheelis's Psychoanalytic and Novelistic Writings." In *Allen Wheelis: An Appreciation of His Work,* ed. Maurice W. DuQuesnay, 29–57. Lafayette: Levy Humanities Series, 1999.
———. *The Talking Cure: Literary Representations of Psychoanalysis.* New York: New York University Press, 1985.
———. *Writing Widowhood: The Landscapes of Bereavement.* Albany: State University of New York Press, 2015.
Breuer, Josef, and Sigmund Freud. *Studies on Hysteria.* In *The Standard Edition of the Complete Psychological Works of Sigmund Freud,* trans. James Strachey, vol. 2. London: The Hogarth Press, 1955.

Brizendine, Louann. *The Female Brain*. New York: Broadway, 2006.
Charon, Rita, and Eric R. Marcus. "A Narrative Transformation of Health and Healthcare." In *The Principles and Practice of Narrative Medicine*, Rita Charon, Sayantani Dasgupta, Nellie Hermann, Craig Irvine, Eric R. Marcus, Edgar Rivera Colon, Danielle Spencer, and Maura Spiegel, 271–291. New York: Oxford University Press, 2017.
Clarke, Terence. "Irvin D. Yalom: A Conversation." *Huffington Post*, May 7, 2015. Https://www.huffingtonpost.com/terence-clarke/irvin-d-yalom-a-conversation. Accessed July 19, 2016.
Damasio, Antonio. *Looking for Spinoza: Joy, Sorrow, and the Feeling Brain*. Orlando: Harcourt, 2003.
Durant, Will. *The Story of Philosophy: The Lives and Opinions of the Greater Philosophers*. New York: Simon and Schuster, 1926.
Eby, Carl P. *Hemingway's Fetishism: Psychoanalysis and the Mirror of Manhood*. Albany: State University of New York Press, 1999.
Elms, Alan C. *Uncovering Lives: The Uneasy Alliance of Biography and Psychology*. New York: Oxford University Press, 1994.
Erikson, Erik H. *Young Man Luther: A Study in Psychoanalysis and History*. New York: Norton, 1962.
Farber, Leslie H. *Lying, Despair, Jealousy, Envy, Sex, Suicide, Drugs, and the Good Life*. New York: Basic Books, 1976.
Fiedler, Leslie A. *Love and Death in the American Novel*, rev. ed. New York: Stein and Day, 1966.
Fitzgerald, F. Scott. *The Crack-Up*. New York: New Directions, 1945.
Frank, Arthur W. *The Wounded Storyteller: Body, Illness, and Ethics*. Chicago: University of Chicago Press, 1995.
Freeman, Lucy. *The Story of Anna O*. New York: Walker and Company, 1972.
Freud, Sigmund. *An Autobiographical Study* (1925). In *The Standard Edition of the Complete Psychological Works of Sigmund Freud*, trans. James Strachey. Vol. 20. London: The Hogarth Press, 1959.
———. *The Complete Letters of Sigmund Freud to Wilhelm Fliess, 1887–1904*. Trans. and ed. Jeffrey Moussaieff Masson. Cambridge: Harvard University Press, 1985.
———. *On the History of the Psycho-Analytic Movement* (1914). In *The Standard Edition of the Complete Psychological Works of Sigmund Freud*, trans. James Strachey. Vol. 14. London: The Hogarth Press, 1957.
———. *Leonardo da Vinci and a Memory of His Childhood* (1910). In *The Standard Edition of the Complete Psychological Works of Sigmund Freud*, trans. James Strachey. Vol. 11. London: The Hogarth Press,1957.
———. *Letters of Sigmund Freud*. Selected and ed. Ernst L. Freud; trans. Tania and James Stern. New York: Basic Books, 1960.
———. "Mourning and Melancholia" (1917). In *The Standard Edition of the Complete Psychological Works of Sigmund Freud*, trans. James Strachey. Vol. 14. London: Hogarth Press, 1957.

———. *Notes Upon a Case of Obsessional Neurosis* (1909). In *The Standard Edition of the Complete Psychological Works of Sigmund Freud*, trans. James Strachey. Vol. 10. London: The Hogarth Press, 1955.

———. "Observations on Transference-Love (Further Recommendations on the Technique of Psychoanalysis" (1915). In *The Standard Edition of the Complete Psychological Works of Sigmund Freud*, trans. James Strachey. Vol. 12. London: The Hogarth Press, 1958.

———. *Totem and Taboo* (1913). In *The Standard Edition of the Complete Psychological Works of Sigmund Freud*, trans. James Strachey. Vol. 13. London: The Hogarth Press, 1953.

Gabbard, Glen O. "Disguise or Consent: Problems and Recommendations Concerning the Publication and Presentation of Clinical Material." *International Journal of Psycho-Analysis* 81 (2000): 1071–1086.

———. "Review of *The Schopenhauer Cure*." *American Journal of Psychiatry* 163 (2006): 1118.

Gisiger, Sabine, dir. *Yalom's Cure: A Guide to Life, Love and Happiness*, 2014.

Godwin, Gail. *The Good Husband*. New York: Ballantine, 1994.

Goethe, Johann Wolfgang von. *The Autobiography of Johann Wolfgang von Goethe*. 2 vols. Trans. John Oxenford. Introduction by Karl J. Weintraub. Chicago: University of Chicago Press, 1974.

Goldstein, Rebecca. *Betraying Spinoza: The Renegade Jew Who Gave Us Modernity*. New York: Schocken, 2006.

Gornick, Lisa. "Why I Never Wrote About My Patients." *New York Times*, May 12, 2015.

Greenberg, Gary. "Should Therapists Write About Patients?" *New York Times*, April 19, 2016.

Hesse, Hermann. *The Glass Bead Game* [*Magister Ludi*]. Trans. Richard and Clara Winston. Foreword by Theodore Ziolkowski. New York: Henry Holt, 1990.

Hirschmüller, Albrecht. *The Life and Work of Josef Breuer: Physiology and Psychoanalysis*. New York: New York University Press, 1989.

Hoffman, Eva. "Tales of Suspense from the Psychiatric Couch." *New York Times*, September 6, 1989.

Horney, Karen. *Neurosis and Human Growth: The Struggle Towards Self-Realization*. New York: Norton, 1950.

James, William. "On a Certain Blindness in Human Beings." In *Talks to Teachers on Psychology: And to Students on Some of Life's Ideals*. Cambridge: Harvard University Press, 1983.

Johnson, Michael. "Revisiting Irvin Yalom's Seductive Novels of Ideas." *Facts & Arts*, July 23, 2015. Http://www.factsandarts.com/literary-essays/revisitingirvin-yaloms-seductivenovels-of-ideas. Accessed November 12, 2016.

Joll, James. "Nietzsche v. Nietzsche." *New York Review of Books*, February 11, 1993.

Jones, Ernest. *The Life and Work of Sigmund Freud*. 3 vols. New York: Basic Books, 1953–1957.

Josselson, Ruthellen. *Irvin D. Yalom: On Psychotherapy and the Human Condition.* New York: Jorge Pinto Books, 2008.
Joyce, James. *A Portrait of the Artist as a Young Man.* New York: Viking, 1968 [1916].
Jung, C. G. *Memories, Dreams, Reflections.* Recorded and ed. Aniela Jaffé. Trans. Richard and Clara Winston. Rev. ed. New York: Vintage, 1989.
Kantrowitz, Judy Leopold. *Writing About Patients: Responsibilities, Risks, and Ramifications.* New York: Other Press, 2006.
Kaufmann, Walter. *Nietzsche: Philosopher, Psychologist, Antichrist.* 3rd ed. Princeton: Princeton University Press, 1968.
Kesey, Ken. *One Flew Over the Cuckoo's Nest.* New York: Berkley, 1963.
Kirsch, Jonathan. "Getting Inside the Mind of a Shrink: A Review of *Lying on the Couch*." *Los Angeles Times*, September 4, 1996.
Kübler-Ross, Elisabeth. *On Death and Dying.* New York: Macmillan, 1970.
———. *On Life after Death* (1991). New foreword by Caroline Myss. Berkeley: Celestial Arts, 2008.
———. *The Wheel of Life: A Memoir of Living and Dying.* New York: Scribner, 1997.
Lichtenstein, Heinz. *The Dilemma of Identity.* New York: Jason Aronson, 1983 [1977].
Lieberman, Morton A., Irvin D. Yalom, and Matthew B. Miles. *Encounter Groups: First Facts.* New York: Basic Books, 1973.
Lindner, Robert. *The Fifty-Minute Hour.* New York: Rinehart, 1955.
Loftus, Elizabeth, and Katherine Ketcham. *The Myth of Repressed Memory: False Memories and Allegations of Sexual Abuse.* New York: St. Martin's Griffin, 1994.
Lynn, Kenneth S. *Hemingway.* New York: Simon and Schuster, 1987.
Magee, Bryan. *Confessions of a Philosopher: A Personal Journey Through Western Philosophy from Plato to Popper.* New York: Modern Library, 1999.
———. *The Philosophy of Schopenhauer.* Oxford: Oxford University Press, 1983.
Mann, Thomas. *Buddenbrooks.* Trans. H. T. Lowe-Porter. New York: Knopf, 1964.
Masserman, Jules. *Principles of Dynamic Psychiatry.* New York: Saunders, 1947.
May, Rollo, Ernest Angel, and Henri F. Ellenberger, eds. *Existence: A New Dimension in Psychiatry and Psychology.* New York: Simon and Schuster, 1958.
McAdams, Dan P. "What Psychobiographers Might Learn from Personality Psychology." In *Handbook of Psychobiography*, ed. William Todd Schultz, 64–83. Oxford: Oxford University Press, 2005.
Merkin, Daphne. "A Neurotic's Neurotic." *New York Times Magazine*, December 30, 2007.
Meyer, Nicholas. *The Seven-Per-Cent Solution.* New York: Ballantine, 1975.
Middlebrook, Diane Wood. *Anne Sexton: A Biography.* Boston: Houghton Mifflin, 1991.
Miller, Laura. "The Last Word; Scheherazade in the Consulting Room." *New York Times*, June 15, 2003.
Moody, Skye K. "Review of *The Schopenhauer Cure.*" *Seattle Times*, February 6, 2005.
Mosher, Paul W., and Jeffrey Berman. *Confidentiality and Its Discontents: Dilemmas of Privacy in Psychotherapy.* New York: Fordham University Press, 2015.

Nabokov, Vladimir. *Lolita*. London: Weidenfeld and Nicolson, 1959.

———. *Speak, Memory*. In *The Portable Nabokov*, selected, with a critical introduction, by Page Stegner. New York: Viking, 1973.

Nadler, Steven. *Spinoza: A Life*. Cambridge: Cambridge University Press, 1999.

Nelson, Leah. "Hatewatch: White Supremacist Arthur Kemp Reprinting Forgotten Racist Texts." *Southern Poverty Law Center*. Http://splcenter.org/hatewatch/2011/07/12/white-supremacist-Arthur. . . . Accessed July 28, 2016.

Nietzsche, Friedrich. *Basic Writings of Friedrich Nietzsche*. Trans. and ed., with commentaries, by Walter Kaufmann. New York: Modern Library, 1992.

———. *Beyond Good and Evil*. Trans. R. J. Hollingdale, with an introduction by Michael Tanner. New York: Penguin, 1990.

———. *Ecce Homo*. In *Basic Writings of Friedrich Nietzsche*, trans. and ed., with commentaries, by Walter Kaufmann. New York: Modern Library, 1992.

———. *The Gay Science with a Prelude in Rhymes and an Appendix of Songs*, trans. with commentary by Walter Kaufmann. New York: Vintage, 1974.

———. *Human, All Too Human: A Book for Free Spirits*, trans. Marion Faber, with Stephen Lehmann. Introduction and notes by Marion Faber. New introduction by Arthur C. Danto. Lincoln: University of Nebraska Press, 1996.

———. "Schopenhauer as Educator." Trans. Adrian Collins. Https://en.wikisource.org/wiki/Schopenhauer_as_educator. Accessed November 12, 2016.

———. *Thus Spake Zarathustra*. In *The Philosophy of Nietzsche*. New York: Modern Library, 1954.

———. *Twilight of the Idols*. In *The Portable Nietzsche*, selected and trans. with an introduction, prefaces, and notes by Walter Kaufmann. New York: Penguin, 1959.

Noël, Barbara, and Kathryn Watterson. *You Must Be Dreaming*. New York: Poseidon Press, 1992.

O'Neill, Eugene. *The Iceman Cometh*. New York: Vintage Books, 1957.

Pattison, E. Mansell. "Review of *Inpatient Group Psychotherapy*." *Psychiatric Services* 35 (1984): 500–501.

Pennebaker, James. *Opening Up: The Healing Power of Expressing Emotions*. New York: Guilford Press, 1997.

———, ed. *Emotion, Disclosure & Health*. Washington, DC: American Psychological Association, 1997.

Pollack, George H. "The Possible Significance of Childhood Object Loss in the Josef Breuer—Bertha Pappenheim (Anna O.)—Sigmund Freud Relationship." *Journal of the American Psychoanalytic Association* 16 (1968): 711–739.

Popkin, Richard. "Spinoza's Excommunication." In *Jewish Themes in Spinoza's Philosophy*, ed. Heidi M. Ravven and Lenn E. Goodman, 263–279. Albany: State University of New York Press, 2002.

Presley, Gary. "Interview with Irvin Yalom." March 5, 2012. Http://www.kirkusreviews.com/features/inside-spinoza-problem. Accessed August 4, 2016.

Raabe, Peter B. *Issues in Philosophical Counseling*. Westport: Praeger, 2002.

Ravven, Heidi M. "Spinoza's Rupture with Tradition—His Hints of a Jewish Modernity." In *Jewish Themes in Spinoza's Philosophy*, ed. Heidi M. Ravven and Lenn E. Goodman, 187–223. Albany: State University of New York Press, 2002.

Reik, Theodor. *Listening with the Third Ear: The Inner Experience of a Psychoanalyst*. New York: Jove/HBJ, 1977.

"Review of *Every Day Gets a Little Closer*." *Kirkus Reviews*, November 8, 1974.

"Review of *Lying on the Couch*." *Kirkus Reviews*, June 15, 1996.

"Review of *Lying on the Couch*." *Publishers Weekly*, July 29, 1996.

Richman, Simmy. "Irvin D. Yalom Interview: The Grand Old Man of American Psychiatry on What He Has Learned about Life (and Death) in His Still-Flourishing Career." *Independent*, March 25, 2015. Http://www.independent.co.uk/news/people/profiles/irvin-d-yalom-interview. Accessed August 13, 2016.

Rosenberg, Alfred. *Memoirs*. Ostara Publications, 2015.

———. *The Myth of the Twentieth Century: An Evaluation of the Spiritual-Intellectual Confrontations of Our Age*. Middletown, DE: 2016.

Roth, Philip. *Portnoy's Complaint*. New York: Random House, 1969.

Rubin, Merle. "Review of *The Schopenhauer Cure*." *Los Angeles Times*, January 8, 2005.

Rudnytsky, Peter L. "Book Review of *Writing About Patients: Responsibilities, Risks, and Ramifications*." *Journal of the American Psychoanalytic Association* 55 (2007): 1406–1411.

Russell, Bertrand. *History of Western Philosophy*. London: George Allen & Unwin, 1946.

Sacks, Oliver. *Hallucinations*. New York: Vintage, 2013.

———. "My Own Life." *New York Times*, February 19, 2015.

Safranski, Rüdiger. *Schopenhauer and the Wild Years of Philosophy*. Trans. Ewald Osers. Cambridge: Harvard University Press, 1991.

Saks, Elyn R. *The Center Cannot Hold*. New York: Hyperion, 2007.

Saks, Elyn R., and Shahrokh Golshan. *Informed Consent in Psychoanalysis: The Law, the Theory, and the Data*. New York: Fordham University Press, 2013.

Schultz, William Todd, ed. *Handbook of Psychobiography*. Oxford: Oxford University Press, 2005.

Schwartz, Daniel B. *The First Modern Jew: Spinoza and the History of an Image*. Princeton: Princeton University Press, 2012.

Schwartz, M. F., L. D. Galperin, and W. H. Masters. "Dissociation and Treatment of Compulsive Reenactment of Trauma Sexual Compulsivity." In *Adult Survivors of Sexual Abuse: Treatment Innovations*, ed. M. Hunter, 174–186. Thousand Oaks: Sage, 1995.

Schwartz, Morrie [Morris S.]. *Letting Go: Morrie's Reflections on Living While Dying*. Introduction by Paul Solman. New York: Walker, 1996.

Sehmi, Sunita. "An Interview with Sabine Gisiger." *Swiss Style Magazine*. Http://www.swissstyle.com/an-interview-with-sabine-gisiger. Accessed October 13, 2016.

Sexton, Anne. *Anne Sexton: A Self-Portrait in Letters*. Ed. Linda Gray Sexton and Lois Ames. Boston: Houghton Mifflin, 1977.

———. *Complete Poems*. Boston: Houghton Mifflin, 1981.
Sexton, Linda Gray. *Searching for Mercy Street: My Journey Back to My Mother, Anne Sexton*. Boston: Little, Brown, 1994.
Sharp, Alan. *A Green Tree in Gedde*. New York: New American Library, 1965.
Shulman, Michael. "'Unavoidable Satisfactions': The Analyst's Pleasure." *Journal of the American Psychoanalytic Association* 64 (2016): 697–727.
Silverman, Phyllis R. *Widow to Widow: How the Bereaved Help One Another*. 2nd ed. New York: Brunner-Routledge, 2004.
Simpson, Eileen. "'I Had Botched This Case Beyond Belief': *Love's Executioner*." *New York Times*, September 3, 1989.
Smith, Joan-Dianne. "Review of *The Schopenhauer Cure*." *International Journal of Group Psychotherapy* 56 (2006): 379–382.
Solomon, Robert C. *Living with Nietzsche: What the Great "Immoralist" Has to Teach Us*. New York: Oxford University Press, 2003.
Spence, Donald P. *Narrative Truth and Historical Truth: Meaning and Interpretation in Psychoanalysis*. New York: Norton, 1984.
Spinoza, Baruch. *A Spinoza Reader: The Ethics and Other Works*. Ed. and trans. Edwin Curley. Princeton: Princeton University Press, 1994.
———. *Tractatus Theologico-Politicus*. Trans. Samuel Shirley. Introduction by Brad S. Gregory. Leiden: E. J. Brill, 1989.
Stanley, Alessandra. "Poet Told All; Therapist Provides the Record." *New York Times*, July 15, 1991.
Stewart, Garrett. *Death Sentences: Styles of Dying in British Fiction*. Cambridge: Harvard University Press, 1984.
Thomas, Lewis. *Lives of a Cell: Notes of a Biology Watcher*. New York: Viking, 1974.
"The Top 10 Most Influential Therapists." *PsychotherapyNetworker* magazine. 2006. Https://www.psychotherapynetworker.org/magazine/article/661/the-top-10. Accessed October 20, 2016.
Tugend, Alina. "Engendering Sons: Is It Doable—or Even Desirable—to Raise Gender-Neutral Children?" *California Magazine*, Winter 2014. Http://alumni.berkeley.edu/california-magazine/winter-2014-gender-assumptions. Accessed October 15, 2016.
Waite, Robert G. L. *The Psychopathic God: Adolf Hitler*. New York: Basic Books, 1977.
Wampold, Bruce E., and Zac E. Imel. *The Great Psychotherapy Debate: The Evidence for What Makes Psychotherapy Work*. 2nd ed. New York: Routledge, 2015.
Weingarten, Randall. Foreword to the Perennial Classics edition of *Love's Executioner and Other Tales of Psychotherapy* by Irvin D. Yalom. New York: Perennial Classics, 2000.
Wheelis, Allen. *The Doctor of Desire*. New York: Norton, 1987.
Winnicott, D. W. "Hate in the Counter-Transference." *International Journal of Psycho-Analysis* 30 (1949): 69–74.

Wolf Man. *The Wolf Man*. With *The Case of the Wolf Man* by Sigmund Freud and *A Supplement* by Ruth Mack Brunswick, ed. with notes, an introduction, and chapters by Muriel Gardiner. New York: Basic Books, 1971.

Worden, J. William. *Grief Counseling and Grief Therapy: A Handbook for the Mental Health Practitioner*. 3rd ed. New York: Springer, 2002.

Wurmser, Léon. "Shame: The Veiled Companion of Narcissism." In *The Many Faces of Shame*, ed. Donald L. Nathanson, 64–92. New York: Guilford Press, 1987.

Yalom, Irvin D. "Autobiographical Note." Http://www.yalom.com/pagemaker.php?nav'bio. Accessed December 25, 2015.

———. *Becoming Myself: A Psychiatrist's Memoir*. New York: Basic Books, 2017.

———. *Creatures of a Day and Other Tales of Psychotherapy*. New York: Basic Books, 2015.

———. *Existential Psychotherapy*. New York: Basic Books, 1980.

———. Foreword. *Studies on Hysteria*, by Josef Breuer and Sigmund Freud. New York: Basic Books, 2000.

———. *The Gift of Therapy: An Open Letter to a New Generation of Therapists and Their Patients*. New York: HarperCollins, 2002.

———. *Inpatient Group Psychotherapy*. New York: Basic Books, 1983.

———. *Love's Executioner and Other Tales of Psychotherapy*. New York: Perennial Classics, 2000.

———. *Lying on the Couch*. New York: Harper Perennial, 1997.

———. *Momma and the Meaning of Life: Tales of Psychotherapy*. New York: Basic Books, 1999.

———. "Religion and Psychiatry." *American Journal of Psychotherapy* 56 (2002): 301–317.

———. *The Schopenhauer Cure*. New York: Harper Perennial, 2006.

———. *The Spinoza Problem*. New York: Basic Books, 2012.

———. *Staring at the Sun: Overcoming the Terror of Death*. San Francisco: Jossey-Bass, 2008.

———. *The Theory and Practice of Group Psychotherapy*. New York: Basic Books, 1970; 4th ed., 1995; 5th ed., with Molyn Leszcz, 2005.

———. *When Nietzsche Wept*. New York: Harper Perennial, 1993.

———. "Writing *The Schopenhauer Cure*." In *The Schopenhauer Cure*. New York: Harper Perennial, 2006.

———. *The Yalom Reader: Selections from the Work of a Master Therapist and Storyteller*. Ed. Ben Yalom. New York: Basic Books, 1998.

———, and Robert L. Brent. *I'm Calling the Police*. New York: Basic Books, 2011.

———, and Ginny Elkin. *Every Day Gets a Little Closer: A Twice-Told Therapy*. New York: Basic Books, 1974.

———, and S. Vinogradov. *Concise Guide to Group Psychotherapy*. Washington, DC: American Psychiatric Association, 1989.

Yalom, Marilyn. *The American Resting Place: Four Hundred Years of History Through Our Cemeteries and Burial Grounds*. Photos by Reid Yalom. New York: Houghton Mifflin Harcourt, 2008.
———. *A History of the Breast*. New York: Knopf, 1997.
———. *A History of the Wife*. New York: HarperCollins, 2001.
———. *How the French Invented Love: Nine Hundred Years of Passion and Romance*. New York: Harper Perennial, 2012.
———. *Maternity, Mortality, and the Literature of Madness*. University Park: Pennsylvania State University Press, 1985.
———, and Theresa Donovan Brown. *The Social Sex: A History of Female Friendship*. New York: Harper Perennial, 2015.
Young, Philip. *Ernest Hemingway: A Reconsideration*. University Park: Pennsylvania State University Press, 1966.
Young, Royal. "Marilyn Yalom and the Language of Love." *Interview Magazine*, October 23, 2012. Http//:www.interviewmagzine.com/culture/marilyn-yalom-how-the-french-invented-love. Accessed October 14, 2016.
Yovel, Yirmiyahu. *Spinoza and Other Heretics: The Adventures of Immanence*. Princeton: Princeton University Press, 1989.

Index

Abraham, Karl, 258
Adams, Henry, 206
"Age States," 165
Albom, Mitch, 213–214
Allport, Gordon, 28
Anderson, Robert, 157
Andreasen, Nancy C., 145
"Anna O." (Bertha Pappenheim), xx, 79, 83, 85–87, 90, 99, 101–102, 294
Anticipating regret, 133–134, 285
Anticipatory mourning, 13
Ars Moriendi, 95, 213–214
Asimov, Isaac, 67
Ataraxia, 208, 238
Auden, W. H., 214
Aurelius, Marcus, 267, 280–281
Austen, Jane, xiv
"Awakening Experience," 211–212

Babacan, Nalan Akgül, 205
Banville, John, 296
Barley, Andrew, 204
Barnes, Julian, 71
Barnett, Laura, 220
Bartlett, Frederic, 183
Bass, Ellen, 183
Beauvoir, Simone de, 293
Beck, Aaron, xv
Beckett, Samuel, 191

Beethoven, Ludwig van, 39
Bellow, Saul, 14, 121, 296
Benefactor-beneficiary relationship, 80, 88
Ben-Gurion, David, 263
Bereavement, 65–66, 94, 130, 153, 156
Berman, Jeffrey, xvi–xviii, 34–35, 156–157, 218
Bibliotherapy, 189, 256
Binswanger, Ludwig, 28
Bleuler, Eugen, 258
Boundary violations, xx, 6, 21, 55, 117–141
Breuer, Josef, xiv, xx, 79–116, 132, 137, 140, 149, 181, 208, 214, 294
Brizendine, Louann, 293–294
Brodsky, Joseph, 155
Brücke, Ernst, 83
Buber, Martin, 40, 174, 195–196

Camus, Albert, 39, 173
Cervantes, Miguel de, 60
Chamberlain, Houston Stewart, 255–256
Charon, Rita, 23
Chaucer, Geoffrey, 239
Child Sexual Abuse, 118, 182
Churchill, Winston, 226
Clarke, Terence, 216, 287

Confidentiality, 15, 17, 46, 51, 125, 132, 134, 137–138, 141, 174, 217–218, 234, 261–262, 272, 275
"Continuing Bonds," 156–157
Counterphobic motivation, 23, 37, 175, 221
Cummings, E. E., 209
"Cyclotherapy," 21–22, 41, 65

Damasio, Antonio, 231
"Death anxiety," ix, xvii, xix, xxi, 27, 29–31, 34–35, 40, 43, 52, 65, 69, 110, 155, 163, 207–209, 218, 221, 223, 241, 267, 269, 272, 278, 291
Dicken, Charles, 65, 67–68, 75, 111, 137, 156, 202, 211, 288
Disraeli, Benjamin, 256
"Dodo bird effect," 38
Dostoevsky, Feodor, xii, 25, 195, 288
Dryden, John, 94
Dual relationships, 174, 181
Duhl, Frederick J., 126
Durant, Will, 246

Eby, Carl P., 35
Einstein, Albert, 173, 226, 231, 259, 263–264
Elkin, Ginny, xiii, xviii, 17–25, 30, 47, 68, 100, 103, 277
Elms, Alan C., 81
Empathy, 38, 47, 94, 105, 132–133, 144, 164, 168, 178, 188, 209, 227, 236, 254, 293
Epictetus, 198
Epicurus, 177, 208, 238–240, 248
Erhard, Werner, 6, 41
Erikson, Eric H., 81, 186, 198
Eternal Recurrence, 110–111
Eudemonia, 238
Existence Pain, xi, xix, 43, 49–77, 80, 268
Existential psychotherapy, xv, xix, 27–42, 119, 277, 291

Farber, Leslie H., 117–118
"Feedback," 8–9, 164–165
Fellow Sufferers, 114, 118
Ferenczi, Sándor, 131–132, 165
Fiedler, Leslie A., 36
"Fishbowling," 46
Fitzgerald, F. Scott, 52
Flaubert, Gustave, xx, 71, 243, 293
Fliess, Wilhelm, 88
Frank, Arthur W., 23–24
Frank, Jerome, xiii, 1, 219
Frankl, Viktor, 19, 28–29
Freeman, Lucy, 86
Freud, Sigmund, xv, xix, xx, 15–16, 19, 24, 30–31, 34, 37–40, 49, 51–53, 59, 75, 79, 81–92, 96–97, 101, 103–107, 111, 115, 117, 131, 135–136, 156, 159, 164, 167, 172, 192–194, 208, 216, 226, 235–236, 250, 258, 260–261, 296
Fromm, Erich, 28, 165, 173
Frost, Robert, 155

Gabbard, Glen O., 12, 204, 217
Gardner, John, 173
Gardner, Patrick, 190
Garwood, Dorothy Semenow, 9
Geertz, Clifford, 101
"Gentling anger," 45
Gide, André, 116
Gisiger, Sabine, 285–287
Giving Feedback, 8–9, 164–165
Godwin, Gail, 203
Goethe, Johann Wolfgang von, 76, 80, 232, 255–258, 261–264
Goldstein, Rebecca, 230, 232
Gornick, Lisa, 216
Gratitude, 19, 73, 79–80, 87–88, 92, 98, 114, 140–141, 173, 200–201, 205, 214–215, 218, 235, 268, 278
"Gratitude visit," 214–215
Greenberg, Gary, 216
Gregory, Brad S., 232

Group Psychotherapy, xix, xxi, 1–14, 43–48, 149–150, 153, 165, 181, 196
Gutheil, T., 12

Hamburg, David, 22
Hamlet, xviii, 123
Hardy, Thomas, 41–42, 155, 195, 295
Hawthorne, Nathaniel, 17
Heidegger, Martin, 27, 39, 173, 208
Héloïse and Abelard, 293
Hemingway, Ernest, x, xix, 28, 35–37, 186
Hesse, Hermann, xviii, 2–4
Hirschmüller, Albrecht, 87
Hitler, Adolf, xxi, 228–229, 231, 252–264
Hoarding, 273
Hoffman, Eva, 76
"Holding Environment," 261
Holly, Buddy, 25
Holmes, Sherlock, xix, 51
Horney, Karen, 28, 119, 164–165
Hotchner, A. E., 37
Hume, David, 201
Hysteria, 83, 90, 102

Intersubjectivity, 168
"I-Thou" relationship, 40, 174, 196

James, Henry, ix, 73
James, William, 82
Johnson, Michael, 265
Joll, James, 116
Jones, Ernest, 84–88, 126
Josselson, Ruthellen, xv, 1, 9, 22, 27, 141, 184
Joyce, James, 50, 243, 290
Jung, C. G., xv, 4, 23, 119, 126, 138–140, 147, 168, 251

Kafka, Franz, 12, 28, 38, 72, 190, 195
Kaiser, Helmuth, 28

Kantrowitz, Judy Leopold, 217
Kaplan, Mordecai, 249
Kaufmann, Walter, 83, 94
Keats, John, 74, 122
Kelly, George, 28
Kemp, Arthur, 254
Kesey, Ken, x, ix, 43
Khan, Masud, 129
Kirsch, Jonathan, 141
Klein, Melanie, 165
Kohut, Hans, 94, 209, 236
Kraus, Karl, xxi
Kübler-Ross, Elisabeth, xix, 32–35, 41, 147

La Rochefoucauld, Francois de, 33, 207, 278
Lewis, Helen Block, 11
libido theory, 30, 34, 156
Lindner, Robert, 49
Loftus, Elizabeth, 183
"Love-as-sickness" and "lovesickness," 57, 104, 290–291, 294
Lynn, Kenneth S., 35

Magee, Bryan, 189–191
Mahler, Gustav, 256
Mann, Thomas, 179–180, 190, 200
Maslow, Abraham, 28
Masserman, Jules, 126–127
Maternal Loss, 107, 151, 232, 245, 256
May, Rollo, xiii, 28, 62, 165, 168, 209, 219–221, 279, 296
McAdams, Dan P., 82
McEwan, Ian, 296
Medeiros, D., 5
Melville, Herman, 18
"Memory wars," 118
Mendelssohn, Felix, 256
Merkin, Daphne, 140
"Methodolatry," 220
Meyer, Nicholas, 51

Middlebrook, Diane Wood, 125–126
Miller, Laura, 296
Minuchin, Salvador, xv
Moody, Skye K., 204
Mortera, Saul Levi, 229, 241–248, 264
Mosher, Paul W., x, 125, 127, 217
Mueller, Claude, 269
"Multiple therapy," 47
Murdoch, Iris, 191
Murphy, Gardner, 28
Murray, Henry, 28
"Mutual analysis," 131–132

Nabokov, Vladimir, 191
Nadler, Steven, 244–246
Narrative medicine, 23
Nelson, Leah, 254
Nietzsche, Friedrich, xi–xii, xviii, xx, 28–31, 39, 79–116, 119–120, 132–133, 137, 144, 146, 149, 159, 169, 172, 181, 186, 188, 190, 192–194, 200, 209, 223, 225–226, 233–236, 250–251, 269, 294–296
Noël, Barbara, 127

"Observer effect," 46
Offenbach, Jacob, 256
O. Henry, 53, 76
O'Neill, Eugene, xviii, 2
"Originalology," 81–82
Orne, Martin, 125
Oskar Pfister award, xv, 229
Ozick, Cynthia, 296

Parloff, M. B., 2
"Past lives therapy," 210
Pattison, E. Mansell, 47
Pedagogical Love, 239
Peltz, James, x
Pennebaker, James, 5
"Perspectivism," 105–106
Petty, Norman, 25

Philosophical counseling, 178–179, 185, 229, 232, 248, 262
Picasso, Pablo, 28, 122
Pindar, 95
Plath, Sylvia, 195, 291
Plato, 178, 190, 238
Pollack, George H., 109–110
Popkin, Richard, 246
Positive psychology movement, 214
Posterity self, 218
Powell, Anthony, 20
Presley, Gary, 225
Protocols of the Elders of Zion, 259–260
Proust, Marcel, 20, 71, 190, 290, 294
Psychiatric Diagnosis, 71, 120, 279
Psychobiography, x, xx, 35, 80–82, 170
Psychotherapy Networker, xv

Raabe, Peter B., 179
Rank, Otto, 28, 63, 85, 126
"Rat Man," 15, 49
Ravven, Heidi M., 250
Reciprocal Healing, 79–11, 149, 151
"Recovered memory movement," 63, 118, 183, 195
Rée, Paul, 84, 92, 112
Reik, Theodor, 20, 49
Rescue fantasies, 34, 152, 162
Richman, Simmy, 268, 295
Rilke, Rainer Maria, 79, 121, 164
"Rippling effect," 212–213, 215, 218
Rogers, Carl, xv, 28, 94, 119, 165, 209
"Rolfing," 168, 210
Rosenberg, Alfred, xxi, 225–265, 281, 294
Rosenzweig, Saul, 38
Roth, Philip, 121, 145, 225, 296
Rubin, Merle, 204
Rudnytsky, Peter L., 217
Russell, Bertrand, 230

Rutherford, R. B., 267
Rycroft, Charles, 167

Sacks, Oliver, 183, 201, 208
Safranski, Rüdiger, 189, 190, 192
Saks, Elyn R., 217
Sartre, Jean-Paul, 115, 173, 178, 186, 191, 293
"Satanic ritual abuse," 118, 183
Schadenfreude, 181
Schopenhauer, Arthur, xi, xiv, xvii–xviii, xxi, 13, 28, 39, 81–82, 90, 108, 139, 160, 165, 168–206, 225–226, 229, 233–235, 250, 271, 294–295
Schultz, William Todd, 80
Schwartz, Daniel B., 230
Schwartz, M. F., 200
Schwartz, Morrie, 213–214
Sehmi, Sunita, 285
Selectivity Error, 198–199
Seligman, Martin, 214, 265
Sexual Addiction, 177, 185, 187, 190, 199–200
Sexton, Anne, x, 125–126
Sexton, Linda Gray, 126
Shadow Self, 12, 139
Shakespeare, William, 52, 296
Shame, 11, 17, 54, 62, 77, 112, 180, 196
Shared written group summary, 46–47
Sharp, Alan, 108
Shelley, Mary, 67
Shulman, Michael, 282
Silverman, Phyllis R., 156
Simpson, Eileen, 76
Singer, Isaac Bashevis, 76
Smith, Joan-Dianne, 204
Smith, Olive, 11, 65, 209, 278–279
Socrates, 115, 171, 178, 232, 236, 240
Sokel, Walter, 188–189

Solomon, Robert C., 105
Spence, Donald C., 117
Spiegel, David, 41
Spinoza, Baruch, xviii, xxi, 28, 39, 81–82, 90, 111, 173, 183, 225–265, 281, 294
"Stage theory of dying," xix, 33–34, 147
Stanley, Alessandra, 126
Steinbeck, John, 288
Stewart, Garret, 202
Stoppard, Tom, 22
Strachey, James, 85–86
Suggestibility, 118
Suicide, xvii, 6–8, 30–31, 35–36, 39, 54, 57, 72–73, 89, 96, 99, 104, 117, 125, 154, 178, 180, 185–186, 192, 199–200, 244
Sullivan, Harry Stack, 47, 165
"Surgical model of psychotherapy," 16
Sybil, 118

"Talking cure," xiv, xvi, xx, 3, 50–51, 85–86, 90, 104, 110, 115, 228, 230, 263
"Teaching novel," xiv, 263
Terence, 173
"Therapeutic hubris," 56, 123, 149, 152
"Therapeutic Incontinency," 128, 159
Therapist self-disclosure, xii, xvii, xx, 13, 63, 128, 130–136, 140
Thomas, Dylan, 69
Thomas, Lewis, 50
The Three Faces of Eve, 118
Time-delayed Intervention, 177
Tolstoy, Leo, xii, 211
Tomkins, Silvan, 11
"Touching of hands," 167
Transference and countertransference, 2, 16, 21, 23, 38, 55, 57, 62, 66, 86, 119, 122, 125, 129, 135–136, 151–152, 157–160, 260–261, 294

Tugend, Alina, 294
Two-person psychology, 168
Two-way mirror, 45–46

Uncertainty principle, 272

Vertical and horizonal self-disclosures, 7–8, 174, 196
Vipassana meditation, 195

Wagner, Richard, 89, 92, 97, 113, 190, 255
Waite, Robert G., 260
Wampold, Bruce E., 38
Watterson, Kathryn, 127
Weingarten, Randall, 49
Wheelis, Allen, xvi, 37, 140, 165
Whitehorn, John, xiii, 146, 149, 219–220
Whittingham, Martyn, 48n.1
"Wild analysis," 81
Wilde, Oscar, 130, 202
Wilder, Thornton, 28, 36
Will, George, 81
Winnicott, D. W., 165, 261
"Wolf Man," 15–16, 24, 49
Woolf, Virginia, 20, 52, 195, 212
Worden, J. William, 156
"Wounded healer," 3–4, 23–24, 54, 59, 138–139, 151, 163, 168, 176, 197, 251
Wurmser, Léon, 11

Yalom, Irvin D. and acknowledging error, 5, 9–10, 55–56, 60, 155, 164; and affirming the here-and-now, 9, 38, 44, 52, 165; and attitude toward "bizarre" therapy, 41, 210; and attitude toward self-disclosure, xv–xvi, xvii, 5, 7, 9, 11–13, 17, 56–57, 77, 165–166, 210, 270–271; and avoiding patient-therapist sex, 137, 194; and awards, xiv–xv; and being Jewish, 238; and being love's executioner, xx, 53–54, 59, 271; and being an octogenarian, 77, 267–296; and being in therapy, xix, 10–11, 23, 29–30, 47, 65, 167–168; and belief that psychotherapy is both a science and art, 2, 57; and childhood, xii, 144, 166, 286–287; and concern about the future of psychotherapy, xxi, 163; and confessing prejudice, 61–63; and conflicted relationship with his mother, 10–11, 67, 144–145, 149, 166, 221–222, 287; and crafting a prose style, xviii, 50, 296; and creativity, 39, 69, 94, 144–145, 263, 277; and death anxiety, xix, xxi, 29–31, 207–210, 221, 267, 288; and the dedication of his books, 291; and demystifying therapy, 1, 12–13, 46, 49; and dual identity, xxii; and evaluation of his career as a writer, 296; and existence pain, xi, xix, 52; and giving feedback, 164–165; and the hazards and privileges of being a therapist, 80, 163–168; and interpreting his own dreams, 145, 166–167, 209; and love for being a psychotherapist, 282–283; and love of reading, xii, 287–288; and love-obsession, 56–57, 68, 77, 100, 294; and lovesickness, 54–57, 290–292; and marriage, xiii, 287–288, 291–292; and medical training, xii–xiii; and the patient-therapist relationship, xv–xvi, 31; and preserving patient-therapist confidentiality, xiii, 17, 21, 51, 215, 217; and private practice, xiv; and relationship to his mentors, xiii, 219–221; and shifting attitude toward psychoanalysis, 168; and the Smiley the Bear dream, 219; and teaching career at Stanford, xiii, xv, 1–2; and teaching empathy, 164; and therapist transparency, 12, 45, 53; and thoughts on aging and death, xxii, 286; and touching patients nonsexually, 164, 167; and viewing patients as fellow travelers, 4, 164; and working with cancer patients, 40–41; and writing goodbye, 295–296; "Autobiographical Note," xii, 139; *Becoming Myself*, xiv, xxii, 116, 139, 285, 295–296; *Concise Guide to Group Psychotherapy*, xviii; *Creatures of a Day and Other Tales of Psychotherapy*, xiv, xxii, 265, 267–283, 291, 295; *Encounter Groups: First Facts*, xiii, xviii, 8, 28; *Every Day Gets a Little Closer*, xiii, xviii, 15–25, 30–31, 47, 68, 90, 100, 103; "Foreword" to *Studies on Hysteria*, 90; *The Gift of Therapy*, xiv, xx–xxi, 3, 137, 163–168, 184, 196, 215, 217, 291; *I'm Calling the Police*, xviii; *Inpatient Group Psychotherapy*, xiii, xix, 43–48, 50, 149–150, 153; *Love's Executioner and Other Tales of Psychotherapy*, xii–xiv, xix–xx, 11–12, 14, 49–77, 90, 95–96, 99, 106, 110, 120, 122, 130, 143–144, 162–163, 215, 285, 291, 294–296; *Lying on the Couch*, xiv, xx, 55, 117–141, 158–162, 170, 172, 175, 194–195, 202, 219, 294, 296; *Momma and the Meaning of Life*, xiv, xx, 143–162, 166–167, 177, 219, 287, 295; "Religion and Psychiatry," xv; *The Schopenhauer Cure*, xi, xiv, xvii, xxi, 13, 139, 160, 165, 168–206, 213, 223, 229, 231, 237, 248, 251, 262, 265, 275, 296; *The Spinoza Problem*, xiv, xxi, 40, 190, 204, 208, 225–265, 278; *Staring at the Sun*, xiii–xiv, xxi, 33, 143, 164, 207–223, 265, 273, 278, 296; *The Theory and Practice of Group Psychotherapy*, xiii, xviii, 1–14, 47, 174; *When Nietzsche Wept*, x, xi–xii, xiv, xx, 14, 79–116, 126, 132–133, 139–140, 149, 163, 185, 214, 222, 248, 262, 265, 269, 291; "Writing *The Schopenhauer Cure*," 169; *The Yalom Reader*, xiv, xxii, 2, 14, 27, 35, 50, 82, 85, 131

Yalom, Marilyn, ix, xiii, xviii, xxii, 20, 35, 38, 41, 286–294

Young, Philip, 36

Young, Royal, 292

Yovel, Yirmihahu, 236, 257

www.ingramcontent.com/pod-product-compliance
Lightning Source LLC
Chambersburg PA
CBHW030009240426
43672CB00007B/882